Beyond Compliance

Studies in Asian Security

A SERIES SPONSORED BY THE EAST-WEST CENTER

Muthiah Alagappa, Chief Editor
Director, East-West Center Washington

The aim of the Asian Security series is to promote analysis, understanding, and explanation of the dynamics of domestic, transnational, and international security challenges in Asia. Books in the series will analyze contemporary security issues and problems to clarify debates in the scholarly and policy communities, provide new insights and perspectives, and identify new research and policy directions related to conflict management and security in Asia. Security is defined broadly to include the traditional political and military dimensions as well as the nontraditional dimensions that affect the survival and well-being of political communities. Asia, too, is defined broadly, to include Northeast, Southeast, South, and Central Asia.

Designed to encourage original and rigorous scholarship, books in the Asian Security series seek to engage scholars, educators, and practitioners. Wide-ranging in scope and method, the series welcomes an extensive array of paradigms, programs, traditions, and methodologies now employed in the social sciences.

★   ★   ★

The East-West Center is an education and research organization established by the U.S. Congress in 1960 to strengthen relations and understanding among the peoples and nations of Asia, the Pacific, and the United States. The Center contributes to a peaceful, prosperous, and just Asia Pacific community by serving as a vigorous hub for cooperative research, education, and dialogue on critical issues of common concern to the Asia Pacific region and the United States. Funding for the Center comes from the U.S. government, with additional support provided by private agencies, individuals, foundations, and corporations and the governments of the region.

Beyond Compliance

CHINA, INTERNATIONAL ORGANIZATIONS,
AND GLOBAL SECURITY

Ann Kent

SPONSORED BY THE EAST–WEST CENTER

Stanford University Press • *Stanford, California*

Stanford University Press
Stanford, California

Library of Congress Cataloging-in-Publication Data

Kent, A. E. (Ann E.)
   Beyond compliance : China, international organizations, and global security / Ann Kent.
      p. cm.
   Includes bibliograpical references and index.
   ISBN-13: 978-0-8047-5551-1 (cloth)
   ISBN-13: 978-0-8047-7382-9 (pbk.)
   1. China—Relations—Foreign countries. 2. International organizations. I. Title.

DS779.27.K46 2007
355'.033051—dc22   2006032137

Typeset by BookMatters in 10.5/13.5 Bembo

For my family

When it comes to laws on the books, no generation has inherited the riches that we have. We are blessed with what amounts to an international bill of human rights. . . . We also enjoy a set of international rules on everything from trade to the law of the sea, from terrorism to the environment and from small arms to weapons of mass destruction. . . . But, without implementation, our declarations ring hollow.

UN Secretary-General Kofi Annan,
21 March 2005, A/59/2005

Cooperation is an effective way to cope with common challenges facing mankind. To strengthen international cooperation, we must champion multilateralism. The UN is the centre of international multilateral mechanisms and the key platform for making multilateralism work. . . . The threats and challenges we face make it imperative to strengthen, rather than weaken, the role of the UN.

Li Zhaoxing, General Debate,
UN General Assembly,
59th Session, 27 September 2004

Contents

Tables

Preface

In 1961, in the mid-winter of the Cold War, the U.S. ambassador to the United Nations, Adlai Stevenson, normally a liberal internationalist, rejected the idea that the People's Republic of China might become a more harmonious member of the international community if it were allowed to participate in the United Nations. By contrast, a handful of diplomats and scholars argued that only when the People's Republic was welcomed into the United Nations could it and would it become a good international citizen. Which side was correct? Thirty-six years after the People's Republic replaced Taiwan as the official representative of China in the United Nations, and then in a host of other international organizations, we have enough distance from events to subject the question to rigorous scrutiny.

During the period I have researched this topic, I have been helped by a swathe of officials in international organizations, in particular the Conference on Disarmament, the World Bank, the International Monetary Fund, the United Nations Environment Programme, the International Labour Organization, and the UN Committee against Torture. First and foremost, however, I am indebted to the Australian Research Council, which made this book possible by awarding me successive fellowships, including generous support for fieldwork. In my first fellowship, held in the Law Program, Research School of Social Sciences, Australian National University (ANU), I enjoyed the support of John Braithwaite, Peter Cane, Jane Stapleton, and Chris Treadwell. Thanks are due in particular to John, who supported the project throughout and made many valuable suggestions. During my second fellowship, in the Centre for International and Public Law, ANU College of Law, I benefited from the wisdom

and warm collegiality of Hilary Charlesworth, Michael Coper, Don Greig, J-P
Fonteyne, Andrew Byrnes, Don Rothwell, Kim Rubenstein, Gerry Simpson,
Madelaine Chiam, Jennifer Braid, John Williams, and Don Anton. At all times,
the staff of the UN Library, the ILO Library, the National Library of Australia,
the Menzies and the Law Libraries of the Australian National University and
the IT office in the Law School provided invaluable assistance. Others who facil-
itated my fieldwork, interviews, and thought processes in Geneva; Washington,
DC; Beijing; and Canberra, apart from the many international civil servants,
diplomats, and public servants who prefer to remain anonymous, include Borge
Bakken, Mac Boot, Pieter Bottelier, Theo van Boven, Frank Frost, John and Sue
Garland, Patricia Hewitson, Rebecca Johnson, David Mason, Diana Millar,
John Pace, Douglas Poulter, James L. Richardson, Brian Rose, Lee Swepston,
Robert de Viana, and Garry Woodard.

My father, the late J. M. Garland, introduced me to the world of international
organizations. I also wish to acknowledge the initial stimulus of Stephen
FitzGerald, Gregory Clark, and the late John Melhuish and Alex Borthwick,
with whom I had lively discussions on many of the issues canvassed in this book
in the Australian Department of External (now Foreign) Affairs prior to China's
UN entry. More recently, I gained insights from discussions with international
lawyers at Peking University and the Foreign Affairs University in Beijing, and
from lawyers attending the International Symposium of the Chinese Society
of Legal History in Kaifeng in October 2005. As a guest of the Centre for China
and International Organization, School of International Relations and Public
Affairs at Fudan University in late 2005, I also had a fruitful exchange of ideas
with international relations scholars from leading Shanghai universities. However, I alone am responsible for the views expressed, and any errors made, in
this book.

Finally, I wish to thank the anonymous readers appointed by Stanford Uni-
versity Press, one of whom revealed his identity as Andrew Nathan, for their
perceptive comments and suggestions. Particular thanks are due to Muthiah
Alagappa and the other members of the *Studies in Asian Security* series Editorial
Committee for their review and encouragement, and to Jeremy Sutherland of
the East-West Center Washington for his assistance. At Stanford University
Press, I am indebted to Muriel Bell, Kirsten Oster, Judith Hibbard, David
Jackson, and Richard Gunde for their excellent work. Closer to home, I am
grateful to Bruce, for his apparently limitless fund of good humour, support and
wisdom, to my mother, for her unfailing interest, and to Rohan and Cris.

Beyond Compliance

Introduction

Compliance and Cooperation in a Changing World

> International relations and foreign policy . . . depend on a legal order,
> operate in a legal framework, assume a host of legal principles and
> concepts that shape the policies of nations and limit national behav-
> ior. If one doubts the significance of this law, one need only imagine
> a world from which it were absent—approximately a situation in
> which all nations were perpetually in a state of war with each other.
> There would be no security of nations or stability of governments;
> territory and airspace would not be respected; vessels could navigate
> only at their constant peril; property—within or without any given
> territory—would be subject to arbitrary seizure; persons would have
> no protection of law or of diplomacy; agreements would not be
> made or observed; diplomatic relations would end; international
> trade would cease; international organizations and arrangements
> would disappear. . . . Attention to the law, in Justice Holmes's phrase,
> may not be a duty but only a necessity.
>
> *Louis Henkin,* How Nations Behave *(1968)*

We stand at a critical juncture in international history. The end of the Cold War, the intensification of globalization, the rise of ethnic tribalism and political sep-aratism within states, the unleashing of fears and threats of terrorism and the spread of weapons of mass destruction, coupled with the perils of global warm-ing and mass migration from poor, authoritarian states to wealthy, metropoli-tan, liberal democracies, have produced unprecedented international challenges and a sense of universal insecurity. Issues of state security have become inex-tricably enmeshed with matters of human security.[1] At the same time, the nor-mal remedies to such problems, sought through multilateral action, the resort to international organizations, and the application of international law, are being increasingly questioned. While such remedies have not been entirely side-lined, their effectiveness, and thus, legitimacy, is under challenge. This state of anomie may prove enduring, or only ephemeral. Much will depend on the an-swers that issue from debate and experience.

In the context of such controversy, this book provides evidence that the multilateral system, whether international or regional, notwithstanding its lack of strong enforcement mechanisms, has made a vital contribution to the international well-being and security of states and their citizens, in particular through its role in "socializing" and reintegrating its more recalcitrant members. It reaches this conclusion by examining the changing relationship of China with key international organizations over three decades and, for purposes of comparison, analyzing its international behavior before it entered those organizations, in particular the United Nations. As I have argued, China constitutes a least-likely case of compliance by virtue of its history, cultural traditions, and power.[2] It has historically considered itself to be the "Middle Kingdom," unconstrained by international society; it lacks a tradition of the rule of law; and it is powerful enough to ignore its international obligations. Therefore, it is least likely to comply with the norms, principles, and rules of international organizations and their associated treaties. If it is nevertheless reasonably compliant with its international obligations, it helps validate the notion that all states, even non-liberal ones, comply with the norms and rules of the international system.[3]

Formerly castigated as a "rogue" or "renegade," China has changed its international behavior under the impact of international institutions.[4] Its rapid integration into the international system since it replaced Taiwan as formal representative of "China" in the UN in 1971 is indicated in the expansion of its membership from only one intergovernmental organization (IGO) and fifty-eight international nongovernmental organizations (INGOs) in 1966, to forty-six conventional IGOs and 1,568 conventional INGOs in 2003.[5] How China has complied with the norms, principles, and rules of these organizations and associated treaties, how it has cooperated with the international community, and how it has changed from an isolated, verbally aggressive state to an increasingly interdependent and compliant one, constitute an important test case of the effectiveness of international multilateralism.

Such questions are not only important as a test of the existing system. They are also important indicators of the future viability of that system. China's unique position as the world's most populous state, as one of the five permanent members (P-5) of the Security Council, as a nuclear power, as an increasingly influential military and economic entity, as the World Bank's largest borrower, and as a "developing" country, underlines its international significance. As a rising power, it will clearly play a vital role in shaping any new world order. This has occurred and will continue to occur largely through its role in key international organizations, through its participation in the negotiation of international treaties, and through its influence over the increasingly assertive group of developing states in international forums. Like other states, China plays a part in influencing how the international organization perceives issues and tackles problems, and in adding to, or subtracting from, the general environment of international cooperation. How it shapes those rules and uses that influence is therefore critical. Since it is argued here that international organizations themselves are capable of "learning" and changing, and since international law continues to develop and its jurisprudence to expand, China's input is an important constituent of the organic process of change, evolution, and decay in the international system. Its continuing support for the norms and rules of international treaties will also be vital to ensuring that, in the future, international standards of sustainable development, labor relations and conditions, and finance and trade are maintained and developed, thereby preventing any diminution in international security and any lowering of global human security standards. By virtue of its size, importance, and influence, China's behavior is, in short, a vital indicator of the shape of things to come.

This book evolved from my work on China's compliance with a range of UN human rights bodies and treaties, which presented the most extreme test of its compliance with its treaty and membership obligations.[6] This specialist study stimulated my interest in China's comparative performance in other international regimes, and in the deceptively simple theoretical question underlying it: why do states comply with international rules? I therefore extended my research to the regimes of international security, the international political economy and the environment, as well as human rights, and tested the reasons for its compliance in each against the main compliance theories. These regimes all pertain to global security—whether state security, the principal subject of the international security regime, or human security, the focus of the latter three regimes.

As my research on these empirical and theoretical questions proceeded, however, it became increasingly clear that, for a fuller account of how the multilateral system worked and how states like China related to it, I needed to go beyond compliance to the more political question of cooperation. While a compliance test was an important indicator of a state's integration into the international system, the measure of its cooperation offered a more comprehensive test of its internalization of international norms.[7] I also needed to garner further insights from international law. For instance, I needed to focus not just on the state and on its responses to the international system, but also on the active part played by international institutions themselves as well as the effect of the state's actions on them. My book therefore brings into the research equation the quality of international rules and their "compliance pull"; the nature of each international organization and its mandate; and the impact that the state is having on those same international organizations and rules. It disaggregates the international system in a way that makes complex outcomes more comprehensible and opens the way for a broader enquiry than compliance studies normally generate.

This approach is new. While scholars of international relations and of China have written cogent studies of China's compliance within international regimes, they have done so largely without reference to international law and to theories of compliance and cooperation.[8] They have also tended to focus more on pressures from within China than on pressures from without. While they have made important contributions to an understanding of domestic political developments, they have largely bypassed the intricate processes of international diplomacy. In failing to focus on the features of international organizations that encourage state compliance, and on the significance of their constituent instruments and associated treaties, they have also failed to adequately explain *why* China complies. Moreover, although excellent singly or jointly authored studies have been made of China's interaction with specific international regimes,[9] there is as yet no single-authored comparative study of China's compliance and cooperation with the international norms, principles, and rules of the wide range of regimes comprising global security. Conversely, as thoughtful international lawyers concede, international law is often silent about the more political aspects of the compliance process,[10] even though it is itself a product of the way rules are formulated through international negotiations. Nor does it inquire into the wider context of the political, economic, and social pressures producing this environment,[11] the political processes inducing international compromise and cooperation, or even, I contend, into the domestic outcomes consequent on the application of compliance mechanisms.

The overall conclusions emerging from my expanded empirical and theoretical investigation have been that:

- In general, China complies with the rules of international organizations and treaties and its compliance has usually improved over time. The initial impetus for its entry into an international organization or its ratification of a treaty has been primarily instrumentalist and has indicated little sympathy for the norms involved. This position has altered with the process of participation, shifting from procedural into a deeper, more meaningful, compliance. However, China's pattern of compliance has not been linear and has been sensitive to the changing international and domestic environment.

- China's compliance, like that of most states, has been determined by a mix of motives, neither wholly instrumental nor wholly based on norms and ideals, and has been impelled by both international and national pressures. The international pressures have been most effectively communicated and applied through the interactive processes of international organizations. The feedback effect of such processes has led to China's gradual reconception of its domestic interests to align more closely with that of the international institution. Its compliance has been deepest when international pressures and its domestic interests have converged.

- At the same time, China also complies differently across and within regimes. For international relations scholars this uneven pattern of compliance may be thought unusual, whereas international lawyers would anticipate such an outcome. Nevertheless, by comparing its responses in different circumstances, common characteristics and patterns of behavior are revealed.

- International organizations and their principles, norms, and rules are themselves active players in the compliance process, not only because of their role in integrating states into the international community, but also because of the variability in their purpose, functions, and enforcement mechanisms and their incentives and disincentives for compliance. This is one reason that states comply differently across and within regimes.

- One set of theories, which I will describe below as "process-based theories," are most useful for explaining China's compliance, while competing liberal and rationalist theories are less helpful, even if they sometimes provide valuable insights.

- Compliance and cooperation are two separate issues that must be considered in their relation to each other. Even the concept of "deep" compliance does not adequately cover the interactive, communicative nature of international politics and the international system. Thus, while China normally "complies" with international norms and rules, it has often not cooperated with them.

- At the same time as complying with existing international rules, China has had an important impact on the international system and on the development of international law. Its part in the negotiation and renegotiation of rules must be understood as a separate category of activity from "compliance" and non-compliance and from "cooperation" and non-cooperation. It is a reflection of the fluid quality of international law, whose function is not only to set rules for state interaction but to continually adjust those rules in response to changing state practice and altered circumstances.

Several of these overall conclusions require elaboration. In particular, there is a need to explore theories of compliance and cooperation and the role, both past and present, played by international law and international organizations in influencing compliance and cooperation within the international system. This will enable a deeper understanding of why China complies, why its compliance record is uneven within and across regimes and why, despite its compliance, it does not necessarily cooperate. The rest of the chapter will consider these issues and will conclude with an analysis of the methodology adopted in this book and a discussion of its organization and trajectory.

Compliance Theories

For decades, scholars have debated the claim of Louis Henkin that "almost all nations observe almost all principles of international law and almost all of their obligations almost all of the time."[12] For the international relations scholar, the question of compliance is at the root of the main question for neoliberal institutionalists as to whether international regimes matter. For the international lawyer, it is critical to the central problem of whether international law makes a difference. In a globalized yet highly differentiated world, the fragility yet critical importance of non-coercive mechanisms renders the question of states' compliance with international rules at once more compelling and more puzzling.

Until recently, there has been almost universal endorsement of Henkin's thesis, and an extensive literature has been produced on the question of why states comply by both international lawyers and international relations specialists.[13] To some extent, as Robert Keohane has observed, both the focus and the approach are dependent on the discipline involved.[14] Obviously, public international lawyers tend to emphasize the nature and legitimacy of rules and of institutional process in facilitating compliance, whereas liberal international relations theorists focus on the interests of the state and its interplay with state and non-state actors as well as with international institutions.

Theories of compliance may be classified in a number of different ways. Harold Koh, for instance, divides them into four strands of thinking that had evolved as early as the end of the nineteenth century: an Austinian, positivistic realist strand, which indicated that states did not "obey" international law, since it was "not really law"; a Hobbesian, utilitarian rationalist strand, which argued that states only followed international law when it was in their interest to do so; a liberal, Kantian strand, which posited that a sense of moral and ethical obligation was the chief source of compliance; and a process-based strand, which attributed compliance to complex patterns of interaction and legal discourse between states. These translate, in contemporary discourse, into a realist strand, a rationalist strand, a Kantian liberal strand, and a process-based strand.[15] Kal Raustiala, on the other hand, distinguishes between rationalist, norm-driven, and liberal theories, while Oona Hathaway, distinguishing beween the rational actor and normative models, situates the "managerial model" within the normative pole, and realism, institutionalism, and liberalism within the rational actor pole.[16] The inherent flexibility of such categories, which may be divided into general and specific theories, demonstrates not only that they are not mutually exclusive but also that they share essential characteristics. Thus, the relationship between norms, institutions, rules, legitimacy, process, and sanctions is a concern of most compliance theorists: they differ, however, on the priority accorded to the various elements and on their interpretation of the nature of the interaction. The majority of theorists argue the case for a particular interpretation. A few, like Louis Henkin and Oran Young, are more eclectic.[17]

For heuristic purposes, the categorization adopted here draws on the Koh taxonomies but concentrates on three main strands: liberalism, process-based theories, and rationalism. Realism is not a useful basis for comparison because it provides no alternative explanation apart from self-interest, a motive already included in most of the other theories, particularly rationalism. This taxonomy facilitates a distinction between international law and international relations theories of compliance that plot a spectrum moving from an almost exclusive emphasis on the nature of norms and rules to an overriding focus on states' interests. However, within the broad spectrum of theories there is considerable overlap and even convergence, particularly between neoliberal institutionalists within the international relations field and some international legal theorists, who concur in underlining the significance of institutional process and the compliance pull of rules and norms. Likewise, the rule–legitimacy strand of liberalism, neoliberal institutionalism, and process-based theories tend to be non-coercive, inclusive theories that attempt to understand why the world, as it currently operates, works. By contrast, for different reasons, international relations realists, some rational choice theorists, and liberal internationalist/identity theorists, discount the significance of both international norms and international institutions. In their different ways, they are more exclusivist, more programmatic, more coercive and potentially interventionist.

Process-based Theories

Process-based theories bring together international law and international relations and have in common a belief in the socializing process of normative discourse and repeated interactions between transnational actors, particularly within an institutional setting. Their proponents are also skeptical, to a lesser or greater extent, of the role played by coercion in achieving compliance. The theories fall into three main categories: the managerial theory of international lawyers Abram and Antonia Chayes, the transnational legal process theory of international lawyer Harold Koh, and the international relations school of constructivism. Together, they provide the main theoretical underpinning for the empirical case studies in this book.

In their book, *The New Sovereignty*, Abram and Antonia Chayes contend that encouraging compliance is a matter of "management," based on procedural fairness and equal and nondiscriminatory application, and harnessing the mutual social pressures operating between states within multilateral institutions. In their view, "not even the so-called hermit state of North Korea has been completely able to resist this kind of escalating pressure."[18] Their theories largely accord with empirical observations of China's diplomatic responses. They argue: (1) that states' compliance with international treaties is quite good and does not owe as much as rational choice advocates believe to enforcement; (2) that a general propensity to comply with treaty rules is engendered by national interest, the need for efficiency, and regime norms; (3) that state compliance tends to be the result of an ongoing interaction between states and the norms, rules, membership, and organizations of international regimes, producing, through reporting procedures, "interacting processes of justification, discourse and persuasion"; (4) that sanctions, while useful in some contexts, are not appropriate for routine enforcement; and (5) that "non-compliance is not necessarily, perhaps not even usually, the result of deliberate defiance of the legal standard,"[19] but, rather, derives from (a) the ambiguity and indeterminacy of treaty language; (b) the limitations on the capacity of states parties; and (c) the temporal aspect of the social, economic, and political changes contemplated by regulatory treaties.[20]

This managerial approach also leads the Chayes to distinguish between the effectiveness of different types of organizations in inducing compliance. However, in some cases their model is not appropriate for China. For instance, they fail to take account of those many cases where self-interest is not endogenous to the treaty but exogenous to it. Their insistence that non-compliance is not usually the result of deliberate defiance of a treaty standard flies in the face of empirical evidence that it is often the state that has the least intention of complying with a treaty, that is, the "least-likely" state, that is most ready to ratify it.[21] They have also been criticized for failing to distinguish between different types of treaties, for setting up a polarity between management and enforcement, for failing to explain how their insights might apply outside the realm of positive, treaty-based law to the growing realm of customary and declaratory international law, and for failing to address the issue of norm and rule internalization.[22]

Many of these theoretical omissions have been remedied in Harold Koh's transnational legal process theory. The internalization of international norms, which has not until recently received much attention from international lawyers, is now a matter of increasing interest.[23] Koh addresses the issue via his theory of the "transmission belt," whereby "the norms created by international society infiltrate into *domestic* society."[24] He focuses on the complex vertical and horizontal process, impelled by global and domestic social pressures, of the translation of international norms into the domestic arena.

> When a nation deviates from [a] pattern of presumptive compliance, frictions are created. To avoid such frictions in a nation's continuing interactions, national leaders may shift over time from a policy of violation to one of compliance. It is through this transnational legal process, this repeated cycle of interaction, interpretation, and internalization, that international law acquires its "stickiness," that nation-states acquire their identity, and that nations come to "obey" international law out of perceived self-interest.[25]

By introducing the notion of "presumptive compliance," Koh addresses the issue of the inherent inertia favoring treaty compliance, explained by other theorists as the phenomenon of "routinization."[26] He also espouses a related notion about states' commitment to "keep the game going." Most importantly, in this particular exposition of his theory, he is agnostic on the question of domestic political structure. Since he sees national identities as socially constructed products of learning, knowledge, cultural practices, and ideology, he claims that states are neither permanently liberal or illiberal, but "make transitions back and forth, from dictatorship to democracy, prodded by norms and regimes of international law."[27] In this respect he specifically cites the experiences of South Africa, Poland, Argentina, Chile, and the Czech Republic.[28] He also argues that management and enforcement are complementary, rather than alternative, facilitators of compliance. As he has observed, "the managerial model sometimes succeeds not solely because of the power of discourse but also because of the shadow of sanctions, however rare and remote that possibility might be."[29] This theory is similar to the enforcement pyramid conceived at the domestic level by Ian Ayres and John Braithwaite.[30]

However, in his 1998 Frankel Lecture, "Bringing International Law Home," Koh elucidates his theory in terms that appear to limit its application to a liberal state. He identifies six key agents in the transnational legal process: (1) transnational norm entrepreneurs; (2) governmental norm sponsors; (3) transnational issue networks; (4) interpretive communities and law-declaring forums; (5) bureaucratic compliance procedures; and (6) issue linkages. He illustrates the way these six processes converge to require the United States and other liberal states to internalize aspects of international law. Of these, the pressures exerted by transnational norm entrepreneurs, transnational issue networks, and domestic NGOs appear the most constant and significant in his case studies, and provide the basis for his prescriptions for future action. However, of these six agents, only (2) and (5) currently apply to a least-likely state such as China, with a minimal opportunity for (4). While Koh affirms that his theory can also serve as a model for "rogue states" such as Iran, North Korea, and China, he fails to identify the precise agents of change in states that lack effective domestic NGOs and are unresponsive to the direct pressures of transnational NGOs. At most, he posits that "strong executives may internalize international rules for an illiberal country, even without judicial or legislative involvement. Yet, once these rules are accepted as domestic law, they begin to trickle into the system and force domestic change, even within illiberal systems."[31] However, even accepting the questionable validity of the "trickle-down" effect, Koh still fails to identify the initial incentives that would motivate the executives and/or citizens of nonliberal states to internalize international norms. Moreover, this version of his theory also fails to explain the reasons behind sudden reversals in the compliance record of liberal states, particularly of the United States, his ostensible model.

Nevertheless, of all the theories analyzed, Koh's is the most comprehensive and the most appropriate for China. It is inclusive theoretically because it incorporates the importance of process in managerial theory, the insights of constructivism, and even a modified acceptance of the role of self-interest and need for the "threat" of enforcement. It is also inclusive in a structural sense, because it comprehends all levels of state and non-state interaction, influence, and compliance—the international and the domestic, the vertical, and the horizontal. Thus, Koh's theory has contributed to the methodology adopted in this book.

Moving to the realm of international relations, constructivists base their ideas on notions of identity formation and international society. Rules and norms are not creations born of states' interests but are themselves constitutive of a state's international identity and interactions. Constructivists argue that the experience of complying with a rule in time may lead a state to redefine its interests, and even reconstruct aspects of its domestic identity, in conformity with that rule. Understanding law as socially constructed, they conceive the main transformative influence as the interaction between the interstate legal structures and the recurrent types of international social interactions to which the laws apply. Thus, according to Andrew Hurrell, "a good deal of the compliance pull of international rules derives from the relationship between individual rules and the broader pattern of international relations: states follow specific rules, even when inconvenient, because they have a longer-term interest in the maintenance of law-impregnated international community."[32] Such a theory has close correlations with China's experience. By contrast, the version of constructivism promoted by Thomas Risse, Stephen Ropp, and Kathryn Sikkink is less appropriate to China. It constructs a spiral theory of five phases in a state's relationship with the transnational human rights network, in which the state is gradually drawn into compliance with human rights norms and rules.[33] But, this theory depends for its realization on domestic political reform, and is thus not applicable to a least-likely, authoritarian state that has not to date responded positively to NGO pressures.

More relevant is a recently developed international relations theory that attempts to bridge the divide between constructivists and rationalists by focusing on persuasion. Its supporters propose a "synthetic approach to compliance that encompasses both rational instrumental choices and social learning, an approach which will help both rationalists and constructivists to refine the scope of their compliance claims."[34] There are strong synergies between this work and that of the Chayes.[35] However, the latter do not scrutinize persuasion in the detail required by the former. Thus, Iain Johnston focuses on the microprocesses of socialization in an attempt to distinguish the internalization of norms from their instrumental adoption.[36] He proposes the testing of socialization by using international institutions as the social environment and individuals and small groups involved in state policy processes as the individual agents of interest. Another contribution made by persuasion theory is its suggestion that there may be different phases in the international socialization of states and that international organizations may have different effects depending on the political constitution of the state involved and the point at which it commenced participation. Such is the burden of two of Jeffrey Checkel's hypotheses borrowed from social psychology. The first is that "argumentative persuasion is more likely to be effective when the persuadee is in a novel and uncertain environment—generated by the newness of the issue, a crisis or serious policy failure—and thus cognitively motivated to analyze new information." The second is that "novice agents with few cognitive priors [prior beliefs] will be relatively open to persuasion."[37] Checkel argues not that uncertainty and inexperience are sufficient for social learning to occur, but that they make it more likely that an agent will be convinced and then learn through processes of persuasion and communication.

These theories correspond, to a greater or lesser extent, to the experience of a revolutionary state. To date, however, few contemporary scholars have sought to explicitly address why nonliberal states comply. Thus, David Armstrong, Charles Ziegler, and Stephen Chan analyze the foreign policy goals, values, and motivations of "revolutionary" states, and their reasons for non-compliance with international norms: but they do not address the reasons why such states comply, when they do.[38] For such theories one has to go back to the earlier ideas of Richard Falk and Inis Claude in the Cold War era.[39] In his 1966 article, Claude espoused an eclectic theory that contains aspects of process-based theory, liberalism, and rationalism. He identified the motivation behind the foreign policy choices of "revolutionary states" as the "collective legitimizing function" of international organizations. According to Claude, collective legitimization is a political, not a legal, process that is "less a matter of purporting either to apply or revise the law than of affixing the stamp of political approval or disapproval."[40] It is an aspect of the verbal rather than the executive functioning of international organizations, in particular, of the United Nations. Thus, admission to the UN has taken on the political meaning, if not the legal implication, of collective recognition.[41] In addition, General Assembly and Security Council resolutions proclaim the legitimacy or illegitimacy of positions or actions taken by states. Even in the case of revolutionary and developing states, "the vigorous effort that states customarily make to prevent the passage of formal denunciations of their positions or policies indicates that they have respect for the significance, if not for the validity, of adverse judgments by international organs."[42] The result is that a state may hesitate to risk Assembly disapproval, not because it accepts the priority of the will of the Assembly over its national interests, but because an adverse judgment by that body makes the pursuit of that policy contrary to the national interest. This legitimizing function applies not only to state actions but also to important, abstract issues that affect the global balance of power.

Revolutionary states identify their national interests with the will of the Assembly because of the benefits they draw from UN participation. By invoking the authority of the UN, Claude claims, revolutionary states have also been able to claim the right to development and control of their own resources. Through the international organizational norm of the sovereign equality of states, such states have enjoyed a voice that on any other criterion of power would be denied them. However, precisely because such a collective legitimizing function empowers as well as constrains revolutionary and developing states, it also has the potential to destabilize international order. The danger, Claude warns, is that "collective legitimization may stimulate legal changes that will make international law more worthy of respect and more likely to be respected, but it may also encourage behavior based upon calculation of what the political situation will permit rather than consideration of what the principles of order require."[43]

This paradox is critical to an analysis of the international behavior of a least-likely state. The same quality of collective legitimization that cements the global order may also be manipulated by such a state to destabilize it. This brings us closer to the nub of the problem and confirms the approach of this study. Not only does a detailed disaggregation of the behavior of a least-likely state test the validity of different theories of compliance, it also helps clarify which aspects are indicative of its compliance and/or cooperation with international norms, principles, and rules, and which are calculated merely to test the bounds of what the political situation will permit.

Alternative Theories

Other theories are less applicable to the situation of China. Liberal theories argue that state decisions cannot be simply explained by the processes of organizational participation and calculations of interests. Explanations must focus on the role of ideas and values. For that reason alone, they are less relevant to the experience of a nonliberal state such as China. As might be anticipated, this category of theory is primarily the domain of international lawyers, and subdivides into the rule-legitimacy theory of Thomas Franck and the liberal internationalist (or rule-identity) theory of Anne-Marie Slaughter.[44] Of the two, Franck's ideas are the more applicable to China, in that he emphasizes the nature and legitimacy of international rules and their capacity to induce compliance. He sets out to establish a "definitive hierarchical ordering of international rules according to how effective they are in evoking a sense of obligation and securing voluntary state compliance."[45] His ideas thus bear a close relation to the more specific compliance theories of those international lawyers who are opposed to the abstract nature of compliance theory and who argue the more practical possibilities of "treaty-induced" compliance within a specific regime.[46]

Franck argues that, in the manifest absence of enforcement powers, the community of states has identified "legitimacy" as "the standard by which the community measures rules' capacity to obligate." One indicator of an international rule's perceived legitimacy is its "compliance pull," itself dependent on four principal indicators: determinacy, symbolic validation, coherence, and adherence. At the same time, he cautions that "compliance pull" is not the same as compliance: "A state may violate a rule because the perception of national advantage to be gained by rule disobedience in a particular instance is so powerful as to overwhelm the most powerful compliance pull."[47] He thus recognizes that self-interest may sometimes act as an exogenous force working against compliance.

Because of his primary attention to the nature of international rules, Franck's broader view has sometimes been obscured by critics. In fact, he argues that legitimacy is determined not only by the text of a rule, but also by the process of text formation and by the nature of the rule-giving institution. In addition, he sees the international community as a "rule community," in that "the usual form of affiliation among states is by rules of conduct and rules that govern the making, interpretation and application of obligating rules." As the reciprocal of the international community's validation of the nation's statehood through participation in international organizations and their treaties, states feel obliged to obey its rules; the highest commitment of states in international forums is "to keep the game from ending."[48]

The strength of Franck's theory is that it disaggregates rules and distinguishes a hierarchy in their effectiveness and legitimating properties. However, in focusing on a rule's "compliance pull," he obscures the fact that rules also differ from each other in terms of the ease, or difficulty, with which they may be implemented. Moreover, he fails to identify the comparative "compliance pull" effected by rules, by rule-giving institutions, and by participation in the international community as a whole. Franck also neglects discussion of different forms of institutional interaction or the means by which norms are internalized into domestic legal systems.[49] His inquiry appears to end abruptly at national borders. More broadly, he does not give sufficient attention to the role of politics within international institutions. Finally, the strength of his argument is vitiated, as Keohane points out, by the fact that it is circular: a rule's compliance pull is an index of its legitimacy, while its legitimacy is said to explain "compliance pull."[50] Aside from such theoretical critiques, the dependence of his rule-legitimacy argument on the shared understandings of a community of liberal states raises questions about its applicability to a least-likely state.

At the more extreme end of the liberal spectrum, the liberal internationalist/identity theory of Anne-Marie Slaughter relies far too heavily on the shared understandings of liberal states.[51] The initial basis of this theory was the idea that state behavior is primarily determined by an aggregation of individual and group preferences.[52] However, as Anne-Marie Slaughter has developed it, the theory "mandates a distinction among different types of states based on their domestic political structure and ideology."[53] Compliance, according to this view, is largely dependent on whether or not the state is a liberal democracy, enjoying representative government, civil and political rights, juridical equality, and a functioning judicial system dedicated to the rule of law.[54] The applicability of this theory to the world's most powerful democracy has already been brilliantly challenged by José Alvarez.[55] However, it is even less applicable to least-likely states. This is because, as in the case of the Ropp, Risse, and Sikkink argument, the "centre" of democratic governance and the "periphery" of illiberal states can only be reconciled, and universal compliance achieved, once the center has succeeded in luring the periphery into its democratic embrace. In principle, therefore, the theory has no applicability until the political structure of the nonliberal state itself has been transformed, at which point the newly liberal-democratic state is self-evidently no longer a least-likely state. Moreover, although like the work of other scholars it addresses the relationship between the international and the domestic,[56] liberal identity theory emphasizes the internationalization of domestic norms rather than the domestication of international norms. As such, it would not appear to have resonances with the situation of a least-likely state.[57]

Rationalism, a third significant theoretical approach, incorporates a range of political positions, but, unlike liberal theory, is primarily the preserve of international relations scholars. It treats states as choice-making entities that accept their interdependence but make rational calculations on the basis of interests rather than norms. Rationalist theories range from the neoliberal institutionalism of Robert Keohane, to the more extreme rational choice model of George Downs et al. Because Keohane's theory is closer to that of the Chayes, it has more relevance to China than does the Downs version. Like the Chayes and the constructivists, he stresses the power of institutions to bring states to redefine their interests in ways that accord with the principles and rules of their particular regime. Applying an instrumental and a normative optic to the question of the impact of norms on states' compliance with international rules, he focuses on three concepts essential to an account of how rules relate to state action: interests, reputation, and institutions. He argues that both interests and concern about reputation are changeable, responsive to alterations in descriptive information and causal and principled beliefs. They can only be reconciled within the context of highly valued international institutions, which are important for the way in which they can alter states' interests and affect how others behave. Thus, "institutions that states strongly value can promote cooperation by linking normatively prescribed behavior, such as fulfilling commitments, to the continued receipt of material or normative benefits from the institutions." Although allocating significance to both interests and norms, he thus, like the Chayes, places international institutions at the top of the hierarchy of causation. Like the Chayes, Keohane also downplays the importance of coercion and underlines the lack of sophistication in the views of crude instrumentalists.[58] His theory, although placing too much emphasis on the need for material incentives, would therefore appear to have some explanatory value for least-likely states, particularly as regards the importance of a state's "reputation."

By contrast, George Downs, David Rocke, and Peter Barsoom have mounted a comprehensive challenge both to the Chayes' managerial position and, by extension, to neoliberal institutionalists such as Keohane. Of all the compliance theories (apart from realism), the rational choice model is the most highly instrumental and, paradoxically perhaps, the least appropriate for China. Whereas Keohane downplays the role of coercion as a "negative incentive," Downs et al. stress its importance. The Downs et al. variant of rationalism starts from the premise that the high level of treaty compliance and the marginality of enforcement result from "the fact that most treaties require states to make only modest departures from what they would have done in the absence of an agreement."

This is because of "state selection," which ensures that states have already selected out those treaties they cannot comply with, since they are "unwilling or unable to pay the costs of enforcement."[59] This position contrasts with the Henkin argument, and the Hathaway findings, that states sometimes ratify treaties with which they have no intention of complying.[60]

To demonstrate their claim, Downs et al. set up an index of "deep compliance" against which they compare a number of empirical cases where enforcement has been present or lacking. The "depth of cooperation" demanded by a treaty is to be determined by "the extent to which it requires states to depart from what they would have done in its absence." The depth is measured by the treaty level and "could be based on the status quo at the time an agreement was signed or on a prediction derived from the year-to-year change rate prior to that time."[61] In contrast to the Chayes, they see significant self-interest as largely exogenous to the treaty-making and treaty-ratifying process (although playing an initial part in treaty selection), and therefore as imposing a constraint on treaty compliance. For this reason, they argue that, to obtain deep compliance with a treaty, not only is enforcement through sanctions necessary, but "the deeper the agreement is, the greater the punishments required to support it."[62] The applicability of such a theory to a powerful, least-likely state, jealous of its sovereignty and of its international status and reputation, is shown in these case studies to be highly questionable.

Compliance and Cooperation

Compliance with international rules, however, is not the whole story. To gain a more complete understanding of the dynamics of state integration into the international system, we must move beyond compliance. The term, "beyond compliance," has been used in the literature in a number of different ways. It has been used to argue that the real questions of international law go "beyond compliance" to questions of the ideology of international law.[63] It can indicate a programmatic goal of continuous improvement "beyond compliance," whereby states are urged to take the lead to promote concepts globally.[64] Conversely, it can mean that, because the international situation is seen as no longer amenable to the application of universal rules, it has moved "beyond compliance." In view of the "shrinking regulatory resources" at the disposal of regulators, scholars devise ways to extract the "biggest bang" from the rapidly diminishing "regulatory buck."[65] In this book, by contrast, "beyond compliance" is used as an analytical concept, designating the need to move beyond sole consideration of formal compliance (and non-compliance) in evaluating the integration of a state into the international system, to the broader political questions of cooperation (and non-cooperation).

Compliance is essentially a legal concept. Formal or "rule" compliance may be defined as a state's implementation and enforcement of the specific norms, principles, and rules required by the international treaty to which it is a party or of the constitutive rules of the international organization of which it is a member.[66] More specifically, as Joseph Grieco has defined it, compliance constitutes "the initiation, modification or cessation of some form of behavior by signatories so that they are in accord with injunctions articulated in code rules."[67] Since the degree of compliance with norms, binding principles, and rules may vary between regimes and even within regimes, compliance is here assessed on the basis of a single regime or part thereof, by taking into account the state's adherence to the major associated treaties to which it is a party. Formal compliance may be instrumental or cognitive/normative.

Cooperation, on the other hand, is a broader political concept defined in more general terms as "collaboration, coordination, joint action and mutual support."[68] Whereas compliance involves the implementation of an existing rule, cooperation is the original motivating force, or act, behind the formation of that rule. In the words of John Braithwaite and Peter Drahos, "cooperation involves one actor helping another actor to satisfy an interest or goal which one or both actors possess [and which] can be reciprocally or non-reciprocally based."[69] However, this broad definition contains within it the option of states collaborating for purposes of self-interest and in possible breach of their obligations under international law.[70] For the purposes of this study, therefore, cooperation is defined more narrowly in relation to international regimes as either individual action by a state that promotes the object and purpose of a treaty or regime, and, in particular, their non-binding norms, or collective action to the same end. Conversely, non-cooperation is reflected in attempts to block, stymie, or impede the object and purpose of an organization or treaty.

The concepts of compliance and cooperation both suggest a "capacity to yield," thereby imputing certain characteristics to the state actor. Both also issue from a complex interplay of constraining variables. The wellsprings of formal compliance include the rules themselves, the institutional process of participation in the organization or treaty regime, the application of incentives or coercive mechanisms, the pressures from within the epistemic community, whether international or domestic, habit, and, finally, the state actors themselves and their perceived international and domestic interests. Cooperation in the positive sense, on the other hand, implies an individual or collective willingness to collaborate, which normally excludes the need for coercive enforcement and which is evaluated less on the basis of obligations entrenched in legal instruments and more on the basis of associated and reinforcing principles that are not strictly legal requirements. Cooperation, like compliance, is a function of a

state's strategic choice but it is generally more reflective of normative internalization than of mere instrumental responses. However, whether or not states
choose cooperation over conflict, or cooperation over instrumental compliance,
also depends on their calculations of the "payoffs," and the behavior and cooperation of other nations, since "self-interest can be assessed individualistically,
relatively or conjointly."[71]

Cooperation may not always lead to compliance with rules, and compliance
can occur without cooperation, for instance, as a consequence of the imposition
of coercive sanctions. However, at the individual level, if a state's compliance with
an international norm or rule is associated with long-term cooperation, it is more
likely to be a function of "deep" compliance whereas, without cooperation, compliance may be merely instrumental. Thus, for instance, a state that has entered
major reservations on its acceptance of a treaty may still be in formal compliance with the remaining provisions, but not be considered "cooperative" with
the object and purpose of the treaty. Cooperation in this sense addresses the spirit,
rather than just the letter, of international law.

As a collective phenomenon, cooperation and, in particular, a pattern of cooperation, also creates an international environment that can assist, and help
explain, compliance.[72] In this sense, cooperation is part of the "circumstantial
penumbra" that forms the international context in which compliance is encouraged. A joint decision to cooperate is, after all, at the basis of the formulation
of international rules and of the establishment of international organizations and
regimes. The continuing effectiveness of such rules, organizations, and regimes
is in itself a confirmation and legitimation of the original cooperative decision
and creates a presumption that states will normally comply with the rules.
Conversely, the defection of significant states from such arrangements is likely
to destabilize the assumption of the legitimacy of their rules, organizations, and
regimes and to alter existing habits of compliance, triggering more unstable
international behavior generally.

The Role of International Law, International Organizations, and International Regimes

As Louis Henkin has pointed out, international law performs a variety of functions. It provides legal concepts of nationality, national territory, property, torts,
contracts, and the rights and duties of states; and it establishes mechanisms, forms,
and procedures whereby states maintain their relations, engage in trade, and
resolve differences. The most important such mechanism is the international
agreement, with its underlying principle of *pacta sunt servanda* ("treaties are to
be obeyed").[73] For the purposes of this study, the most significant of these agreements are those promoting cooperation for some global aim—international

treaties in a wide variety of regimes, and the constituent instruments governing the establishment, administration, and jurisdiction of international organizations such as the United Nations and its specialized agencies.

International organizations or, more precisely, intergovernmental organizations (IGOs),[74] have a shorter history than international law, although they are
intertwined with, and governed by, as well as developing, it.[75] They are normally
created between states, by treaty or the legal act of an already existing organization, for some purpose, and possess a will distinct from that of their member
states.[76]

Although the late nineteenth and early twentieth centuries saw the establishment of functional bodies such as the International Trade Organization
(ITO) and the Hague Conferences that regulated the conduct of war, the main
spur to international organizational development came from the United States
in the course of the two world wars. The Paris Peace Conference of 1919,
presided over by President Wilson, undertook the dual responsibility of making a peace settlement and fashioning an international system that would ensure
that the devastating conflict of 1914–18 could never be repeated. To promote
international cooperation, peace, and security, it had to address not only collective security matters and the relations between states, but pressing economic
and social questions that had been highlighted by the growth of the trade
union and socialist movements in the previous half century. The Covenant of
the League of Nations, based on Wilson's vision, underwrote the establishment
of the League of Nations, the Permanent Court of International Justice, itself
originally inspired by the Hague Conferences, and the International Labour
Organization. These institutions represented the nursery slopes of the fully
functioning international system that was fathered by Franklin D. Roosevelt in
the 1940s. Apart from its goals of collective security and of liberalizing international trade in an equitable manner, its foundations were strengthened by its
amalgamation of U.S. domestic norms of social justice, derived from the New
Deal, with those of European welfare states. As manifested in the robust international institutions to which it gave rise, namely the United Nations and the
Bretton Woods institutions of international development, finance, and trade—
the World Bank, the International Monetary Fund, and the concept of an
International Trade Organization—it provided a holistic system of international norms incorporating individual and collective values of democracy, civil
rights, and social justice.

This vision was incorporated into the provisions of the UN Charter, which
established in workable equilibrium the requirements of sovereignty, peace and
security, and individual human rights. It was also formalized in the 1948
Universal Declaration of Human Rights, which integrated civil, political, social,

economic, and cultural rights, in both individual and collective forms, and was implemented as binding international legal instruments in the International Covenant on Civil and Political Rights and the International Covenant on Economic, Social, and Cultural Rights. With the onset of the Cold War, the social justice component of Roosevelt's initial conception was whittled away, and the norms of civil and political rights assumed ascendancy. As a result, the proposed International Trade Organization, an institution designed by John Maynard Keynes to achieve fair trade, was sidelined, and one part of it, the General Agreement on Tariffs and Trade (GATT), which was initially simply a temporary multilateral agreement to facilitate the reduction of trade barriers, became the principal forum of international trade regulation.[77]

Since those early days, international organizations have evolved along more pragmatic and less idealistic paths. Their principal role is now seen "not as the *deus ex machina* of yesteryear, entering the scene in order to save the day or to save the world, but rather as a type of bounded political community which facilitates discussion and debate; no longer as regulatory agencies *par excellence*, but simply (and most importantly) as places where international politics is conducted."[78] At a more abstract level, however, they are also understood as the institutional representations of internationalization and interdependence. They represent an "organizing process of conflict management at the supranational level" and a "collective organizing response to a multiplicity of 'traffic' control problems in a world of contradictory trends."[79] In reducing the autonomy of the state and reshaping the international system, they are today seen as both constitutive of, and responsive to, the processes of globalization.

At the same time, international organizations have a less commonly observed role: in an era of globalization, they also empower states. As Dinah Shelton observes, "If globalization is a process mostly structured by private actors, then states must cooperate to exercise public power. It is largely through intergovernmental organizations that this cooperation takes place."[80] This empowering function is reflected in the main reasons states seek to enter the United Nations. The first reason, as we have already pointed out, is international legitimization. This includes the specific legal goal of recognition, insofar as membership of the UN, according to Martin Dixon, "entail[s] a presumption of statehood which it would be very difficult to dislodge,"[81] and the principle of the sovereign equality of states, which empowers developing and unequal states as well as protecting their sovereignty. The second reason is the need for community. Even revolutionary actors depend upon mutual contact and communication, not only with developing, but also with developed, states. Related benefits of this community are that it helps "stabilize identities, codify interests,

enshrine moral principles and resolve cooperation problems."[82] As Richard Falk
has pointed out:

> The dependence of *every* international actor upon mutual contact and communication
> is the most basic form of interdependence. Such interdependence presupposes a mini-
> mally reliable system of international order, despite the fact that revolutionary and
> nonrevolutionary actors are engaged in a struggle for supremacy and containment,
> and adhere to contradictory values and proceed toward incompatible goals.[83]

The third reason is the requirement of a rule-based system. A minimally reliable system of international order requires a rule-impregnated international society.[84] As palpable entities with formal hierarchies of decision making and sets
of established rules, norms, and governing procedures, international organizations fulfill this need. For their part, once they have entered the organization,
new member states become aware, if they have not already done so, that the
international institution exists not just as a forum to promote their goals, but
also as a source of duties and obligations. To realize their goals on a continuing
basis, states must exhibit a degree of reciprocity by complying reasonably with
the norms, principles, and rules of the international organization and its associated treaties. In other words, a pressure to comply is already built into the existing system. Thus, in joining international organizations and becoming a party
to international treaties, member states freely consent to the obligations
entrenched in the norms and rules of the specific organization and accept the
need for reciprocity.

International organizations are not only important in themselves: they constitute a vital means of shaping and accessing the international regimes operating in different issue areas and their associated community of states. As Abram
and Antonia Chayes have argued, international organizations constitute some
of the chief sources of pressure for obtaining states' compliance with regime
norms.[85] They and their treaty regimes not only encourage transparency, cut
transaction costs, build capacity, and enhance settlement, but also, through a
process of "jawboning," *persuade* parties to "explore, redefine and sometimes discover" their own, and mutual, interests.[86] They subject states to a process of strategic interaction and mutual pressure for consensus that helps regulate their conduct. They not only help define, but also legitimize, the activity regulated by a
regime.[87]

Regimes, on the other hand, are customarily defined as "sets of implicit or
explicit principles, norms, rules and decision-making procedures around which
actors' expectations converge in a given area of international relations."[88]
Norms, to adopt the terminology used by John Braithwaite and Peter Drahos,
constitute a "generic category which includes rules, principles, standards and

guidelines." Principles are "settled agreements on conduct, recognized by a group," which are abstract and can conflict. Rules, on the other hand, prescribe relatively specific acts.[89] Principles may be constitutive of international rules, whether as general principles of law or as legal requirements within a treaty. Where, on the other hand, principles are not legal requirements in a particular treaty or regime, they may give rise to rules, may provide the context in which rules may be interpreted, or may have the function of programmatic goals.[90] The difference between these two types of principles is not always self-evident, and to distinguish between those that require compliance and those that could be described as nonbinding requires careful analysis.

Because regimes incorporate a matrix of values, rules, and institutions, they are commonly seen as transcending a strictly organizational framework. However, international organizations provide a wide range of pressures that may appeal as much to a state's short-term interests as to its ideals. They are sources of power, status, information, finance, technical assistance, and technology transfer; they submit the state to the approval or disapproval of its peers; and they provide the crucial source of constraints and incentives that regulate the conduct of wavering states within international regimes. They and their associated treaty bodies also provide the mechanisms for monitoring state compliance with a treaty's norms, principles, and rules, and for arriving at authoritative judgments. In the opinion of international lawyer Don Greig,

> the existence of an organizational structure will usually provide an added dimension to limitations upon State sovereignty. Whereas any treaty regime impinges upon that sovereignty to the extent agreed upon in the terms of the treaty, if the treaty establishes an organization, it will often bestow powers directly or indirectly upon that organization which will enable it to create obligations for States, in some circumstances against their will.[91]

The study of international organizations may thus be said to be both narrower and broader than the study of regimes.

According to international lawyer David Kennedy, the norms and institutional structures of international organizations reflect the particular context of international jurisprudence from which they emerged.[92] Thus, the ILO, with its tripartite structure and strong egalitarian and socioeconomic focus, was a product of the movement for economic democracy in the West and of the post–World War I Wilsonian idealism that also gave rise to the League of Nations. The UN, World Bank, and IMF embody the formal institutional machinery, generalized norms, and vertical enforcement mechanisms forged by statesmen and international lawyers during the 1940s. Although the GATT was formed in the same period, it was, as we have observed, originally only part of a projected International Trade Organization that was intended to combine free trade with international socioeconomic fair dealing.[93] Today, the GATT and WTO offer a total contrast to that vision. They represent the second wave in two centuries of free trade, seeking neomercantilist freedom from the yoke of the state, and eschewing vertical authority. Likewise, the UN human rights bodies have evolved to combine formal institutional machinery and generalized norms with a more horizontal emphasis on participation by NGOs and on the right of individual petition. The environmental regime initially mirrored the human rights regime in setting up vertical institutions and conferences, beginning with the Stockholm Conference in 1972. At the same time, it instituted a more horizontal "process" rather than "rights" orientation, favoring the use of principles and standards rather than formal rules, expanding participation from states to NGOs, forgoing "vertical" in favor of "horizontal" institutions, and adopting a wider variety of pressures for compliance than were available in the earlier regimes.[94]

Certain consequences flow from this historical and structural, as well as thematic, differentiation. First is the degree to which an international organization is coextensive with its overall international regime. For instance, despite efforts to integrate labor standards into the WTO, the ILO, the earliest international human rights organization, remains the principal body setting and promoting such standards. On the other hand, the World Bank, the IMF, and the WTO form only part of the international political economy regime, that is, the overall investment, finance, and trade institutions. Other international organizations influential in this area include the OECD, the Basle Committee on Banking Supervision, the Bank for International Settlements (BIS), the Financial Action Task Force, the EC, and the G-7/8.[95] The overall human rights regime comprises UN bodies, UN specialized agencies like the ILO, regional bodies, NGOs, and some bilateral mechanisms. In arms control, the Conference on Disarmament is the main multilateral negotiating forum, but the overall regime includes the International Atomic Energy Agency (IAEA), the UN First Committee, the UN Disarmament Commission, special sessions of UNGA, specific conferences such as the NPT extension conferences, regional multilateral organizations like the ASEAN Regional Forum (ARF), and bilateral negotiations. In the environmental regime, UNEP is one of a number of international organizations presiding over a horizontal sweep of treaty secretariats. Others influential in environmental matters include the OECD, EU, G-7, IMO, CSD, UNDP, UNIDO, and the World Bank.[96] Such organizational complexity has been increased by the expansion of the specific mandates and normative structures of international organizations in response to the globalization of ideas, with the result that these institutions now include a host of activities not originally anticipated in their constituent instruments.

Second, international organizations differ in their recognition of a key international legal principle, the sovereign equality of states. While the UN proper reflects this principle in most bodies apart from the Security Council, the ILO through its tripartite structure distributes power between states, businesses, and workers. Power in the IMF and World Bank, on the other hand, is hierarchical and broadly reflects the economic power of the state. Power in the GATT and WTO is bilateralized and horizontal, while in UNEP, it is diffused into developmental, regional, or interest groups.[97]

Third, the regimes associated with international organizations differ in their degree of "hardness" and "softness." In international relations, as distinct from international law, human rights and the environment are often represented as "soft" regimes, on the basis of the argument that they do not directly and immediately affect the security of the state, or the interests of other states.[98] However, such understandings are incomplete. In both cases, sovereignty and security issues become important over time when transboundary "externalities" affect neighbors. In the case of the environment, for instance, it is precisely the increase in their transboundary impact that distinguishes current environmental issues from those in the past.[99] Moreover, both human rights and the environment are vital issues bearing on human security, whether between or within states. This situation has given rise to a notion of "collective goods," which is used by environmentalists to persuade states that doing good for oneself can also mean doing good for others.[100] Despite the persuasiveness of this concept, there still appears to be no initial international presumption in favor of environmental protection.[101] The conflict between economic development, sovereignty, and the environment places constraints on the power of international law to extend its protection, so that political intervention is required.[102] However, because of the need for state consent, the likelihood of progress on issues such as climate change, which presents states with such challenges and conflicts of interest, is highly questionable.[103]

In the case of human rights, refugee flows are an obvious example of the "externalities" that impact on other states and undermine state and human security. Unlike the environment regime, the international human rights regime benefits from an initial presumption in its favor. Nevertheless, partly for this reason, and partly because it addresses itself to the well-being of the citizenry, bypassing the authority and interests of the state, it is seen by many states to threaten their sovereignty and even national security. In fact, most breaches of human rights are caused by states acting against their own citizens or against those in their jurisdiction. Therefore, as Robert McCorquodale and Martin Dixon observe, much of international human rights law operates outside the national legal system to provide both an international standard by which state practice can be judged and redress for the infringement of human rights.[104]

Nevertheless, it is true that the "externalities" of the international environmental and human rights regimes are not as immediate or as obvious as are those of the international security and political economy regimes. The latter are more open to management through the use of reciprocal mechanisms and even through enforcement. The norms, principles, and rules of the international political economy regime are particularly "sticky," in that they both inhere in, and regulate, the processes of globalization.[105] By contrast, the international human rights and environmental regimes normally lack the bargaining counter of reciprocity, at least as that concept is understood in the international security and political economy regimes, and differ in the degree to which they are vulnerable to external sanctions. The human rights regime offers enhanced moral status in exchange for compliance, and long-term, non-specific gain in exchange for short-term, specific pain. However, even this minimal incentive may be ineffective, in the light of the notion that moral status can accrue to states simply as the result of ratifying a human rights treaty, whereas the additional status flowing from the treaty's implementation is not sufficient to offset the huge costs involved.[106] The environment can offer more financial and marketing rewards, but also suffers from strong, if short-term, material disincentives.

It follows that international regimes and their organizations differ markedly in the type of compliance and accountability mechanisms entrenched in their treaties and constituent instruments. For instance, in the international security regime, the IAEA can report back on cases of non-compliance to the Security Council, which has a range of sanctions at its disposal. Under their Articles of Agreement, the IMF and the World Bank can threaten withdrawal of financial or developmental benefits in the event of non-compliance, while the WTO offers the incentive of mutual benefits in exchange for compliance, as well as the disincentive of trade sanctions approved by WTO panels. By contrast, human rights are normally only open to bilateral and multilateral enforcement in the form of trade sanctions in crisis situations. Otherwise, universal enforcement is achieved mainly through mechanisms of varying effectiveness. These include public naming and shaming, and accountability mechanisms such as reporting and on-site inspections, which rely heavily on the state's voluntary acceptance of scrutiny. Environmental cooperation similarly relies on international consensus rather than enforcement: reciprocal trade-offs exist, but, apart from exclusion from those rewards, and resort to shaming, reciprocal sanctions are lacking. The difference between compliance mechanisms means that there is also a difference in the way compliance, deep compliance, and cooperation are most effectively measured in each regime.

At the same time, as has been noted, these international organizations and regimes are not strictly separate and discrete: increasingly they are characterized by issue linkages and functional overlap. Just as it is recognized that each issue area has an impact on other issue areas, so international institutions have expanded to reflect the new consciousness. Thus, the World Bank is no longer just a development institution, but includes in its mandate responsibility for administering environmental funds and for ensuring that its projects meet criteria of good governance and anticorruption. Again, while not all regimes impose the same pressures and incentives to achieve compliance, there may be an overall trade-off on issues between the international organizations constituting them. There is often such a trade-off between states within different regimes, particularly the human rights, environment, and trade regimes. For instance, states have traded off an agreement not to pursue a resolution against China in the UN Human Rights Commission in exchange for an agreement to commence bilateral "human rights dialogue." States may also buy and sell emissions credits in the climate change regime.

Measuring and Explaining Compliance and Cooperation

Richard Falk has argued that, to assess a state's compliance, it is only necessary to judge its behavior.[107] To the extent that we are dealing at the international level with policy as formally articulated by a state's agents and as implemented internationally and domestically by state and non-state agents, behavioral measures are more reliable as indicators of compliance than policy statements alone. Behavioral analysis, however, involves three main analytical problems. How, on the one hand, may compliance with international rules be identified? And how, on the other, does one distinguish between the sufficient conditions leading to compliance, and the necessary ones? Furthermore, as José Alvarez has put it, at what point is compliance proven? At the point of signature of a treaty; at the point of reservations entered into the treaty; at the point of ratification of the treaty; or at the post-acceptance stage?[108]

In order to surmount the difficulties of evaluation and to avoid judgments that are too narrow or subjective, this book assesses a state's behavior by four main criteria. These are its formal (or "rule") compliance with organizational rules and the international and national treaty obligations arising therefrom; the "depth" of its domestic compliance; the "depth" of its international compliance; and the degree of its cooperation in promoting the interests of the regime.

The evaluation of formal compliance is facilitated by a distinction drawn between five inter-related manifestations of compliant behavior at the international and domestic levels. These are: (1) accession to a treaty or agreement; (2) procedural compliance with reporting and other requirements; (3) substantive compliance with the rules and principles promulgated by the multilateral body, exhibited in international or domestic behavior; (4) de jure formal legal compliance, or the implementation of international norms in domestic legislative provisions, in judicial incorporation, or in institutional development; and (5) practical compliance, or compliance at the level of domestic implementation and enforcement.[109]

To further refine the fifth level, it is helpful to distinguish, in the manner of Harold Koh, between political implementation, or what he calls, "political internalization," which indicates government policy responding to an international norm, and social implementation (or what he calls "social internalization"), which indicates widespread civil obedience to a norm.[110] Whereas political implementation (5a) may be indicative of either instrumental adaptation or genuine norm internalization, social implementation (5b) is a more reliable indicator of "deep compliance" or norm internalization at the domestic level. These five levels form a spectrum rather than a continuum. For instance, a state may comply at levels 1, 3, or 5, and not necessarily at 2 and 4. The levels are also of different significance, depending on whether one is measuring international or domestic compliance.

The depth of a state's *international* compliance, on the other hand, is indicated, according to the Chayes, other process-based theorists, and Keohane, by the extent to which participation in international organizations leads that state to redefine its interests in terms that correspond with treaty norms.[111] Here, the critical point to discover is whether organizational and treaty norms initially constituted part of a state's perceived interests, and, if not, whether participation in international organizations gradually altered its perception of its interests, disposing it to accept and internalize those norms. A second indicator of deep compliance, also an outcome of the process of institutional participation, is a state's increasing preparedness to renegotiate its sovereignty and move to a more restrictive interpretation of the principle in practice. The third process-based indicator is the extent to which the state has gradually accepted the "costs" of participation in the regime. Needless to say, these indicators often overlap, and each may apply more usefully in different regimes.

Finally, an important indicator of a state's cooperation, as distinct from its compliance, is its readiness to promote the object and purpose of the constitutive rules of an organization and its associated treaties, by, for instance, ratifying treaties without introducing excessive reservations, assuming non-mandatory obligations, and encouraging other states to follow suit. Conversely, non-cooperation is evaluated not only on the basis of domestic responses, but on the basis of a state's failure to respect the object and purpose of the organization/treaty, its introduction of excessive reservations on ratification of a treaty, or even its attempt to undermine international norms and principles. However, such non-cooperation and spoiling activity must not be confused with the legitimate, democratic exchanges of differing opinion and policy that form the basis of the ongoing development of international law and diplomacy.

As has been suggested, there is no set or immutable standard of compliance, whether with respect to the substantive issues or to the record of other states. Any assessment about the extent to which states such as China comply with their treaty obligations and with the norms and procedures of international organizations depends, in the first place, on the standards against which compliance is measured.[112] This book assesses compliance with reference to the way in which norms are currently operationalized in the monitoring procedures of each regime. It deals not with prescriptions, but with empirical reality. China is adjudged to change as it adapts to, and internalizes, prevailing rules, norms, and procedures of international organizations and their treaties.

Secondly, as the Chayes have pointed out, the provisions of international treaties and the constituent instruments of international organizations provide abstract and ideal standards, but in practice perfect compliance with them is never attained. Instead, there is a level of "overall compliance" that is judged "acceptable" in the light of the provisions of each treaty or international organization.[113] Or, as John Jackson has observed in relation to the law of the GATT, it is a matter of whether a state has achieved a "reasonable degree of compliance with the obligation."[114] This "acceptable" or "reasonable" level is also subject to variation across different parts of the regime, and according to different periods and situations.[115]

The relative and environment-dependent nature of compliance and cooperation is exemplified by the contrast between the present international policies of the United States and those of the 1940s, or, more recently, between the more multilateralist outlook of the Clinton administration and the unilateralism of President George W. Bush.[116] Many critics, including former President Jimmy Carter and Senator Robert Byrd, have remarked on the contradiction between the long-held liberal foreign policy norms of a powerful liberal democracy and its actual realist behavior, while others decry the inexplicable shift now occurring from multilateralism to unilateralism.[117] Realists may seek to justify this situation by arguing that, even though a hegemonic state may have been one of the principal architects of the liberal international system, realism will trump liberalism in its foreign policy.[118] However, they would have more difficulty in explaining the double paradox that, in recent years, both the Chinese and U.S. governments have reversed their previous approaches to multilateralism.[119] Six years ago, China was seen as a country that had not yet integrated smoothly into the international system, and that questioned many of its rules and practices, whereas the United States was seen as a benevolent, if sole, superpower that was largely respectful of international law and institutions. Today, the United States is increasingly invoking raison d'état for its foreign policy decisions and China is appealing to many of the international norms it had previously rejected. International organizations have provided the forum for such appeals, and a means by which the relations between unequal states have been formally equalized. Particularly in the arms control regime and in debates in the UN Security Council, China has called on the United States, explicitly or implicitly, to respect the obligations under international law that it is seen to be breaching.[120] In other words, compliance (and cooperation) are measured not only by absolute standards, but also in relation to the behavior of other states and/or the same state over time.

A further complication is that most regimes allow for a "time lag between undertaking and performance."[121] The time factor, as Risse, Ropp, and Sikkink have also pointed out, is therefore significant in this respect too.[122] Finally, there is rarely a perfect fit between international and national/municipal law. This is because, although according to the concept of *pacta sunt servanda* treaties are acknowledged to be legally binding on the states that ratify them, they do not automatically become a part of the law of the land unless they are self-executing. This is so, whether in common law or civil law jurisdictions, or in the case of liberal-democratic or nonliberal states.[123] In countries with a dualist system, international obligations will not usually trump municipal rules, while even in those that adopt a monist system (where, in theory, obligations assumed under international treaties automatically become part of the law of the land), the situation is rarely so simple in practice.[124] Where international law does not automatically become part of the law of the land, implementing legislation must be passed by national legislatures to harmonize domestic law with international legal obligations. As Dixon and McCorquodale observe:

> The resolution of this struggle [between international law and national/municipal law] is usually determined by the constitution of each State—the constitution having been created by political acts—and by the interpretation of the constitution and national laws by the national courts of each State. As a consequence, the application of international law within a national system will vary from State to State. Further, the lack of significant enforcement measures in international law has meant that it is often through national courts that international law is enforced, and therefore national law can often determine the effectiveness of international legal decisions and the lawfulness of international actions.[125]

An important aspect of this book's methodology is that, in conjunction with the above four-level analysis, it uses diplomatic history to reveal the process of change. Because standards of compliance are relative and dependent on a judgment of "reasonable expectations," the assessment of a state's compliance is more effective if it is based on such comparative qualitative/historical, rather than quantitative, criteria. While compliance may be approached quantitatively by means of a comparative analysis of the behavior of a number of states across a variety of treaties in an issue area, such analyses of the behavior of a single state are less helpful, because they gloss over vital historical, cultural, and international contexts.[126] This historical micro-macro approach is undertaken through a combination of documentary analysis and interviews with the principal actors in different international organizations or, as Marc Levy and others have put it, "'natural or quasi-experiments' involving comparisons across different issue areas over time."[127] This is achieved in a number of ways, for instance, by comparing China's initial attitude to the norms of each international organization with its later attitude, and its policy on international organizations and international law before and after it entered the United Nations. Such an approach explains how China interacts over time with different international organizations; how its views and interests in those international organizations change over the decades; how it achieves its organizational ends; how its organizational behavior compares with that of other states; what effects the international organization has on the state's domestic institutions; which are the endogenous and exogenous pressures promoting China's compliance and those constraints limiting it; and what has been China's impact in shaping the norms and rules of the international organization over time.

Structure and Sources

The choice of international organizations in this study is dependent on the significance of their role in the different issue areas relating both to state security and human security, and on a history of Chinese participation that is sufficiently long—two decades at least—to provide substantial evidence for the inquiry. China and the international security regime will be examined through the Conference on Disarmament (CD), and, to a lesser extent, the IAEA; China and the international political economy regime through the World Bank (IBRD/WB) and the International Monetary Fund (IMF); China and the international environmental regime through the United Nations Environment Programme (UNEP) as well as the World Bank; and China and the international human rights regime through the International Labour Organization (ILO) and the UN Committee against Torture (CAT). Since there is as yet no adequate history of China's participation in the WTO, which began on 11 December 2001, discussion of its lengthy negotiations to join that organization, of the benefits and costs its entry entails, and of its compliance since entry, are not the main subject of a specific chapter but, like its relations with the World Health Organization (WHO), are included in mini case studies testing the overall findings in the Conclusion.

Research on international organizations is inevitably affected by issues of accessibility and transparency. Here there is also enormous variation. In general, UN bodies proper are more transparent than specialized agencies like the IMF. This is because their documentation of plenary sessions is comprehensive and identifies the name and country of speakers. UN bodies proper are also normally open to the involvement of NGOs, even though their right to participate is often contested by nonliberal states members. However, there are notable exceptions to this general observation. Of the particular international organizations examined here, the ILO stands out as a specialized agency that is extremely transparent. Its annual conference and committee and other activities are well documented, as are the activities of its member states. As an institution, it is also physically accessible. Although it does not allow for NGO participation, its tripartite organization, comprising government, business, and workers, is broadly representative of the civil society of the industrial sector. On the other hand, UNEP, which is a UN body, is less transparent. Its documentation of state activity is generally disguised under the regional, rather than individual, identity of the state (for instance, "the Group of 77 and China"), making it difficult to identify the particular contribution of a specific state. The main transparency is provided by the summarized accounts of UNEP's meetings by a Canadian NGO, the International Institute for Sustainable Development. One reason for the opacity of the international environmental regime is the extreme sensitivity of environmental issues, and the concern of the secretariats of international environmental bodies not to deter states' participation by singling them out for attention, unless they are found to be abnormally non-compliant. In this case, an implementation committee may publicize breaches of obligations.

By contrast, the Conference on Disarmament provides extensive documentation identifying the position taken by states at its open sessions. However, a great deal of its activity is conducted in closed sessions. In this context, the unremitting activity of Rebecca Johnson, Executive Director of the international security NGO called the Acronym Institute, has done much to offset areas of organizational opacity. For their part, the World Bank and the IMF conduct most of their business in confidential Executive Board meetings. Only their official historians gain access to their records.[128] Nevertheless, their published reports on country performance in a variety of issue areas provide essential transparency, disgorging a wealth of information on the progress and problems of a member state's economic, financial, health, and environmental development, as well as on the success of World Bank and IMF country programs. Finally, as a UN treaty body, the Committee against Torture is highly accessible despite its sensitive subject matter. It publishes detailed reports and, through its close relations with NGOs, communicates freely with international civil society.

In analyzing and comparing the historical record of China's compliance with the norms and rules of these different international organizations, this book highlights the usefulness of process-based compliance theories as an explanatory tool. Chapter 1 situates China in its historical, political, and legal culture and describes the early history of its interaction with international law and international organizations from the nineteenth century until the establishment of the People's Republic in 1949. It also compares the early history of the PRC's attempt to replace Taiwan as the official representative of China in the United Nations with the history of its participation in the UN and its specialized agencies immediately after November 1971. The succeeding Chapters 2 to 5 track the complex interaction, from the point of entry, between the PRC and principal international organizations within the significant regimes that are being scrutinized, illuminating the extent to which it has implemented the norms, principles, and rules of each organization and associated treaty/treaties. In the process, they analyze each institution and its rules; the history of China's participation; and its internalization of institutional norms and rules through the interacting processes of domestic legislation, institution building, leadership policy, and social implementation. Finally, the Conclusion relates the findings of the chapters and the brief record of China's compliance with the WTO and WHO to the questions and compliance theories under analysis. The patterns and sequences of China's compliance and cooperation are identified. Conversely, the implications of China's imprint on the negotiation of specific international treaties and on the development of international law are explored.

As a "least-likely" case study and as a formerly designated "rogue state," China offers an important test of the effectiveness of international organizations and their treaties in achieving compliance with their norms, principles, and rules. It thereby highlights the explanatory power of process-based theories. In its potential to destabilize the underlying consensus that gives legitimacy to these formal and informal constraints, China is also a "most-likely" case study. This book will therefore provide a guide not only to the sources of compliance for a state that has the power to make or break regimes, but also to the way in which that state has sought to influence their shape and development. More broadly, the inquiry will go beyond compliance to consider the nature, extent, and sources of China's international cooperation, without which there can be no ultimate guarantee of international order and little assurance of global security.

I

China and International Organizations
From Alienation to Integration

> There are some who acknowledge the illegal and aggressive conduct
> of the Chinese Communists, but who believe that the United Nations
> can somehow accommodate this unbridled power, and bring it in
> some measure under the control—or at least the influence—of the
> community of nations. They maintain that this can be accomplished
> by bringing Communist China unconditionally into participation
> in the United Nations. By this step—so we are told—the interplay
> of ideas and interests in the United Nations would sooner or later
> cause these latter-day empire builders to abandon their warlike ways
> and accommodate themselves to the rule of law and the comity of
> nations. . . . [But], the United States earnestly believes that it is im-
> possible to speak seriously today of "bringing Communist China
> into the United Nations."
>
> *U.S. Ambassador Adlai Stevenson,*
> *United Nations, 1 December 1961*

In 1961, U.S. Ambassador Adlai Stevenson summarized the prevailing arguments
about the best ways to handle recalcitrant states, arguments that continue to this
day, and expressed his skepticism of process-based compliance theories. A decade
later, that skepticism was tested by the changing behavior of the People's
Republic of China, when it belatedly gained widespread diplomatic recognition and took its first tentative steps toward participation in international organizations. The impact of China's gradual institutional reintegration is thrown
into relief by the manner in which its roller-coaster relationship with other
nations and its negative experience of international law and organizations from
the early nineteenth century contributed to its reputation from the 1950s as a
"rogue state."

China's modern international experience oscillated between the tempestu-
ous interaction of imperial times and the calmer waters of the Republican period,
when it began to integrate imperceptibly into the international community via
its participation in international organizations and its increasing tendency to
invoke international law. Thereafter, the two traumatic decades of exclusion that

followed the establishment of the People's Republic in 1949 illustrate the negative effects of nonparticipation in international organizations. Contrary to general impressions, the PRC's gradual alienation from the international community from 1949 to 1971 was due less to the policies of the newly established communist government and more to the rejection by UN members of its efforts to become the official representative of "China." After it was finally admitted to the UN in 1971, its initially cautious behavior bespoke a state whose international policies were still largely overshadowed by its own history and its domestic, ideological struggles. From 1978, however, economic modernization policies and the lessons it had absorbed from its involvement in the UN over the preceding seven years encouraged its greater openness, confidence, and support for multilateralism. Finally, it advanced into a new era in which it became willing not only to comply with international rules but also to actively support the multilateral system and to accept the costs, as well as the benefits, of participation. This chapter documents the long, drawn-out process of China's gradual reintegration into the international community. By comparing and contrasting its attitudes to international organizations and international law in the different periods until the present, it uses history to provide a benchmark of the power of international institutions to help socialize and transform states.

Imperial and Republican China: From Isolation and Conflict to International Apprenticeship

Until the early twentieth century, China's interaction with the international community was inhibited by its exceptionalist notion of itself—not entirely dissipated to this day—as the "Middle Kingdom" at the apex of a hierarchically based system of tributary states. The Chinese emperor was, according to this view, "responsible for all peoples under heaven and . . . their rulers were viewed as his appointed representatives."[1] Before 1860, even the increasingly assertive Western powers were obliged, as Tseng Yu-hao pointed out in 1930, to "struggle for equality, as the Chinese of the present day are fighting for justice."[2] On the other hand, to China's rulers, European public international law, as a mechanism used to justify foreign incursions into China and the imposition of unequal treaties upon the country, appeared as the West then conceived it, as an instrument confined to "civilized" Western states that was designed to consolidate power in the hands of the powerful and undermine states that were militarily weak.

It was therefore not surprising that China's early attitude to international law was, at worst, dismissive and, at best, instrumental. Qing dynasty officials had been apprised of the "law of nations" by representatives of the Dutch East India Company in the seventeenth century and its principles had influenced the one-off Treaty of Nerchinsk of 1689.[3] Yet China's first invocation of international law in the modern era was largely a reflex response to the series of "unequal treaties" imposed by Britain in the wake of the Opium Wars of 1842 and 1860.[4] The Qing court's acceptance of international law as a defensive weapon against the marauding West encouraged the Tsungli Yamen's publication of a translation of Henry Wheaton's *Elements of International Law* in 1864, and informed its successful protest against Prussia's arrest of three Danish vessels in the Bohai Sea, on the grounds that this "inner ocean" fell under exclusive Chinese jurisdiction.[5] However, it was not until the founding of the Republic in 1911 that Chinese authorities began to appeal regularly to international law to promote their interests.[6]

China's closest encounter with international institutions in these years was through multilateral bodies such as the Shanghai International Settlement.[7] The latter was established in 1863 to regulate the intrusion of foreign "barbarians" into Chinese society, and was administered by a Council of American and British merchants, the Shanghai Mixed Court, presided over by a Chinese magistrate but with a foreign co-judge, and the Chinese Imperial Maritime Customs Service. Again, this early experience, reflecting the effective inequality of states, was hardly a favorable one. By the late nineteenth century, the gap between China's assumption of cultural and political superiority, and the reality of its military and political subordination at the hands of Western powers, had widened, giving rise to severe national trauma.

From the turn of the century, China began to participate in genuinely multilateral organizations by joining the Universal Postal Union in 1897, and sending delegations to the 1899 and 1907 Hague Conferences. Its decisive emergence onto the international stage occurred with the participation of the fledgling Republican government in the Paris Peace Conference in 1919, when it helped draft the Covenant of the League of Nations, and its foundation membership of the International Labour Organization. Nevertheless, these ventures in international citizenship did little to mitigate its maltreatment by the major powers, as evidenced by the destructive military intervention and indemnity imposed in response to the Boxer Rebellion and the transfer of Germany's concession in Shandong to Japan, which sparked the seminal patriotic May Fourth Movement of 1919. Relations with the West were further soured by Britain's repression of protests against the exploitation of Chinese workers in Japanese cotton factories in Shanghai in 1925. Finally, China's initial faith in the League of Nations was shattered by the latter's ineffectual response to its appeal for assistance against Japan's attack on Manchuria in September 1931.[8]

The collapse of the League and the devastation wrought by World War II rekindled hopes for the establishment of a new and stronger organization to guarantee world peace. Because of its critical role in the war against Japan, the

Republic of China was invited to participate, for the first time on an equal basis with the great powers,[9] in the Moscow talks of 1943 about the creation of such a body. The following year, representatives of China, the United States, the United Kingdom, and the Soviet Union met at Dumbarton Oaks for exploratory talks on the new organization and, in October 1944, agreed upon the Dumbarton Oaks Proposals.[10] At Yalta, in February 1945, it was decided that China, the United States, the UK, the Soviet Union, and France should be invited to be foundation members of the new body and the Republic of China thereupon accepted an invitation to become a sponsor of the San Francisco Conference, which drew up the UN Charter.[11] Its new prominence was largely the result of the intervention and foresight of U.S. President Franklin D. Roosevelt. Although he was concerned to keep China fighting the Japanese, he also wanted it to be one of the "Big Four" who would guarantee the postwar collective security system, and hoped that its involvement would encourage it to become a democracy at the end of the war.[12]

The People's Republic of China, and the Consequences of Exclusion

The international organizational apprenticeship of the Chinese leadership was rudely interrupted by a twenty-year deadlock that developed from 1949 over whether the Nationalist regime in Taiwan or the People's Republic on the mainland was the legitimate representative of the Chinese people in the UN and its associated organizations. In 1949, the newly established People's Republic had fully expected that the UN and its specialized international agencies would legitimize its power and status by voting for its replacement of Taiwan. This assumption prompted China's new Foreign Minister, Zhou Enlai, in accordance with a September 1949 resolution of the Chinese People's Political Consultative Conference, to demand the expulsion of the Nationalist delegation to the UN headed by Dr. T. F. Tsiang.[13] The PRC's numerous overtures to the UN, directly and through intermediaries, followed logically from pre-1949 policies.[14] Although the Chinese Communist Party had shared the Nationalist government's disappointment in the League of Nations, it had also supported the Republic's hopes of the United Nations. In 1945, Mao Zedong had welcomed the San Francisco Conference with a declaration that his party fully agreed with the proposals of the Dumbarton Oaks and Yalta Conferences on "the establishment of an organization to safeguard international peace and security after the war" and that it was appointing "its own representative on China's delegation to this conference in order to express the will of the Chinese people."[15] As a result of pressure from Zhou Enlai and the Allies, Dong Biwu, a senior Party member, together with his colleague Qiao Guanhua, had taken part in the proceedings of the conference and had personally signed the UN Charter.

The immediate problem facing the PRC, however, was that there were no guidelines in the Charter with respect to the representation of a nation whose political regime had changed. Even more important was that the Western bloc, headed by the United States, was not ready to extend diplomatic recognition to the PRC. Thus, although the United States did not initially regard the question of the PRC's admission *vice* Taiwan as a substantive issue subject to its veto, a Soviet proposal, made on 10 January 1950 in response to further representations from Zhou Enlai, that the Security Council expel "the Chinese Kuomintang reactionary remnant clique," was defeated on 13 January by 6 votes to 3 with two abstentions.[16]

Nevertheless, PRC hopes were bolstered when the UN Secretary-General, Trygve Lie, circulated a memorandum on 8 March that concluded that the question of China's representation, "unique in the history of the United Nations," should be determined on the basis of whichever government had the power to "employ the resources and direct the people of the State in fulfillment of the obligations of membership."[17] Since five members of the Security Council (India, Britain, Norway, Yugoslavia, and the USSR) had already recognized Beijing, and since it was generally accepted that the veto would not apply on a question of credentials, only two more votes would have been required to transfer China's credentials to Beijing.[18] Lie therefore persisted in urging PRC representation, and sought to obtain the necessary votes from among Egypt, Ecuador, and France.[19] Since even the United States was prepared to accept the decision of the majority in the Security Council, there was every likelihood in the first half of 1950 that the People's Republic could have emerged as the official representative of China in the UN.[20]

The history of China's relations with the United Nations, and with international organizations in general, might thus have been very different had it not been for the outbreak of the Korean War on 25 June 1950.[21] Ironically, the Soviet boycott of the Security Council between 13 January and 1 August, allegedly in support of the PRC, weakened the long-term standing of the latter by enabling the Council, freed from the threat of a Soviet veto, to authorize an international force to repel North Korea's attack on South Korea.[22] In fact, whether Stalin was indirectly trying to put obstacles in the way of China's integration into the international community at that point is currently a matter of intense scholarly speculation. To make matters worse, in the midst of the Council's discussion on 1 August of the "Complaint of Aggression against the Republic of Korea," the Soviet Union, which had returned to the Council, took over its presidency and presented a provisional agenda in which the issue of recognition of the People's Republic of China preceded the issue of the peaceful settlement of the Korean question.[23] This deliberate linkage of the Korean crisis with the problem of China's representation did not assist the effective handling of either matter. The majority of delegates felt that a study of possible uniform procedures on representation questions should first be initiated by the UN General Assembly, to which body further debate was then transferred. In the meantime, in mid-October 1950, as the U.S.-led international force moved north toward China's border, Chinese troops entered North Korea. In late November, when General MacArthur reached the Yalu River, Chinese and North Korean forces counterattacked in huge numbers.

Against this background, in December 1950, after prolonged negotiations, General Assembly Resolution 396 (V) recommended that whenever more than one authority claimed to be the government entitled to represent a member state, the question should be considered "in the light of the Purposes and Principles of the Charter and the circumstances of each case." Any such question had to be decided by the General Assembly or its Interim Committee, while other organs of the UN and specialized agencies had to take into account the position taken by the General Assembly or its Interim Committee on any representation question. This recommendation left the PRC's claim to UN representation a hostage to circumstance. From 1951 to 1953, the General Assembly supported the American proposal to postpone the question and, from 1954 to 1960, it agreed to the U.S. proposal "not to consider" any move to seat China or expel the Nationalists. In this way, the issue of Beijing's UN representation became one of the casualties of the Cold War, only to emerge as a real possibility two decades later.[24]

As a result, when the first delegation of the People's Republic of China to the United Nations, headed by General Wu Xiuquan, landed in New York on 14 November 1950, it came not as the representative of "China," but in response to an invitation to attend the Security Council meeting on the Draft Resolution on U.S. Aggression against Taiwan, presented by the government of the People's Republic of China.[25] Under Article 32 of the Charter, any state that was not a member of the United Nations or the Security Council could be invited in a non-voting capacity to discussions concerning a dispute to which it was a party. The Security Council's subsequent rebuff to the PRC's delegation, together with the adoption of Resolution 498 (V) charging the PRC with aggression in Korea, profoundly shocked China and provoked a subsequent change in its attitude to ad hoc participation. Thus, in 1955, it rejected the Security Council's invitation to participate in discussions concerning hostilities with the Republic of China (ROC).[26]

Although it was questionable whether, as Chinese scholars claim, U.S. pressure was as significant as the Korean War in blocking China's UN entry in 1950, there is no doubt that it subsequently became the main impediment to that entry.[27] Until the end of 1953, China continued to seek representation, even making support for its seat in the United Nations a precondition of diplomatic recognition.[28] However, from the spring of 1954, learning from its failures, it adopted a more indirect approach.[29] By that time, the rebuffs it had suffered had altered its view of the UN. While continuing to support the principles of the UN Charter, it now differentiated between the formal entity, the UN of the Charter, and the political reality of the UN under U.S. control. As a Chinese scholar observed,

> The Charter of the United Nations itself contains many democratic principles and reflects the will of the people of the world. However, no matter how perfect the Charter is, if the members of the United Nations do not observe the Charter, the United Nations cannot realize the purposes and principles of the Charter.[30]

This distinction allowed China to inveigh against UN policies and resolutions, as dominated by the United States, while at the same time continuing to insist on its right to the "restoration" of its UN seat. In 1955, looking back from the vantage point of the tenth anniversary of the founding of the UN, Dong Biwu expressed China's disappointment:

> After the establishment of the United Nations, people all over the world hoped sincerely that the United Nations would become an effective organization capable of maintaining international justice and world peace, and that it would play its proper part in international affairs. . . . China is one of the original members of the United Nations. She is one of the five permanent members of its Security Council. Since the overthrow of imperialist and Chiang Kai-shek reactionary rule by the Chinese people and the founding of the People's Republic of China, our country has been illegally deprived of its legitimate position and rights in this regard. This is due to the constant obstruction of the United States, in defiance of the wishes of the majority of member states of the United Nations.[31]

Evolving Policies on International Organizations and International Law

China's sense of loss of sovereignty at the hands of the United States and other Western states echoed the humiliation experienced in its earlier relations with Western powers. It also ensured that there were no offsetting international incentives that might persuade it to soften the dogmatic application of its socialist ideology. From the establishment of the People's Republic of China in October 1949, China's view of the world developed into a complex amalgam of its historical and cultural legacy, its ideology and related tactics, and its perception of international encirclement. Mao's interpretation of Marxism-Leninism was premised on an explicit philosophy of flexible strategies and tactics, drawn

from the communists' guerrilla war experiences and designed both to protect
China as a revolutionary society perceived to be under siege and to realize its
new, revolutionary goals. At a subliminal level, China's new policies also reflected
the traditional reliance of its domestic political culture on ethics rather than law,
moral consensus rather than judicial procedure, and benevolent government
rather than checks and balances, as well as notions of hierarchy, power, and personal relationships (*guanxi*).[32]

Like its domestic ideology, China's foreign policy strategies were mapped and
remapped according to the "major" and "minor" contradictions generated by
changes in the international environment.[33] Over the years, until the onset of
a more global consciousness from 1978, its policies variously reflected Marxist
internationalism, opposition to social imperialism, which cast the Soviet Union
as an ideological enemy, and the notion of the "Three Worlds," which distinguished between the First World, or two superpowers, the Second World, or
developed states, and the Third World, or developing states. The new foreign policy was informed by a Marxist view of international law, itself an outgrowth of
socialist conceptions of municipal law. According to Marxist theory, law, like
politics, is part of the superstructure of a state produced by its economic base
and representing the interests of the ruling class. In a socialist society, it was seen
as an instrument of the state. By extension, international law was conceived as
an instrument of a state's foreign policy,[34] a view reinforced by China's earlier
experiences with Western powers. The close interrelationship between China's
view of international law and its foreign policy was later reflected in a critique
by Chinese international lawyer Huan Xiang:

> Principles and rules of international law since Hugo Grotius' time [in general] re-
> flected the interests and demands of the bourgeoisie, the colonialists and in particular,
> of the imperialists. The big and strong powers have long been bullying the small and
> weak nations, sometimes even resorting to armed aggression. International law has
> often been used by the imperialists and hegemonists as a means to carry out aggres-
> sion, oppression and exploitation and to further their reactionary foreign policies.
> Apologies for aggression and oppression can often be found in the writings on inter-
> national law.[35]

For this reason, as in the late nineteenth and early twentieth centuries, international law continued to be seen by China's spokesmen as a tool to promote
China's foreign policy interests rather than as a set of universal norms, principles, and rules that provided the foundation of international order:

> International law is one of the instruments of settling international problems. If this
> instrument is useful to our country, to socialist enterprise, or to the peace enterprise
> of the people of the world, we will use it. However, if this instrument is not advanta-
> geous to our country . . . we will not use it and should create a new instrument to
> replace it.[36]

This new, revolutionary perspective was a radical departure from the former Nationalist government's adoption of Western models of municipal and international law.[37] Although the PRC's understanding of international law was heavily influenced by Soviet theorists, it did not share the latter's increasingly generous interpretation of the formal sources of international law, which over time began to resemble the Western view. Learning from its own international organizational experience, by the mid 1960s, the Soviet Union had moved from its early emphasis on treaties as the most important source of international law to recognizing the role of general principles of international law and the decisions of international organizations and, as subsidiary sources, judicial decisions and the writings of scholars. By contrast, China recognized treaties and implicitly accepted custom as sources of international law, but did not appear to recognize the decisions of international organizations, judicial decisions, or scholarly opinion.[38] It considered that the subjects of international law were states, and did not include international organizations or individuals. International organizations also had no law-making role. Thus,

> The United Nations Organization is one form of international organization of sovereign states. Its resolutions in general have only the character of a recommendation (with the exception of Security Council decisions to maintain peace, taken under Chapter VII of the Charter). Such resolutions cannot ipso facto bind member countries. The United Nations definitely does not possess legislative power. Even the legal drafts prepared by the International Law Commission and adopted by the General Assembly must still go through the procedure of an international conference and the conclusion of a treaty before they acquire binding force. . . . The United Nations is an international organization among sovereign states, not a "world government" above them.[39]

International treaties themselves were valued as "an important means for adjusting mutual relations between states and for securing their independence and mutual interests." However, they were divided into "equal treaties" and "unequal treaties." This was because "the contents of an international treaty are decided by the ratio of the relative strength of the contracting states and the prevailing general international situation at the time of concluding the treaty."[40] Nevertheless, in practice China still tolerated some unequal treaties, as its preparedness to negotiate new land boundaries with the Soviet Union based on such treaties indicated.[41] It also chose to recognize some of the international treaties signed by the former ROC government, such as the 1949 Geneva Conventions.[42]

At the same time, China's scholars recognized international law as the repository of valuable principles, foremost of which was sovereignty:

> The principle of sovereignty is . . . the core of all fundamental principles of international law. The principles of nonintervention in internal affairs, mutual non-

aggression, equality and mutual benefit and so forth, are all based on the principle of mutual respect for sovereignty. At the same time, the principle of sovereignty also has important links with other norms of international law. . . . For example, the principle of pacific settlement of disputes, the principle of *pacta sunt servanda*, the system of diplomatic privileges and immunities, and so forth, are all based on the premise of respect for each other's sovereignty and nonimpairment of each other's independence. Therefore, in many problems of international law the principle of sovereignty becomes a legal criterion for judging the legality or illegality of a given act. Because of the foregoing, the struggle revolving around the principle of sovereignty in international law is often very sharp and fierce.[43]

China distinguished its own view of sovereignty both from "absolute sovereignty," or the theory that "a state may, without being subject to any restriction, do anything it wishes to other states," and from "restrictive sovereignty," according to which, it alleged, "sovereignty is relative, divisible, and subject to restriction and abandonment."[44] It advocated instead the "principle of mutual respect for sovereignty," or what could be termed "reciprocal sovereignty," according to which "respect for sovereignty must be mutual: the principle that other states respect our sovereignty and we respect the sovereignty of other states. The exercise of sovereignty should be based upon the premise of not impairing the sovereignty of other states."[45] There were several flaws in this line of reasoning. First, the principle of sovereignty has never been so absolute that it has supported the notion of total impunity with regard to the treatment of other states. Secondly, the principle of *pacta sunt servanda*, which China claimed to support, was itself an expression of restrictive sovereignty, a concept China officially rejected.

Although, as time passed, this view of sovereignty was somewhat modified, Chinese scholars still resiled from a restrictive interpretation.[46] Sovereignty was understood as comprising internal sovereignty, expressed as the supreme power of the state, and external sovereignty, expressed as the right to independence.[47] The third element in the troika, popular sovereignty, was absent. Even half a century later, Chinese scholars still conceived a radical difference between their interpretation of sovereignty and that of the West, claiming that whereas developing states stressed the legal aspect of sovereignty as a shield to protect state interests, developed states emphasized the interdependence of states.[48] The Chinese interpretation thus continued to conflict with the morality of the international order as it is commonly understood. The act of ratifying treaties, complying with their provisions, and cooperating with international regimes and their norms usually entails the ceding and restricting of a state's sovereignty. According to this interpretation, the exercise of sovereignty is not manifested in the use of executive power to refuse obligations, but rather, in the state's autonomous decision to permit the restriction of its authority for a given, collective purpose.

The exclusion of the People's Republic from the principal forum of world opinion and debate had a number of serious consequences, not least for the United Nations itself. The absence from its membership, and from that of its specialized agencies, of a government representing, by the mid-1960s, at least 800 million people, had far-reaching implications for the authority and legitimacy of that body. The fact that the Republic of China was generally regarded as a cooperative member that shared the values of the organization and participated dutifully in the shaping of international law and international organizations,[49] in no way obscured the absurdity of its claims to represent "China," particularly given its role as a Permanent Member of the Security Council armed with a veto. Even Taiwanese international relations scholars indirectly acknowledged this at the time.[50] The perceived injustice provoked a particularly trenchant opinion by an Indian legal scholar in 1958:

> As the United Nations is not inspired by any single idea or motive and is universal in its membership, including Communist Governments as well as other types of new and revolutionary ones, the exclusion of China by refusing its effective mouthpiece the right of representation is a clear illegality involving: (i) disregard of international law and the commission of an international wrong; (ii) violation of the United Nations Charter; (iii) adoption of an unconstitutional procedure; (iv) conclusions being reached which are impossible to sustain; (v) resort to discriminatory treatment which is forbidden according to international standards; (vi) loss of potency and effectiveness of the United Nations from the organizational viewpoint; and (vii) a complete confusion of the principles of recognition as accepted by international law.[51]

For the People's Republic, the consequences of its exclusion from the UN were not just serious, but disastrous. Exclusion deprived it not only of an essential aspect of external legitimation but also of the countless benefits and socializing effects of participation in, and mutual interaction with, the global community. Moreover, the resulting sense of national grievance became permanent. Even after China's entry into the UN in 1971, an observer remarked that "it suffers, more or less consciously, from having been rejected by the UN for twenty-two years and ignored by other international institutions, from being recognized by a minority of states, and from being slandered and vilified by the others."[52] As Chinese scholars indicated, the most damaging effect of its exclusion was the weakening of China's sovereignty.[53] The PRC had some opportunities for multilateral interaction, notably through its participation in the Geneva Conference of 1954, the 1955 Bandung Conference, and the Enlarged Geneva Conference on the Laotian Question.[54] It also joined or sent observers to various communist intergovernmental organizations and, by 1960, had succeeded in joining two international intergovernmental organizations and thirty nongovernmental organizations.[55]

However, full and meaningful access to the international community lay through entry into the United Nations and thence through the doors of its specialized agencies, in particular the Bretton Woods institutions. Deprived of that source of empowerment, China's foreign policy gradually shrank into a narrow and self-regarding preoccupation with ideological issues and Cold War competition, heavily colored by its paranoia about containment and encirclement, through which its perceptions of the outside world were distorted and refracted. Even though it continued to express its views on UN activities and resolutions from the outside,[56] it was unable to influence and shape them. Its bilateral relations were primarily limited to extensive contacts with other socialist and developing states, with whom it joined common cause in the expression of its grievances. Its frustration and sense of alienation were reflected in the standards it began to impose for its participation in international organizations. Apart from the expulsion of Taiwan, which had always been a prerequisite, each organization was now required to have a "correct" ideological orientation, a favorable political climate, and institutional safeguards.[57]

The arguments used in the UN to justify the annual vote to exclude China, moreover, created increasing pressures on that state. From 1950 to 1961, in the annual agenda item on the question of China's representation, the U.S. delegation proposed, and obtained, the postponement of debate. The U.S. legal argument was based on two main claims: that the People's Republic had not yet been recognized by the United States and many other members of the United Nations; and that the UN General Assembly had passed a resolution that identified China as an "aggressor."[58] However, although the matter of China's UN representation related solely to the credentials of the PRC to represent China, the United States and like-minded states also invoked Article 4 of the Charter relating to new membership. This article stipulated that membership was open to all "peace-loving states which accept the obligations contained in the present Charter and, in the judgment of the Organization, [were] able and willing to carry out these obligations." This provided UN members the opportunity to annually appraise China's leaders and its socialist system, to challenge their "peace-loving" qualifications, to submit China to comparison with some idealized state, and to reject it as wanting. Particularly offensive to the Chinese was the allegation that their country "despised" the UN and that, if supported in its bid, it would not comply with UN resolutions. In response to this, an eminent Chinese scholar insisted in 1956 that China's peaceful foreign policy was entirely consistent with the provisions of the UN Charter, and that its only argument was with actions that had been forced on the UN by the United States.[59]

China's exclusion led it to an almost dismissive view of the UN between 1958 and 1961. According to another scholar, Kong Meng:

The various international organizations are only a form of cooperation among states: they are neither members of international society nor subjects of international law. Even the functions of an international organization like the United Nations are limited to the scope prescribed by the agreement (the Charter of the United Nations) among member states, and, hence, such an organization is not comparable to a state which possesses sovereignty. The specialized agencies of the United Nations . . . are merely organs of cooperation among states in various specialized fields; the scope of their activities is restricted by their constitutions (agreements among states). They, also, are not subjects of international law.[60]

In this constricted and punitive international environment, Chinese legal scholars supported only a limited role for the UN and became critical of international organizations in general. As Kong Meng claimed, "after the Second World War, the imperialists have done their best to enhance the status of international organizations . . . to establish world domination through them."[61]

In 1961, China's UN prospects further deteriorated. The United States, supported by Australia, Colombia, Italy, and Japan, erected another obstacle to its membership by invoking Article 18 of the UN Charter, according to which the election of new members and the expulsion of members became an "important question," requiring a two-thirds majority for a change in the status quo rather than, as before, a simple majority.[62] In his speech supporting the resolution sponsored by these states, U.S. Ambassador Adlai Stevenson denounced China's "illegal and aggressive conduct" and argued:

With such a record and with such a philosophy of violence and of fanaticism, no wonder this [PRC] regime after twelve years still has no diplomatic relations with almost two-thirds of the Governments of the world. One cannot help wondering what the representatives of such a predatory regime would contribute in our United Nations councils to the solution of the many dangerous questions which confront us.[63]

The adoption of the "important question" procedure, combined with Indonesia's withdrawal from the UN in December 1964, led China to challenge the very foundations of the UN, and of international order as a whole, and to even call for the UN to be replaced.[64] On 24 January 1965, Premier Zhou Enlai declared:

The UN has committed too many mistakes. . . . In these circumstances, another UN, a revolutionary one, may well be set up so that rival dramas may be staged in competition with that body which calls itself the UN but which is under the manipulation of United States imperialism and therefore can only make mischief and do nothing good.[65]

Adding fuel to the flames, in September 1965, in his speech "Long Live the Victory of People's War," Defense Minister Lin Biao revived China's foreign policy strategy of the mid- to late 1950s promoting the idea of "encircling the developed areas from the underdeveloped areas," thereby heightening Western anti-communist fears.[66] In this embattled atmosphere, China's movement to reform international institutions merged seamlessly with extreme domestic revolutionary fervor, manifested in the Cultural Revolution, which developed from early 1966 into an attack on domestic "capitalist tendencies." Launched by an ageing Mao to rekindle the revolutionary spirit of the civil war period, it set citizen against citizen and humiliated, summarily tortured, killed, or drove to suicide many leading cadres and intellectuals. In the ensuing chaos, the judiciary was dismantled and the Public Security organs were attacked by Red Guards. Even in the case of prolonged detention or sentencing, normal legal procedures were ignored. So, too, were the norms and conventions of diplomacy.[67] The spill-over effects of the Cultural Revolution destabilized China's relations, not only with the West, but also with the Soviet Union and a number of Third World states.[68] In the short term, China's converging pressures for both domestic and international revolution only made it less likely that it could assume its seat in the UN. The increasing perception of China as a "rogue state" had a dramatic impact on its support. Whereas the 1965 vote on its admission was a tie (47 against, 47 in favor, 20 abstentions, and 3 absent), in 1966, following the outbreak of the Cultural Revolution, it slumped to 57 against, 47 in favor, 17 abstentions, and 1 absent.

The PRC's Integration into the International Community, 1971–1978

Paradoxically, it was the extreme nature of the Cultural Revolution that eventually persuaded many Western states that the policy of excluding China from international forums was counterproductive and destructive of world peace. In 1966, a National Policy Panel established by the United Nations Association of the USA recommended the seating of both China and Taiwan on the basis that "the recent hardening of Maoist extremism in Peking and the xenophobic excesses of the Red Guards convincingly demonstrate, in our view, the need to provide this fresh and timely encouragement to those moderate influences that still remain in China."[69] More broadly, a shift in opinion began to be detected in the United States that had as its slogan "containment without isolation."[70] Beijing's nuclear test in the same year simply underscored the need to engage China.

By the late 1960s, China had also begun to mend its fences with the outside world. The Chinese Foreign Ministry, whose numbers had been decimated and policies shattered by Cultural Revolution purges, recommenced diplomatic activity in mid-1969.[71] As China's most outward-looking Ministry, it was aware that the Cultural Revolution had alienated even those among China's still narrow circle of friends.[72] However, the new policy had an even more authoritative source. In 1969 and 1970, Mao openly declared to foreign guests his wish to improve and develop relations with both the Third World and the United States.[73] China's initiation of ping-pong diplomacy with the United States and elsewhere in the West was followed by two visits of Henry Kissinger in 1971, prompting a flurry of announcements of diplomatic recognition by other states. Whereas China had established diplomatic relations with only thirty-nine countries a decade earlier, seventy countries had recognized it by 1971, fourteen of them between October 1970 and October 1971.[74]

These bilateral developments, combined with progress toward winding up the Vietnam War, provided an auspicious atmosphere for a renewed PRC effort to assume its "rightful place" in the United Nations and other international organizations. The drive to obtain recognition of the PRC's sovereignty also united some unlikely allies within China. Internationalists within the Chinese political elite formed a common bond with more hard-headed and conservative nationalists, who were persuaded that the resolution of the Taiwan issue could be indirectly facilitated via the United Nations.[75] By 1970, international support for the Albanian resolution calling for the admission of the PRC and the expulsion of the ROC had increased for the first time from 48 in favor, 55 against, and 21 abstaining in 1969, to a simple majority of 51 in favor, 49 against, and 25 abstaining.[76] China now became quietly hopeful, if not overly confident, of success and embarked on a multipronged diplomatic strategy, which included extensive "banquet" diplomacy, people-to-people diplomacy from the Bandung era, and increased aid diplomacy.[77]

From 18 to 26 October 1971, the twenty-sixth session of UNGA debated the question of the restoration of China's seat to the PRC. While the United States no longer contested the PRC's right to participate in UNGA and to assume its rights and responsibilities as a permanent member of the Security Council, it also supported the ROC's continued participation in UNGA, a plan vigorously opposed by the People's Republic. There followed a series of byzantine twists and turns that included a U.S. draft resolution to promote a "two Chinas" solution. On the evening of 25 October, ironically on the same day that Henry Kissinger was meeting Chinese leaders in Beijing, the U.S.-sponsored resolution to declare the issue of China's representation an "important question" was defeated for the first time, by a vote of 59 to 55, with 15 abstentions.[78] Soon after, in an atmosphere of gathering tension, the Albanian draft resolution was adopted by the Assembly by 76 votes to 35, with 17 abstentions.[79] According to an eyewitness account, UN delegates then rose, cheering and applauding the vote for several minutes, while the United States Ambassador, George Bush, Sr., slumped in his seat, "as if a great defeat of U.S. policy had just occurred."[80] In an attempt to defuse the tension, the UN Secretary-General, U Thant, insisted that the vote "should not be considered in terms of either victory or defeat, but as an essential step toward a more effective and realistic international system."[81]

On 26 October 1971, the Secretary-General transmitted the text of UNGA Resolution 2758 (XXVI) of 25 October to the executive heads of all the organs and agencies of the UN. This decided to restore to the People's Republic of China all of its rights, to recognize the representatives of its government as the only legitimate representatives of China to the United Nations, and to expel forthwith the representatives of Chiang Kai-shek from the place that they unlawfully occupied at the United Nations and in all the organizations related to it.[82] The Secretary-General also referred the executive heads of such organizations to General Assembly Resolution 396 (V) of December 1950, which had recommended that other organs of the UN and specialized agencies should take into account the position taken by the General Assembly or its Interim Committee on any representation question.[83]

The formal adoption of Resolution 2758 marked, as Vice-Premier Qian Qichen was to declare nearly three decades later, the effective entry of the People's Republic of China into the global community.[84] It also marked China's transfer from a "system-transforming" approach during the exclusion period of 1949–1970 to a selective "system-reforming" one.[85] The PRC's entry brought near universality of membership and, for the first time, gave developing states a permanent voice on the Security Council.[86] As Chinese officials insisted, "without China's participation, the United Nations could not become a real 'United Nations.'"[87] Subsequently, China's scholars attributed their country's sudden success not only to the decline of U.S. power, to Western Europe's increasing independence, to the support of an increasing number of Third World states, to their country's diplomacy, and to internal factors, but also to the UN's need to strengthen its legitimacy by supporting the representation of the government of one-fifth of the world's population.[88]

For its part, the international community was generally welcoming of China's accreditation. Any initial concern about the potential problems associated with the PRC's entry was, moreover, soon dispelled by the gradual waning of the Cultural Revolution, the lure of the Chinese market, and the role China subsequently adopted in global affairs.

Amid the euphoria of the moment, the cautious but confident tone of Premier Zhou Enlai's interview with a Japanese journalist foreshadowed the tenor of China's behavior over the next decade. As he said,

> We do not have too much knowledge about the United Nations, and are not too conversant with the new situation which has arisen in the United Nations. We must be

very cautious. This does not mean, however, that we do not have self-confidence; it means that caution is required and that we must not be indiscreet and haphazard.[89]

As a mark of China's assurance, Ambassador Huang Hua quickly urged the UN Secretariat to ensure that the United Nations and all its related organizations immediately cease all contacts with Taiwan; that all assistance and contacts of UNDP and the Office of Technical Cooperation to the Republic should cease; and that the PRC Permanent Mission should be informed of the results of relevant actions taken.[90] In a clever move that clearly obviated the difficulty of finding its own trained and experienced staff, China also encouraged all the Taiwanese in the UN Secretariat to protect their jobs by becoming Chinese citizens, which most of them did. China thereby achieved an automatic presence in the Secretariat that was immediately exploited as UN Departments enthusiastically promoted Chinese staff.[91]

In the PRC's first week as a new member of the UN General Assembly, its representatives were also politically assertive.[92] During his maiden speech on 15 November 1971, Deputy Foreign Minister Qiao Guanhua stated that China would not behave as a superpower in the UN and that it opposed "the power politics and hegemony of big nations bullying small ones or strong nations bullying weak ones."[93] A week later, as China took its seat in the Security Council, its Permanent Representative, Ambassador Huang, made a speech critical of "one or two superpowers."[94] More generally, Beijing indicated that it would continue to follow the policy of opposition to colonialism, imperialism, and racism that it had followed during the period of its exclusion.[95]

In its subsequent activity within the UN, however, China soon confounded the ominous predictions of Adlai Stevenson by adopting a modest, self-assigned role as a learner. As Samuel Kim's 1979 study of its early years in the UN has shown, it followed a deliberate policy of selective, incremental engagement and non-aggressive assertion of its interests, whether in budgetary matters or in studying the rules of the game. As a UN official at the time has since remarked, China's progress within the organization occurred in "slow, big waves."[96] This moderate course was justified, since, as Philippe Ardant observed in 1972, as "a newcomer in 1949 to an international order which was constructed without it and where its place was contested, China does not always know its rules and does not willingly make an effort to assimilate them."[97] Kim's analysis of China's voting pattern in the UNGA plenary session from 1971 to 1976 reveals that, while favoring the Third World, its record accorded with the UN consensus on about 65 percent of the recorded or roll-call votes, and never registered more than 9.1 percent negative votes.[98] Although China sent the third largest diplomatic contingent to New York, increasing from twenty-four personnel in January 1972 to over forty in the mid 1970s, the delegation adopted a modest, sociable, and low-profile approach that was accessible to smaller states. China avoided a leadership role in UNGA committees and adopted a selective approach to participation, involving itself primarily in the General Committee and least of all in the Sixth (Legal) Committee.[99]

The PRC was most assertive in the Fifth Committee (Administrative and Budgetary) over the question of the ROC debt of US$30 million.[100] In May 1972, it refused to pay for past UN peacekeeping operations of which it disapproved and, in early October 1972, denied any liability for ROC debts, on the basis that they were incurred when the Nationalists "usurped" the China seat.[101] On the other hand, it not only paid its regular budget contributions due for 1971 and 1972 promptly, but offered in October 1972 to raise its rate of contribution from 4 percent to 7 percent over the next five years.[102] This gesture was coupled with a request for the UN to accept Chinese as an official UN language, thereby assuming indefinite financial responsibility for the required Chinese interpreters and translators.[103] Subsequently, in December 1972, both the Fifth Committee and the General Assembly moved to create a "special account" for China's pre-entry debts and to regard the amount as "a part of the short-term deficit of the Organization."[104] Although scholars have expressed surprise at China's unusual October initiative, it may well have been related to the reciprocal UN decision to remove China's burden of pre-entry debt and to return the situation to the status quo ante. Importantly, this UN decision provided a precedent for similar budgetary concessions to China by other international organizations.

In its subsequent relations with UN specialized agencies and other functional international organizations, China's experience varied. Within six months of its entry, the PRC was recognized, under a variety of formulae, as the only official representative of China by the International Labour Organization (ILO), the International Atomic Energy Agency (IAEA), the United Nations Educational, Scientific and Cultural Organization (UNESCO), the Food and Agricultural Organization (FAO), the General Agreement on Tariffs and Trade (GATT), the International Civil Aviation Organization (ICAO), the World Health Organization (WHO), the World Meteorological Organization (WMO), the International Maritime Organization (IMO), and the International Telecommunication Union (ITU).[105] China did not initially respond to overtures from the ILO, IAEA, and the GATT.[106] On the other hand, the International Monetary Fund (IMF), World Bank, International Development Association (IDA), International Finance Corporation (IFC), and the World Intellectual Property Organization (WIPO) preferred to leave the initiative to the PRC. Rather than pursuing all the openings that immediately became available, China assessed its priorities on the basis of its still limited capabilities and expertise and its preparedness to comply with the obligations of membership entrenched both in the constituent instruments of each organization and in treaties or conventions. Until 1979, when the United States finally established formal diplomatic ties with China, it also had to contend with America's influence and opposition, particularly in the UN specialized agencies.

China's entry into international organizations occurred in three main stages. In the pre-1978 stages, its foreign policy was still inhibited by the ongoing Cultural Revolution, yet tinged with a degree of idealism.[107] The organizations that the PRC initially chose to join were technical, scientific, and educational IGOs and basic IGOs such as the ILO, the United Nations Environment Programme (UNEP), UNESCO, the FAO, the ICAO, and the WMO. Its behavior in these bodies reflected a reluctance to be heavily involved in politics or in the organizations' secretariats; and its presence was more symbolic than substantive and, as in the UN proper, geared to learning.[108] In this period, it was primarily interested in intergovernmental organizations, both because they conferred legitimacy and because many international nongovernmental organizations were unacceptably apolitical and quite happy to maintain "two Chinas" as members.[109] By 1977, China's membership of intergovernmental organizations had increased from one in 1966 to twenty-one. By contrast, the second stage of its entry, between 1977 and 1983, saw a greater percentage increase in its membership of international nongovernmental organizations, from 71 to 307.[110] These included the International Olympic Committee, the International Committee of the Red Cross, PEN International, and the International Council of Scientific Unions.[111]

Only after the Third Plenum of the Eleventh Party Congress in 1978 had officially sanctioned the policies of greater openness and economic modernization, and after formal Sino-U.S. relations had been established, did China move toward full-scale organizational participation. It was at this point that its international and domestic interests converged. Its greater self-confidence and the loosening of ideological constraints in the country at large allowed it to seek entry into the more politically sensitive and strategically important bodies, such as the World Bank and the IMF, as well as the Conference on Disarmament and UN human rights bodies. It also began to participate fully in the ILO. Since each body had an independent secretariat, each had to be approached separately on the question of Taiwan. In addition, entry into the World Bank and the IMF required the negotiation of complicated organizational and financial issues.[112] The date of China's formal entry onto the international stage thus determined the particular set of challenges it faced. On the one hand, it was obliged to negotiate its way to the top of well-established specialized agencies like the World Bank and the ILO, and largely inherited the vertical structure of the UN human rights regime. On the other hand, it was able to take an active part in the formation of the security and environment regimes, which were still in the process of either reconstitution or establishment. It was also involved in the nego- tiation of some human rights instruments.

In all three stages of China's integration, national self-interest, and in partic- ular, considerations of sovereignty in ousting Taiwan, were all-important.[113] Its obligations, as opposed to rights, as a member of international organizations were not uppermost in its leaders' minds. Even general norms were not a priority. Some have argued that there was a certain noblesse oblige in China's early UN participation, instanced in its initial offer to contribute more than its share of UN dues, and its offer in 1986 of a voluntary payment of $4.4 million "solely to help the financial crisis now facing the United Nations."[114] This generosity, however, usually also had a rational, instrumental basis, as the case of its offer to assume a greater share of UN dues demonstrated. Because of the newly recep- tive environment, the executive bodies of international organizations were also initially focused on China's rights rather than on its obligations. In their relief at reversing what had become an untenable position for internationally repre- sentative bodies, they were prepared to exempt China from the normal financial and other requirements of membership. Therefore, China represents not only an important test case for compliance, but also a unique one. Given its special treatment on entry, the extent to which it subsequently moved to alter its pol- icy and moderate its behavior is all the more significant.

The PRC's Evolving Participation in International Organizations from 1978

As we have already noted, China's effective integration into the international system was the product not only of its international experience but also of domestic pressures. By 1978, seven years after entering the UN and two years after the death of Mao, it began to take leave of its revolution, via the Third Plenum of the 11th CCP Central Committee, which introduced qualitative changes in all areas of policy-making. Starting with a program of decollectiv- ization in the countryside, China's leadership initiated the wide-ranging eco- nomic reforms that were to move it into a new political and developmental era. While Mao was not repudiated, his mistakes were recognized and his revolu- tionary policies were modified. As Benjamin Schwartz observed, China's social- ist ideology began to resemble "a retreating glacier flowing into the sea . . . [that] continues to flow and to shape the terrain over which it flows."[115] On this shift- ing terrain, the goal of reforming international society for the sake of the rev- olution was subtly transmuted into one of influencing that society to better pro- mote China's interests. A new "four modernizations" agenda entailed a variety of new objectives: an enhanced position in the international community, and particularly in international organizations; modernization of the Chinese economy; and maintenance of a credible nuclear deterrent. Foremost among its aims, therefore, was the preservation of a peaceful international environment. This agenda had a critical impact on its view of the world and its foreign policy. It provided the domestic context for a new phase in its interaction with international organizations, marked by its more confident entry into strategic international security and international political economy bodies.

The pattern of China's entry into UN-affiliated international organizations after 1978 reflected the lessons it had learned from its early experience. Its negotiating agenda continued to be dominated by the issue of credentials and the ouster of the Republic of China. Yet it was also more cautious about expressing its interest in joining international organizations than it had been in the 1950s. First, it embarked in each case upon a careful examination of the costs and benefits of entry, a process that did not imply acceptance of their norms. Secondly, its final decision to participate was usually only reached once its expressions of interest were reciprocated by the organization in question.[116] Finally, having decided to press ahead, it set conditions on its participation, foremost of which was the expulsion of Taiwan from each organization.

The most important influence on its behavior was the new receptivity of the international community. Having been treated as a renegade or rogue state during the Cultural Revolution, China now received red-carpet treatment. In this newly hospitable environment, China became a seller in a seller's market. Its discriminating sense of priorities, its renewed self-confidence, and its hard-headed projection of its interests only served to increase its appeal. For instance, in the ILO, World Bank, the IMF, UNESCO, and FAO, the negotiations for entry were initiated by the heads of the international organization involved. Indeed, some chief executives like Robert McNamara, President of the World Bank, and Francis Blanchard, Director-General of the ILO, regarded China's entry, or full participation, as an achievement to cap their approaching retirement. For this reason, they made concessions over and above their treatment of other large states, except in the case of the Bank's initial treatment of India.[117]

Having entered an international organization, China usually enunciated the principles underlying its membership and its intended future policies.[118] Thereafter, as in the UN proper, it normally assumed and pursued narrow, self-interested goals and became more proactive only as its understanding of the culture and workings of each organization matured. Over the years, as its officials made a more sober assessment of the benefits of intensifying participation, they became more likely to engage in tough and hard-headed bargaining. China now moved from its "system-reforming" approach in the 1970s toward a "system-maintaining and system-exploiting" position.[119] If, in the process, it still fell back on traditional tactics and responses, it was nevertheless using more modern techniques.[120] Its tendency was to seek satisfaction for national goals within and through international organizations, rather than outside them. However, in practice it still exhibited a preference for using bilateral mechanisms to resolve interstate or intrastate conflict.

The 1990s ushered in yet another phase in China's interaction with international organizations in which its participation and multilateral activity deepened and began not only to complement, but even to replace, bilateral interaction as the main avenue of international diplomacy. Just as the initial phase of its involvement was an outcome of the Cultural Revolution, so, paradoxically, this development grew out of the government's suppression of China's Democracy Movement in June 1989. Multilateral activity became a means of compensating for the decline in its bilateral relations resulting from the crackdown. Although international organizations, in particular the World Bank and the ILO, also imposed sanctions on China for attacking its own citizens, they tended to return to the status quo ante more quickly than did individual states, and provided a public stage on which China could exhibit a responsible internationalism, offsetting fears aroused by its often maladroit and misconceived bilateral diplomacy. They helped restore China's shattered reputation and provided more neutral territory within which it could continue to pursue its national interests.[121] Over the decade, China recognized that multilateralism could indeed serve a wide variety of its strategic interests. In the late 1990s, this recognition was also reflected in an intensified regional multilateralism, which prompted Chinese participation in new ASEAN security, trade, and financial institutions.[122] In June 2001, China even cosponsored its first regional multilateral organization, in the shape of the Shanghai Cooperation Organization (SCO), a formalization of the informal Shanghai Five forum established in Shanghai in 1996.[123] As a Chinese scholar has observed, with a degree of overstatement, the main change was that, where once China was a revolutionary state operating outside the international system, it was now an economically developing country operating within the system to preserve stability.[124] It had thereby entered the fully international phase of its interaction with the world.

By the beginning of the twenty-first century, China had moved into an enhanced phase of multilateralism, bespeaking a new flexibility, confidence, and maturity in a globalized environment in which it sought to boost its role as a key international player. This new confidence followed the 11 September 2001 terrorist attack on the United States which, for the first time since World War II, united the United States and China against a common enemy, the threat of terrorism.[125] Although China at first feared it could be the hidden target behind the "axis of evil" concept subsequently invoked by President Bush, the attack had the beneficial effect of diverting the new administration's attention away from potential U.S.-China competition and disputes to a subject of mutual concern. By emphasizing this new threat, and concluding an anti-terrorist agreement with the United States, China was able, at least temporarily, to contain some of the tensions in the relationship. It even began to assume the role of peacemaker and intermediary between developed and developing states, whether in bilateral or multilateral forums, notably in the six-party arms talks on North Korea, intercession in peace talks between India and Pakistan, and between the different interest groups in the Doha round of WTO negotiations.[126] This rise in its status saw President George W. Bush even acknowledging it as a "partner in diplomacy."[127] China also began to take a more active role in UN peacekeeping than in the past, dispatching the first contingent of a total of 500 armed personnel to Liberia.

This greater sophistication was partly due to the increasing openness of Chinese society. China's international policies were now informed by a variety of sources, including government think tanks, in particular interagency coordinating bodies, scholarly advisory bodies, and NGOs in limited and specific areas.[128] The growth of civil society had also expanded the parameters of discourse.[129] The result was a more open, mature, and cosmopolitan approach to international affairs and a level of policy communication that was more modern than in the past, harnessing international media opportunities, leaders' press conferences and visits abroad, and the Internet.[130]

In response to its greater assurance and relaxation, China's international image also began to change. The state once conceived as a "rogue," "renegade" or "revolutionary,"[131] was now seen by some as "post-revolutionary"[132] or even "capitalist."[133] In fact, China fell into none of these extreme categories. Rather, it now had the characteristics of a quasi-revolutionary state, a polity retaining its Leninist structure and strategy even though much of its substantive revolutionary content had been effectively jettisoned. Despite China's support for multilateralism, it remained concerned with protecting its sovereignty and security through the expansion of national military power and, within the multilateral system, maintained a weak version of the system-reforming approach of the 1970s. The latter approach was linked to its attempts to counter U.S. hegemony and to encourage multipolarity, now for reasons of nationalism and national interest rather than revolution. Moreover, its foreign policy was still constrained by political institutions enduring from the revolutionary period. Its authoritarian political system still attempted to limit the flow of information from outside and to compartmentalize its dissemination.[134] Indeed, by 2005, Western technology companies were even being accused of acquiescing in its attempt to control the Internet.[135] The parameters of intellectual debate, if much wider than before, were still restricted, and control of the press and Internet access, secrecy, and a lack of interest-group participation still inhibited the responsiveness of the state to public opinion.[136] In addition, China continued to manifest a range of habitual tactical responses.[137] To that extent, and to the extent that, as a Leninist political system, it could still in theory shift to a more aggressive and uncooperative international stance, it retained its "least-likely" status. The incomplete nature of its political transformation was thus significant insofar as it helped maintain the outer garments of revolutionary policy, while at the same time bolstering traditional cultural responses that survived the revolution, enabling the continuation of some tried and true foreign policy responses. A number of different foreign policy traditions combined to form a repertoire from which China's leaders chose their strategy and tactics to meet problems as they arose.

These traditions included a typically Marxist approach to the analysis of foreign policy, which utilized similar analytical categories and analytical techniques to those adopted in pre-1978 China. Although Chinese scholars of international relations were increasingly interested in constructivist and liberal schools of thought, policy analysts advising government made the same detached, systematic and strategic assessments of the totality of international political, social, and economic forces as before, evaluating major issues and problems, minor and major contradictions, and the changing distribution of power.[138] Their thinking, which remained realist in its outlook, reflected a world view still characterized in theory by Marxist values of opposition to hegemony, racism, inequality, and exploitation, as well as of continued support for states seen as victims of these problems. It also included elements of China's cultural past, a China-centered perspective, and diplomatic strategies and habits of negotiation based on classical writings, such as Sunzi's *The Art of War*.

Paradoxically, while it was once more difficult for revolutionary states to promote revolution internationally than domestically, it has proved easier for quasi-revolutionary states such as China to accommodate to the international rule of law than to a domestic one.[139] However, most theories of compliance are based on the assumption of shared liberal norms, both international and domestic, and a common understanding about the principles of conduct necessary to uphold them.[140] These understandings are not shared by China. The apparent similarity of Chinese goals of economic modernization to the market principles underlying Western capitalism and its more open international policies should not be read as evidence that its domestic political and social policies or its foreign policy have experienced wholesale liberalization. Despite some hopeful theorizing to the contrary, Chinese officialdom still embraces different goals, worldviews, and strategies from Western liberal democracies and even from the post-revolutionary states of Eastern Europe.

Approach to International Organizations

Having said this, nothing better demonstrates the integrating effects of China's involvement in international organizations than the changes that have occurred since 1978 in its attitude to those bodies and its behavior within them.[141] International organizations have profoundly changed not only China's view of the world, but also its view of itself. They not only encompass China from without, but also from within, by dint of their establishment of branch offices in China that liaise with Chinese counterparts. In addition, the obligations China has accepted in ratifying their rules and associated treaties have been entrenched in its domestic law. Today, China's leaders acknowledge that membership of international organizations enhances their country's power and that it is essential to effective participation in globalization and modernization. They look to these organizations to confer prestige, status, and international and domestic legitimacy on China[142] as well as to help solve the problems inherent in globalization. China draws support from international organizations to promote and protect its national interests, to develop its economy, and to further its international influence.[143] Participation has also entrenched and confirmed China's reform and economic modernization policies.[144]

As two leading Chinese scholars have observed, international organizations constitute a bridge from which to establish friendly relations with the world. China uses them not only to establish wide-ranging international contacts and connections, and thereby to enhance its "legal position" (*qude hefa de diwei*), but also to make contributions to the organizations themselves.[145] These contributions are seen to include activities with a strong normative dimension—to strengthen world peace and security by opposing hegemonism and great power politics, to promote dialogue between North and South, to facilitate South-South cooperation and to resolve the "common problems of mankind."[146] Participation is thus driven by normative concerns as well as domestic needs, sovereign needs, and the long-term need to strengthen and develop China.[147]

The importance China attaches to international organizations is highlighted by the dominant role of the Chinese Foreign Ministry (Waijiao bu) in all matters relating to them. The mechanics of its participation are primarily the responsibility of the Ministry's International Organizations and Conferences Department (Guoji si). One of the largest central bureaucracies, the Ministry is subordinate to the State Council but reports directly to the Standing Committee of the Political Bureau through the Group Leader of the CCP Central Committee Foreign Affairs Leading Small Group (LSG). It consists of the General Office and eighteen external affairs departments and offices of departmental rank and five internal affairs departments. The eighteen external affairs departments are made up of a group of seven regional departments and two regional offices (*diqu si*), and nine external functional departments and offices (*yewu si*), of which the International Organizations and Conferences Department is one.[148] Although other relevant and powerful bureaucracies, such as the Ministry of Trade, the Ministry of Public Security, the Ministry of Defense, the Ministry of Health, and the Ministry of Finance, are also closely involved in China's activities in international organizations, MFA oversight is enhanced by a central joint directive requiring that all matters concerning countries designated as sensitive must have policy clearance from it.[149] While broad policies on international organizations are made by the central leaders, it is the role of the Ministry and its Department of International Organizations and Conferences to make tactical policy choices and work out the detailed plans for the realization of the leaders' goals.[150] The close control of the Ministry over its diplomats in international organizations is reflected in their almost total dependence on instructions from Beijing. Whether in New York or Geneva, China's official representatives have even been known to hold up UN proceedings while they await instructions.[151]

At the same time, China's relationship with international organizations is not without its domestic critics. While emphasizing the crucial importance of that relationship, Chinese scholars point out that their country's membership of intergovernmental organizations falls short of the fuller participation enjoyed by developed states.[152] Moreover, they observe, while branch offices have been established in China, no headquarters have been set up there. While China is seen as a "decisive force" (*juzu qingzhong*) in the UN, in a handful of international organizations its competitive strength is viewed as weak, and its level of activity as insufficient. Furthermore, critics claim, it has too few senior figures employed in international organizations and lacks a sufficient number of qualified candidates to be appointed as international civil servants. Finally, Chinese research and teaching on international organizations is described by some scholars as poor.[153] Such inadequacies, in the eyes of these domestic critics, arise from China's lack of a tradition of open contact with the world, national and international obstacles, its failure to emphasize participation in international organizations, its late entry into these organizations, and its historical passivity.[154] International obstacles include its realist, or, as some would have it, cultural realist, rather than liberal, foreign policy perspective,[155] and its emphasis on retaining its autonomy in a globalized and interdependent world.

Some Western analyses also question the significance of China's global presence. The 2003 A.T. Kearney/*Foreign Policy* Magazine Globalization Index, for instance, which measures a country's global participation, from trade, foreign direct investment, and participation in international organizations to international travel, telephone traffic, and Internet servers, ranked China only fifty-first in the globalization stakes, as compared to the United States in eleventh place.[156] At the same time, it acknowledged the "continuing integration of Russia and China into the international system."[157]

For China, whose international status rose dramatically upon its entry into the United Nations and other international organizations after 1971, the problems posed by international institutional participation are relatively recent. In the 1990s, President Jiang Zemin both welcomed the world's increasing interdependence and warned of the threats it posed to North-South relations, the centrifugal and centripetal pressures that it exerted on the economy, the social and environmental ills that it entailed, and its possible impact on economic growth. Yet he also acknowledged the responsibility that interdependence placed on China to broaden its understanding of the world.[158] However, other, more defensive reactions within China's leadership have continued to stress the way in which international cooperation and interdependence protect and promote U.S. hegemonic interests.[159] These leaders are particularly ambivalent about globalization (*quanqiuhua*) which, unlike the concept of modernization (*xiandaihua*), is seen to place China at serious risk of losing control over its own policies.[160]

China's international relations scholars and diplomats are also divided about post–Cold War politics and the effects of globalization. The majority recognize the role of international organizations, and particularly the UN, in enhancing China's international status and insist both that "the world needs the UN" (*shijie xuyao Lianheguo*) and that the UN cannot be replaced.[161] However, echoing past concerns, the more pessimistic claim that, since the end of the Cold War, the predominance of the United States has meant that the UN has gradually bent its policies to the will of "the hegemon." Their pessimism has been deepened by the war in Kosovo, particularly by the UN's failure to prevent NATO from bypassing its authority.[162] A weakening of the UN's authority has been seen as largely due to the loss of political will among states members and to the existence of the veto power in the Security Council, which gives excessive power to the Permanent Five. The pessimists criticize Western states for using the UN when it suits them, but otherwise treating it with contempt.[163] Other scholars claim that the UN is still able to exert ultimate control and promote global security because it continues to promote the norms of sovereignty and non-aggression, and remains, in the last resort, indispensable for the United States and other Western states. The UN is also able to curb the worst excesses of these states and is thus of vital importance for the developing world.[164] In between these opposing views stands the middle position, which sees the UN as a contradictory mélange of the ideal and the real, and as an organization with an ambiguous mandate, struggling to reconcile its dual roles of serving its member states while governing them.[165]

The situation, in the eyes of such scholars, has been further complicated by the post-2001 unilateralism of the United States. However, because of China's reluctance to jeopardize its all-important economic modernization program, the apparent unwillingness of other states to attempt to balance U.S. power, and the costs involved in confrontation with the United States, China has initially chosen to adopt Deng Xiaoping's *taoguang yanghui* strategy of "conceal[ing] capacities and bid[ing] our time."[166] It has sought to counter U.S. and regional suspicions of its intent by promoting the notion of China's "peaceful rise" and, more recently, "peaceful development." It has also opted to balance U.S. power indirectly by strengthening ties with Russia and its regional neighbors and by protecting its vital interests, particularly in the Asia-Pacific region.[167] At the multilateral level, its dependence on the UN and on its position in the UN Security Council and other international bodies to restrain and mediate the exercise of U.S. power has been highlighted. Rather than reacting defensively to U.S. unilateralism by withdrawing its own support for the UN, since 2001 China has reinforced its commitment to multilateralism and has insisted, even more than before, on the need to rely on the UN to make universally binding decisions rather than constituting ad hoc groups of states, often led by the United States, to resolve global problems. This emphasis was reflected in China's Position Paper on the question of UN reform, circulated in June 2005, in which it placed priority on the values of multilateralism, universality, the resolution of international disputes by peaceful means, and the role of the Security Council as "the only body that can decide the use of force."[168]

Approach to International Law and Treaty Harmonization

China's attitude to international law has also changed substantially in the post-1978 era. By the beginning of the twenty-first century, it had become a party to 273 multilateral international treaties, of which 239 had become applicable to China only after 1979. In its new, quasi-revolutionary mode, it now acknowledges the universal applicability of generally recognized international law, even if it still plays down the importance of customary international law.[169] It also acknowledges the doctrine of *pacta sunt servanda* ("treaties must be obeyed"). It emphasizes the principles of international law, and regards those contained in the UN Charter, in particular as they relate to state sovereignty, as basic.[170] It formally recognizes international organizations as subjects of international law, while some scholarly opinions also recognize them as "supranational."[171] International law is seen to offer a universally accepted path to achieving its objectives and, rather than flouting it, China's representatives often insist on a positivist interpretation of the letter of international law to promote and defend their policies. Indeed, international law is now seen not merely as an instrument of power and interests, but as the foundation of international order necessary for the international community as a whole.

Domestically, however, the obstacles to the implementation and enforcement of international law within China remain immense. They include the institutional defects of China's domestic rule-making system.[172] The harmonization of international legal obligations with domestic law, as in other states, is a complex process. It is sometimes assumed that, in China's formally monist system, international law should automatically prevail over its national laws.[173] This is because Article 142 of the General Principles of Civil Law provides that "if any international treaty concluded or acceded to by the People's Republic of China contains provisions differing from those in the civil laws of the People's Republic of China, the provisions of the international treaty shall apply, unless the provisions are ones on which the People's Republic of China has announced reservations."[174] This prompted China's delegate before the Committee against Torture (CAT) to insist that, for China, "international instruments t[ake] precedence over domestic law."[175]

Significantly, however, the Chinese Constitution, which prevails over national laws if there is any inconsistency between their provisions and constitutional provisions, remains silent as to the legal status of an international treaty in domestic law.[176] The result has been that, in legislative and judicial practice, China has, like many other states, adopted a mixed monist and dualist system. It incorporates provisions of international treaties and rules into domestic laws; issues general stipulations on the application of international treaties; and revises or amends domestic laws in accordance with the international treaties that it has ratified or acceded to.[177] However, its approach differs from area to area. Whereas it directly applies international treaties in civil, commercial, and economic domains, it requires international human rights treaties to be harmonized with domestic law through domestic legislation enacted before ratification.[178]

In addition, a Chinese international law scholar has observed that

> the provisions (of the General Principles of Civil Law) appear to limit the effect of international treaties in the domestic legal order. They suggest that an international treaty is applied only when the relevant law is inconsistent with the treaty. In other words, framers of these laws would be pleased to see that domestic law plays the main role where the issue concerned is covered by both an international treaty and a relevant law. Therefore, inherently, there is a risk that courts do not bother seeing if the relevant law is consistent with a treaty before determining the appropriate "applicable law."[179]

The lack of effective oversight by the National People's Congress (NPC) presents a further obstacle to harmonization. According to the Chinese Constitution, the NPC Standing Committee has the power to ratify and abrogate treaties. In practice, however, the decision to negotiate or enter into a treaty is made by China's Party leadership with the Politburo at its apex, and the NPC Standing Committee has never to date refused to ratify an international treaty that has been submitted to it.[180] This situation creates a wide gap between the process of ratification and that of harmonization. In the event that harmonizing legislation is promulgated, further domestic institutional obstacles arise. Laws and regulations are promulgated by many different ministries and local governments, resulting in a lack of clear and consistent rules.[181] Equally, legislation is implemented by different parts of the bureaucracy, and this inconsistency gives rise to the problem of discretionary application.[182] Moreover, because the judicial system itself is open to political influence, the enforceability of the laws incorporating the norms and rules of the international treaties that China has ratified is problematic. At the critical grass-roots level, the conflict between central government powers and local political interests also hinders the implementation of legislation.[183] Finally, a more abstract cultural mindset comes into play. The emphasis of Chinese culture on form rather than substance, on the appearance of things rather than on their reality, tends to concentrate official attention on the outward forms of compliance, in the sense of institutional and legal implementation and even political rhetoric, rather than on the way those laws and rules are enforced, implemented, and internalized in social practice.

Conclusion

This chapter has revealed a broad pattern of China's interaction with the international community marked by extremes. Thus, the country has ricocheted from a violent reaction against foreign exploitation in the nineteenth and early twentieth centuries to the apprenticeship of Republican China within international organizations, and from the abrupt international exclusion and isolation of the People's Republic after 1949, to its increasing inclusion after 1971. Three principal periods of the PRC's post-1949 relations with international organizations have been distinguished: the years between 1949 and 1971, when it struggled unavailingly for international acceptance and ended by rejecting the whole structure of the international system; the 1971–78 period, following its replacement of Taiwan as official representative of "China," when, in the midst of its Cultural Revolution, it maintained its revolutionary rhetoric in the United Nations but built a careful foundation for future participation; and the subsequent years, when the dual pressures of domestic and international interests converged to encourage its more meaningful and deeply engaged participation.

Consistent with its previous experiences of international interaction, the initial period of the PRC's participation in international organizations largely reflected an instrumentalist approach. Whereas its entry into the UN provided it with the golden key to international legitimacy and acceptance, its integration into the other international organizations was more pragmatic, reflecting both its continuing need to entrench its sovereignty vis-à-vis Taiwan and its specific functional interests. Concern for its status and international reputation and a sensitivity to its historical setbacks obliged China to behave as a modest learner in international affairs. The same concerns, however, also generated some rigorous bargaining behind the scenes, which arguably elicited more generous concessions, particularly financial ones, from international organizations than other large states had enjoyed. This was because, by 1971, China's membership of these organizations had become equally critical for the global community. Just as China's legitimacy was enhanced by its membership, so also was the legitimacy and authority of the international organizations it joined.

For that reason, a mutually advantageous outcome was not achieved without cost. As this chapter has shown, well before the founding of the PRC, President Roosevelt had been prepared to make special concessions to China because of its status as a significant wartime ally. However, far more sacrifices were arguably made in 1971 and after than would have been the case had the PRC's bid in 1950 to replace Taiwan in the UN been accepted by the international community. Despite the belief of some scholars that the international community did not make more sacrifices to encourage China to participate than it would have for any other large power, the facts speak otherwise. Having been humiliated for twenty-two years, China was prepared to exact its pound of flesh when it was formally welcomed into the fold. The special treatment given to it by the United Nations and other international bodies in the 1970s and 1980s was evidence of that price. The costs, however, were not merely material ones. Had China been able to participate in the UN from the early 1950s, at a time when it nurtured a positive, hopeful, and even idealistic view of that body, it is arguable that much of the bitterness and anguish that subsequently infected Chinese relations with the rest of the world might have been averted.

As a corollary of its instrumental approach, China initially showed little interest in, or respect for, the norms, principles, and even rules of the international organizations it joined. It was only after 1978—when it had finally submitted without reservation to the interacting processes of "justification, discourse and persuasion" within international organizations; when it had become part of the democratic effort to find consensus within those organizations; and when it began to fulfill its role as a Permanent Member of the Security Council and as one of the nuclear weapon states (NWS), or conversely, as one of the voices of the developing states—that it began to reassess its interests in the light of organizational norms, to acknowledge, if only in practice, the negotiability of its sovereignty, and to accept the costs as well as the advantages of organizational participation. Most important, it was only after 1978 that China learnt the importance of reciprocal compliance as a foundation of international trust and cooperation.

By comparing the isolating effects of China's nonparticipation in international organizations with the increasingly engaged nature of its subsequent participation, this chapter has highlighted the value of process-based institutional interaction. It has also shown that China has been more likely to engage and participate when a favorable international environment has prevailed and when international pressures and its national interests have converged. The case studies that follow will detail the complex processes of interaction, diplomatic bargaining, institutional pressures, and the repeated cycles of negotiation, interpretation, and internalization that gradually led China to translate its international obligations into its laws and institutions, its formal policies and, to a variable extent, its social practice. In this way, during three decades of interaction, it changed from an alienated and angry critic of the United Nations, to a semiengaged member sizing up the game, and thence to an active participant, at once promoting its national interests and demonstrating increasing support for the multilateral system.

2

China and the International Security Regime

The Conference on Disarmament

> The Chinese Government attaches great importance to the role of
> the Conference on Disarmament and has taken an active part in its
> work. . . . The institution of the Conference on Disarmament has
> changed the situation in which only a few countries monopolized
> disarmament negotiations and it has provided the small and medium-
> sized countries with an important forum for participation in the
> settlement of disarmament questions. As the sole international body
> for multilateral disarmament negotiations, the Conference on Dis-
> armament has over the past few years done a great deal of useful
> work in pushing forward the international disarmament process.
>
> *China's Foreign Minister, Wu Xueqian, at commencement*
> *of the 1987 session of the Conference on Disarmament*
> *(CD/PV.385, 3 Feb. 1987)*

> This year marks the 25th anniversary of the first special session of
> the General Assembly devoted to disarmament, and the 25th session
> of the Conference on Disarmament. This is a significant milestone,
> but . . . international peace and security continue to face profound
> challenges in the form of weapons of mass destruction and their
> delivery vehicles, rising military expenditures, the prospect of an
> arms race in outer space, and the continual development of new
> weapons systems. I hope, therefore, that 2003 will mark a turning
> point in the history of this Conference.
>
> *UN Secretary-General Kofi Annan, 21 January 2003*

The Conference on Disarmament (CD) has been described, somewhat face-
tiously, by a departing ambassador as "the best club in town." The crucial nature
of its mandate to achieve global nuclear nonproliferation and disarmament means
that it has certainly been one of the most important international forums,
enjoying a high degree of legitimacy while remaining peculiarly vulnerable to
the changing strategic environment. This mix of authority and fragility is already implicit in the setting in which states members convene. The soaring architecture of the Council Chamber of the Palais des Nations in Geneva provides

a fitting framework for the majestic gold, sepia, and black murals painted in 1935 and 1936 by the Spanish artist José Maria Sert. Starting out from the very simple notion of "what separates men and what unites them," Sert depicted, through the surging, gargantuan figures of men and women, the extremes of the human condition—the diversity of races, conflicts and wars, ruin and destruction, and the struggles and counsels of men, from which would emerge, Phoenix-like, a new order of peace, humanity, and scientific and social progress.[1] His sense of doom, tragedy, and renewal hangs over the Conference, heavy with foreboding, yet infused with hope.

As the only nuclear weapon state (NWS) apart from France outside the arms control and disarmament regime in the 1960s and 1970s, China's entry into the CD in 1980 held a special significance. Its decision to join was all the more remarkable because of its initial insistence on the right of all sovereign states to develop nuclear weapons. Today, it has signed or acceded to the major arms control and disarmament treaties.[2] It also participates fully in the main international and regional nuclear nonproliferation and arms control organizations, the Conference on Disarmament (CD), the UN First Committee, the UN Disarmament Commission, the International Atomic Energy Agency (IAEA), the Nuclear Suppliers Group (NSG), and the Zangger Committee. Of these, it has until recently seen the Conference on Disarmament as the principal institution promoting arms control, or rather, as successive Chinese ambassadors have claimed, as the only universal multilateral disarmament negotiating body.

This chapter evaluates China's compliance and cooperation with the norms, principles, and rules of the treaties that the CD has negotiated and that China has signed and/or ratified. Within the context of the ongoing discussion, debate, and treaty negotiations held under CD auspices, it identifies the specific turning points in China's progress since 1980 in arms control and disarmament in response to the multiple pressures of the participation process, and analyses its compliance with its treaty obligations, its overall contribution to global security, and the role of the CD in facilitating its progress. It assesses the degree of China's internalization of regime norms by examining its domestic legislation, institution building, and readiness to make the adjustments identified in the process-based indicators. Finally, it analyzes the degree of its cooperation with the norms of the regime and assesses its impact upon it. Since 1980, the proceedings of this body have documented one of the most dramatic and surprising conceptual about-turns in China's short history of participation in international organizations, engendered by the process of normative discourse and repeated interactions between transnational actors within an institutional setting, and based on the principle of reciprocity. It is perhaps the most outstanding example of how international organizational processes and principles have altered China's perceptions of its national interests to coincide with the norms of a regime.

Institutional and Historical Context

The UN Charter contained two specific mandates to further the cause of disarmament. Under Article 11, the UN General Assembly was assigned the responsibility of considering and making recommendations on "the principles governing disarmament and the regulation of armaments." Article 26 provided for the Security Council to submit to the Members of the Organization "plans . . . for the establishment of a system for the regulation of armaments." Although the Security Council never submitted such plans, the Conference on Disarmament became the "sole multilateral body for negotiating measures of disarmament."[3] Unlike other international organizations such as the ILO, however, which has almost exclusive international jurisdiction over workers' rights, the Conference forms only part of a web of arms control and disarmament organizations.[4] The function of verifying compliance with the Nuclear Nonproliferation Treaty (NPT), for instance, is assumed by the IAEA, and many of the actual arms control negotiations have occurred bilaterally. Thus, the primary role of the CD is one of "socialization"—of "jawboning," persuading, and pressuring—rather than of monitoring.

At the same time, the CD, and its antecedent bodies, have been the *fons et origo* of the major international nonproliferation and disarmament treaties. Leading multilateral treaties such as the Nuclear Nonproliferation Treaty (NPT), the Seabed Arms Control Treaty, the Biological Weapons Convention (BWC), the Chemical Weapons Convention (CWC), and the Comprehensive Test Ban Treaty (CTBT) have been negotiated under their auspices. The CD's meetings deal with the most difficult issues in arms control, and it is often made responsible for matters in the world's "too hard basket."[5] Fundamental concepts involved in the stated role and purpose of the CD are a common responsibility for disarmament and a recognition that success requires participation by the wider international community and a process of multilateral arms control and disarmament agreements.[6] Its key functions have historically included discussions and negotiations on the following ten agenda items: nuclear weapons; chemical weapons; weapons of mass destruction; conventional weapons; reduction of military budgets; reduction of military forces; disarmament and development; disarmament and international security; confidence-building measures; and comprehensive disarmament under international control.

Although it is funded entirely by UN contributions and meets under UN auspices, the CD is technically separate from the UN and enjoys an independence cherished by its members.[7] Originally comprising forty member states and now an organization of sixty-five states, it evolved from the Disarmament Commission, set up in January 1952, and the Eighteen-Nation Committee on Disarmament (ENDC), established in 1961. Under the name Committee on Disarmament, it was brought into existence by the Final Document of the First Special Session on Disarmament (UNSSOD1) held by the UN General Assembly (UNGA) in 1978. In 1984, it was renamed the Conference on Disarmament.[8]

The CD adopts its own rules of procedure and its own agenda, taking into account the recommendations made by the UN General Assembly. It conducts its work and adopts its decisions by consensus. It convenes in plenary meetings, held in public unless it decides otherwise. It may establish subsidiary bodies, such as ad hoc committees, working groups, technical groups, or groups of governmental members, open to all member states of the Conference. Representatives of non-member states may have reserved seats in the Conference and may submit proposals and working documents on measures under discussion. Communications from NGOs are retained by the Secretariat and made available to delegations upon request, while NGOs and individuals may attend open plenary sessions in the Visitor's Gallery, but not the frequent closed sessions. The CD submits annual reports of its activities at the end of each session to the UNGA.[9] Its annual session is divided into three parts of ten weeks, seven weeks, and seven weeks respectively, starting from the penultimate week of January every year. When the Conference is in session, its Presidency rotates among all its members on the basis of the English alphabetical list of membership, with each President presiding for a four-working-week period. The Secretary-General of the Conference, for many years Vladimir Petrovsky and currently Sergei Ordzhonikidze, is appointed by the UN Secretary-General.

Scholarly views on China and arms control and disarmament have changed over recent years.[10] While China was initially depicted as a primary violator of the international nonproliferation regime, scholars now perceive an evolution in its attitude to nuclear nonproliferation and a readiness to learn and change. However, even among the more optimistic Western specialists, there are some who have argued that, because of its realist calculations of its interests, it has not internalized norms, but rather, utilizes them for its own advantage. Iain Johnston and Michael Swaine, for instance, have distinguished between China's instrumentalist "realpolitik" approach and the "common security" approach that indicates meaningful socialization.[11] Even compliance based on China's wish to be seen as a responsible power has been judged by Johnston and Paul Evans to be "coerced," in the sense that "the image costs of opposing the treaty or agreement were weighted heavily in the decision to accede."[12] More recently, though, Johnston has adopted a more positive view, contrasting China's concern about status and reputation, which underlay its signing of the CTBT, with the more instrumental relative power position it could have adopted.[13]

This book views concern about reputation and image as a prerequisite of international socialization.[14] Such concern encourages a state to transcend its most powerful urge to satisfy those national goals that may be judged selfish or internationally anti-social. It is one of the few positive motivations that can still constrain a powerful state. Conversely, when states lack this concern, international law is most likely to be violated or, at the very least, ignored. China's motivations are understood as not very different from those of other nuclear states. Its compliance is therefore judged less by its perceived motivation and more by its behavior—its readiness to implement its obligations internationally and domestically, to redefine its interests, to renegotiate its sovereignty, and to accept costs. Apart from its preparedness to ratify major disarmament treaties, one indicator of China's acceptance of costs in this regime has been its membership of the IAEA. States party to the NPT rely on IAEA safeguards for assurance of compliance by other states with their nonproliferation undertakings, as well as to provide proof of their own compliance.[15] Membership therefore subjects China's peaceful nuclear facilities to the oversight of an international body and entails a potential loss of sovereignty. As Hans Blix has remarked, "China's taking up membership in the IAEA is indicative of the practical usefulness which that country attaches to peaceful nuclear cooperation."[16] The history of China's membership of the IAEA, and of other institutions having a bearing on sovereignty, is therefore also woven into this account.

China's Entry

China began participating in the CD in February 1980. The initial stages of its entry bore witness to its lack of support for regime norms. Prior to that point, China's changing policies had largely reflected its assessment of the state of the strategic environment. Thus, before 1978, its attitude to disarmament and nonproliferation had been largely shaped by its political and strategic Cold War concerns, in particular its changing relationship with the two superpowers, the Soviet Union and the United States. Because its foreign and defense policies had been strongly influenced by the Soviet Union, before 1962 it had supported the Soviet policy of thoroughgoing disarmament and arms control. Not only did Zhou Enlai, in a speech to the 1954 Geneva Indochina Conference, express support for these principles, but the joint communiqué of the Bandung Conference in 1955, strongly endorsed by China, stated that "all States should cooperate, especially through the United Nations, in bringing about the reduction of armaments and the elimination of nuclear weapons under effective international control."[17]

At the same time, China was less supportive of the norm of nuclear non-proliferation. It believed that any sovereign state had a right to develop nuclear weapons, and, in the mid-1950s, in the context of perceived encirclement by hostile U.S. forces and tensions over Taiwan, and anticipating the support of the Soviet Union, it decided to embark on its own nuclear weapons program.[18] Its primary purpose, it claimed, was defensive: to prevent external attack and intimidation, and to secure a strategic retaliatory capability in case of nuclear war. However, nuclear weapons capability was also seen as a means of promoting China's international status and independence.

From the late 1950s, China's faith in the Soviet Union was undermined by the development of the Sino-Soviet dispute. Following the deterioration of Sino-Soviet relations in 1959, the Kremlin suddenly recalled thousands of Soviet experts, in a single move undermining China's nuclear ambitions. Soviet signature of the Partial Test Ban Treaty (PTBT) with the United States in 1963 completed China's disillusionment.[19] China became increasingly concerned to build up its own nuclear capability to cope with the nuclear threat presented by the superpowers, both of which were now seen as hostile. It viewed arms control treaties like the PTBT or the Nuclear Nonproliferation Treaty (NPT) simply as a means of consolidating superpower monopoly of nuclear weapons or, later, as in the strategic arms limitation talks (SALT), to gain qualitative nuclear superiority.[20] Statements by Mao pointed to his belief in the inevitability of nuclear war, as well as in China's capacity to recover therefrom. On 16 October 1964, China detonated its first atom bomb. It fired its first nuclear-capable ballistic missile in 1966 and successfully tested a hydrogen bomb in 1967. However, even though it continued to insist on the right of "peace-loving" states to develop their own nuclear capacity, it declared publicly that it would avoid nuclear proliferation itself and would not help other states in their efforts to develop nuclear weapons.[21] From 1964, its own tests were justified on a "no-first-use principle" and on the basis of its policy that only universal and total disarmament would solve the problem of nuclear proliferation.

By 1978, however, as China began to open to the outside world, its leaders revised their earlier belief in the inevitability of war. The perception that the Soviet threat was diminishing inspired a new confidence and independence in foreign affairs. Encouraged by states in the Non-Aligned Movement (NAM), on 29 May 1978, Foreign Minister Huang Hua declared China's interest in participating in UN deliberations on disarmament and its readiness to negotiate on the total destruction of nuclear weapons with the two principal nuclear powers.[22] Deng Xiaoping was reportedly the architect of this new policy.[23] China also made inquiries about possible participation in the IAEA. It did not, however, join the CD in 1979 as it felt it needed more time to prepare.[24] When it did so the following year, it was motivated by considerations of status, by its wish to build up its reputation as an advocate of peace, and by its concern to protect its interests in disarmament negotiations. It was also influenced in the timing of its participation by its organizational ambitions. Had it delayed entry by another month, it would have had to wait another six years before it assumed chairmanship of the CD. Its formal entry was welcomed by a number of member states, who were relieved that the CD could now legitimately claim to represent all the nuclear powers and make universally valid decisions.[25] It was significant that, in the same year, without any public announcement, China quietly ceased atmospheric nuclear testing. While willing to cooperate, at that very early period it was not prepared to publicize its effective renegotiation of its sovereignty.

China's entry into the CD marked its awareness that sovereignty could be strengthened by the legitimizing effect of membership in international organizations, even though at the same time participation had the potential to constrain that sovereignty. The attraction of the CD was its representativeness, its role in promoting multilateral dialogue, and its mandate to negotiate treaties. These features distinguished it from, for instance, the UN First Committee, which proposed resolutions for UNGA but had no negotiating mandate. Any disarmament agreements concluded under the CD's auspices were seen by China to have "great significance." It also viewed the CD as a universal body, unlike, for instance, the later Ottawa process banning anti-personnel landmines (APLs) in which, China has alleged, the treaty was concluded quickly, outside the auspices of the CD, and hence without the support of a number of important states, including itself and the United States.[26] While emphasizing the importance of the CD as a forum for negotiating disarmament agreements, China also saw "consensus" as vital to its effective working. The consensus principle, in fact, was established in the CD with the intention of bringing in states like China. However, other CD members have observed that the consensus requirement often acted as a form of veto by a single state, a fact that China was also later to deplore.

In 1998, a senior Chinese official commented that, just as appropriate physical conditions were necessary to ensure the success of agricultural crops, so the CD had flourished in different periods, depending on the international strategic environment. While the CD's effect could be measured by the treaties it concluded, he observed, it could not be expected to spawn "a production line of treaties." Thus, under earlier disarmament bodies, the NPT had been produced in 1968, the Sea Bed Treaty in 1971, the Biological Weapons Convention in 1972, the Environmental Modification Treaty in 1976, and yet, during the early 1980s, there had been no agreement in the CD. With a change in the international situation at the end of the Cold War, conditions had become propitious for the negotiation of the Chemical Weapons Convention (CWC) and the CTBT. Then, in the late 1990s, progress had once again stalled. Even so, China's Ambassador for Disarmament Affairs, Li Changhe, commented in 1999 that the CD was "irreplaceable in terms of its status and role." He insisted that, "though it has not been able to get down to treaty negotiations for the time being, the Conference can still function as an important forum where dialogue can be conducted on major issues of international peace and security, and on some specific disarmament items."[27] By contrast with China's claims of normative support for the organization, some Western observers have contended that China took the CD seriously primarily because the issues it debated and negotiated posed a potential threat to China's security.

Progress in China's disarmament and nuclear nonproliferation policies occurred over three main periods between 1980 and 2001, as it became bound ever more tightly into the diplomacy of international security organizations and conferences, and as it responded to the pressures of the nonnuclear, non-aligned states to represent their interests in the counsels of the Permanent Five (P-5).

Power Politics and Conceptual Ambiguity: 1980–1985

In the first years of its participation, China appeared more concerned with disputation with other socialist states, in particular with the Soviet Union and Vietnam, than with promoting the norms of the regime.[28] While supporting the disarmament of the two superpowers, it closely aligned its policies with the Group of Twenty-One (G-21) non-aligned states and continued to insist on the right of states to develop nuclear capability. Despite this, its entry was greeted with enthusiasm by almost all members of the CD apart from the Soviet Union.[29] When, for instance, in 1982, together with France, China announced it would not participate in the Working Group on a Nuclear Test Ban, in a thinly veiled attack, the Soviet representative accused "the United States of America and certain other states" of blocking work on the cessation of the nuclear arms race and nuclear disarmament and of "trying to distort the very content and nature of negotiations in the Committee."[30] In response, China's representative, Tian Jin, accused the Soviet representative of trying to "make us believe that China is a 'negative factor' in the field of disarmament."[31]

Procedurally and conceptually, China was embarked on a steep learning curve, having been catapulted into the presidency of the CD in March 1980, within a month of joining. China's initial position on arms control was influenced by the insistence of the G-21 that the refusal of the Permanent Four (P-4) to countenance the spread of nuclear weapons was discriminatory toward developing countries. China also opposed policies of nuclear deterrence, claiming that they were "based on the first use of nuclear weapons." The main issues it emphasized in its first five years in the CD were the need for the complete prohibition and destruction of nuclear weapons and chemical weapons and for a comprehensive program of disarmament, as well as for security assurances for nonnuclear weapon states and the prevention of an arms race in outer space.[32] Under a policy of "three cessations and one reduction," that is, cessation of testing, development, and production of nuclear weapons as well as reduction of nuclear weapons, it saw itself as sharing a common objective with the policies of the G-21. However, it differed in holding that, "at the present stage, the United States and the Soviet Union, which possess more than 95 percent of the world's nuclear weapons, should take the lead in taking actions to be followed by the other nuclear states."[33]

Nevertheless, over the next five years, China modified its initial policy on the immediate cessation of testing and accepted that reduction could occur gradually. It also balanced its requirement that the two superpowers take primary responsibility with an acknowledgment that multilateral and bilateral negotiations were complementary, and that the disarmament process could not be allowed to hang solely on agreement between the superpowers, but had to be accompanied by collective international efforts.[34] It accepted its own responsibility for nuclear disarmament and declared, as it had in the past, that "at no time and in no circumstances" would it be "the first to use nuclear weapons."[35] Its support for multilateral negotiations as a complement to bilateral agreements signaled a change from its historical preference for the latter, particularly in relation to security matters.[36] As we shall see, another change, in view of its heavy emphasis on sovereignty, was its insistence on strong verification procedures in relation to chemical weapons.

From the beginning, China's identity and policies in the CD were unique. It was never a member of any formal Western or Eastern group or even the G-21. In 1986, Australia's Ambassador for Peace, Richard Butler, commented that "one member of our Conference does not take part in group meetings organized under the aegis of the Conference. In this particular sense, China stands alone."[37] Twelve years later, China's Ambassador for Disarmament Measures referred proudly to China's status as a "one nation group." As a permanent member of the Security Council and as one of the five formal nuclear powers, China shared status and aspirations with the nuclear weapon states (NWS). As a developing Asian state, it also identified with some of the interests of Third World states, and often adopted their rhetoric. Whether in policy statements within the CD or in interviews, Chinese representatives invoked the position of the developing states on disarmament and arms control. And yet, increasingly over the years Western observers were struck by the growing ease with which China participated in the counsels of the NWS and by its unquestioning assumption of its P-5 status and the economic clout it entailed. Even so, within the P-5 China emphasized the large technology and capability gap between itself, the United States, and the Soviet Union, while at the same time it did not wish to be treated on a par with the UK and France. The key to this complicated state of affairs was strategic. China's status as a "club of one" maximized its negotiating flexibility and allowed it to associate either with the NWS or with the non-nuclear weapon states (NNWS), depending on the issue involved. In addition, the NNWS were useful to China in advocating positions in the CD with which China agreed but which it did not wish to openly espouse.

According to both Chinese and Western negotiators, there were a number of practical turning points in this first phase of China's involvement in the CD, which occurred against the background of the escalating superpower arms race. The first was its decision in July 1983 to appoint a Special Ambassador for Disarmament Measures, marking the special status of disarmament issues within the Chinese bureaucracy as compared to the Soviet Union, which had created no other Special Ambassadors in its Foreign Ministry. The next was its partic-ipation in the negotiations for the Chemical Weapons Convention (CWC), where it pressed for "international on-site inspection measures with regard to charges on the use of chemical weapons, the destruction of chemical weapon stockpiles and the dismantling of facilities for their production."[38]

In 1982, it also ratified the Inhumane Weapons Convention. It put forward an influential proposal on the essential measures for an immediate halt to the arms race and for disarmament at the second special session on disarmament of UNGA, once again requiring the superpowers to take the lead in disarma-ment. It recommended that all nuclear weapon states should reach an agree-ment on the non-use of nuclear weapons and that the Soviet Union and the United States reduce by 50 percent all types of nuclear weapons and their means of delivery. Thereafter, it insisted, "*all nuclear-weapon states should cease all nuclear tests*, stop the qualitative improvement and manufacturing of nuclear weapons and reduce their respective nuclear arsenals according to agreed proportions and procedures."[39] It also produced five working papers for the CD.[40] At the thirty-ninth session of UNGA, together with fifteen other countries, it cosponsored a resolution on the prevention of an arms race in outer space (PAROS), which was unanimously adopted with only one abstention.[41] Its concern about this issue was fuelled by U.S. President Ronald Reagan's Strategic Defense Initiative (SDI) Program, introduced in 1983. This was seen not only as accelerating the superpower strategic arms race but as detrimental to China's four moderniza-tion goals.

Another breakthrough in the first phase occurred in 1984, when China acceded to the Biological Weapons Convention (BWC), a treaty that had been opened for signature in April 1972 and that it had originally criticized as a "fraud of sham disarmament."[42] In its accession to the BWC, it stipulated that the Convention would only be binding in relation to other parties, and would cease to be binding in relation to enemy states that did not observe the Convention's provisions.[43] Finally, having applied for membership of the IAEA in 1983, China became a member in 1984. Subsequently, it also became a member of the IAEA Board of Governors. Thus began a process in which China accepted increasing reporting responsibilities and IAEA oversight.[44] A further symbol of its progress was its appointment to the so-called Group of Seven Wise Men, which reported on how to improve the functioning of the CD.[45]

Conceptual Change: 1985–1992

The second phase in China's participation marked a considerable conceptual advance, again triggered by changes in the international environment, in this case an easing in tensions between the superpowers. This was evident almost from the moment of the meeting in Geneva in January 1985 between the Soviet Foreign Minister and the U.S. Secretary of State, at which agreement was reached on the reopening of disarmament negotiations after President Ronald Reagan had accused the Soviet Union of violating its commitment to observe the Strategic Arms Limitation Treaty (SALT) II. In their joint statement of 8 January, the two sides agreed to "work out effective agreements aimed at preventing an arms race in space, and terminating it on earth, at limiting and reducing nuclear arms and at strengthening strategic stability." After hailing this as a "positive development," China's Ambassador for Disarmament Affairs, Qian Jiadong, announced that, despite China's tardiness in participation, if a nuclear test ban body were to be established in 1985, "the Chinese delegation would be willing to reconsider its position."[46] In July 1985, he also addressed the CD on China's decision, in view of its need to concentrate on economic development, to cut back its conventional armaments and reduce its armed forces by one million men.[47]

Concrete proposals for China's own participation in the disarmament process were also mooted. Welcoming the resumption of bilateral negotiations between the United States and the Soviet Union as a "positive development,"[48] China reiterated in the CD its proposal to UNSSOD that, after the United States and the Soviet Union had reduced by 50 percent all types of their respective nuclear weapons and means of delivery, all other nuclear states should also stop testing, improving, or manufacturing nuclear weapons and should reduce their respective nuclear arsenals.[49] Furthermore, celebrating the UN's designation of 1986 as the International Year of Peace, on 21 March Premier Zhao Ziyang formally announced that China had "not conducted nuclear tests in the atmosphere for many years and would no longer conduct atmospheric tests in the future." In a nine-point policy, he outlined China's basic position on disarmament.[50]

From 1986, Chinese statements in the CD became increasingly buoyant and optimistic. They emphasized the importance of arms control for developing states, called for increased discussion in multilateral forums, and acknowledged China's own responsibility to disarm.[51] The CD reciprocated by vesting greater responsibilities and authority in China, elevating it to the position of Chairman of the Group of Seven.[52] Retrospectively, Ambassador Fan Guoxiang commented favorably on the experience that, "in spite of the fact that each member had his own proposals and preferences, everyone adopted a positive attitude to discussions in order to seek common ground while setting aside differences, and to try to achieve concrete results."[53] In this period, China also expanded its bilateral and regional dialogue on security issues and became an official dialogue partner in the ASEAN Regional Forum (ARF). However, in 1988 it raised its benchmark for the participation of the P-3 (France, the UK, and China) in nuclear arms control talks, from its "50 percent position" to a requirement for "drastic reductions."[54]

At the same time, China was making increasing progress on nuclear nonproliferation. Against a background in which developing states were themselves moving toward acceptance of this norm and actively lobbying China to join them, Chinese policy-makers were persuaded that their existing position did not enhance global security. According to a senior official, by the late 1980s China had become a strong supporter of the nonproliferation of nuclear weapons and other weapons of mass destruction. As early as 1985, it announced its decision to voluntarily put part of its civilian nuclear facilities under the safeguards of IAEA and guaranteed that it would require recipients of Chinese nuclear exports to accept IAEA safeguards.[55] In 1989, China and the IAEA concluded the Agreement for the Application of Safeguards in China, and in 1991, China undertook to report on a continuing basis to the IAEA any export to, or import from, non-nuclear states of nuclear materials of one effective kilogram or above.

In the meantime, Chinese initiatives in the CD included the submission of a working paper on the prevention of an arms race in outer space, an intervention followed a month later by the finalization of the mandate of the Ad Hoc Committee on the Prevention of an Arms Race in Outer Space (PAROS), at which Qian expressed his delight.[56] China's new optimism was also reflected in a statement by Qian's successor, Fan Guoxiang, on the achievements of UNSSOD III in 1988. Somewhat unexpectedly, Fan expressed support for the activities of NGOs and for the usefulness of multilateral discussions. Any shortcomings in the session, he found, were due to the "tendency to concentrate too much on bilateral relations between the superpowers and to give inadequate attention to the multilateral efforts in disarmament, and in particular to adopt the rigid position of having one's own way while ignoring the reasonable demands of the great majority."[57]

China's upbeat mood reflected not only the favorable strategic environment, but also a new confidence arising from its improved international status. Its optimism even survived the unfavorable international reaction to its suppression of the Democracy Movement in June 1989. In August, already buoyed by the conclusion of the agreement between the United States and the USSR on the Intermediate Range Nuclear Forces Treaty in December 1987 and by the subsequent January 1989 Paris conference on the prohibition of chemical weapons, Ambassador Fan noted that "in international affairs the trend of confrontation moving towards dialogue, and tension turning toward relaxation, has kept up its momentum [and] has had positive effects on progress in the field of disarmament."[58] The importance for China of multilateral negotiations and a favorable strategic environment was increasingly emphasized. In an address to mark the tenth anniversary of China's entry into the CD, Foreign Minister Qian Qichen announced that the Chinese delegation was ready to join in the work of the Ad Hoc Committee on a nuclear test ban as soon as it was established by the CD and that it was giving consideration to sending an observer delegation to the Fourth Review Conference of the Parties to the Nuclear Nonproliferation Treaty in August 1990.[59]

Internalization of Norms: 1992–2001

The conceptual shifts of the 1980s were followed in the 1990s by concrete policy changes in the wake of the relaxation of Cold War tensions, when China ratified or signed the major international nonproliferation and arms control treaties. This decade brought it to what might be called a "plateau of receptivity" to the norms, principles, and rules of the regime, before the advent of the tensions that followed the inauguration of the second Bush administration. In this period, China not only began to comply formally with its treaty obligations, but also internalized those norms both internationally and domestically. According to the process-based indicators outlined in the Introduction, it did so internationally by accepting constraints on its sovereignty, by reconceiving its interests to conform with treaty norms, and by accepting the costs, as well as the benefits, of ratifying, and complying with, relevant treaties. At the domestic level, it accepted IAEA and CWC verification processes, including on-site inspections (OSI), and the internal constraints involved in the cessation of nuclear testing. On the other hand, it was accused in some quarters of breaching specific obligations under the Nuclear Nonproliferation Treaty (NPT).

In 1990, as foreshadowed, China attended the fourth NPT Review Conference and in 1991, announced its intention to accede to the NPT while voicing reservations about the treaty's discriminatory nature.[60] Its major policy advance, according to its negotiators, occurred with its accession to the NPT in March 1992. Western observers also saw the accession as a turning point. Once in the NPT, according to one, China was "more part of the non-proliferation and disarmament debate."[61] The NPT, which was designed to prevent the spread of nuclear weapons, to encourage disarmament, and to promote the peaceful uses of nuclear energy, had been opened for signature on 1 July 1968. In finally agreeing to accede to it, China was motivated both by strategic interests and political pressures. These included the U.S.-Soviet arms race, the announcement of France's decision to ratify, its own need to improve its image after Tiananmen, its interest in securing aid from Japan,[62] and pressures from within its own scientific and academic community.[63] The declaration accompanying its accession in March 1992 expressed support for the norms and principles of the treaty and stated China's policy of "not advocating, encouraging or engaging in the proliferation of nuclear weapons, nor helping other countries to develop nuclear weapons." It also articulated China's unique view of the relationship between nonproliferation, disarmament, and its ultimate objective of the total elimination of nuclear weapons.[64]

At the 1995 Nonproliferation Treaty Review and Extension Conference, China supported the decision to extend the treaty indefinitely. Although it would have preferred a twenty-five-year extension, its unwillingness to undermine consensus meant that it was not in favor of the extension decision being put to a vote.[65] It was also at pains to emphasize its compliance with the treaty, producing a national report on its implementation to date, and its first White Paper on arms control and disarmament.[66]

The NPT concluded a double bargain. It offered assistance to nonnuclear weapon states (NNWS) to develop nuclear energy in exchange for their undertaking not to develop nuclear weapons, and it proposed nuclear disarmament by the five declared nuclear weapon states (NWS) in return for the renunciation of nuclear arms development by all other states.[67] Under Article I of the NPT, China and the other NWS agreed not to transfer nuclear weapons or devices and not to assist NNWS in acquiring nuclear weapons. Under Article III.2, they undertook not to provide source or special fissionable material or equipment or material for the processing, use, or production of special fissionable material to any NNWS for peaceful purposes, unless that state agreed to the application of IAEA safeguards. Under Article VI, they undertook to seek an early end to the nuclear arms race and to pursue nuclear disarmament as well as general and complete disarmament, "under strict and effective international control."

It was this last obligation that was to create the greatest conflict between NWS and NNWS, which were subsequently to claim that the NWS were placing too much emphasis on nonproliferation and too little on their own responsibility to disarm.[68] Unlike the NNWS, the nuclear weapon states were not required to submit the peaceful nuclear activities within their territories to the safeguards required by Article III. Nevertheless, like the other NWS, China subsequently accepted IAEA safeguards on two of its civilian nuclear reactors (Qinshan-1 nuclear power reactor and HWRR-2 research reactor at the China Institute of Atomic Energy [CIAE], Beijing). The motive behind this entirely voluntary commitment was to provide a model to the NNWS and to prevent charges of discriminatory treatment.[69]

However, China still experienced difficulties with problems arising from inadequate implementation, the technology gap, and the issue of transparency. As observers remarked, China was "already initiated into the lore [of disarmament], but not fully immersed." It found the NPT difficult to implement in terms of export controls, especially vis-à-vis Pakistan, and therefore had considerable problems with its other treaty partners.[70] The situation improved from 1995, when, following its promulgation of necessary legislation, Beijing gained more control over its arms exporting industry. Transparency, however, became a problem when, along with 129 other countries, China signed the Chemical Weapons Convention on 13 January 1993. Under Article VI, Activities Not Prohibited under This Convention, each state party was required to subject toxic chemicals and related facilities in the Verification Annex to data monitoring and on-site verification, to make an initial declaration on those chemicals, and thereafter to make an annual declaration. Under Article IX, states parties also had the right to request an on-site challenge inspection of any facility or location in the territory of another state party concerning possible non-compliance with the Convention's provisions. It thus represented a considerable cost to the state and a constraint on sovereignty.

Because of its uncertainty about U.S. intentions to accede to the CWC, China delayed ratification.[71] But, in December 1996, the Standing Committee of the Eighth NPC approved ratification, and on 25 April 1997, just four days before the treaty entered into force, the instrument was duly deposited with the UN. China attached two declarations, the one on signature, the other on ratification. Both asserted its support for the norms and principles of the Convention but opposed "any act of abusing the verification provisions which endangers [China's] sovereignty and security."[72] China also became a founding member of the Organization for the Prohibition of Chemical Weapons (OPCW), and a member of its Executive Council, which directed the CWC's verification regime. It delivered the initial declaration and annual declaration required under the Convention and, by June 2005, had received ninety-five on-site inspections by OPCW personnel to verify submitted declarations, as well as participating in the conferences of states parties.[73] In addition, from 1988, it annually provided the United Nations with information on convention-related matters and on confidence-building measures in regard to the Biological Weapons Convention (BWC). It participated in the BWC Review Conferences and submitted reports on its compliance with the Convention.[74]

Concessions of sovereignty were made in other areas. Although there was no UN treaty controlling missile proliferation and although China was not a member of the Missile Technology Control Regime (MTCR), it began to issue statements in the early 1990s supporting the principle of missile nonproliferation and, in November 1991, undertook not to violate MTCR guidelines. In October 1994, it signed a bilateral agreement with the United States to refrain from selling MTCR-class missiles, despite its objection that the MTCR was only a "time-winning device" that lacked a legal basis in international law.[75] From 1992, China also began to supply information to the UN Register on Conventional Arms (UNROCA). Following the U.S. listing of arms exports to Taiwan in 1997, however, it withdrew from participation. In April 1995, China and the P-4 issued UN Security Council Resolution 984, providing Positive Security Assurances to NPT nonnuclear states.

Throughout this period, however, China had continued the development of its nuclear arsenal. In the late 1980s and early 1990s this had taken the form of the modernization of its nuclear forces. For this reason, its integration into the arms control and disarmament regime could not be completed until it had signed and ratified the CTBT. China had been in the middle of its nuclear weapons testing when negotiations on the CTBT began, unlike the United States, Russia, and Britain, which had already completed several development cycles.[76] Its provocative decision to continue testing while participating in negotiations did not go unchallenged, and it suffered a degree of international disapproval in the CD that, though at first subdued, became more vocal after the recommencement of French testing in the Pacific.[77] As Zou Yunhua has ably documented, on 5 October 1993 China conducted its first test since the moratorium adopted by the other nuclear weapon states just prior to the beginning of CTBT negotiations.[78] Its subsequent test was held on 10 June 1994 during a session of the CD, where it was again criticized.

As a member of the CD, China was clearly subjected to stronger pressures and disapproval than if it had been outside that body. Time and again in the CD, it was obliged to defend its testing program.[79] Less than two days after the end of the Nonproliferation Treaty Review and Extension Conference, and before delegates had departed, on 15 May 1995 it held another test. This time, the Non-

Aligned Movement made clear its displeasure. Japan also imposed aid sanctions on China. After two more tests, on 8 June 1996 China announced it would hold only one more. This subsequent test, conducted shortly before the last negotiating session for the CTBT, was the occasion for China's announcement that it would henceforth cease all nuclear testing. While reflecting China's taste for political symbolism, the timing of the announcement also demonstrated its concern to be seen as a cooperative member of the disarmament community. Such an outcome was clear evidence of its responsiveness to widespread international pressure, although it is not clear why that pressure was not imposed more unequivocally prior to France's renewed tests.

Despite such progress, China regretted the level of transparency it had accepted under the CWC and was not prepared to accept the same level in the CTBT. Thus, it found the negotiation process to establish the CTBT difficult, although it participated fully.[80] China quickly established its position on all the issues by issuing a formal working paper, "Basic Structure of a Comprehensive Test-Ban Treaty," dated 30 March 1994. Its readiness to cooperate, despite its firm declaratory position, was borne out by the compromises it made during the CTBT negotiations, and by the costs it accepted in signing the treaty. During the negotiations, it gave up its requirements for a no-first-use policy and security assurances, for a policy allowing peaceful nuclear explosions (PNE), and for its position that entry into force of the CTBT should require ratification by all CTBT members and by all nuclear capable states identified by the IAEA.[81] In particular, having been allowed peaceful nuclear explosions under the NPT, China was baffled by the logic that the rules of the CTBT should supersede the norms of the NPT. Yet, as an interviewee commented, "having lost the debate, China gave in gracefully."[82] On some issues, on the other hand, it was not prepared to concede. As in the human rights regime, the issue that proved most difficult for it was on-site inspection (OSI), including the trigger mechanism for OSI and its decision-making procedure.

Because of the challenge OSI represented to the sovereignty of the inspected state, the Chinese delegation held that it should only be triggered under extreme circumstances and should be the last resort of the verification system. Thus, China opposed the Western proposal that on-site inspections should be triggered not only by the International Monitoring System (IMS) of seismological monitoring stations, but also by national technical means (NTM). China saw the OSI as a key issue for its fundamental national security interests and held steadfastly to its position until just before the completion of negotiations. In the end, the CTBT was only passed by an Australian initiative that took the treaty text out of the CD to UNGA in New York.[83] Even in the CTBT negotiations, China engaged in free-riding, allowing Russia to argue the position against on-site inspections, but standing exposed when Russia unexpectedly accepted the inspections regime.[84] China refused to sign the CTBT if the United States persisted in its policy that a "green light" to proceed with OSI should require only a simple majority. Instead, it promoted the idea of a process requiring approval by three-fifths of the Executive Council members. The United States finally accepted a compromise requiring authorization of "at least thirty affirmative votes" in the fifty-one-member council. In return, China agreed that NTM should have a supplementary role in triggering an OSI.[85]

Although opinion differs on the degree to which China accepted costs in this regime, there is general agreement that, in becoming the second signatory of the CTBT after the United States in March 1996, it allowed a significant diminution of its sovereignty. Certainly, Chinese officials consider this to have been the case. In conjunction with its Article VI obligations under the NPT, signature of this instrument entrenched China's obligation to limit its weapons capability. The decision required an enormous effort of coordination among Chinese ministries and reflected Ambassador Sha Zukang's personal "pull."[86] According to Bates Gill, the People's Liberation Army and the defense-industrial complex argued that China was "not technically ready" to sign, whereas the Chinese Foreign Ministry argued that China's international stature and reputation as a responsible power required its signature. In the end, pressures from the international community, including from several of China's Asian neighbors, in conjunction with Ministry of Foreign Affairs (MFA) arguments, convinced China's leadership.[87] Once again, China showed itself accessible to persuasion and debate.

Having already accepted many compromises during negotiations, China, in signing the treaty, was obliged by Article 18 of the Vienna Convention on the Law of Treaties "to refrain from acts which would defeat the object and purpose" of the treaty. The treaty imposed a freeze on China's nuclear weapons program when it was at a less-developed stage than any of the other nuclear weapon states, limiting the further modernization of its arsenal. When negotiations for the CTBT began in 1994, the United States had already conducted 1,032 nuclear tests, Russia, 715, Britain, 45, France, 191, and China, only 39.[88] By 1996, when it ceased testing, China had conducted just 46 tests. A freeze represented a special problem for China because of its technology gap. Its development was far behind that of the United States and Russia, but, with status considerations always paramount in its policy, it still did not wish to be treated on a par with the United Kingdom and France.[89] As a Western diplomat has conceded, the freeze also represented a more severe cost to China than to the United States because, unlike China, the United States could use simulation techniques as a substitute for testing.[90] China was also not under the protection of any nuclear umbrella.

China's signature of the CTBT was therefore widely seen as evidence that its role in disarmament had become "more positive, constructive and active."[91] At the 1999 Conference on Facilitating the Entry into Force of the Comprehensive Nuclear Test Ban Treaty to urge countries to sign and ratify the CTBT, China also promised to speed up its ratification, based on a full review of the treaty and the international security environment.[92] Despite the U.S. congressional rejection of the CTBT in October 1999, and despite President George Bush's subsequent opposition to it, the treaty was duly submitted to China's National People's Congress for ratification.[93] Yet, both the original statement accompanying its signature and other formal policy documents indicated that the failure of the United States to ratify the treaty presented a major obstacle to China's own ratification.[94] As a Chinese official remarked in 2002, although it had always been China's policy to have a comprehensive ban, the success of a ban "also depend[ed] on other countries."[95]

It was particularly important for both the United States and China to ratify the CTBT. This was because both states were nuclear powers belonging to the group of forty-four that had to ratify the treaty for it to take effect, and because a time limit was incorporated into Article 18 of the Vienna Convention on the Law of Treaties. Pending the CTBT's entry into force, ratifying states were obliged to refrain from acts that would defeat the treaty's object and purpose. However, this obligation pertained, in the words of the Vienna Convention, "pending the entry into force of the treaty and *provided that such entry into force is not unduly delayed.*" In other words, as Patricia Hewitson has observed, even ratifying states like Russia and France could decide to resume nuclear testing if there were any undue delay in its entry into force. More significantly for our purposes, China as a signatory could also argue that undue delay would relieve it of its interim obligation.[96]

Why did China sign the CTBT? Senior Colonel Zou Yunhua has suggested a number of reasons: the post–Cold War international situation favored support for the CTBT; China needed to "maintain its image in the Third World countries"; a peaceful international environment was indispensable for China's rapid economic development; China had the capability to undertake the obligations of the treaty; massive U.S. and Russian nuclear arsenals had become a heavy burden to the world, convincing China of the correctness of its decision to build only a small nuclear arsenal; and China saw a need to create the right international atmosphere for its resumption of sovereignty over Hong Kong.[97] Besides such specific reasons were the more general considerations of international pressure, the high legitimacy of the nonproliferation and disarmament regime, China's concern about its international status and reputation, and internal policy dynamics.[98] In the face of such pressures and incentives, China was prepared to accept the clear constraints the treaty imposed both on its sovereignty and on its status as a nuclear power.

Signature of the CTBT prefigured other advances. In May 1996, China also promised it would not offer to assist the nuclear facilities of those nonnuclear weapon states that had not accepted the IAEA's safeguards.[99] In May 1997, it published the Circular on Questions Pertaining to the Strict Implementation of China's Nuclear Exports Policy, with strict provisions regarding exports of dual-use nuclear materials, including the requirement of IAEA safeguards. In 1997, it also sent observers to attend a meeting of the Zangger Committee, a mechanism of international nuclear export control, and joined it in October 1997, albeit without accepting full-scope safeguards. Other milestones identified in this period by interviewees included a greater openness to the disarmament community, in particular disarmament NGOs, a change that Rebecca Johnson, the Executive Director of the Acronym Institute for Disarmament Diplomacy, traced from the appointment of Ambassador Sha Zukang as fourth Special Ambassador for Disarmament Measures to Geneva in 1994. As another interviewee put it, Ambassador Sha "fought the good fight" in the CD, an organization in which the personality of the state's representative sometimes played a critical role. Under Sha's guidance, China's policy also became more clear-cut and consistent. Before that time, it had been seen by one Western participant as "not so focused or well led," and as "divided in inter-agency fights," between the Foreign Ministry, the PLA, and the Defense Ministry.[100]

Through Ambassador Sha's vigorous campaigning and advocacy, at a time of considerable financial stringency in all capitals of the world, including Beijing, a special Department of Arms Control and Disarmament was created in the Chinese Foreign Ministry in 1997, directly responsible to the Minister and equivalent in status to the Department of International Organizations, of which it was formerly the Fourth Office. One of the functions of the new Department was to serve as a bridge between the Foreign Ministry and the military. Ambassador Sha realized that China needed not just to hold to its position but to advance its interests, and to do this he needed staff with technical and scientific expertise and better liaison with international NGOs.[101] In Beijing, his Department developed the reputation of being one of the areas in the Foreign Ministry most accessible to the foreign press and to scholars.[102] In another policy advance, China participated in negotiations for a protocol to the BWC, initiated in 1996, which addressed the problem of a verification framework for that treaty.

Even the shock of the Indian and Pakistani tests in May 1998 merely strengthened China's conviction that it was following the correct nonproliferation and disarmament policy and hardened its resolve to continue to conclude relevant agreements.[103] The tests did, however, affect China's perception of its strategic environment. The possibility that India in particular might catch up with, and even surpass, its nuclear capability represented a challenge for China's effective policy of minimum deterrence and did not augur well for future peace.[104] However, China articulated its primary concern as being the threat the tests represented to the NPT and the CTBT. As Sha Zukang later observed, they represented "a litmus test for the effectiveness of the international nonproliferation regime."[105]

Thus, on 15 May 1998, China transmitted to the CD the Foreign Ministry's condemnation of the Indian tests, rejecting them as "nothing but an outrageous contempt for the common will of the international community for the comprehensive ban on nuclear tests and a hard blow on the international effort to prevent nuclear weapon proliferation."[106] Members of the CD were almost unanimous in regretting the deleterious effects the tests would have on the arms control regime.[107] The Pakistani Ambassador subsequently retorted that "for the five nuclear states to tell other states not to proliferate is like five drunkards preaching abstinence to the rest of the world."[108] Nevertheless, China took the unusual initiative of drafting the 4 June 1998 joint communiqué of the P-5 condemning the nuclear tests by India and Pakistan, rather than leaving it to others to act. Two years later, China's sense of security and its evolving nuclear disarmament policy were to be even more seriously tested.

Within the CD, apart from coping with the constant pressures on it before 1996 to explain its continued nuclear testing, China continued to struggle with the issue of transparency. Adopting a notion of "asymmetrical transparency," it argued that because it was a weaker nuclear state it had less of an obligation to be transparent than the others. However, as usual it was careful to frame its position in legally correct forms. Thus, it invoked the rules of procedure of the CD to criticize the Chairman of the Ad Hoc Committee on Transparency in Armaments for allegedly inappropriate behavior.[109] In 1997, China's attitude on this thorny issue was spelt out in an illuminating statement that reflected its view of the costs it had accepted in the regime:

[Our] delegation is not against transparency as a matter of principle. We only feel that all transparency measures are in fact treaty-specific. For instance, China, like many other countries, accepts the IAEA safeguards. That in itself constitutes a transparency measure. We have accepted the on-site inspection provision under the CWC. That, of course, is also a transparency measure. Furthermore, China has concluded bilateral or regional multilateral agreements on confidence building with some neighboring countries. An important component of these agreements is the transparency measures. For the reasons listed above . . . it is not necessary to re-establish the Ad Hoc Committee on Transparency in Armaments in this year's session of the CD.[110]

China was equally defensive about its policy on anti-personnel landmines (APLs). Although it was "not opposed to the objective of prohibition of APLs in a phased approach," it could not, for reasons of "legitimate territorial defense requirements," agree to an immediate total ban.[111] For its part, it sought unavailingly to encourage the nuclear weapon states to conclude a treaty against the first use of nuclear weapons.[112] Despite such difficulties, as one of the elite P-5, it took an increasing pride in its membership of the CD, and participated ever more freely in the give-and-take of discussions. By contrast with its earlier tendency to free-ride, its disarmament diplomacy was now described as "relatively open," involving frequent interventions in debates.[113] Over time, it showed a growing readiness to accept the costs of participation in the organization and to accede to associated treaties.

China also joined a number of bilateral and multilateral confidence and security-building institutions apart from the ARF. As a result of its proposal to convene a meeting on security policies, in November 2004 the first ARF Security Policy Conference was held in Beijing. China also supported protocols for the establishment of various nuclear weapon free zones (NWFZs).[114] In December 1998, it signed with the IAEA the Additional Protocol to the Safeguards Agreement, aimed at strengthening the effectiveness of the IAEA safeguard system, undertaking to report to the IAEA on its nuclear cooperation with nonnuclear weapon states.[115] In 2000, it received a full-scope IAEA international regulatory review team mission in China and a peer review of radiation safety infrastructure. At the end of March 2002, it notified the IAEA that it had completed the required legal procedures to become a party to the Additional Protocol and for its entry into force for China.[116]

China's readiness to bend to international opinion and accept the norms of nuclear nonproliferation and disarmament was further demonstrated by its changing policy on fissile materials. Originally, it had not supported the 1993 UN General Assembly resolution calling for a Fissile Material Cutoff Treaty (FMCT) and, in March 1994, had opposed the creation of an Ad Hoc Committee in the CD to begin negotiations for a FMCT. This was because it wished to link negotiations on FMCT with progress on nuclear disarmament and the establishment of an Ad Hoc Committee on the Prevention of an Arms Race in Outer Space (PAROS). It also believed that a cut-off treaty should deal only with future production, should be universal, and should include verification measures.[117] Despite these initial concerns, by 1998 it had withdrawn its objections to negotiations and, in the CD session in late 1998, voted for the reconstitu-tion of the Ad Hoc Committee.[118]

By late 1998, China appeared well satisfied with the achievements of the CD. A senior Chinese official praised the CD's transformation from a place of polit-ical confrontation between two blocs to a genuine forum for multilateral nego-tiation, which had successfully negotiated the CWC and the CTBT. At the same time, he expressed concern about its future effectiveness with regard to the ad hoc committees on the FMCT and on the PAROS.[119] Within the CD, China saw the main difference between itself and the P-4 and NAM states as being the issue of nuclear disarmament.[120] Through its no-first-use policy, it rejected, at least in theory, the doctrine of nuclear deterrence, and identified itself as the only nuclear weapon state standing for the complete prohibition and destruc-tion of nuclear weapons—a position that in 1998 it believed the P-4 were begin-ning to accept themselves. On the other hand, according to China, the NAM states believed that the possession of any nuclear weapons was immoral, a posi-tion China could not accept. Some NAM states also failed to distinguish between the policies of the different states in the P-5, and proposed a time-bound nuclear disarmament program that, the official said, was "not realistic."

In China's own judgment, and that of the wider scholarly arms control community, its nuclear arsenal was small, both qualitatively and quantitatively.[121] As of 1998, it was estimated at about 400–450 devices and aimed primarily at meeting its peripheral security requirements. Its strategic force, which it was in the process of modernizing, was land-based, with only a few intercontinental ballistic missiles (between six and twenty-four) capable of reaching interconti-nental targets. It had the capability of deploying multiple warheads on its ICBM force but had chosen not to do so.[122] It therefore did not believe that its nuclear arsenal represented a global threat. For that reason, together with France, and over the objections of the G-21, China still refused to "multilateralize" the strate-gic arms reduction talks (START) process.[123] Although the reduction of the arse-nal of the big powers "to a certain level" closer to that of the P-3 was a pre-requisite to broadening the process, it was still considering alternatives such as U.S. and Russian acceptance of the principle of "no first use."[124]

Uncertainty and Reaction: 2001–

The next, and still current, phase of China's CD participation highlighted the critical importance of the principle of reciprocity in the international security regime. It suggested that all the benefits of the organizational process could be undermined by the loss of mutual trust essential to maintain states' faith in the norms, processes, and predictability of that regime. In 2001, following the election of U.S. President George Bush, China's evolving position on nuclear disarmament and nonproliferation suffered a major setback. A succession of U.S. foreign policy shifts, from the new administration's decision not to ratify the Kyoto Protocol to its questioning of the ABM (Anti-Ballistic Missile) Treaty and the CTBT, led China and many other states to the reluctant conclusion that widely shared norms of international behavior, an assumption of interdependence, and even the fragile authority of international rules were under threat, paradoxically from one of the original architects and strongest champions of the international legal system.[125] States were not the only entities adversely affected by the changes in U.S. policy. Increasingly, the authority and effectiveness of the Conference on Disarmament were undermined.

Deeply worrying to China were the new U.S. projection of its unipolar power and its apparent indifference to the opinion of the international community. In particular, U.S. plans to introduce a National Missile Defense System and Theater Missile Defense System, briefly flagged by President Clinton in his final year as President and resurfacing under the new President, and the possible abrogation of the ABM Treaty by the United States, represented a new threat to China's security and a potential threat to its economic modernization. They also revived the fears provoked by Reagan's 1983 SDI initiative. U.S. actions undermining the Biological Weapons Convention, through the blocking of an international attempt to strengthen its inspection powers, created further insecurity, as did indications that it was involved in renewed research on biological weapons.[126]

The more assertive manner in which the United States now wielded its power, and, in particular, its identification of states belonging to "the axis of evil," reinforced China's long-held conviction that progress in disarmament was largely a function of the international strategic environment. In the conventional military arena, for instance, as a result of the high-tech strategy adopted by the United States in the Gulf War in 1991, the PLA had changed its approach from "defense as the overall posture, offence as the supplement," to "adroit response based on a combination of offensive and defensive capabilities."[127] The threatened abrogation of the ABM Treaty now appeared to create similar pressures to rethink the nonproliferation and disarmament regime, potentially undermining not only the START process, but also the CTBT and even the NPT, and possibly affecting nuclear proliferation dynamics in Central and South Asia.[128]

Initially, China's response to these perceived threats was to adopt a two-pronged strategy. On the one hand, it stepped up its support for multilateralism and, on the other, launched a diplomatic offensive to counter the threats, joining with Russia to work against abrogation of the ABM Treaty. Sha Zukang in particular was vociferous in every possible multilateral forum about the need to preserve the treaty that was seen as the backbone of the disarmament regime.[129] In an apparent recasting of its security and foreign policy persona, China argued that for the United States to undermine the authority of a legitimately constituted disarmament agreement was to embark on a new global arms race and weaken the arms control and disarmament consensus.[130] The paradoxical result was that, whereas China had once been seen as a major threat to the regime, it now became a major bastion of support for it. China's fears for the stability of the legal foundations underpinning the regime were also sounded in April 2002 by Foreign Minister Tang Jiaxuan at a disarmament conference jointly hosted in Beijing by the Chinese Foreign Ministry and the UN Department of Disarmament Affairs. Significantly, he appealed to states to demonstrate a proper respect for common security and to recognize the destructive effects of a realpolitik approach to disarmament:

> Thanks to joint efforts over the years, the international community has established a relatively complete legal system for arms control and disarmament. As an important component of the global security framework with the UN at its centre, this system has increased the predictability of international relations and played an important role in safeguarding international peace, security and stability. Under the new circumstances, it is vital to maintain the existing arms control legal system and continue to promote the arms control and disarmament process. Only by so doing, can the international community enhance mutual trust and cooperation in a joint effort to cope with various new threats. The practice of abandoning or weakening this process and seeking security through expanding unilateral military advantages will not only fail to address the problems, but instead will exert serious impact on international strategic stability. Arms control and disarmament are at a crucial moment when failure to advance would mean retrogression.[131]

In the CD, Ambassador Hu's 7 February 2002 statement offered an unusually frank exposition of China's concerns about the new U.S. policies, even though it did not mention the United States by name, and about the way in which these had irrevocably altered the balance of global security:

> The ABM Treaty, which was recognized by the international community at the NPT Review Conference as the cornerstone of strategic stability, is about to be rendered null and void. The seven-year long negotiations on a protocol to strengthen the BWC have been set at naught and the ad hoc group has suspended its work, its future uncertain. The CTBT has been rejected and its future prospects are dismal and there is now even a possibility that nuclear tests will resume. . . . This legal regime has become an essential component of the global collective security structure centered on the United Nations and also plays a crucial role in maintaining global and regional security and stability. . . . [And yet] we have witnessed such developments as . . . the pursuit of self-interest and the application of double standards in non-proliferation issues; the adoption by a country of a strict position to others in matters of treaty compliance, but a lenient one to itself, to the extent of passing domestic legislation which distorts the obligations provided for in international treaties; insistence on the speedy conclusion

of a treaty with an extremely strict verification regime during negotiations, followed by a volte-face on conclusion of the treaty and categorical refusal to ratify it. *All these actions have not only eroded the stature and impartiality of international arms control and disarmament treaties, but also impaired confidence among States.*[132]

On the eve of the ABM decision, Chinese officials in Beijing appeared anxious, but nevertheless refrained from direct criticism of the parties.[133] This was partly in reaction to the subdued Russian response.[134] However, the officials observed that it was vital for the international community to maintain multilateral arms control norms, "otherwise we live in chaos." They added that "these norms are good for everyone, including China."[135] Arms control agreements were seen as different from other issues because of their strategic sensitivity. An "appropriate balance" had to be found between "common security and legitimate interests." When the abrogation of the treaty was finally announced in late May 2002, like the rest of the international community, China did not express outrage, but, publicly at least, sought to put the best interpretation on the outcome. Its position was that, because of the vital importance of international strategic stability, it was better to keep dialogue open and, together with other concerned countries, to try to slowly change the U.S. attitude.

Within the CD, China's Ambassador for Disarmament Affairs continued to intervene in ways that reflected both concern about the existing treaties and increasing alarm about U.S. intentions on missile defense. Together with Russia, China lobbied for the reestablishment of an Ad Hoc Committee to negotiate a treaty on the Prevention of an Arms Race in Outer Space[136] and submitted a joint working paper on the prevention of the deployment of weapons in outer space.[137] Hu also called for an early entry into force of the CTBT and introduced a document, Draft Decision on the Establishment of an Ad Hoc Committee on Prevention of an Arms Race in Outer Space and its Mandate.[138] However, in an ironic twist, U.S. opposition to these proposals led Chinese officials themselves to bemoan the veto-like powers imposed by the "consensus principle."[139]

Progress in the CD was clearly impeded by U.S.-China disagreement. While the United States saw no need to negotiate a new outer space treaty, it wished to negotiate a fissile material cut-off treaty: China, on the other hand, wished to negotiate a new outer space treaty and, even though still calling for the negotiation of the FMCT, in the light of the new uncertainty about U.S. missile defense plans, now wanted to keep its options open. While observing that China was often seen as the main obstacle to progress, Acronym Executive Director Rebecca Johnson concluded that "the present impasse is equally the responsibility of the United States and China—a strange combination perhaps, but one more than sufficient to suffocate the CD."[140] The compelling need for the negotiation of an outer space treaty was to be further underlined by China's successful completion of its first space mission in October the following year and another in 2005.

Given such developments, in August 2002, Ambassador Hu flagged the necessity for an entire rethink of arms control and disarmament and the establishment of "a new global security framework." He enunciated certain "indispensable" principles that should underlie this new framework: continuous efforts to promote nuclear disarmament and a diminishing role for nuclear weapons; prevention of the weaponization of outer space and an arms race in outer space; nonproliferation of weapons of mass destruction; and efforts to ensure that the missile defense system did not disrupt global strategic stability or lead to missile proliferation.[141] Progress in nuclear disarmament was seen to hinge both on the maintenance of global strategic balance and on the possibility of "undiminished security for all."

There was little doubt that China's concerns were also shared by other members of the CD, and complaints proliferated that progress in the disarmament body had reached a stalemate.[142] Already, the need to move the negotiation of the CTBT to New York had raised questions about the CD's effectiveness.[143] Now, fewer and fewer delegations bothered to make policy statements before the Conference and an increasing number of governments began cutting the resources necessary for participation.[144] Such complaints continued in 2003, despite the UN Secretary-General's rousing call to revitalize the Conference at the opening of its twenty-fifth session. Some meeting of minds occurred as China and the United States made some minor concessions on the matters of fissile material and PAROS. However, the 2003 CD session concluded on the depressing note that, despite increasing threats to international peace and security, for seven straight years the conference had not been able to end the stalemate on disarmament negotiations.[145] China's relative silence during the open plenaries of the 2004 and 2005 Conference proceedings reflected its disillusionment. By December 2004, it had concluded that "the key to pushing forward the international arms control and disarmament process is to break the deadlock at the Conference on Disarmament."[146]

Notwithstanding such setbacks, China's overt, and uncharacteristic, moderation, and its continued declaratory support for the arms control and disarmament regime in the face of radical changes in U.S. policy, were potent indicators not only of its support for, but of its increased dependence on, the regime. Significantly, too, China's support was now couched not in the language of realpolitik, but in the language of common security. Also notable was its increasing emphasis on the international legal underpinnings of the global collective security regime. On the other hand, because it opposed the use of force as a means of handling nonproliferation issues, it continued to use its P-5 status to discourage the use of sanctions in cases of breach. Despite its declared support for verification measures when it ratified each treaty, it was still reluctant in practice to accept any initiative either by the Security Council or the IAEA that could lead to the use of force, whether with respect to Iraq, Iran, or North Korea. Thus, it hailed Libya's voluntary disarmament as a case study of the success of China's preferred policy of patient diplomacy. In this case, it opened itself to the charge of undermining the UN's ultimate authority to enforce its rules, even though in China's view this cautious approach was one which best respected and protected the purposes of the UN Charter.[147]

Apart from its enhanced support for multilateral mechanisms, China's concern about terrorism by weapons of mass destruction and about new U.S. initiatives like the Proliferation Security Initiative (PSI), set up by the United States in conjunction with a number of other states on 31 May 2003, was translated into some new areas of cooperation. Its formal application on 26 January 2004 to join the Nuclear Suppliers Group (NSG) was evidence of its heightened concern about nuclear proliferation.[148] Soon after joining the NSG, China also expressed interest in joining the Missile Technology Control Regime (MTCR), which promised to give "positive consideration" to its application.[149]

The downside to this apparent progress, however, has been that, in a context of continuing strategic uncertainty, China has still not ratified the CTBT. As Rebecca Johnson has commented, China's declaration at the 2005 NPT Review Conference that it "support[ed] an early-entry-into-force of the CTBT and [wa]s now working actively on its internal legal proceedings for ratifying the treaty" would have been more credible had it not used a similar excuse at the 2000 Review Conference.[150] Clues to its failure to proceed to ratification lay in its continuing complaint about the "uncertain, unstable and unpredictable factors affecting international security."[151] China's growing concern about the strategic environment, already aroused by the Gulf War, the Indian and Pakistani nuclear tests, and the 2003 war in Iraq, was intensified by reports that the United States was rebuilding its nuclear stockpile and intended to conclude a nuclear pact with India. Such developments led China to strengthen its own defenses and to further modernize its nuclear force, even though it still insisted that it would not recommence nuclear testing.[152] It even began an internal policy debate on its own "no first use" policy. Chinese analysts also speculated that China might move from its strategic nuclear posture of minimum deterrence to a more rigorous one of limited deterrence.[153] Thus, whereas in 1998 it had between 400 and 450 nuclear weapons, some strategic analysts now claim it has 490 and that it is building up its short- and long-range ballistic missile production.[154] Such estimates would suggest that, while its declaratory support for multilateralism has intensified, in practice China is beginning to lose faith in the multilateral process and to take defensive measures that are contrary, if not to the letter, then at least to the spirit, of disarmament norms. In the complex balancing act between "common security and legitimate interests," China has reluctantly begun to give precedence to the latter.[155]

This shift in China's policy is all the more disturbing in view of the steps it had taken over the preceding twenty-five years toward the institutional and legal implementation of treaty norms and rules and, to a lesser degree, the implementation and enforcement in practice of the obligations it had assumed under the treaties to which it was a party.

Legislative and Institutional Implementation

From the 1990s, China's international compliance was mirrored domestically in the steps it took to harmonize its domestic laws and institutions with its international obligations under the Biological Weapons Convention, the Chemical Weapons Convention, and the NPT. By 2003, it had established a systematic policy framework. Apart from the post of Special Ambassador for Disarmament and the new Department of Arms Control and Disarmament in the Chinese Foreign Ministry, it set up a web of interagency institutions to absorb, disseminate, and debate the increasingly complex technological and scientific developments in the arms control regime, as well as the array of strategic doctrines relevant to its participation in the CD and the UN First Committee.[156] These new institutions included the Commission on Science, Technology and Industry for National Defense (COSTIND) and the General Armaments Department (GAD), itself established in 1998. They brought together not just officials, but arms control specialists and scholars from within and outside China. The result was a more open, pragmatic, and sophisticated approach that expanded the debate within China and eroded the normal barriers between China and the international strategic community. While the Ministry of Foreign Affairs usually presided over the "jawboning" process, particularly when it involved leading delegations of officials from different Chinese ministries abroad, the input of government agencies such as the Ministry of Defense was often reflected in China's negotiating positions in international forums. Other institution building occurred as a direct outcome of China's accession to a treaty. For instance, Article VII.4 of the Chemical Weapons Convention required states parties to establish or designate a national authority to serve as the point of liaison with the OPCW. In response to the NPT, China also established a Military Production Export Small Group.

Following its ratification of the NPT, China also introduced a series of laws, regulations, and decrees on export controls, beginning with the May 1994 Foreign Trade Law and including the 1997 Regulations of the PRC on the Control of Nuclear Export, the 1997 Regulations on the Administration of Arms Export (amended in October 2002); the Military Products Export Control List (promulgated in November 2002); the 1998 Regulations on the Control of the Export of Dual-Use Nuclear Materials and Related Technologies Export; and the 2001 amended Nuclear Export Control List.[157] In November 2002, it promulgated Measures on the Administration of Export Registration for Sensitive Items and Technologies, and in December 2003, an Export Licensing Catalogue of Sensitive Items and Technologies. After ratifying the CWC, it also issued the December 1995 Regulations of the People's Republic of China on the Supervision and Control of Chemicals; the March 1997 supplement to the regulations; the August 1997 Ministerial Circular on strengthening chemical export controls; the 1998 Decree No. 1 of the State Petroleum and Chemical Industry Administration; and the October 2002 Measures on Export Control of Certain Chemicals and Related Equipment and Technologies and Certain Chemicals and Related Equipment and Technologies Export Control List.

Likewise, in October 2002, China promulgated the Regulations of the People's Republic of China on Export Control of Dual-Use Biological Agents and Related Equipment and Technologies and Dual-Use Biological Agents and Related Technologies Export Control List. As well as verbal and written commitments to adhere to the Missile Technology Control Regime, in August 2002, it promulgated the Regulations of the People's Republic of China on Export Control of Missiles and Missile-related Items and Technologies, based on MTCR guidelines.[158] By 2005, its international export control measures included an export registration system, end-user and end-use certification system, a licensing system and "catch-all" principle, and corresponding penalties for breaches of these laws and regulations. It had also set up an inter-agency approval and coordination mechanism on export control.[159]

This ongoing program of legislation and institution building, which was maintained even over periods of heightened global tension, aimed at a more rule-based, transparent system that would be more in keeping with international standards and practice.[160] Transparency was also enhanced by China's publication of eight White Papers on arms control and defense: its December 2004 and September 2005 Papers were considered great improvements in this regard.[161] Critics, however, observed that there was still room for China's fuller participation in and adherence to international nonproliferation export control regimes, clearer bureaucratic processes and division of labor, the further development of its legal framework for export controls and stricter export license procedures, sterner enforcement, customs inspections and punitive measures, and more rigorous pre-license checks and post-shipment verification systems.[162]

Compliance and Cooperation

Despite such institutional progress, a question mark has hung over China's practical implementation and enforcement of some of its treaty obligations in the international security regime. Contention, particularly between the United States and China, revolved primarily around the issue of weapons proliferation, involving China's alleged breaches of the NPT and, to a lesser extent, of the CWC. Particularly alarmist was the May 1999 Cox report, which has been described by arms control specialists as sensational and ahistorical.[163] On different occasions over the years, the United States alleged that China was helping Pakistan to develop nuclear weapons; that it had contributed to North Korea's nuclear weapons research program; that it had supplied a nuclear reactor to Algeria; that it was indirectly contributing to Iran's development of a nuclear weapons program by helping it safeguard a uranium conversion facility; that it had sold SCUD missiles to Iran, Iraq, and North Korea; that it had supplied Iran and North Korea with chemicals that could contribute to possible chemical weapons research programs; and that it continued to cooperate with Saudi Arabia on ballistic missiles and with Pakistan on nuclear technology and missiles.[164] Consequently, the United States frequently imposed sanctions on China for alleged breaches.[165] For instance, in August 2001, it imposed trade sanctions on a major Chinese arms manufacturer believed to have transferred missile parts and technology to Pakistan; on 2 April 2004, it imposed further penalties on five Chinese companies; and on 27 December 2005, it announced sanctions against state-owned Chinese companies it accused of aiding Iran's missile and chemical programs.[166]

However, in evaluating the claims against China, a distinction must be made for the purposes of this study between its alleged breaches prior to its accession to a treaty, in particular the NPT, and those alleged to have occurred subsequently. The former allegations are not relevant to an evaluation of "compliance," just as allegations pertaining to the MTCR, which is not an international agreement and has no legal authority, are not relevant.[167] Many of the charges against China are made by the United States and refer to China's full compliance with *U.S.* nonproliferation policy, rather than universally accepted *global* nonproliferation norms as embodied in the NPT and CWC, which are the only standards relevant here. For instance, China resisted U.S. pressures to suspend nuclear exports to Iran, since the sale in fact complied with IAEA safeguard provisions.[168] The fact that it finally cancelled the sale of nuclear reactors to Iran in 1997 was due not to its non-compliance but to its political concerns about the U.S.-China relationship.

Of the claims made against China since it ratified the NPT in 1992, the most worrying appear to be that in early 1996 it sold unsafeguarded ring magnets to Pakistan for use in its uranium enrichment program; that it sold a "special industrial furnace" and "high-tech diagnostic equipment" to unsafeguarded nuclear facilities in Pakistan in 1996; and that PRC technicians built an electromagnetic isotope separation system for enriching uranium in Iran in 1997.[169] However, apart from ring magnets to Pakistan, there has been no independent confirmation of most of these allegations. In addition, ring magnets, being dual-use items, are not on the nuclear trigger list. In 2004, Beijing was also embarrassed by the revelation that Chinese nuclear weapons blueprints, supplied to Pakistani scientists in the early 1980s, had been discovered in Libya.[170] Since this transfer predated China's signature of the NPT, however, it was not in itself evidence of a breach. Only if, as U.S. officials allege, China is still providing assistance to Pakistan or helping Iran and Saudi Arabia,[171] might it be in breach of its treaty obligations.

However, the question as to whether or not China has been "compliant" in this regime is highly complex. This is not only because of the lack of transparency in China's policy,[172] but because there is no set benchmark for compliance. Since no state has been fully compliant with all the norms and rules of arms control and disarmament treaties, the question has turned on an evaluation of what is a "reasonable" or "acceptable" level of compliance.[173] Reflecting this lack of clarity, opinion on China's record has differed. On the one hand, Johnston and Swaine have observed cautiously that "China's existing record of arms control behavior *does not show a clear pattern of noncompliance*," but only because it has "yet to enter into regimes with strict verification or compliance procedures."[174] In 2002, CRS expert Shirley Kan highlighted as significant China's failure to commit to the full-scope safeguards required by the Nuclear Suppliers Group.[175] On the other hand, Gary Klintworth has argued that, at least in its recent record, China has generally upheld its arms control commitments.[176]

Likewise, Yuan Jingdong has noted the "sharp contrast" between China's "arms-transfer practice in the 1980s, when it was a major supplier to developing countries, including nuclear and missile-related transfers," and its "gradual, yet significant, progress in its nonproliferation policy" since that time. He has concluded that, since the 1980s, China has acceded to most international arms control treaties and conventions that are broadly based with universal membership and that it has "by and large, complied with their norms and rules." Since its ratification of the NPT, he observes, China's proliferation activities have narrowed in terms of their scope and character, so that it no longer transfers complete missile systems but, rather, largely dual-use nuclear, chemical, and missile components and technologies, and then only to Iran, Pakistan, and North Korea.[177] At the time of writing in 2002, Yuan also shared reservations about China's refusal to join the key multilateral export-control regimes such as the Nuclear Suppliers Group (nuclear export control), the Australia Group (chemical weapons), the Wassenaar Arrangement, and the Missile Technology Control Regime.[178] However, such criticisms relate to the question of cooperation, since they involve voluntary undertakings, rather than of compliance. In any case, China's entry into the Nuclear Suppliers Group in June 2004, its participation in the UN Group of Governmental Experts on Missiles, and its application in September 2004 to join the MTCR have gone some way to meeting such criticisms.[179]

A further difficulty in evaluating compliance is that it is a moving target. Because historically China's attitude to disarmament has been determined very much by the changing international strategic environment, and because issues of sovereignty and national interest are so critical to the regime, there has always been "an interactive relationship between U.S. decisions on missile defense deployments and the end-state of China's nuclear modernization."[180] As we have seen, from the 1950s American and Soviet/Russian policies played a determining role in China's decision as to whether to react defensively to its strategic environment or to cooperate in promoting arms control and disarmament. Thus, its decisions to ratify crucial treaties like the NPT and to sign the CTBT were invariably associated with a propitious international strategic environment and the cooperation of the other NWS. Conversely, its noncooperation has been associated with periods of downturn and mistrust in the U.S.-China relationship in particular.[181] China's dependence on continuing reciprocal compliance by other powerful states therefore signals that its current compliance will not guarantee its cooperation in the future under changed international circumstances. In 2003, for instance, when China assumed a significant role in mediating on the North Korean nuclear crisis, U.S. and Japanese plans to set up missile defense shields were reported to have prompted it to expand its ballistic missile program.[182] Indeed, acknowledging the reciprocal effect of U.S. policy decisions on China, in February 2002, the Swedish Foreign Minister, Anna Lindh, charged China with "using the American missile defense plans as an argument for expanding its own nuclear arms program," a charge China's Ambassador strongly denied.[183]

Taking into account these important qualifications, to date China may be deemed to have complied at a reasonable level with the broad range of its arms control and disarmament treaty obligations. While the jury is still out on some of its alleged post-1992 breaches, whether on its alleged transfer of nuclear technology to Pakistan, Saudi Arabia, and Iran or its ability to implement the domestic laws it has promulgated, the majority of allegations stem from its activities before it had acceded to the NPT, and to a lesser extent, the CWC, and therefore do not appear to involve breaches of its treaty obligations. Assessing its behavior in terms of the depth of compliance criteria, China has shown a readiness in this regime to redefine its interests, to renegotiate its sovereignty, and to accept the costs, as well as the benefits, of participation in arms control treaties and organizations.

Putting aside the issue of *compliance with rules*, however, China's broader *cooperation* with the regime, in the sense that concept has been defined, is debatable. First, while generally compliant with the letter of the norms, principles, and rules of the regime, with some signal exceptions China has normally interpreted them narrowly, has been inclined to exploit any gray area, and has failed to commit itself to voluntary and extended controls that accord with the spirit of its obligations and with the requirements of cooperation.[184] In this sense, its recent participation in the Nuclear Suppliers Group and its application to join the MTCR have foreshadowed the beginning of a more cooperative approach. As we have noted, until that point, it had refused to require full-scope safeguards (FSS) as a condition for supply of nuclear exports, something it was now obliged to do as a member of the NSG.[185] Another optimistic sign is the normative content of its new declaratory policy, in which it openly proclaims that the rules governing nonproliferation and disarmament benefit both China and the world.[186]

Second, China's cooperation has clearly been affected by its sensitivity about sovereignty. As its participation in arms control and disarmament negotiations reveals, even though it has accepted the oversight of the IAEA, its continued concern about verification and the requirements of transparency has, with some significant exceptions, led it to be uncooperative in these areas, in particular in relation to the national technical means of verification. It has also been guilty of footdragging about its own responsibility in arguing against the disarmament of smaller nuclear powers until the United States and the Soviet Union have largely disarmed. This conflicts with the declaration of the Director-General of the IAEA, Mohamed ElBaradie, that "a key part of the bargain is the commitment of the *five* nuclear states in the nonproliferation treaty—Britain, China, France, Russia and the US—to move towards disarmament."[187]

This same sensitivity underlay China's uncertainty in November 2002 about participating in the proposed voluntary International Code of Conduct against Missile Proliferation. It had actively participated in discussions over the code, and had agreed with its principles, but had objected to its provisions requiring missile states to provide advance notice of ballistic missile tests and to provide an annual report on missile tests in the previous year.[188] Yet, compliance with processes of verification and the principle of transparency is critical to the success of the arms control regime. As Jayantha Dhanapala, President of the NPT Review and Extension Conference in 1995, warned, "A good regime requires verification, enforcement, transparency and reciprocity. . . . Maximalist interpretations of sovereignty will hinder the achievement of all of these qualities of stable and effective regimes. And such interpretations will only contribute to the triumph of minimalist expectations about the nuclear regime."[189]

This leads us to the final question, the effect China has had on the international security regime. Clearly, it has been influential in persuading other states to emphasize the initial responsibility of the two most powerful nuclear states to disarm, and it has raised the bar on the P-3's obligations to join disarmament negotiations. Similarly, its insistence on asymmetric transparency and its sensitivity on verification issues have placed limits on the effectiveness of the regime. These policies have been ongoing influences and are at the root of China's difficulties with it. Other policies that have had a decisive impact have been its circumstantial reactions to the growing concerns it has felt in the face of U.S. unilateralism since 2001. In particular, the Bush administration's policies like the PSI and the U.S. Missile Defense System have been seen as indirectly targeting China itself.[190] China's responses to this new situation have had both a positive and negative effect on nuclear disarmament. On the one hand, its championing of the UN and its insistence that the global community must depend on UN nonproliferation bodies, in preference to embarking on unilateral initiatives, have helped strengthen the UN's role. On the other hand, its concerns about the Missile Defense System have led to the current impasse in the CD about reconstituting the ad hoc committees on FMCT and PAROS, while its simultaneous insistence on dialogue and diplomacy and opposition to the imposition of sanctions as a means of combating proliferation are seen by some as constraining the effectiveness of UN disarmament bodies. Most important, its recent reported expansion of nuclear weapons production and its failure to ratify the CTBT bear witness to its loss of trust in the stability and predictability of the strategic environment.

Conclusion

This chapter has documented the important changes in China's arms control policies as the result of its deepening involvement with international arms control institutions, its ratification of a host of international security treaties, and its efforts to harmonize its domestic laws, institutions, and practice with its obligations under those treaties. China joined the Conference on Disarmament for reasons of self-interest, even though at that stage it still did not accept one of its principal norms, nuclear nonproliferation. Yet, today, it has become an integral part of the CD and of the arms control and disarmament regime more generally. It has moved from narrow, instrumental policies contrary to arms control norms to accepting the norms, principles, and rules of the nuclear nonproliferation and disarmament regime. It has even consented to verification procedures that potentially compromise its sovereignty. It has become one of the chief supporters of the international security regime in an era in which many of the basic tenets of that regime are being questioned or placed in jeopardy.

This transition has been gradual, an outcome of the interacting processes of institutional jawboning—negotiation, persuasion, compromise, self-justification, mutual learning—and other international and domestic pressures. At the outset, China tended to be passive and resorted to free-riding, falling in behind states like India and the Soviet Union. Nevertheless, during the 1980s, under pressure from NNWS, it made conceptual adjustments, joined the IAEA, acceded to the BWC, and proposed agreements limiting naval forces, conventional arms, and weapons in outer space. During the 1990s, its disarmament diplomacy became increasingly open and involved frequent interventions in CD debates.[191] In this period, it ratified the NPT and the CWC, signed the CTBT, and was active in official security dialogues and negotiations. It internalized arms control and disarmament norms in its domestic institutions and laws and largely abided by its treaty obligations. Arguably, it showed acceptable compliance at all five levels of compliance, whether in terms of accession to treaties, procedural and substantive compliance, or of legislative and practical implementation. It also achieved deep compliance, in terms of its preparedness to redefine its interests to accord with the norms it had previously rejected, to renegotiate its sovereignty, and to accept the costs, as well as the benefits, of international organizational participation. Costs that it has accepted include its signature of the CTBT in 1996, despite the rejection of its request for "no first use" and the right to continue peaceful nuclear explosions, and despite its unilateral commitment to a global moratorium on testing. Other undertakings it has shouldered include the acceptance of full-scope safeguards implied in its membership of the NSG and its application to join the MTCR. Even on the issues of transparency and verification, it has accepted intrusive domestic controls and verification missions from IAEA and OPCW. Its commitments under the NPT have involved not only a diminution of its sovereignty but also the extensive material costs of foregone profits from otherwise uncontrolled arms exports.

Why is this so and what has been the role of the CD in its transition? A more favorable strategic environment, increasing self-confidence, international and domestic pressures, concern about its international reputation, and growing international experience have been important in encouraging China's compliance. As Zhu Mingquan has noted, even the development of its own nuclear arsenal helped deepen its understanding of the dangers of proliferation.[192] To a large extent, however, China's compliance has been the outcome of the process of participation in multilateral forums, principally, in its own estimation, in the CD.

Within the CD, we have documented the painful process of China's gradual evolution of thinking, the many instances of its concessions to majority opinion in CD debates and in treaty negotiations sponsored by the CD, and the role of this specialized forum in promoting discussion, disseminating information, and applying multilateral pressures. Interaction with other states members, and the expertise it has required, have persuaded China to ratify treaties that in turn have generated arms control activities and stimulated domestic legislation and institution building to harmonize with its international obligations.[193] These multiple pressures and a web of reciprocal responsibilities have in turn entrenched China's sense of obligation. Even when general agreement was impossible, China still saw the CD as an important forum for dialogue. Participation also created a negative incentive, in that the difficulty of disengaging from an organization after joining it produced a momentum favoring, if not presuming, compliance.[194] Having set out to use the CD for its own purposes, China has ended up being drawn into compliance with, and acceptance of, its basic norms and principles.

Conversely, China's impact on the CD has been significant, both positively and negatively. First, other CD members felt that its entry had brought enhanced legitimacy and universal authority to that body. Its presence also gave members a confidence-building forum within which they could attempt to influence China's nuclear policies and, in particular, express their disapproval of its nuclear testing within a multilateral setting. In addition, its participation gave the G-21 an often sympathetic, if not representative, voice within the P-5. In particular, its opposition to the abrogation of the ABM Treaty expressed both G-21 and Russian concerns. Apart from its critical role in the negotiation of treaties, China's specific contribution to debate included its insistence on the need for the United States and the Soviet Union/Russia to make progress in disarmament and nuclear nonproliferation before other NWS were obliged to follow suit. Its "no first use" policy and position on the "complete prohibition and destruction of nuclear weapons" were other specifically Chinese inputs. Its participation in the CD debates also helped mitigate its own shocked response to the Indian and Pakistani tests and thereby helped obviate excessive international tensions. Less positively, its policy of "asymmetrical transparency" has also influenced the G-21, while the recent tensions between the United States and China within the CD have arguably undermined that body's effectiveness.

However, China's interaction with the international security regime has not been just a simple matter of mutual learning or of compliance and noncompliance. As in the case of other regimes, China has been more compliant in some areas of the regime and less in others. When we look beyond compliance, moreover, to the question of cooperation—its readiness to promote the object and purpose of international treaties—in matters affecting sovereignty, such as verification and transparency, it has been less than cooperative. This is partly—but not wholly—because, in the arms control and disarmament regime, cooperation, like compliance, is a highly contingent affair. In a regime peculiarly dependent on reciprocity and trust, the problem cannot be reduced to the claim, made in some quarters, that China "says one thing and does another."[195] Rather, while its increasing instinct has been to cooperate with the international community, and to demonstrate its peaceful and law-abiding intentions, China's concern about sovereignty and its physical vulnerability have led it to react quickly to any adverse changes in the "circumstantial penumbra" of the external strategic environment. Where change has been perceived as threatening, its cooperation and compliance have been undermined. China, however, is not alone in this response.[196]

Since the late 1990s, from China's point of view, the international environment has been destabilized, first by the nuclear tests of India and Pakistan, and, more recently, by the unilateral policies adopted by the Bush administration, in particular on NMD, TMD, the ABM Treaty and the CTBT, as well as on a host of other, and unrelated, international instruments. The politics within the CD have inevitably reflected this loss of certainty. Ironically, China's mature and measured response to the increasing unpredictability of the international security regime reflects the real progress it has made in its commitment to arms control and disarmament. However, its continuing compliance and cooperation with regime norms, principles, and rules remain dependent on the maintenance of a favorable strategic environment and on the continuing reciprocal compliance of other states. While international organizations disseminate information, pressure states to comply with international norms and rules, and provide the medium through which such rules are formulated, the effectiveness of the arms control and disarmament regime depends ultimately, as China has reminded us, on the willingness of all states, and particularly the most powerful nuclear ones, to cooperate with others and to comply with the international norms, principles, and rules that they themselves have negotiated so painfully over decades.

China and the International Political Economy Regime

The World Bank and the International Monetary Fund

> China's decision to be associated with the IMF and the World Bank
> marked the first critical step toward economic integration with the
> global economy. . . . Our experience with these two institutions
> as the gateway to the world reinforced our conviction that active
> engagement with the international community could benefit China's
> economic development which in turn contributes to the develop-
> ment of the world economy.
>
> *Jin Liqun, Vice-Minister of Finance,*
> *Washington, DC, 22 October 2002*

The World Bank (IBRD) and the International Monetary Fund (IMF), created
at Bretton Woods in 1944, and the General Agreement on Tariffs and Trade
(GATT), established after it, together form the pillars of the Bretton Woods system, and the keystone international economic organizations (KIEOs) of the
international political economy.[1] Although there is little resemblance between
the present functions and operation of the Bank and Fund and the way they
were conceived at Bretton Woods,[2] they were based on the still-current idea
that international economic prosperity would be best guaranteed under liberal
rules of free trade, free payments, monetary stability, and capital mobility. All three
organizations were established outside the UN framework, but were subsequently brought into the UN as specialized agencies under the formal coordinating authority of the Economic and Social Council (ECOSOC). They are
freestanding intergovernmental organizations established by intergovernmental agreement, with budgets separate from the UN organization. Between them,
they create legal norms in international finance and development, in international monetary relations (the IMF), and in international trade (GATT/WTO),
through treaty-making and non-treaty processes including promotion of codes
of conduct; generation of rules of customary international economic law; and
the development of administrative rules.[3]

The international political economy regime as a whole extends beyond the
KIEOs and their specialized agreements. In accordance with Article 55 of the
UN Charter, a number of UN organizations and specialized agencies have been

set up to promote higher standards of living, development, and the solution of international economic problems. Apart from the Economic and Social Council (ECOSOC), these include the United Nations Conference on Trade and Development (UNCTAD), the United Nations Industrial Development Organization (UNIDO), the United Nations Development Programme (UNDP), the World Food Council (WFC), and the World Intellectual Property Organization (WIPO). The market also acts as a powerful and extra-organizational source of behavioral norms.[4] At the same time, it is the source of practices that may conflict with the efficient workings of the regime, as the capital flight from Asia in late 1997 demonstrated.

This chapter provides further evidence of the validity of the process-based argument that continuing normative discourse and repeated interaction between transnational actors in a multilateral setting is a critical source of state compliance. It documents the cycle of negotiation, interpretation, and internalization leading to the PRC's growing integration into the World Bank and the IMF, which it entered in 1980 when it replaced Taiwan as official representative of China, and monitors the extent and depth of its compliance. Conversely, it undermines the claim by rational choice theorists George Downs and others that coercive sanctions are the main reason for "deep" compliance. At the same time, compliance itself comes under the spotlight in this case study: paradoxically, and controversially, China's compliance with World Bank rules has not necessarily benefited China's human security, whereas its non-compliance with one aspect of IMF norms has protected human security not only in China but the Asia-Pacific region more generally.

One reason for this, as will become clear, is that in this part of the international political economy regime, the emphasis is less on the importance of reciprocal compliance between states parties to treaties, as it is in the CD, and more on each member state's compliance and cooperation with the international institution itself and its constituent rules. Compliance in this case is primarily determined by a state's willingness to reflect the regime norms of transparency and accountability, to abide by the Articles of Agreement under which the Bank and Fund were established, to meet the conditions of loans, and to realize the organizations' expectations that it will optimize its use of loans, advice, and technical assistance. In the sense that the Bank is usually the source of substantial benefits to the state, compliance is more readily forthcoming in this organization than in many others: the IMF, on the other hand, which places more conditions and sovereignty constraints on member states, constitutes a more rigorous compliance test. While considering the influence of international organizational rules, we will also examine the paradoxical outcome of China's compliance/non-compliance. Beyond this, we will look for signs that China has cooperated with both organizations and that it has taken steps to promote the object and purpose of their constituent instruments, norms, and principles. Finally, we will evaluate China's own impact upon them.

China's Entry

As an Allied power, the Republic of China had been a founding member of both the World Bank and the IMF in 1945 and had been given a powerful position at Bretton Woods. There, because President Roosevelt had promised wartime ally China that its quota in the IMF would rank fourth, the U.S. Treasury official responsible for drawing up the quotas subsequently confessed to having "exercised a certain amount of freedom in order to achieve the predetermined quotas."[5] As a result, China's IMF quota of US$550 million, which determined its voting power, exceeded that of France by US$100 million. Such special treatment was based on the legal position that the ROC was the representative of mainland China, since it depended on a generous reading of the size of the mainland's, rather than of Taiwan's, economy. From that time until 1980, the ROC, on the tiny island of Taiwan, acted as the official representative of China in both the IMF and the World Bank.

Soon after replacing Taiwan in the United Nations in 1971, the People's Republic declared that aid giving should respect the sovereignty of the recipient countries, "attach no conditions, ask for no privileges, genuinely help them develop an independent national economy and not add to their burden."[6] It also called for the reform of the international monetary system, criticized the quota system in the IMF, which, it claimed, flouted the principle of the sovereign equality of states, and requested compensation for losses occasioned by the realignment of major currencies. Its initial position was therefore clearly at odds with the norms, principles, and rules of both the World Bank and the IMF.

Nevertheless, as Michel Oksenberg and Harold Jacobson have documented, in 1972 China set up a United Nations Small Group in the Bank of China to analyze the possibility of membership in all UN financial agencies.[7] In 1973, as it had done in 1950, the Chinese Foreign Ministry requested both the World Bank and the IMF to expel Taiwan.[8] In response, World Bank President Robert McNamara sent a telegram to Beijing stating that an application from China to join would be welcome. However, a June 1974 report prepared by the Ministry of Finance (MOF) and the Ministry of Foreign Affairs recommended against doing so. Its reasons were uneasiness about the weighted voting formula in the IMF and the Bank and a belief that the Articles of Agreement of the IMF were not only contrary to the norms of a socialist monetary system, but would also undermine China's policy of self-reliance. However, following major changes in China's foreign trade policies, the decision at the Third Plenum to undertake major economic reform, and complicated domestic politicking, Deng Xiaoping announced in February 1979 that "there would be no hitch on China's part in joining the IMF if the Taiwan issue is settled."[9]

China's final achievement of representation in the Fund and Bank was not just the product of its 1978 policy to open up and develop its economy. It was also due to the strenuous efforts of McNamara, acting against the wishes of the U.S. Treasury, as well as to the greater receptiveness of the international community as a whole. In the late 1970s, McNamara has recalled, the U.S. administration tried to prevent him from visiting China to negotiate its entry. Yet, from his point of view, the world's greatest development institution needed its largest developing country as a member, especially at a time when China appeared more receptive to entry.[10] McNamara was reportedly impressed by the purposeful way his Chinese partners, in particular Deng, indicated the assistance they expected from the Bank.[11]

As in the case of other organizations, the initial motives behind China's involvement were almost entirely instrumental. Membership of the Bank was a logical extension of its UN membership; it would enhance China's status and would entail the expulsion of Taiwan. Membership would also strengthen China's bilateral foreign and trade relations and facilitate access to information on international finance and economics, as well as to concessional interest rate loans and IMF drawing privileges.[12] Finally, it would strengthen the hand of domestic reformers. Unlike its accession to other international organizations, in this case China was already aware of the onerous obligations it would incur on entry. It would have to open up highly confidential data and receive frequent IMF and World Bank missions. And it would have to make large financial contributions to meet its IMF quota and World Bank subscription.

First, however, political barriers would have to be overcome. It was only after the United States had extended formal recognition and most-favored-nation trading status to China that, in February 1980, the Chinese Ambassador to Washington, Chai Zemin, approached the World Bank President. Because states were required by the Articles of Agreement to first become members of the IMF, negotiations were set in train during two IMF missions to China in March and April.

Initial discussion between the IMF and the Chinese government to transfer China's credentials to the PRC revolved around the question of the quota and China's rights and obligations within the Fund, including the matter of the Fund's holdings of gold contributed by Taiwan. Since the ROC authorities had asked that China's subscription not be increased from its US$550 million, by 1960 "China's" quota had fallen to the point where it had lost the right to appoint an Executive Director. Early in the Fund's negotiations with the PRC, it was understood that the quota would be renegotiated upwards. In 1980, China's quota therefore rose to SDR1.8 billion; and in 1983 it was further increased to SDR2.39 billion, the ninth largest in the IMF. China thereby regained the right to constitute a single constituency and to elect its own Executive Director. However, the gold was not transferred to the PRC: to China's chagrin, Taiwan was permitted to purchase it at the official price. Because of its still influential policy of self-reliance, China also indicated that it would not borrow money from the IMF but would still pay its quota. On 17 April 1980, the IMF Executive Board decided that henceforth the People's Republic would represent China in the Fund.

China's negotiations with the Bank were equally exacting and fraught with complications. McNamara personally expedited the process because he realized the importance of marshalling the support of the Carter administration, then in its last year. According to Bank sources, any obstacle at that point would have delayed China's entry for a long time.[13] An official who accompanied McNamara on his first visit in April reported that he had never seen him so excited as in these discussions.[14] The Mission established the broad outlines of an agreement. Not only did the Bank accede to China's requests for project assistance, technical assistance, and broad, strategic advice, it also increased China's share of the votes and, as in the case of the IMF, agreed that it would constitute a single-state constituency and be represented by its own Executive Director on the Board of the Bank. Thus, China was given 12,250 votes in the World Bank, or 2.84 percent of the total; 4,404 votes in IFC, or 0.83 percent of the total; and 91,311 votes in IDA, or 2.07 percent of the total.[15] China made other "multiple and insistent demands" upon the Bank.[16] It required it to obtain PRC approval for the hiring of Taiwanese nationals, for the publication of data on Taiwan, and for the determination of Taiwan-related nomenclature. It also insisted that Bank lending to China should not exceed China's receipt of IDA credits and that Bank publications mapping or discussing Chinese borders in dispute with other countries should first obtain PRC clearance.[17]

The People's Republic became a member of the World Bank on 15 May 1980, only a month after it had joined the IMF. Despite the difficulties, McNamara subsequently judged China's entry as one of his greatest political achievements. The entry process also brought out the "creative originality" of which the Bank was capable. The early work of the Bank's China Department, the excellence of its knowledge and expertise, and the professionalism of its reports, had, in the words of a former official, "probably not been matched in any other substantial geographical region."

The World Bank

The headquarters of the World Bank, at 1818 H St., Washington, DC, appears from the street as massive and solid as any other monumental public building. But upon entry, the visitor is transported into a cathedral of glass, steel, and polished marble floors, with five vast columns soaring like a giant umbrella to support the glass roof. Like the institution it houses, it is a building designed to impress, inspire, and illuminate. As the largest source of international development assistance, the Bank's main goals are to help reduce global poverty and promote sustainable development. While its basic mandate has not altered, it has evolved in six overlapping phases, from its inception as a reconstruction bank in the late 1940s to a conservative lender in the 1950s, and thence to a development agency in the 1960s, an advocate for the poor in the 1970s, a policy reformer in the 1980s and, most recently, to a more holistic development body. Its focus has changed over the years from individual projects to the policies, strategies, and institutions that ensure the success of these projects. In short, it has extended its concern, if not as rapidly as its critics would wish, to human and social development.[18]

The Bank now provides nearly US$30 billion in loans annually to its client countries for the purposes of: investing in basic health and education; protecting the environment; encouraging private business development; strengthening the ability of governments to deliver quality services; promoting reforms to create a stable macroeconomic environment; overcoming problems of fraud and corruption; and encouraging sustainable development, inclusion, good governance, and institution building as key elements of poverty reduction.[19] Its involvement in such a variety of issue areas illustrates the cross-linkages now blurring the previously sharp functional differentiation between specialist international organizations.

The "Bank Group" today consists of five closely associated institutions: the International Bank for Reconstruction and Development (IBRD) (normally known as the World Bank); the International Development Association (IDA), which supports the poverty reduction mission with soft loans; the International Finance Corporation (IFC); the Multilateral Investment Guarantee Agency (MIGA), which helps encourage investment in developing countries by providing guarantees to foreign investors against loss caused by noncommercial risks; and the International Centre for Settlement of Investment Disputes (ICSID). The Bank constitutes an open partnership of 184 member countries, which has been compared to a global cooperative.

A country's shareholding in the Bank is decided by the size of its economy relative to the world economy. The United States has the largest shareholding of

16.41 percent and wields a great deal of power. Although almost all decisions are made by a majority of the votes cast by all members of the Bank, some important decisions require an 85 percent majority vote, which gives the United States the equivalent of a veto. Loans are made to developing countries only. They are tailored either for developing countries that are able to pay near-market rates, or for low-income countries with per capita incomes of less than US$885 (as of 1999) or US$1,445 (as of 2000). The latter, dispensed by the International Development Association (IDA), are free of interest, carry a mere 0.75% annual administrative charge and are very long term—thirty-five to forty years, including ten years' grace.[20] Under its Articles of Agreement, the Bank can only lend to a member government or under a member government's guarantee.[21]

Organization, Rules, and Management

The Bank's President, normally an American national, chairs meetings of the Executive Directors and is responsible for overall management. Key Bank policies are decided by the Governors or Alternate Governors, who meet twice a year and are elected by each member nation. The bulk of their responsibilities is delegated to the board of Executive Directors. The five largest shareholders, France, Germany, Japan, the UK, and the United States, each appoint an Executive Director, while the remaining countries are represented by nineteen Executive Directors elected by groups of countries. Of these, only China, Russia, Costa Rica, and Saudi Arabia have formed single-country constituencies.

The Bretton Woods system is treaty based, with the major part of its law originating in the specialized agencies. The Articles of Agreement of both the Bank and Fund grant the Executive Directors the power to interpret their own Articles. The Bank is an operational rather than normative body, but its lending practices have normative implications.[22] Its eleven Articles of Agreement deal primarily with the rights and duties of membership, lending practices and the use of loans.[23] A specific body of rules also regulates loans.[24] Because Bank membership involves privileges rather than costs, the sanctions entrenched in its rules involve loss or suspension of those privileges. The Articles of Agreement include the requirement that loans should not be used for any other purpose than that for which the loan was granted (III.5.b); that a member state has the right to withdraw from membership of the Bank at any time (VII); that if a member state fails to fulfill any of its obligations to the Bank, the Bank may suspend its membership by decision of a majority of the Governors exercising a majority of total voting power (VI.2); that, while under suspension, a member shall not exercise any rights of membership but shall remain subject to all obligations (VI.2); that the member so suspended will automatically cease to be a member one year from the date of its suspension unless a decision is taken by the same majority to restore the member to good standing (VI.2); that, in an emergency, Executive Directors may temporarily suspend operations in respect of new loans or, in the case of a decision by a majority of the Governors, permanently (VI.5.a and b); that each member must make effective in terms of its own law the principles in Article VII on the Status, Immunities, and Privileges of the Bank (VII.10); and that any question of interpretation of the provisions of the Agreement arising between any member and the Bank shall be submitted to the Executive Directors for their decision (IX.a). For its part, the Bank and its officers may not interfere in a country's political affairs and must take only economic considerations into account in their loan decisions (IV.10).[25]

In practice, because states are unwilling to transfer economic sovereignty to international organizations, the Bank eschews coercive sanctions. At most, it enforces the rules governing lending and use of loan proceeds by withholding future loans from non-compliant members or canceling or suspending disbursements, rather than engaging in arbitration or suspending members.[26] Occasionally, loans have been cancelled, but more often disbursements have simply been suspended to pressure the borrower to fulfill the obligations of the loan agreement. Because a formal suspension requires a Board decision, in practice it is difficult to suspend disbursements once a project is ongoing. Rather, Bank staff threatens to take formal steps *toward* suspension if the borrower does not cooperate. To avoid an "embarrassing" Board meeting on suspension, lender and borrower may then agree to informally suspend until the problem is resolved. Where the Bank is not satisfied with the way resources are spent, it may also cease offering advice and withdraw staff. But even if it halts all activity in a country, the country may continue to be a member and to have a say in Bank affairs, since it is thought that the poor may suffer more if the Bank withdraws.[27] It is notable that the Bank's use of the "threat" of sanctions, rather than their actual imposition, corresponds to Harold Koh's transnational legal process theory, rather than to the idea of coercive sanctions advocated by one type of rational choice theory.

Another major issue for the Bank is whether its loans are put to good use. Its criteria are strict, requiring a 10 percent return before a project can be considered successful.[28] The Bank's lending for projects is evaluated after it finishes its loan disbursements. First, there is an evaluation of each operation by the staff responsible for it; then the Operations Evaluation Department (OED) evaluates the operations independently. Satisfactory performance means that an operation has achieved most of its goals without major shortcomings and that it constitutes sustainable development.[29]

Although the Bank is not meant to involve itself in internal politics, its lending policies often have political consequences. This is because both the World

Bank and the IMF have also typically insisted that, in order to qualify for loans, states must accept a large number of quite broad "conditions," particularly in the case of structural adjustment loans (SALs), which provide funds for overall budgetary and balance of payments support, rather than financing a particular project. These conditions have often involved pressure on states to move toward trade liberalization, privatization, and macroeconomic stability.

The appropriateness of both specific conditions and conditionality in general is constantly under dispute. On the one hand, international NGOs like Amnesty International call for increased conditionality, so that human rights may also be included among the preconditions for granting loans.[30] On the other hand, developing countries oppose the use of conditionality. More broadly, both the Bank and the IMF have become the targets of a generalized international dissatisfaction with globalization, or at least with globalization as it currently operates. Critics point to the increase in global inequity that has resulted from Bank and Fund policies, leading to the indebtedness of developing states. They question the two institutions' failure over half a century to appreciably improve distributional equity and social justice within developing states.[31] In particular, the IMF faced public criticism following the Asian financial crisis in 1997 and the political and financial collapse of Argentina in 2002.[32] Both organizations have sought to rebut such criticisms.[33]

Nevertheless, in partial response to such criticisms, and to soften the impact of conditionality, the Bank's support for developing states carrying out structural reforms has in recent years generally included social safety nets to ease temporary pain, with grants to finance unemployment compensation, job creation schemes, and retraining programs. Since the late 1990s, the Bank has also been working with developing countries to pilot a more integrated approach to its mission—the Comprehensive Development Framework (CDF). This calls for a development plan to be "owned" by the country itself, and to be supported by strong partnerships among governments, donors, civil society, the private sector, and other development actors.[34] The Bank's emphasis has shifted from "conditionality" to "selectivity," to adapting policies to the specific situation of each state, to rewarding countries with proven track records, and to putting the country "in the driver's seat."[35] The Bank has even taken upon itself the role of social prophet, warning of an environmental catastrophe, social breakdown, and lower living standards for all if problems of consumption, sustainable development, and equity are not tackled.[36] Former Chief Economist of the World Bank Joseph Stiglitz has praised the Bank under its previous President, James Wolfensohn, for recognizing the need for countries to have more input into the decision-making and management processes. He contends that the Bank has made far more progress toward reform than the Fund and predicts that its future focus will be on capacity- and consensus-building. Part and parcel of this approach is the recognition that funds are fungible and that the Bank may use its loans as "leverage" that helps attract private capital, and to finance projects that can be scaled up.

China and the Bank

The World Bank is the major international institution assisting China's economic development.[37] In the 1990s, its operations in China eclipsed all other multi-lateral development assistance programs, notwithstanding the objections of the Bank's largest shareholder, the United States. China thus replaced India as the Bank's largest borrower and major success story,[38] and the Bank became China's largest single source of long-term foreign capital in the early and mid-1990s.[39] As of 30 June 2005, it had financed 263 development projects in all major sectors and most regions of China, of which about 90 were still under implementation, lending US$38.9 billion, including over US$26 billion in IBRD loans and about US$10 billion in IDA credits.[40] From the mid-1990s, there was a World Bank office in most Chinese counties. About 10,000 Chinese citizens were involved in administering and supervising its programs, and about ten times that number were employed on the actual projects and studies at any one time. Average disbursements for Bank/IDA supported projects amounted to some US$10 million on a typical working day. The Bank's historians have enthusiastically endorsed its relationship with China:

> The most sensational performance of all in the 1980s came from China. In little more than a decade, it transformed itself from a centrally planned economy to a dynamic, market-oriented one, whose burgeoning exports gave it a massive trade surplus with the United States by the early 1990s. . . . China adapted Bank advice to its own ends and succeeded in pushing GDP growth into double digits. It proved that rapid growth need not be limited to small countries like Singapore—good policies work everywhere.[41]

China's special relationship with the Bank resulted from the intersection between its developmental trajectory and the Bank's changing modus operandi. While it is true, as Michel Oksenberg and Harold Jacobson have written, that "the *separate* developmental paths of China and the KIEOs converged,"[42] this parallel development was not entirely coincidental. China joined the two institutions when both were in a period of transition, and more accessible to its influence. This timing coincided with China's gradual, but ultimately almost total, transition away from a socialist command economy to a free market system, albeit one with some residual "Chinese characteristics." Paradoxically, as it began to place the Chinese economy under a microscope, the Bank in turn showed that it was impressed by the progress that China had made over the preceding decades in its social policy, whether in education, health, or its egalitarian redistribution policies. It initially made a comprehensive and influential study of the Chinese economy that arguably reflected many Chinese ideas of social justice and that was published in seven volumes in mid-1981.[43] Although such an approach was doubtless part of the mutual accommodation of views between the Bank and its new client, it nevertheless appeared genuine. As a result, although the Bank's first assistance to China was in relatively narrow projects, it gave more emphasis to social issues.[44] Indeed, the first Bank loan to China, approved in June 1981, was for a project on higher education. One of the main lessons it drew from its interaction with China was also "that growth alone was not likely to solve the problem of deeper reform; and that, in China's case, the establishment of a universal social safety net was critical to the success of China's reforms." More generally, the vital lesson was that "*political economy, rather than simple economic theories, lies at the heart of the process of socialist transition.*"[45]

Yet, from the beginning, even before country "ownership" became accepted Bank policy, China sought control over the Bank's China projects, and insisted on close supervision of them. In this sense it was unlike other developing states.[46] As early as 1984, China's Finance Minister laid down ground rules for interaction:

> The Minister explained [to the Bank] China's view that assistance to the developing countries should be unconditional. . . . [T]his did not mean that the Bank could not offer advice and ideas. The World Bank could put these forward and they would be considered if they were useful. But the Bank should not impose its views.[47]

For this reason, and because the Bank became increasingly dependent on continued Chinese borrowing, China's new-found enthusiasm for the free market began to prevail over the Bank's initial instincts about its need for a social safety net. The Bank accepted China's refusal to distinguish between projects aimed at growth and those aimed at alleviating poverty. It also tolerated China's refusal to use its IBRD loans for poverty alleviation or social justice projects. Aside from these initial differences in developmental approaches, a mutual learning process was engendered. China has paid tribute to the Bank's role in instructing a generation of Chinese economic managers, and to its research unit's provision of technical training needed to establish or implement plans.[48] World Bank historians have also identified the areas in which China learned most from the Bank:

> When China started its transition it had little idea of how to go about it and was eager to absorb lessons from abroad. It used the World Bank as its main sounding board for changes in policy and organizational structures, and a highly productive dialogue ensued. The Bank trained many Chinese personnel at the EDI [Economic Development Institute] and translated its economic policy research into Chinese. Its role was far more important in the realm of ideas than in finance.[49]

The Bank's role in the realm of ideas was particularly valued by China for its political neutrality.[50] Likewise, the Bank has acknowledged its own debt:

> The Bank has learned important lessons from its engagement with China. These include lessons of process, of the value of open discussion and debate, and of the need to disseminate ideas to all levels to effect change. The Bank has also learned from China that where circumstances permit, there are merits in a gradual approach to economic change.[51]

More specifically, a World Bank working paper listed a number of other important lessons garnered from the interaction with China: that partial reform could be successful in raising productivity in agriculture and industry, more in the non-state sector but also in the state sector; that a "big bang" in development was not necessary for economic reasons, unless addressing initial macro-imbalances justified it; that there could be virtue in a decentralized "bottom-up" approach to reform rather than taking a "dogmatic, centralized view"; that rapid privatization was not necessary for successful reform but that diversifying ownership and encouraging entry were very important; that small-scale privatization and the liberalization of distribution and service sectors were likely to have the fastest pay-off in the reform of property rights; and that expatriate investors were a potentially important source of linkage with the world economy.[52]

Thus, from the beginning, China's interaction with the Bank was unique. The negotiating process for its initial loan revealed a preparedness on both sides to make adjustments which held promise for the future success of the relationship.[53] Until 1983, however, China's borrowing was quite modest. From that year, its growing political power, linked with its status as a densely populated developing country, enabled it to borrow more. Its innovative ideas, capacity, and managerial skills also unquestionably had an input in determining the Bank's readiness to lend.[54] However, China's entry into the Bank also created a need to place restrictions on borrowing by large states. While India had previously enjoyed a 40 percent share of IDA, a scarce resource reserved for low-income countries, from 1989 China and India together shared a 30 percent slice of IDA more or less equally. This equality of distribution was surprising, given the Bank's estimate in 1980 that China's GNP per capita was more than twice India's and that, by the late 1980s, China's output per head was generally estimated to have been growing much faster than India's.[55] On the other hand, on a per capita basis, Bank sources pointed out that China's IDA share amounted to about US$2.50 per person, the *"lowest proportion of lending per capita in the entire East Asia region."*[56]

The Bank's program was carried out through three main mechanisms: loans for physical investments; loans or grants, often provided by bilateral partners and administered by the World Bank, for technical assistance; and nonfinancial services in the form of analytical reports, policy advice, workshops, and training.[57] All Bank loans and IDA credits were subject to conditionality and the project/loan/credit negotiations would sometimes be quite difficult. However, the Bank did not always enforce conditions in China's case because the relationship was mostly a reasonable one and problems could usually be resolved without confrontation. Two examples where it could have imposed stronger restrictions on the use and allocation of funds were the Rural Sector Adjustment Loan of the mid-1980s and the Bank's consent to China channeling loans into higher education rather than the Bank's priority area of primary school education.[58]

World Bank assistance to China included projects in poverty reduction and human development, agricultural productivity, and infrastructure development. Its social assistance was channeled through soft IDA loans, as China refused to use IBRD money to finance such projects. By the 1990s, its program included technical assistance for fiscal modernization, banking reform, development of the legal system, development of accountancy standards, promotion of private investment, reform of state-owned enterprises (SOEs), and environmental assistance.[59] According to the Bank, its projects played "a unique role in supporting China's economic reform and modernization process, targeting poverty alleviation, infrastructure development and human resources development."[60] The value of these projects was enhanced by the fact that, according to former Chief of the Bank's resident mission in China, Pieter Bottelier, the resources devoted by the Chinese government itself to poverty reduction projects were insufficient.[61] The Bank was especially influential during turning points in China's reform, in particular the partial recentralization of the Chinese economy that occurred after the Dalian Conference in 1993. This resulted in a macroeconomic stabilization program and a gradual reduction of economic overheating. It also marked the point at which the reform in China became "irreversible and integral in scope."[62]

The high point in lending occurred in the 1990s, when China's annual loans from the IBRD spiraled to as high as US$3 billion. Other sources of finance contributed to China's high rate of economic growth. Already assisted by its high rate of domestic savings,[63] China was quick to join the newly formed Multilateral Investment Guarantee Agency (MIGA) in 1988, so that foreigners could obtain greater assurances for their investment. Between 1988 and 1997, MIGA concluded eighteen contracts of guarantee in eleven projects in China, totaling over US$63.44 million.[64] China also became the ninth largest country portfolio of the International Financial Corporation (IFC), the private lending arm of the World Bank. Finally, foreign direct investment (FDI) became increasingly critical to China's success. By 1997, China was attracting a greater volume of private capital than any other developing country.[65] In 2002, it became the world's largest FDI recipient, taking the lead over the United States and attaining a record amount of US$52.7 billion, or 37 percent of the developing countries' total.[66]

These developments, and a related eligibility issue, prefigured a further adjustment in China's relations with the Bank. From July 1999, China ceased to be eligible for soft loans from the IDA, as opposed to IBRD loans. IBRD loans, which incur interest, cannot be rescheduled and are shorter term. This shift created potential problems of repayment for China's poorer provinces. Controversy about China's ineligibility was heightened by the fact that, although by 1999 its average income level was close to US$800 per year, poverty was still widespread.[67] Thus, a former Bank official has claimed that China only ceased to be eligible for IDA funds because of its sharply improved creditworthiness: on poverty and performance grounds it would otherwise have remained eligible.[68]

The battle over IDA lasted several years and was fought behind closed doors between the United States and the UK on one side, and the Japanese, most Europeans, Canada, and Australia on the other. Although its IDA access was continued for an extra year, from mid-1998 to mid-1999, China continued to feel it had been unfairly treated. In the end, the decision to exclude China was made by IDA donors. China's reaction was mixed. On the one hand, it would have preferred concessional funds for as long as possible, and suspected the United States of influencing the decision: on the other, it enjoyed the prestige of not being one of the poorest countries.[69] According to an interviewee, China's final agreement was facilitated by a Bank decision that India would "graduate" at the same time.[70] Equal treatment thus allegedly eased the pain of financial loss.

After July 1999, the Bank reduced its annual lending to China to US$2 billion, compared with US$3.1 billion in 1993.[71] By 2000, Bank lending had fallen from US$2.8 billion in 1997 to US$1.7 billion, and was further reduced to US$3 billion over the three years from 2002 to 2004.[72] This decline was seen as due to China's loss of IDA credits; the increased costs of IBRD loans; the central government's use of expansionary fiscal policy and low interest rates in the aftermath of the Asian financial crisis; the cost of doing business with the Bank due to lengthy procedures and safeguard requirements; disengagement from areas that could be served by the private sector; cessation of Bank lending in areas where past projects had proved "problematic"; and reduction in the average size of loans.[73] Above all, the decline was due to the Bank rule that one donor could not be granted more than 10 percent of its loan portfolio. At the rate China was borrowing from early to mid-1990s, this exposure ceiling would have been reached by the turn of the century. To avoid the need to suddenly throttle back, as interviews have made clear, the Bank began to reduce new commitments sharply from around 1998.

Nevertheless, controversy raged over the Bank's need to continue lending to China at all. Critics argued that since China was attracting over US$40 billion of net private capital flows, it did not need Bank loans. They further argued that lending to China undermined the Bank's new strategic compact, wherein it adjusted its role to a new world environment in which private capital flows had expanded to five times the amount of official assistance. However, President Wolfensohn responded that China's economy still needed investment in areas that did not attract private capital.[74] It was also pointed out that Bank lending was a vehicle not only to transfer resources but to transfer knowledge and build institutions.[75] A new "country assistance strategy" for China was formulated.[76] The Bank's operational strategy for China was to be planned around three main themes that sought: to improve the business environment and help accelerate China's transition to a market economy; to address the needs of the poorer and disadvantaged people and lagging regions, particularly in the west; and to facilitate environmentally sustainable development.[77]

China's Developmental Challenges

Despite the Bank's generous assistance and China's extraordinary economic progress, Chinese authorities faced serious developmental challenges as a result of the double transition from central planning to the market and from a rural agricultural to an urban industrial economy.[78] The growth-oriented policies of the 1980s and 1990s had not resulted in equitable outcomes conducive to human security. The enormity of China's social problems was reflected in the Bank's December 2001 report, *China and the Knowledge Economy*, which, in the context of China's entry into the WTO on 11 December, advised it to create "at minimum" 100 million jobs by 2010, particularly in service industries, for people moving out of agriculture and those laid off by state-owned enterprises.[79] The gravity of the situation had already been indicated in the 1997 report, *China: 2020*. This described China as one of the most polluted countries in the world. It found that its spending on education lagged far behind many other countries; that access to health care was declining; and that social services were minimal. As the World Bank's China Program Director, Yukon Huang, observed, "China's economy looks like a huge giant perched upon a three-legged stool." As he saw it, the three legs—financial reform, state enterprise reform, and social protection—were interrelated and could not be improved in isolation from each other.[80] In the financial sector, China's state banks suffered declining capital-asset ratios and losses on loans to state enterprises. The rationalization of expensive state-owned enterprises created major problems of "urban labor adjustment," requiring new arrangements for pension and housing reform and health care financing. Public finance needed to be reformed to provide basic public services and develop a new tax administration. Income inequality and poverty reduction needed to be attacked.[81] The loss of agricultural productivity and infrastructure bottlenecks also posed a threat to future growth, while rapid industrialization had degraded the environment.

The result was that, although the number of people in absolute poverty in rural areas had dropped from 250 million before modernization to 26.1 million, by 2002 China's Gini coefficient of the inequality of income distribution had risen from 0.30 in 1982 to 0.46 (including the migrant population in urban areas). China thus ranked ninetieth among 131 countries for which data were available, leaving only 31 countries with a greater income inequality than China.[82] For this reason, by 2003, the Bank had become preoccupied with issues of human security in China, assessing that its greatest needs were to reform core market institutions and to address deep-rooted structural problems related to poverty, globalization, governance, and sustainable development.[83] A year later, it highlighted the challenge of "over 200 million Chinese, many in remote and resource-poor areas in the Western and interior regions, [who] still live on less than US$1 a day, often without access to clean water, arable land or adequate health and education services."[84] Casting his mind to the future, as he left China in 2004, Yukon Huang highlighted sources of social discontent and China's need for "a system to cushion the people, to soften the widening inequality."[85]

Another critical emerging challenge was the environment. Here also the Bank assumed an important advisory, managerial, and regulatory role. Apart from supporting both "green" and "brown" (energy, urban, and health) policies in China, the Bank became one of the three Executing Agencies for the Global Environment Facility (GEF).[86] While UNEP disseminated environmental information and UNDP identified and managed a series of technical assistance projects, GEF Investment Projects were managed by the Bank, which controlled 45 percent of the GEF funds. The Bank's role in global climate change was particularly important, as the Framework Convention on Climate Change had designated the GEF as its funding mechanism.[87] The Bank was also an implementing agency with the United Nations Industrial Development Organization (UNIDO) for the Multilateral Fund (MLF), which helped fund the phase-out of ozone-depleting substances (ODS).

From 1993, the Bank was involved in many of China's environmental projects. It awarded China $US150,000 MLF funds to target CFC production, one of the first projects under the Montreal Protocol to do so. This was in addition to a China/World Bank halon production/consumption project that had already phased out 32,000 ODP (ozone-depleting potential) tons.[88] In July 2004, a joint study involving China, Switzerland, and the World Bank was launched

in Beijing on the Clean Development Mechanism (CDM) for reducing carbon emissions, which allowed developed countries to earn Certified Emissions
Reduction (CER) credits. In confirming China's support for, and application of,
CDM strategies, it represented an important milestone for a country whose share
of the world carbon market was potentially around 50 percent.[89]

The Bank's direct lending to China in this sector, on the other hand, has been
described as "a drop in the bucket" in comparison to its crucial input of introducing new ideas and technologies. In particular, the Bank has been used by
China to raise domestic awareness of environmental issues.[90] It has also produced
periodic "state of the environment" studies that, in associating the State
Environment Protection Agency (SEPA) with the Bank, enhanced the status and
prestige of the Chinese body and encouraged close inter-organizational communication.[91] Other social projects assisted by the World Bank as part of its new,
expanded agenda, have included support for Good Development Governance,
a China Country Gender Review, and a China Private Sector Development
Strategy, supported by the IFC.[92] With its Small Grants Program, it also supported
the activities of Chinese NGOs.[93] In July 2003, the Bank even intervened in
partnership with other agencies to launch the SARS and Infectious Disease
Response Program in China.[94]

Despite the extent of China's developmental challenges, Joseph Stiglitz has
compared the success of its transition over the previous decade favorably with
that of others. China's strategy of gradual reform, he concludes, has been a pragmatic one that has stressed job and enterprise creation and competition among
various localities, encouraging learning from both successes and failures. It has
also established effective corporate governance based on localities.[95] This has contrasted with many countries where privatization without corporate governance
has led to asset stripping rather than wealth creation.[96] Such a positive assessment, however, has not gone unchallenged. Some argue that China's development has been too slow, others that it has not been gradual enough.[97] Among
the latter, Han Dongfang, labor dissident and editor of *China Labour Bulletin* in
Hong Kong, has complained that "the activities of the World Bank and foreign
investors in China are providing endless opportunities for officials to become
extremely rich [while] Chinese workers do not even enjoy minimum social guarantees and our demands have already reached the stage of calling for the right
to eat."[98] In short, Bank policies themselves are regarded by some as responsible for the existence of many of China's "developmental challenges." However,
such a critique is to oversimplify what appears to have been the outcome of
China's own preference, argued at length in the Bank, for growth over more equitable development, and for the Bank's grudging acceptance of those priorities.

China in the Bank

On 1818 H Street, China is seen as well integrated into Bank operations. However, despite its declared concern with developing country issues, China is regarded as advancing its own interests rather than representing the developing country, or G-77, group. India, Brazil, and Malaysia are regarded as more representative of the G-77. China's main source of influence in the Bank is the volume and scale of its borrowing, at one time comprising 35–40 percent of IDA resources.[99] Within discrete Bank contexts, moreover, as a big environmental player China commands substantial authority. At the same time, it straddles the natural divergence between Part I countries (developed) and Part II countries (developing).

As one of the twenty-four members of the World Bank Executive Board and one of the five largest members, China has a chair in its own right. Its total subscription is 4,479.9, that is, 0.4 more than Canada's, comprising 2.85 percent of the total.[100] It commands 45,049 votes, or 2.79 percent of the total.[101] Within the Board, the Chinese Executive Director is a member in good standing and, since Board members deal with each other every day, there is a great deal of mutual accommodation of views.[102] In general, Country Directors are seen to be more moderate in their dealings than the countries they represent, and in this the Chinese Directors have been no exception.

This is not to claim that China has not had differences with the Bank that, to use the expression of a former Chief of Mission in China, have been the subject of "lively and intensive exchange" over the years.[103] While China values the role of the Bank in its development, it has also urged the Bank to follow certain priorities in its lending policies. In 1998, it opposed the increase in the price of IBRD loans "against the will of all borrowing members," because such an increase departed from the Bank's "long-standing principle."[104] While supporting the increased emphasis on social sector issues by the Bank and Fund, China nevertheless argued that economic growth was still a precondition of solutions to problems of poverty alleviation and social issues. Thus, China's Governor in the Bank, Xiang Huaicheng, insisted that the two institutions "should help developing countries achieve stable and steady growth, which in turn will help reduce poverty and solve social issues."[105] To this end, he urged the Bank to provide more concessional funds and promote capital flows, and to maintain its political neutrality.

Specific areas of contention between China and the Bank have included the termination of China's access to IDA funds; its unhappiness over the quality and timeliness of some of the Bank's policy advice and technical assistance; and its concern that assistance programs and the policy agenda have become more strongly influenced by political pressures from Western states and NGOs, thereby allegedly undermining the neutrality of the Bank as required by its Articles of Agreement.[106] China has also expressed a degree of irritation about procedural issues, in particular project complexity, arising from multiple objectives and conditionality; the cost of the Bank's time-consuming preparation, documentation, and clearance requirements; implementation procedures that do not sufficiently recognize China's own growing capacity; and complex, unclear, and costly safeguards requirements.[107] In some cases, such as disagreement over the conditions of a loan in the 1990s to help finance Shanghai's new wastewater facility, there were even fights over conditionality, which led the Bank to informally withhold disbursements. In another case, when corruption was discovered by a Bank supervisory mission in the use of funds for a Guangdong agricultural development project, Guangdong was required to repay the misappropriated funds at once and the Bank succeeded, with the support of the Ministry of Finance, in enforcing procurement conditionality within that province.

In the late 1990s, President Wolfensohn's decision to place corruption and the relationship between democracy and development high on the agenda further disturbed China's leaders, who felt, particularly in relation to the latter issue, that the Bank was straying beyond its mandate. China was also initially not in favor of Wolfensohn's plan to reorganize and decentralize Bank staff. The Ministry of Finance was concerned that Beijing-based sector chiefs would do their business directly with the sector ministries rather than with itself.

Finally, a more subtle problem pervaded the relationship. From the beginning, as we have argued, China was accorded special consideration by the Bank, ranging from the upgrading of its quota standing in the 1940s and 1980s to the policy adjustments made to entice the PRC to join the Bank and Fund. From time to time, the Bank's peculiar sensitivity on China attracted comment, notably from the *Times* (London), which in 1997 called the Bank "an institution in strategic denial":

> A new World Bank report, *China 2020*, was published to great fanfare yesterday but the launch bordered on the farcical. Every time the Bank staff appeared to feel that a question might annoy Beijing, embarrassed giggles rippled down the podium and the reply was left to the one official who no longer has any dealings with China. . . . There is real fear of China's massive economic potential and the Bank clearly feels that, only by feeding Beijing a diet of unquestioning praise, will the rest of the world have a chance of harnessing some of its success to its own interests.[108]

Similar sensitivity was manifested in the Bank's rebuttal in August 2001 of an article in the *Wall Street Journal* criticizing its loans to China. In a letter to the editor, the Bank's China Program Director insisted that, as a consequence of the size of China's population, its projected $900 million in loans in 2001 to China amounted to only about 72 cents per person. He asserted that China was borrowing from the Bank at market rates, that it "pays every cent back" and that "a closer, more balanced look would reveal a great amount of good done for a large number of poor people."[109]

Such organizational sensitivity is a problem not only because it may hamper the institutional goal of fair treatment of all member states, but also because it could possibly affect the Bank's evaluation of China's record of compliance. Thus, there are those who claim that the Bank's attitude differs from that of the Asian Development Bank, which, because of its location in Asia and its closer cultural affinities, seems capable of a greater frankness and transparency in its approach to China.

Institutional and Legislative Implementation

At the international level, the China-Bank relationship is based on China's harmonization of its domestic laws and institutions with Bank norms and principles. Indeed, it has been argued that institution building is perhaps the Bank's greatest contribution to China's development and modernization.[110] The importance of this foundation for the success of future economic development is obvious. Laws, rules and regulations, courts, and law enforcement agencies protect citizens' legal, including property and contractual, rights, while stable government institutions ensure the effectiveness and implementation of those laws, rules, and regulations.[111] Thus, in addition to the laws detailed later in the section on the IMF, China established a special division in the Ministry of Finance, the World Bank Department, to coordinate its interaction with the Bank. The idea behind this counterpart agency (CPA) was to protect China's national security and prestige; to monitor the flow of foreign exchange, technology, and foreign values; to require Bank donors to accept China's national priorities; and to limit foreign interests. The CPA was also expected to help define the country program and to monitor compliance. In its mission to defend China's interests it was largely successful, although some weakening of CPA control occurred in the 1990s. By giving the World Bank Department in the Ministry of Finance control over Bank projects, moreover, China was able to avoid a serious debt problem that could have rendered it more vulnerable to IMF conditionality.[112] China also created the China Investment Bank in 1981 to control allocation of funds provided by the Bank; and it established a nonbank financial institution, the China Trust and Investment Corporation for Foreign Economic Relations and Trade, to manage concessionary bilateral loans.[113]

To facilitate trade and investment, China also reorganized its foreign economic affairs institutions, empowering the Ministry of Foreign Trade and Economic Cooperation within the central bureaucracy and allowing the World Bank, the

IMF, and GATT to interact with the foreign trade bureaucracies of the People's Bank, the Ministry of Finance, and MOFTEC.[114] In 1987, the Bank decentralized its operations, and the core China country team was relocated to Beijing. Thus, the presence in China of much of the Bank's organizational structure cemented the relationship and internalized Bank norms. By 2000, 120 projects were under way, and the representatives of every related sector and of the World Bank's affiliates were present in Beijing.[115] This institutional intertwining meant that the Ministry of Finance sometimes used the Bank as an instrument to achieve policy or behavioral changes at lower levels of government. Occasionally, it even persuaded the Bank to adopt a tougher policy toward lower level government sub-borrowers than it might otherwise have been inclined to do.

Compliance and Cooperation

Initially, just as it has baulked at the procedural requirements of other international organizations, China faced problems in observing some Bank conditions. As we have seen, the Chinese were initially unwilling to move from a fifty-fifty blend of IDA and IBRD loans to accepting a higher proportion of the tougher IBRD loans. Some officials were reluctant to raise two dollars from central government discretionary funds for every dollar borrowed from the Bank. The Chinese side complained about the lengthy and complex initial steps in the generation of acceptable project proposals with the Bank. When negotiating its Structural Adjustment Loan (SAL) with the Bank, it rejected the imposition of conditionality. Whereas the Bank usually disbursed loans in installments and attached conditions to succeeding tranches, China "evidenced a deep reluctance to be put in a position of having to take domestic action in response to an external authority." Its first SAL of US$200 million plus $US93.2 million IDA for a Rural Sector Adjustment Loan was to be disbursed in 1989, but China requested the second disbursement of US$100 million without having to meet any conditions.[116] In the event, the rapid disbursement of the initial funds of the RSAL led the Bank to admit that "the attraction of moving forward on policy-based lending in China may have convinced the Bank to compromise its own policies."[117] For China, such a negative experience ensured that this was its first and only SAL.[118] On the other hand, after initial resistance, it accepted the World Bank's demand that awards for major bank-funded projects be subject to international competitive bidding. It now adopts this procedure for domestically financed projects and to bid for external projects.[119]

If the Bank was initially susceptible to China's pleas of special status, the situation changed, at least on the surface, after the Tiananmen Square massacre. Prior to June 1989, the World Bank and IDA had approved loans and credits of $US8.6 billion to China. Seven additional loans and credits totaling $US786 million were scheduled for consideration by 30 June 1989.[120] Following the crackdown, and in response to a call from President George Bush, the Bank's management decided on 20 June that the Board of Executive Directors' discussion of new loans for China should be deferred.[121] World Bank personnel in the Beijing office were also withdrawn.[122] Yet, the Bank resisted U.S. prodding to make future loans conditional on China's civil and political rights, arguing that its proper role was to advance the economic human rights of the poor.[123] Bank President Barber Conable even authorized the dispatch of a small high-level mission to Beijing within weeks of the crackdown to discuss how the reform and development momentum might be maintained. This overture reportedly cemented the Bank-China relationship more than any loan could have done and cushioned the blow of the loan deferral. The Bank made no further loans to China until February 1990 when, following a severe earthquake, three loans meeting a basic needs criterion were submitted, with U.S. approval, to the Board.[124] Disbursements from previously committed loans also continued at almost the same level as in previous years, and new lending recommenced in 1991.[125]

Despite these ups and downs, the China-Bank relationship has generally been seen by both sides as harmonious and cooperative, particularly with respect to liaison over project implementation.[126] Under the procedure for deciding projects, the World Bank Office, Beijing, liaises with its chief government CPA, the Ministry of Finance, and with the State Development Planning Commission. Project proposals may be submitted by either side and are thoroughly appraised by both before being submitted for final approval. A three-year rolling lending program is reviewed and updated annually.[127] The criteria for assessment are not "mechanistic," but, like those for all country programs, include the physical aspects of the projects, their timeliness, their role in capacity building, the quality of the monitoring system, and the prices.[128] In terms of project implementation, China, according to the official Bank publicity, is one of its "best performing member countries."[129] The project failure rate is comparatively low and projects are generally well implemented, within budget, on time, and achieve their objectives.[130]

More generally, China knows very clearly what it wants but, at the same time, exhibits a "strong sense of accountability" to the Bank. It takes pride in the fact that its programs have a "high success rate." In all, interviewees conclude, its record has been "outstanding."[131] Reasons for this success, according to Yukon Huang, are that projects are well managed; policies are implemented "more or less" uniformly through the country since there are "no differences of views, priorities or objectives"; the government takes ownership of its projects; and competition occurs between provinces, thereby improving quality and keeping costs down.[132] In the words of former Chief of the Bank's Mission in

China, Pieter Bottelier, China has taken the World Bank seriously, has tried to comply with agreed conditions, and has been respectful of Bank regulations and legal requirements. It has made effective use of the Bank's financial resources and technical assistance and has serviced its large debt to the Bank punctually.[133] It has also publicly supported this collaboration.[134]

The enthusiasm of oral testimony, however, is slightly offset by the more sober assessments that have been the result of a revised disclosure policy encouraging increased Bank transparency from August 2001. This policy has only recently made public Bank reports of annual project implementation review meetings to identify and correct systemic implementation issues across sectors and geographic areas. Reports on a Country Assistance Strategy (CAS) of the World Bank Group for China also contain overall project evaluations.[135] According to the 2003 Country Assistance Evaluation report, the success rate of the Chinese projects has varied over the years:

> In terms of the number of projects (over 100), the China portfolio is by far the largest in the Bank, some 50 percent larger than the next tier of borrowers. . . . The quality of the portfolio deteriorated in the mid-90s. This was due to a variety of factors relating in part to the rapid build-up of the portfolio. With a concerted effort to address these issues and through project closures, the proportion of satisfactory projects has returned to its traditionally high levels. This was reconfirmed by OED [Operations Evaluation Department] evaluations of completed projects since 1980, which rated 9 percent as unsatisfactory, compared with the Bank-wide average of 31 percent.[136]

According to the report's figures, from 1990 to 1992, unsatisfactory projects stood at 4 percent, rising as high as 13 percent between 1996 and 1997, and finally falling to 3 percent in 2000, with a slight rise in 2001. In addition, Quality Assessment Group (QAG) ratings of supervision and project quality at entry to the portfolio "normally rank China in line with or, more often, above, Bank-wide averages." Furthermore, QAG and OED evaluations of activities for poverty reduction, forestry, the environment, involuntary resettlement, energy, and transport "found strategies to be well directed generally and projects that either in whole or in part set the standard for best practice." More "problematic," however, were projects supporting industry-specific restructuring, agro-processing, and credit lines to state commercial banks (SCBs).[137] Yet, while noting Chinese criticisms of Bank policies, the 2003 report did not directly address problems in the China-Bank relationship.

By contrast, the Asian Development Bank (ADB) has for some time publicly identified problems in its country assistance program for China. The core problem has been China's attempt to maintain control over all stages of the program. According to a 1998 ADB report, Chinese executive agencies are required by their own planning procedures to prepare detailed feasibility studies for externally funded investments, which are reviewed through a rigid internal screening process before consideration by an external funding agency. Therefore, "most of the key design issues are decided upon before funding agency involvement." Although this system contributes to project quality and to China's ownership of projects, it has meant that there is "only limited scope for the Bank [ADB] to express its ideas and suggestions at an early stage in the project formulation process." This is particularly a problem since, as in the case of the World Bank, the PRC authorities do not agree with the ADB's project classification distinguishing between projects aimed at growth and those meant to alleviate poverty. The result has been that China's "own plans and priorities and assessment of the readiness and quality of project preparation have largely determined the final selection" of projects. The government mainly borrowed for industrial development and "none of the loans approved from 1991 to 1997 had poverty alleviation as a primary objective."[138] The government's insistence that executing agencies be responsible for loan repayment has also "significantly limited" the choice of sectors for ADB lending. The outcome has been that not all projects have had a satisfactory assessment rate. Of the eight China projects approved by the ADB from 1986 to 1990, two were evaluated as unsuccessful, one was terminated, and four were generally successful. While this ratio of success appeared to differ from that in the World Bank, the problems with initial project selection and differences in project priorities and values were very likely similar.

Within the World Bank, China is subject not only to the constraints of the Bank's Articles of Agreement, loan regulations, and project evaluations but also to the norms, principles, and rules of the environmental regime. The last are invoked not just through environmental projects, but also through the environmental impact assessments required of all projects. In the latter case, permission to proceed has not always been automatic:

> Projects and programs we have rejected have tended to die, from [several hundred a year] misconceived micro-level investments . . . to large, dangerous programs, such as reconversion of areas to communal farming, programs of investments in huge Russian-style slaughterhouses, expansions of irrigation pumping to uneconomic elevations, construction of plants without toxic effluent control systems, unsustainable exploitation of natural resources . . . construction of uneconomic dams, etc.[139]

On specifically environmental projects, Bank officials believe they have no special "leverage" on China. Rather, the country itself is seen to be aware of the huge environmental problems it faces, and of the advantages offered by compliance. Thus, "they ask, we lend." In environmental matters, China is regarded as having "the best implementation record in the whole of the Bank," with no extensive corruption.[140] On the other hand, as we shall see in the next chapter, China's differential compliance with the Montreal Protocol and the Framework Agreement on Climate Change illustrates the significance of issue, quality of rules, and nature of incentives in determining compliance with the norms and rules of specific environmental instruments.

The Qinghai Project

One particular project marred China's generally positive record of compliance and cooperation with the World Bank. The fallout from the collapse of the Qinghai component of the Western Poverty Reduction Project underlined the close interrelationship between politics, the environment, and economic development in Bank policies, irrespective of the Articles of Agreement guidelines, and provided a unique opportunity to view the relationship between the Bank and China at a time of acute stress. For China, the collapse was seen as "close to the last straw."[141] It not only provoked some of China's most strenuous criticisms of the Bank, but also initiated a period of sustained tension between the two.[142]

In 1999, World Bank funding of US$40 million approved for a poverty relief scheme that would move Chinese farmers into traditional Tibetan lands met strong opposition from Tibetan exiles, human rights groups, and U.S. officials. The plan involved moving 57,775 Chinese farmers (40 percent Han and 60 percent minorities) from hillsides in Qinghai province to more fertile land in Dulan County to the west near Tibet. Objections, transmitted by NGOs to the United States, focused on the proposed resettlement in the area of large numbers of non-Tibetans and on the alleged environmental damage that the project would cause. The project had passed the Bank's ecological and social impact tests. However, U.S. doubts about the plan set it against China, which warned that it would rethink its ties with the Bank if the loans were not approved.[143] In an unprecedented divided vote, on 24 June the Bank Board reached an agreement that "no work be done and no funds be disbursed for the US$40 million Qinghai component until the Board decided on the results of any review by the independent Inspection Panel."[144] China was reportedly reluctant to have the Inspection Panel appointed, and complained of interference. According to interviewees, China's views were expressed clearly and unequivocally, but it did not "grandstand"; it recognized pragmatically that there was a problem and that there was a need to find a compromise that could be lived with.[145] Following a negative finding by the Inspection Panel, on 7 July 2000 the majority of the Bank's Board of Executive Directors decided not to adopt Management's recommendations as originally formulated. The Chinese Executive Director, Zhu Xian, responded:

> China accepts no conditions beyond Management's original recommendations that had been agreed between Management and my authorities. . . . It is unacceptable to my authorities that other Bank shareholders would insist on imposing additional conditions on Management's recommendations—namely coming back to the Board for approval again for a project that was already approved last year. If that is the case, China

will therefore turn to its own resources to implement the Qinghai component of the project, and in its own way. . . . *Compliance policies have been interpreted by some to an extreme and used for political purposes.*[146]

China thus challenged Article VI. 5.a and .b of the Articles of Agreement allowing loans to be temporarily or permanently suspended, invoking in preference Article IV.10 requiring political neutrality in Bank decisions. Speaking in Prague after the decision, China's Governor in the IMF, Dai Xianglong, insisted:

> The Bank should keep lending operations as its core business, complemented by country assistance strategy and problem diagnosis. We have consistently held that the Bank should operate in accordance with its Articles of Agreement, instead of catering to the political needs of a few members. However, the political orientation of the Bank has become increasingly evident in recent years. The Bank will eventually change itself from a development institution into a political tool of a few countries if it falls in with their political intentions and succumbs to pressures from interest groups at the expense of development objectives. This would rock the foundations of the Bank, compromise the fundamental interests of its developing members and endanger the cause of world development.[147]

In an implicit threat, he complained that "unrealistic requirements and arbitrary increases in safeguard standards have. . . . contributed to the recent decline in the Bank's loan commitment." In interviews in Washington conducted soon after the Prague Meeting, Bank officials expressed uncertainty and even nervousness about whether China intended to continue borrowing. They privately admitted that "the Bank needs China more than China needs the Bank."[148] When in November China recommended borrowing, they expressed considerable relief. Nevertheless, it was noteworthy that, for the variety of reasons canvassed above, China was now borrowing at a diminished rate. Conversely, it began borrowing more from the Asian Development Bank.[149] The possibility that it was engaging in forum-hopping could not be excluded. The Qinghai case highlighted the continued priority placed by the Chinese government on state sovereignty, the more so because it occurred in relation to an international organization and regime where its interests were normally so well served. It further suggested that, far from China being amenable to Bank sanctions, the Bank itself was vulnerable to China. In such a situation, state compliance could only be achieved at best through a sustained process of interaction, negotiation, and persuasion.

International Monetary Fund

The IMF is located on Pennsylvania Avenue, but its main working entrance is at 700 Nineteenth Street, at the rear of the World Bank. Housed in a more conventional office building, it likewise exhibits a distinctly more formal and conservative official culture. It was established to promote international monetary cooperation, exchange stability, and orderly exchange arrangements; to foster economic growth and high levels of employment; and to provide temporary financial assistance to countries to ease balance of payments adjustments. In pursuit of these goals, it exercises surveillance over the exchange rate policies of its members and oversees the elimination of exchange restrictions. Like the World Bank, its modus operandi has evolved to meet the needs of a changing world economy. Otherwise, the differences between the two institutions are manifold. In particular, as we have seen, for a country to become a member of the Bank, it must first be a member of the Fund. This is because membership in the Bank involves primarily a benefit—it qualifies a country for Bank loans. Membership of the Fund, on the other hand, is seen as entailing not only rights (access to credit) but also more stringent obligations, in particular, observance of the agreed rules on exchange rates and currency restrictions.[150]

Initially, the two institutions also had quite different tasks and different sources of finance. The Fund's function was to be guardian of the international monetary system, while the Bank's was development. The bulk of Bank lending is funded on the world's capital markets, is guaranteed by the uncalled portion of its capital, and demonstrates no connection between a country's shareholding and the amount of credit it can receive. In the Fund, on the other hand, member countries contribute an amount equal to their quota, partly in SDRs (special drawing rights) but primarily in their own currency. These quotas determine both voting rights and access to IMF credit. Initially, if the Bank found that the country's creditworthiness was insufficient, it would refuse to lend for even the best project. By contrast, if a country was deemed not creditworthy, the Fund had the explicit authority to require change in a country's policies before it was prepared to lend. Over time, however, the distinct functional separation between the two organizations blurred, and the Fund moved toward structural conditionality while the Bank moved some way toward macroeconomic management. Despite this, criticism of IMF conditionality continues.[151] In particular, Joseph Stiglitz has argued that conditionality has engendered resentment rather than development. Not only has the Fund's approach to developing countries had the "feel of a colonial rule," but the countries that have pursued independent policies, including the United States, China, Malaysia, and Poland, are precisely those that have weathered financial crises most successfully. Particularly deplorable, in Stiglitz's view, have been IMF policies requiring countries to accelerate trade liberalization and to achieve excessively rapid financial and capital market deregulation.

Organization, Rules, and Management

Because the IMF imposes more obligations on its members than does the World Bank, its thirty-one Articles of Agreement are more numerous and detailed. Three explicitly address the obligations of members and participants (IV, VIII, XXII), two govern the rules of membership (II and III), three govern termination of participation, withdrawal from membership, or temporary suspension (XXIV, XXVI, XXVII), and ten govern Special Drawing Rights. The General Obligations (VIII) include avoidance of restrictions on current payments; avoidance of discriminatory currency practices; convertibility of foreign-held balances; and the furnishing of information. The last requirement applies to twelve categories of information on such matters as foreign exchange, total exports and imports, international balance of payments, international investment position, national income, price indices, and exchange controls, with the proviso that "in requesting information the Fund shall take into account the varying ability of members to furnish the data requested" (VIII.5.b). Provisions on withdrawal from membership include a stipulation that, "if a member fails to fulfill any of its obligations under this Agreement" (XXVI.2-3), it may be liable to compulsory withdrawal, following the expiration of a reasonable period, a decision of the majority of members, and an 85 percent vote by a majority of Governors.[152]

Compliance monitoring procedures are also more complicated and rigorous in the Fund than in the Bank. The Fund monitors compliance with its norms in different ways: country surveillance, global surveillance, and regional surveillance over monetary unions. There are also biennial reviews and external evaluations of IMF surveillance. In addition, the Fund has developed and strengthened standards, including the Special Data Dissemination Standards (SDDS), the Code of Good Practices on Transparency in Monetary and Financial Policies, and the Basle Core Principles (BCP). Reports of members' observance of standards are assessed through the experimental Financial Sector Assessment Program (FSAP) and Reports on the Observance of Standards and Codes (ROSCs).[153] Country surveillance takes the form of regular consultations with member countries over their policies, primarily through the "Article IV Consultations." Under Article IV of the IMF's Articles of Agreement, the IMF holds bilateral discussions with individual member states, usually annually. A staff team, usually accompanied by the Executive Director of each country, visits the country to collect economic and financial information and hold discussions with the responsible officials. Their concluding statement summarizing the discussions may be publicly released if the country in question agrees.

China and the IMF

From the beginning, partly because of China's policy of self-sufficiency regarding loans, its relationship with the Fund was less intense than it was with the Bank. For every fifty man-weeks that the Bank spent on China in the mid-1990s, the Fund spent one. Likewise, in the same period, the Bank's office in Beijing had sixty-five members of staff, as against two in the Fund office. In 1981, China drew from the Fund a first credit tranche of SDR450 million and a Trust Fund loan of SDR309 million, in total SDR759 million, to support its economic stabilization program. It drew its reserve tranche in 1981 and repaid both in 1984.[154] In November 1986, it drew a further SDR597.3 million. Apart from these loans, which it fully repaid, China took pride in the fact that it did not have to borrow subsequently.[155] This meant that it was less subject to IMF conditionality than most other developing states. Its underlying assumption, remarked on by other Executive Directors, was that countries should not need to borrow from the IMF and it was proud that it could rely upon its domestic savings.[156] This self-sufficiency was commended by IMF Managing Director Michel Camdessus, who in 1998 observed that he did not believe that China would need IMF support in the years to come, other than technical assistance in macroeconomic matters.[157]

China was in fact to become the Fund's largest recipient of technical assistance.[158] In its eagerness to modernize it found the Fund a useful source of advice and information, particularly via the annual Article IV Consultations on the economy, growth, and inflation. IMF policy advice, particularly on balance of payments, and its technical assistance, were seen as useful adjuncts to that obtainable from the World Bank, the Asian Development Bank, and from sources in Hong Kong. The Fund's provision of technical assistance to China covered all sectors—economic statistics, fiscal reform, taxation, balance of payments, and budgetary and monetary operations. One of the most important sources of training was the IMF Institute. China implemented some of the Fund's advice, and the government maintained particularly close relations with the Fund's Fiscal Affairs and Monetary Exchange Departments. It also appreciated interacting with the many international bankers at senior levels from commercial banks and other financial institutions who attended the annual meeting, and the expansion of business this brought to China. The provision of important information on country matters to Chinese ministries was also seen as valuable. This was because, as a large country with huge technical assistance needs, China had a well-developed curiosity about how other states addressed the type of problems it faced. To strengthen its ownership of each project, when looking at an issue, it normally set up three committees. These investigated: (1) how other countries had tackled the problem; (2) how the proposed reform fitted with the tax regime in each province in China; and (3) the nature of the issues involved in the reform.[159]

China in the IMF

By contrast with its role in the Bank, China perceived its role in the Fund as "subdued," and incommensurate with its size and importance.[160] Within the

Fund, China was a Deputy Director in the Asia and Pacific Department and a Senior Adviser, IMF Institute, but, as of 2000, the Chinese Executive Director was still only appointed at junior level. In that year, China's quota, which determined the amount of its subscription, voting weight, access to IMF financing, and share in the allocation of SDRs was SDR3,385.2 million. Its total votes were 47,122, amounting to 2.20 percent of the Fund total. This compared with the 2.42 percent of the country grouping of Bangladesh, Bhutan, India, and Sri Lanka. During the Asian financial crisis, China had helped play a part in the IMF rescue package for stricken Asian economies by lending Thailand US$1 billion, Indonesia US$200 million, and funds to South Korea supporting its exports. It also took pride in having adopted fiscally responsible policies during the crisis by not devaluing its currency. Moreover, although it qualified for the Enhanced Structural Adjustment Facility program (ESAF),[161] China, like India, volunteered to give up its rights. It even contributed to the fund. In the sense that its role in the IMF was that of a creditor country, it had an attitude similar to that of developed states on what was required to have funds repaid.[162]

Nevertheless, it complained of a generalized inequity. The significance of the quota system was that developing countries commanded only 31 percent of the quotas, whereas industrialized countries disposed of 60 percent. Fund decisions to change membership quotas required 85 percent majority support, other decisions needed 70 percent, while for lending programs, 50 percent support was necessary. China believed that, given their current quotas, developing states lacked sufficient votes to effect changes in Fund policies. For these reasons, as interviews in 2000 made clear, China wanted more active participation in the IMF, with its quotas increased to 2.8 percent, particularly in view of its takeover of Hong Kong in 1997. To achieve this, it was prepared to shoulder increased contributions.

In 2000, Chinese respondents also offered some polite but firm criticisms of Fund policies. In the Fund, as one commented, "developing countries" sometimes believed management was too influenced by G-7 countries: they held that reforms should be initiated by the Board, not by the G-7 countries, which were the creditors. Moreover, although most IMF programs were successful, there was a need to analyze whether failed programs were the fault of the Fund or of the countries concerned. Finally, since there had hitherto been little cost-benefit analysis, China saw the introduction of an Independent Evaluation Office (IEO) as a positive development.

For their part, some IMF respondents saw China as still "too old fashioned." They noted its belief that governments required a margin for maneuver in their decision making. They contended that China attempted to keep some information to itself and imposed certain "speed limits" on its interaction. Thus, China was seen as almost alone in having to check all decisions with its home government. Interviewees observed that while Japanese representatives in the IMF were allowed leeway in their decision making, China and the United States had the least scope.[163]

Chinese criticisms of the Fund largely reflected concerns that had emerged after the outbreak of the Asian financial crisis in July 1997. In October 1998, at the Annual Meeting of the Bank and Fund, Dai Xianglong had paid tribute to the role of both Fund and Bank in preventing and solving financial crises in some regions and countries, in maintaining the stability of the international monetary system, and in assisting member countries to develop in a sustainable manner. But, he added, "the main cause of the crisis [was] that international cooperation and the evolution of the international financial system lag[ged] far behind economic globalization and the financial integration process." He added:

> We hope that the Fund and other international financial institutions can play a more effective role in resolving financial crises. By encouraging the deregulation and liberalization of domestic markets, they should be vigilant to the risks posed by international capital flows; and when designing and implementing assistance programs, they should pay more attention to the specific circumstances of the countries concerned. The Fund should formulate and establish the mechanism for monitoring short-term capital flows, and the movements of speculative capital.[164]

Dai expressed support for the strengthening of the Fund's early warning system on the basis of enhanced information disclosure and transparency. However, a year later, at the 1999 Annual Meetings, Xiang Huaicheng insisted that "increasing transparency of all market participants will help efficiency and prevent crisis. But lack of transparency is not the main cause of the financial crisis. We are not in favor of mandatory enforcement in any form."[165]

Subsequently, Premier Zhu Rongji voiced his support for Malaysian Prime Minister Mahathir Mohamad's call to reform the global financial system.[166] This followed Foreign Ministry spokesman Sun Yuxi's statement that China was willing to consider the proposal to establish an East Asia Monetary Fund.[167] It also followed China's initiative in proposing the establishment in March 1998 of the ASEAN-China, Japan-ROK Dialogue of Finance and Central Bank Deputies, launched under the auspices of ASEAN. By November 1999, the regional states had already met twice to discuss how to monitor and regulate the short-term capital flow and reform the international financial system. To deepen this dialogue mechanism, China suggested three further proposals: to institutionalize the Meeting, and convene meetings of finance ministers and central bank governors; to share information and experience on financial reforms and set up an ad hoc committee for an in-depth study of the supervision and regulation of international capital flow and the restructuring of the international financial system; and to coordinate the positions of East Asian countries on major international financial and economic issues through this mechanism "so that East Asia may do its part for the reform of the international financial system."[168]

Nevertheless, China insisted it was not attempting to promote regional competition with the Fund: rather, it saw regional financial cooperation as a "helpful complement" to the existing financial system. In this context, Dai Xianglong announced that China would be an active participant in financial cooperation based on the currency swap arrangements introduced among ASEAN countries and China, Japan, and Korea. He also invoked the interests of developing states in proposing "a win-win globalization characterized by equality." He called for Fund standards and codes to be disseminated and implemented based on "voluntary and progressive principles," and for improved transparency in the private sector, in order to "deter the massive, disorderly and disruptive flows of short-term capital."[169]

By January 2001, at least one of China's differences with the Fund had been resolved. On 4 January, Horst Kohler, Managing Director of the IMF, announced that the Executive Board had proposed to the IMF Board of Governors an increase in China's quota to SDR6,369.2 million (about US$8.4 billion), up from SDR4,687.2 million (almost US$6.1 billion). He stated: "The proposal responds to a request by China for a special increase in its quota to better reflect its position in the world economy following the resumption of Chinese sovereignty over Hong Kong." The proposed quota represented about 3.0 percent of total quotas and 2.95 percent of total votes, up from 2.19 percent of the total.[170] On 8 February, this proposal was approved by the Board of Governors. It represented a 0.2 percent increase on the preferred increase mentioned during interviews in the previous year, and made China's quota, along with Canada's, the eighth largest.[171] Five years later, on 14 September 2006, in a report to the International Monetary and Financial Committee on IMF Quota and Voice Reform, the Managing Director of the Fund proposed new measures realigning members' quotas with their relative positions in the world economy. The first stage would be ad hoc quota increases for "a small group of the most clearly underrepresented states," China, Korea, Mexico, and Turkey.

Institutional and Legislative Implementation

China moved early to entrench its integration into the Fund by harmonizing domestic legislation and institutions with Fund norms and rules. In the mid-1980s, it set up a central banking system under the People's Bank of China, which adopted measures to increase the flexibility and credibility of its monetary policy. These included measures diversifying monetary policy instruments; adjusting credit policy; stabilizing the balance of payments and the RMB exchange rate; restructuring nonbanking financial institutions; accelerating financial reform and restructuring of state-owned enterprises; reorganizing management; undertaking commercial bank reform; and further opening financial markets. Legislative implementation followed in the form of the Commercial Bank Law, effective as of 1 July 1995; the Law of the PRC on the People's Bank of China; the Guarantee Law of the PRC; the Insurance Law of the PRC; the Price Law of the PRC; regulations on foreign exchange; and twenty-six laws and regulations on foreign investment.[172] These laws and regulations brought China closer to standard international financial practice. The People's Bank of China also issued new regulations that adopted standards from international banking accords, such as the Basle Accord standard of capital adequacy.[173]

In 1998, China recapitalized state commercial banks (SCBs) and, in 1999 and 2000, transferred nonperforming loans totaling 15.5 percent of GDP to asset management companies (AMCs). The latter resolved bad debts through asset sales and debt equity swaps. In the state-owned enterprise (SOE) sector, efforts were made to reduce excess capacity, improve efficiency, and transform ownership structures. In particular, attempts were made to introduce modern enterprise systems, establish independent Boards of Directors and Supervisors, separate government functions from enterprise management, and improve incentive and internal control mechanisms.[174] IMF presence in China was also entrenched through the establishment in 1991 of the IMF's Resident Representative Office in Beijing. This coordinated technical assistance programs, maintained an ongoing policy dialogue with Chinese authorities, and monitored China's economic development. In recognition of the role of Hong Kong as a major financial center, on 11 January 2001 the IMF also set up a Hong Kong SAR sub-office of the main Beijing Office. Hong Kong in 2001 was still seen by the IMF as a "standard setter for corporate governance and transparency."[175]

Compliance and Cooperation

In general, China sees itself as a good member of the Fund that has met its obligations under the IMF Articles, has participated in all activities, and has good relations with management.[176] However, as was the case with its entry to the World Bank, in the initial stage of its participation it was not clear that China had understood all the obligations of membership. In late 1980, the leadership decided to establish an internal settlement price or rate of exchange. Hearing of this indirectly, a visiting Fund mission pointed out that, under the Fund regulations, prior Fund approval was required for what amounted to a dual exchange rate. Chinese officials insisted that the decision was an internal matter.[177] In January 1985, China discontinued the internal settlement rate for its own reasons.

Another misreading of its obligations was reflected in China's treatment of Yang Hong, an IMF employee seconded from China, who, during an IMF mission to China in December 1995, was arrested in a meeting at the People's Bank and subsequently imprisoned for five years. Strenuous efforts by Michel Camdessus failed to secure Yang's release.[178] The Yang Hong case introduced a chill in China's relationship with the Fund, just as the Qinghai case later undermined its relationship with the Bank. It raised the possibility of China being in breach of the provision for diplomatic immunity of international civil servants required by Article IX of the IMF's Articles of Agreement.[179]

In general, however, the process of its organizational participation and the marketization of its domestic economy brought China into line with the Fund's institutional and market norms and rules. China adopted some of the policies recommended by the IMF, in particular its advice since the early 1980s on exchange rate policy. These included the 1986 devaluation of the yuan by 15.8 percent; and, in 1994, its move toward a unitary exchange rate. The IMF was also influential in persuading China to achieve *current account* convertibility.[180] On 4 December 1996, China became the 134th country to notify the IMF that it had accepted the obligations of Sections 2, 3, and 4 of Article VIII, the principal article spelling out the obligations of IMF membership, with effect from 1 December 1996. According to these sections, China undertook to "refrain from imposing restrictions on the making of payments and transfers for current international transactions or from engaging in discriminatory currency arrangements or multiple currency practices without IMF approval."[181] Welcoming both these initiatives, Michel Camdessus observed: "This marks yet another milestone in China's historic transformation and decisive progress toward further integration in the world market economy. The achievement of current account convertibility will further strengthen domestic and international confidence in a very promising reform process."[182]

Before China could achieve *capital account* liberalization, however, under IMF surveillance and guidelines, it had first to reform its financial system and state-owned enterprises (SOEs).[183] Since it had not yet achieved this goal, it was shielded from the full effect of the financial collapse in Asia. Its stock market was also relatively small and the regulatory structure of its foreign trade regime meant that the SOEs were sheltered from outside competition.[184] Indeed, it was precisely this policy independence that, in Joseph Stiglitz's view, enabled China to survive the crisis, while others succumbed.[185] China had basically ploughed its own financial policy furrow, accepting outside advice which it judged sound, but adhering primarily to policies with "Chinese characteristics."[186] The paradoxical result was that its non-compliance with IMF norms in this specific area, albeit involuntary, had not only helped protect human security in China but, as the result of China's financial stability and its decision not to devalue its currency, had also contributed to the human security of the Asia-Pacific region.

China's own reaction to the regional turmoil passed through three phases: self-congratulation at having been spared, followed by a period of "sober reflection" and, finally, "serious action."[187] Realizing that it suffered from many of the same weaknesses that had grounded other Asian economies, its leaders drew a number of lessons from the crisis. They saw that the need for increased attention to macroeconomic management was paramount. In view of the evidence of economic overheating, they concluded that China should pay more attention to the financial sector; that it needed to obtain a good balance in the economy; and that the opening of offshore business would be beneficial.[188] They therefore moved to strengthen China's financial system and regulatory framework, concentrating in particular on the Central Bank's role and regulatory powers, commercializing its other banks, and reducing exposure to foreign currency loans. At the same time, they recognized that their decision not to devalue China's currency had not only buttressed regional stability, a fact acknowledged by both the Bank and Fund, but had also maintained domestic confidence, essential in a situation where domestic banks were primarily funded by China's households.[189]

Despite the IMF's influential role, some scholars have speculated that markets may have been even more important than international financial institutions in educating China in the principal norms of the international financial system.[190] This is partly because the former have imposed penalties automatically when the behavior of Chinese firms and financial institutions has deviated from their expectations. Market forces have also encouraged transparency. To exploit the public international capital market, for instance, required Chinese listing entities to divulge greater information in the 1990s than they had in the past. In much the same way, disappointment in levels of investment in the 1980s had pressured Chinese reformers to liberalize controls on foreign investment.[191]

However, markets do not adopt policies, set programmatic standards, provide advice and technical assistance, and measure progress. As already observed, markets may also work against the interests of the international political economy. In all the above areas, by contrast, the IMF assumed an important role with respect to China, especially in regard to policy advice.[192] In particular, the interactive, continuing process of Article IV Consultations helped guide and encourage China in the direction of compliance. IMF Directors measured both the progress China had made in meeting its IMF obligations, and the distance it still had to cover. Discussion focused on macroeconomic policies to cushion the impact of the Asian financial crisis and medium-term growth, as well as structural reforms in the financial sector, external sector, and state-owned enterprises (SOEs). For its part, China saw the importance of its relationship with the IMF as lying precisely in "effective communication through Article IV Consultation."[193] The Consultations and their reports normally involved a fine balance of strong commendation and detailed criticism and recommendation.[194] They increasingly emphasized the social aspects of Chinese reform, something the IMF has not normally been noted for. Most importantly, they revealed the effectiveness of the organizational process by documenting the progressive change in China's policies in response to the Directors' persuasive advice and policy recommendations.

Thus, at the 2001 Consultations, Directors commended China's skilful macroeconomic management and structural reforms and welcomed the determination and increasing transparency with which authorities were approaching problems in the financial sector. However, they urged China to conduct further work on the "unfinished reform agenda," in particular to reduce the fiscal deficit; to gradually move to greater flexibility in the exchange rate policy; to make further progress in rehabilitating the State Commercial Banks (SCBs); to further bolster the authority and legal environment of the asset management companies (AMCs); to tighten budget constraints on SOEs; to improve market fundamentals; to strengthen the social safety net; and to reduce widening regional income disparities. In particular, they emphasized the need for China to submit to greater IMF surveillance and to exhibit increased transparency:

> Directors encouraged China's early participation in the Financial Sector Assessment Program (FSAP) . . . [and] stressed the need for substantial further improvements to facilitate analysis and IMF surveillance. They . . . noted that, notwithstanding some strengthening in data provision to the IMF, there remained considerable scope for improvement in a number of areas of key importance to IMF surveillance under Article IV. Directors looked forward to China's participation in the General Data Dissemination System.[195]

The following year, at the 2002 Consultations, Directors acknowledged China's progress in joining the General Data Dissemination System (GDDS) on 19 April 2002, but reiterated its need to participate in the FSAP. They also noted the pressing issue of unemployment, which exacerbated regional income disparity, and the need to address rural-urban and regional income disparities. They therefore welcomed China's progress on "a critical component of the SOE reform process," the strengthening of the social safety net.[196] A number of these recommendations were reiterated, in a tone of greater urgency, in the 2003 Article IV Consultations. While again welcoming China's participation in the GDDS and approving its establishment of a new China Banking Regulatory Commission, the Directors called for greater exchange rate flexibility, once again recommended China's participation in the Financial Sector Assessment Program and again argued the need for China to address the employment and social aspects of the reform process and to strengthen the social safety net.[197]

According to its Deputy Finance Minister, following its accession to the

GDDS, China began taking "concrete measures to improve the accounting standards and information disclosure in related sectors."[198] In furtherance of these goals, the IMF also assisted China to develop a Government Financial Management Information System. IMF transparency requirements clearly presented a sharp learning curve, since previously much of China's statistical information had been a state secret. Both the question of China's transparency and its observance of standards were viewed within the Fund as a "huge problem."[199] For instance, in the case of the Article IV Consultations, although China began to participate in releasing the Public Information Notice (PIN), unlike one-third of IMF members, it was not willing to publish the initial, more detailed staff report.[200] This unwillingness was explained by Chinese officials in the following way: it was *not* "illegal" *not* to do so; change occurred gradually in China; and, even if there had been "no leaps" in its development, China had made "strong progress."[201] More generally, China insisted that "Article IV Consultations should not be linked with transparency assessment."[202]

However, the 2004 and 2005 Consultations revealed significant progress in China's cooperation and transparency.[203] In 2004, for the first time China allowed the publication not only of the PIN of China's Article IV Consultation, but also of the more detailed staff report. In addition, Directors acknowledged China's advances in structural reforms in the banking sector and in strengthening the social safety net, while at the same time reiterating China's need to participate in the FSAP "in the near future." Finally, in 2005, Directors applauded China for its new "shift in expenditure from investment to social spending," its adjustment of the exchange rate, and its "decision to participate in an FSAP."

In other words, as a senior Chinese official pointed out, for China, "meeting all the [IMF] commitments [wa]s a work in process."[204] China's accession to the GDDS was just one indicator of its willingness to renegotiate its sovereignty and become more open and transparent in its dealings with the Fund. Another was its decision, after years of negotiation and persuasion, to participate in the FSAP. While not yet showing total compliance with the Fund's Articles of Agreement or manifesting complete cooperation in promoting their object and purpose, under the benign guidance and repeated recommendations of the Directors, China was making definable progress in that direction.

Conclusion

This chapter attests to the explanatory power of process-based theories of compliance. Through its ongoing interaction with other states in these multilateral institutions, through repeated admonitions and recurring pressures having a feedback effect into the domestic polity, China has come to a gradual acceptance of the need to comply with their norms, principles, and rules. Negotiation, persuasion, and modeling, rather than the Downs's notion of coercive sanctions, have been the medium of norm internalization. At most, as Harold Koh's process-based theory would anticipate, China has responded to the "threat" of sanctions. Yet, as the case study shows, such threats have been rare. This is partly because China has managed to avoid engagement with both bodies in areas that involve the imposition of heavy conditionality, whether in the use of SALs in the World Bank or acceptance of loans from the IMF. Despite this, and although initially it did not support the norms and rules of either organization and had difficulty adapting to them, China has nevertheless complied with them reasonably, whether at international or national levels. For the most part, it has abided by the Articles of Agreement under which the Bank and Fund were established, has met the conditions of loans, and has realized the organizations' expectations that member states would optimize their use of loans, advice, and technical assistance. In the case of the Bank, China has enjoyed an exemplary record of project management and repayment of loans, in part because of the many incentives associated with Bank membership. On the other hand, as this case study shows, the Bank has been dependent on China as a major borrower (see p. 141). Even in the case of the IMF, where incentives have been less apparent and costs more burdensome, China has increasingly complied with its obligations.

At the domestic level, China has internalized Bank and IMF rules in legislation and institution building. It has also complied deeply, in that it has accepted the constraints on sovereignty consequent upon the restructuring of its economy, has shouldered the costs of participation by making increased contributions, and has reassessed many of its interests in terms of the dominant norms of the institutions. As elsewhere, China's underlying motivations to conform have reflected a mix of instrumental and normative concerns.

Such compliance is all the more interesting in view of the special treatment accorded to China by the two organizations. Both at the point of entry and as its participation progressed, China was given privileged treatment, whether in terms of special policies or of an unusual preparedness to adopt a tolerant and sensitive attitude toward its unique situation. Such special treatment included the early political decision to reward China for its contribution to World War II with the fourth highest quota in the Bank and Fund, acceptance of PRC conditions for its entry into both organizations in 1980, and efforts to meet China's needs once it became a member. The last included a reassessment of its Bank quota allocation, the continuation for a year of its access to IDA despite its growing affluence, and the upgrading of its IMF quotas. For these reasons, it is difficult to agree with Oksenberg and Jacobson that "the rules of the two institutions have not been bent for China any more than they normally are for large new entrants."[205] One has only to compare the differential treatment accorded other large states like India. As a result of this treatment, China's gains have sometimes resulted in disadvantage to other developing member states, particularly India. In cases where China's claims have been made in the name of developing states, moreover, the benefits of such strategies have often been monopolized, rather than shared. On some issues, such as the repayment of loans, China has even aligned itself with the developed against the developing states. It has thus made strategic use of its dual status as a developing state and rising power to exploit the advantages of each identity in specific contexts. Otherwise, the basis of China's power and influence lies in its economic strength and potential, reflected in its high quotas and single country constituency status. While continuing to borrow from the Bank, its recent promotion to lower-middle-income status is just one indicator of its ever closer alignment with the developed world within this regime.

Both organizations have also been extraordinarily respectful of China's sensitivities about sovereignty, about its status, and about the authoritarian nature of its political system, since these issues have generally formed the basis of the recurring strains in the relationship, just as they have in its relations with other international organizations. Such sensitivity has been partly due to China's growing political and economic importance, and to the fact that the Bank needs China at least as much as (if not more than) China needs the Bank. At a time of increased public scrutiny of Bank and IMF policies, the Bank needs both to lend China money and to bask in the success story that it represents for its policies toward developing states. For the most part, therefore, both the Bank and Fund have been adroit in sidestepping disputes with China, and in smoothing over any unavoidable disagreements. Where they have not been successful, as in the cases of the Qinghai project and the IMF objections to China's arrest of Yang Hong, they have faced considerable unpleasantness and complaints. In the end, however, China has normally accepted the new situation and has not acted on its threats to stop borrowing or to reassess its membership. Despite its special treatment, it has not been tempted to transgress institutional rules.

Conversely, while China's criticisms of the Bank and Fund may have resulted in some adjustment of their policies, it has not undermined their basic norms, rules, and principles.[206] Rather, it has assisted in their development. How may one explain the apparent contradiction involved in simultaneously asserting that Bank and Fund rules have been bent in China's favor, but that China has not changed the regime in any deleterious way? The answer appears to lie in the strength, legitimacy, and flexibility of the key international organizations underpinning the political economy regime. China's size and status have allowed it special treatment in the Bank and Fund without arousing excessive objections from other member states, and without the requests for equal treatment that might otherwise have destabilized the regime. In general, there has been an implicit acceptance by member states of special treatment for China as the necessary price of its entry and integration. Such flexibility has been made possible by the robustness of the organizations' norms and principles as well as by the flexibility of their Articles of Agreement. The latter allow Executive Directors and Directors considerable discretion in their rule interpretation and policy-making. At the same time, these rules have protected the organizations from excessive demands by China and have lent weight to the value of modeling, that is, the positive example set by other complying states. The norms of related international organizations and of the market, operating independently, have exerted complementary pressures on China. Finally, mandatory provisions, such as the Fund's Article IV Consultations, have had a socializing, educative impact.

The result is that China has established a new model of state–Bank/IMF interaction. Despite initial reservations on the part of the international community, its relations with the World Bank and the IMF have proved to be mutually beneficial. This is partly because, unlike other developing states, from the beginning China was already powerful enough to set the outer limits on both relationships. The mutual interaction therefore assumed more the form of a professional partnership than an institution-client relationship. Integration into the Bank and Fund benefited China in many different ways. In the realm of ideas and advice, in technical training, in infrastructure building, in poverty reduction, in technology transfer, in the provision of managerial experience, as a sounding board for policy development, and as the provider of financial and monetary advice, the two international organizations have performed a critical role integrating China into the international political economy regime. For their part, the Bank and Fund have not only derived increased legitimacy from China's membership but have learned new ways of conceiving development and of interacting with member states.

Paradoxically, however, not all these developments have had positive results for human security in China. The normal criticisms leveled at Bank and IMF policies for a lack of concern about human welfare have not been an issue, as in China's case both bodies have been increasingly concerned about such matters. Yet, China's insistence on ownership of its projects, made possible by its special relationship with the Bank in particular, has, quite within the bounds of compliance, allowed it to sidestep Bank and IMF advice in specific areas and to pursue its priority of growth over more equitable development. While the results in terms of GDP have been impressive, the outcome in terms of overall human well-being has been less so, as both Bank and IMF reports have made clear. By contrast, when China was not yet at a stage where it could comply with IMF requirements for capital account convertibility, it remained protected from the capital flight that, in 1997, so devastated the human security of those Asian states that had complied. Human security, in other words, is not necessarily synonymous with compliance.

While China has complied with its mandatory obligations overall, its *cooperation* with this regime has been questionable. Although it has begun to participate in the GDDS, and to evince an interest in voluntary arrangements such as the Fund's Financial Sector Assessment Program, its very emphasis on legality makes it slow to accept such non-mandatory undertakings. It has also avoided obligations with the strings of conditionality attached. It prefers to adhere almost exclusively to the letter of the law, rather than to develop its institutional relationships in a cooperative manner according to the spirit of membership and the object and purpose of the Articles of Agreement. To that extent, although it has accepted many of the costs of membership, it has not yet accepted the sovereignty constraints entailed in full integration into the Bank and Fund. Significantly, for all their recognition of China's significant progress, IMF Directors continue to press China on its inadequate levels of transparency and its reluctance to submit to voluntary constraints on its activities.

Some may argue that China's full integration into both organizations is bound to occur with the passage of time: but its ongoing, historical attachment to the reciprocal interpretation of sovereignty and, to a lesser extent, the principle of self-reliance in its relations with both organizations, suggest that, in some specific areas, it is still only prepared to sacrifice its sovereignty within them when its sovereign interests demand it. On the other hand, critics of both the IMF and the World Bank applaud China's independence in areas such as financial deregulation, and argue that had it been more compliant with Fund and Bank requirements, its economy could well have suffered the same fate as that of other member states in the Asia-Pacific region.[207] In the process of "owning" its own projects and deliberately adopting an independent and gradualist approach to development, such critics argue, China has not only assisted its own economy, but has steered both the Bank and Fund in new and timely policy directions.

4

China and the Atmospheric Environment
The United Nations Environment Programme

The contribution made by the United Nations Environment
Programme towards the protection of the ozone layer constitutes
a magnificent feat of mankind in modern times, which is comparable
to the daring act of Nu Wa who "mended the sky" for the benefit
of mankind. The significant progress and successes achieved by UNEP
in this field have proved that the international community has made
a correct choice in taking resolute actions in response to recognized
problems. Through this process, an outstanding model of North-
South cooperation has thus been created.

> *Qu Geping, "The Mending of the Sky by Present-Day Nu Wa—*
> *A Magnificent Feat of Our Time," 5 October 2000*

As the world's largest developing country and a major player in
environment protection, China is an important force in international
environment cooperation. We are deeply aware of the responsibilities
on our shoulders.

> *Premier Zhu Rongji, World Summit on*
> *Sustainable Development, Johannesburg, 3 September 2002*

The international environmental regime places pressure on all states to balance
their particular developmental goals against the greater good of global environmental sustainability. But, in China's case, the pressures and contradictions involved
in these dual responsibilities are more extreme, because both literally entail
national survival. The difference between the two goals is that whereas in China
economic development is a matter of immediate as well as long-term survival,
the urgency of problems of environmental survival appears to some of its policy-
makers, as it does to those in other states, to be less immediate. With a population of 1.3 billion people, or 22 percent of the world's population, but only 7
percent of its arable land, and an economy growing at an exponential rate, the
balance achieved between its economic development and environmental protection is critical, and not only for China. As a Chinese NGO has put it: "China's
choice on the environment will affect the future of the whole world."[1]

For that reason, international environmental treaties and organizations, in particular the United Nations Environment Programme (UNEP), are of great importance. They have introduced ideas of "sustainable development" into China's domestic policy agenda, persuaded its leaders to modify unfettered economic development and exploitation of natural resources, trained its environmental specialists, facilitated and financed the transfer of new technologies, and educated the Chinese public to become more environmentally sensitive. How great a difference they have made to China's environmental policies, how compliant and cooperative it has been, and why, are the subjects of this chapter. Conversely, in a regime where China is generally perceived as assuming the role of a "leader" of the developing world in environmental negotiations, its impact on the development of international environmental law is also evaluated.

The United Nations Environment Programme is a product both of its time and subject area. Established in January 1973, it was not conceived like the earlier Bretton Woods institutions, as a large operating agency that would administer its own programs, but as a catalyst and coordinator of environmental activities and programs within international organizations and member states. It has been called "the environmental conscience within the United Nations system."[2] While UNEP has permanent headquarters in Nairobi, Kenya, it is a horizontal organization whose diverse activities are administered by a variety of agencies and diffused through different geographical locations. It is conceived as "the leading global environment authority that sets the global environment agenda, that promotes the coherent implementation of the environmental dimension of sustainable development within the United Nations system and that serves as an authoritative advocate for the global environment."[3] It assists governments and the international community to identify global problems; builds consensus on viable solutions; sponsors the negotiation of environmental treaties; and, in partnership with governments, other UN bodies such as UNDP and UNIDO, and specialized agencies like the World Bank, as well as NGOs, encourages the implementation of protective measures by promoting international cooperation and the provision of technical and training assistance. Its specific functions include the initiation, negotiation, and supervision of global treaties governing ozone depletion, trade in hazardous waste, and biodiversity, and the establishment and implementation of the Regional Seas Programme, which is the subject of about thirty regional treaties. Through its involvement with the Intergovernmental Panel on Climate Change, organized jointly by UNEP and the World Meteorological Organization, it also assisted in the establishment of the UN Framework Convention on Climate Change (UNFCCC).

This chapter examines China's environmental compliance within the overall context of its relations with UNEP and, to a lesser extent, the World Bank.

Specifically, it focuses on China's policies on atmospheric pollution, in particular, the issue of ozone depletion. There has been no shortage of research on China and the atmospheric environment.[4] However, it has tended to emphasize the domestic dimensions of the regime, as it impacts on the process of foreign policy formation within China or on domestic policy outcomes.[5] While domestic policies are analyzed as important indices of domestic implementation, the chapter highlights China's interactions with international environmental organizations, and the long drawn out process leading to its gradual reconception of its interests, its increasing compliance with its obligations under international environmental law, and its internalization of environmental norms. It thereby further underlines the significance of process-based theories of compliance, stressing as they do the feedback effects of international organizational pressures upon domestic laws and policies.

The focus here on the ozone issue has been largely determined by its significance to the global community as well as to China, its centrality to UNEP, and its usefulness as a test case. The main instruments of the regime, the Vienna Convention for the Protection of the Ozone Layer and the Montreal Protocol on Substances That Deplete the Ozone Layer and its Amendments, are generally regarded, by practitioners and scholars alike, as among the more successful international environmental agreements.[6] The Montreal Protocol is notable for providing a formal compliance mechanism. In addition, both the Convention and its Protocol offer an instructive comparison with the related Framework Convention on Climate Change and the Kyoto Protocol, which address more complex and critical problems of global warming. As the largest emitter of ozone-depleting substances (ODS) and the second highest emitter, after the United States, of greenhouse gases in the world, China is an important subject of these atmospheric pollution instruments. However, while the Framework Convention came into effect some time ago, the Kyoto Protocol has only recently done so. The ozone treaties therefore provide a useful comparison with the climate change treaties and an example against which to measure the effectiveness of different incentive and compliance mechanisms.[7] They also provide a unique perspective from which to view the China-UNEP relationship.

The importance of China's involvement in the global regulation of the atmospheric environment is highlighted by the dramatic increase that has occurred in its contribution to ozone depletion and global warming. By 1995, China had become the world's largest ODS producer and consumer. By contrast, its contribution to global warming was initially minimal, by comparison with major offenders. By 1991, however, its contributions had risen to roughly 10 percent of the world's total (coming third after the USA and the USSR, at 23.7 percent and 18.6 percent respectively),[8] even though, with a population of 1.3 billion, its emissions per head were just over one-tenth those of the United States. According to calculations in this period, if no other state raised its emissions, and China raised its per capita emissions to half the U.S. level, total world emissions would have risen by about 40 percent.[9] By 2002, China had graduated to the position of the world's second largest emitter of greenhouse gases.

In the atmospheric environment, as in other environmental areas, China sees its interests as closely aligned with those of other developing states. Like them, it sees itself as trapped in the modernization time lag: it is seeking to modernize its economy and to expand its industrial production just as the developed world is calling for limits on the manner of development. Therefore, while acknowledging the need for environmental protection, particularly in areas such as desertification and air quality, since the early 1990s it has taken a proactive role in shaping international environmental law in a direction requiring the developed world to take greater initial responsibility and to provide financial and technical assistance to developing countries to enable them to contribute to protection over time.

Establishment and Administration of UNEP

Although the nineteenth century saw efforts to regulate the international environment, and although the "greening" of international law was ushered in by the United Nations, the World Meteorological Organization (WMO), the World Health Organization (WHO), and the Food and Agriculture Organization (FAO), the development of environmental organization was piecemeal and uncoordinated until the 1970s. This decade witnessed the establishment of a specialist environmental institution, the proliferation of treaties and soft-law instruments, a body of state practice, and the increasing involvement of developing states.[10]

UNEP, established in 1973, was the product of a growing international concern about the environment from the late 1960s, and of a realization that the existing institutional mechanisms for coping with the problems of population growth, radioactive contamination, the dispersal of toxic substances, and damage to forests and marine environments were inadequate. At the initiative of Sweden, the twenty-third session of the UN General Assembly held in 1968 decided to convene a United Nations Conference on the Environment in Stockholm in 1972. Since none of the existing UN agencies was prepared to shoulder principal responsibility for implementing the plan of action and recommendations adopted at the Conference, UNGA subsequently established UNEP as the specialist agency for environmental activities in the UN system, reporting to UNGA through the Economic and Social Council (ECOSOC).[11] A Governing Council, comprising fifty-eight members elected by the General

Assembly for a four-year term, was established to carry out its work.[12] It also set up an Environment Fund. However, to avoid overlap with the responsibilities already shouldered by other international organizations, UNEP's role was largely limited to the initiation of treaties and the coordination of environmental activities. The devolution of environmental responsibility occurring as a result of the early piecemeal approach, the complex nature of environmental problems, and the late arrival of a modest organization operating on an annual budget of less than US$40 million into a world of already powerful international institutions, gave rise to some of the problems of jurisdiction, authority, and enforcement with which UNEP would be required to wrestle.[13]

These problems were, and remain, forbidding. Today, international organizations, NGOs, and individual scholars exert an important impact on this regime, despite their potential intrusion into the domestic jurisdiction of states, and the peculiar nature of the issue. Nevertheless, many of the instruments regulating the protection of the environment are not binding, and are not enforceable by any international body. The apparent absence of an initial presumption in favor of protecting the environment is partly because the right to a clean environment is seen by some not as an individual right but as a generational right.[14] International environmental law also challenges many core concepts of traditional international law. In the words of one authority, "it puts new limits on State sovereignty, it intrudes into the domestic jurisdiction and territorial integrity of States, it creates greater responsibilities for States and it involves many non-State entities in the process of international law."[15]

UNEP is unique in other ways. Its physical location in Nairobi rather than Geneva and the harmonious, African-inspired design of its buildings were aimed as a gesture to both the environment and developing states.[16] The initial controversy over its siting highlighted the primary political division in this regime between developed and developing states. Thus, "its creation was at best somewhat half-hearted—reflecting on the one hand a lack of conviction on the part of the most powerful decision makers about the urgency of environmental issues . . . and, on the other, the opposition of certain less-developed states that perceived a direct contradiction between the then emerging environmental demands and the requirements of rapid development."[17]

In line with its initial mandate, UNEP's major activities in the development and implementation of international legal instruments were focused on the Convention on Biological Diversity; the Basel Convention (Transboundary Movement of Hazardous Wastes and Their Disposal); the Convention on the Conservation of Migratory Species of Wild Animals (CMS); the Convention on International Trade in Endangered Species of Wild Fauna and Flora (CITES); and the coordination of secretariats of environmental conventions.[18] Within the context of the ozone protection regime, UNEP also sponsored a policy meeting of governments and international agencies, which drafted a World Plan of Action on the Ozone Layer. This led to the adoption of the 1985 Vienna Convention and, in 1987, to the Montreal Protocol. With its modest resources, UNEP also operated a "remarkably varied and important set of programmes."[19] Like the World Bank, UNEP's role evolved, expanded, and occasionally contracted over time, as it met new challenges.

Despite this expansion of its portfolio, developing states were initially suspicious that UNEP was too focused on the environmental concerns of developed states, such as ozone pollution and climate change, rather than on issues such as desertification, land erosion, and the challenges of economic development.[20] Later, developed states became concerned that UNEP was too close to developing states and too unwilling to criticize them. In addition, while the effectiveness of UNEP as a catalyst of atmospheric environmental action was recognized, its inability to receive and comment on complaints of member states and to create binding environmental standards was seen as a weakness.[21] By the 1990s, this had provoked the UN General Assembly to leapfrog over UNEP to vest responsibility for climate change negotiations in a special negotiating committee, and to create a new body, the Intergovernmental Panel on Climate Change (IPCC), to implement the Earth Summit's *Agenda 21*, to investigate climate change, and to issue ongoing reports and recommendations on mitigation.

Subsequently, debate raged over UNEP's role. This was partly because of the communications and security problems at Nairobi and the decision to locate the secretariats of the subsequent Rio conventions elsewhere.[22] The nineteenth session of UNEP's Governing Council in 1997 nevertheless adopted the Nairobi Declaration on the Role and Mandate of UNEP, which identified it as the principal UN body in the field of the environment and as an authoritative advocate for the global environment. At the twentieth session, the appointment of Klaus Topfer as Executive Director confirmed the revival of UNEP's fortunes.[23] Yet, the demands of the expanding environmental regime continued to raise questions about institutional restructuring. Prior to the World Summit on Sustainable Development (WSSD) in August 2002, UNEP's Intergovernmental Working Group on International Environment Governance (IEG) discussed whether this reform should be achieved by establishing a World Environment Organization or by enhancing UNEP's powers to make it a specialized or a centralized UN agency.[24]

China's Entry

Because its relations with UNEP dated from the latter's formative years, China was able to have a greater impact on both the organization and its associated treaties than was the case with other bodies examined here. This impact was, moreover, shaped by China's tendency to emphasize its identity as a developing state, and the circumstance that, at the time of its entry into the UN, it was still governed by a Stalinist ideology exalting heavy industry, in the context of which its environmental sympathies were at a discount.[25] China's awareness of the potential conflict between environmental protection and a state's freedom to develop, in short, prompted it to seek to shape international environmental law in ways which protected the interests of the South.

China's position was reflected in the support of its small delegation to the Stockholm Conference for the Indian view that poverty was the greatest polluter. It also supported the initial proclamation in the Draft Declaration that "in the developing countries most of the environmental problems were caused by underdevelopment." However, its position was not just a passive one. It also took a leadership role, requesting the conference to set up an ad hoc committee to discuss the draft, which it criticized for failing to acknowledge that "the major social root cause of environmental pollution is the policies of plunder, aggression and war pursued by imperialism, colonialism and neocolonialism and in particular the superpowers."[26] A spokesman for the Chinese delegation itemized ten main principles to be considered in revising the Draft Declaration. These were: the need to distinguish between the environmental responsibility of developed and developing states; the need for a more optimistic view of the relationship between population growth and environment conservation; the need to emphasize the close relationship between war and the environment; the need to recognize the social causes of environmental pollution; the right of states to exploit as well as protect their own natural resources; the need for domestic measures to fight pollution; the right to compensation for international pollution; the need for international exchanges in scientific and technical knowledge on environment conservation; the necessity of establishing an international environment fund; and the need for widespread cooperation in the conservation of the human environment. In the articulation of all these needs, a subtext was the importance of respecting state sovereignty.[27] The statement at once set the pattern for China's future involvement in the environmental regime and highlighted its profound ambivalence about the norms of environmental protection. While still harboring "grave reservations" about the final text of the Declaration, China also did not participate when the final vote was taken on it.[28] However, no country opposed the Declaration's adoption.

Following the Stockholm Conference, and despite its lack of sympathy with environmental norms at the time, China joined UNEP in 1973, and was elected a member of its Governing Council in the same year by the UN General Assembly. Having argued vociferously at Stockholm in defense of the positions

fully entrenched in China's legal system, the practice of torture in China will remain systemic.

Because their norms represent peculiar obstacles to China's integration into the international community, the ILO and CAT may be understood as institutions that would be least likely to engender its compliance. China's refusal to fully legislate for, and practically implement, the right to freedom of association and the prohibition against torture is an indication of its unwillingness to give up the practices of coercive control that have their origins in Chinese history and tradition. These human rights that, as will be seen, also have critical synergies, thus represent the promise for China's future that is currently blocked by its past. China's implementation of such norms in its domestic legislation, institutions, and, most importantly, its social practice, would be a powerful indicator of its international socialization, its preparedness to renegotiate its sovereignty, and its determination to become a modernized economy underpinned by a genuine rule of law. Currently, however, whatever its formal declaratory policy, China regards the norms and principles of both the ILO and the CAT as diametrically opposed to its national and sovereign interests.

This chapter examines how China has related to these bodies, whether and to what extent it has complied with their rules, principles, and procedures, and why. These are questions fundamental to an understanding not only of its attitude to human rights, but of its responsiveness to different compliance mechanisms and its preparedness to weather what it conceives as assaults on its national sovereignty for the sake of international cooperation.[10] Such questions provide a critical test of the validity of process-based compliance theories. The case studies that follow demonstrate, on the one hand, the latter's impressive explanatory power and, on the other, the outer limits of organizational process in influencing the compliance of an authoritarian "least-likely" state.

The International Labour Organization

In June 1926, five years after its establishment, the ILO moved into the historic building, now known as Centre William Rappard, built for it below the Palais des Nations and on the shores of Lake Geneva. Almost half a century later, in November 1974, it transferred to a more modern, capacious building, this time overlooking the UN. This distancing and elevation reflected the considerable lineage and standing of the ILO which, notwithstanding its formal position as a UN specialized agency, was not prepared to subsume its identity under that of the UN, which was seen as a more recent, and sometimes competing, institution. The impersonal appearance of the International Labour Office, with its lofty, semi-industrial, gray facade, is only somewhat offset by the bronze statues of workers, gifts of the government of Belgium in 1925 and other states in the 1930s and

1940s, in the surrounding gardens. Nevertheless, unlike the UN proper, the World Bank, and the IMF, which are closely guarded and security-conscious institutions, the ILO is distinguished by a more relaxed bureaucratic culture, a greater physical openness, and an accessibility to visitors of all kinds. While it is not as available as the United Nations to nonoccupational NGOs, its tripartite system of representatives of governments, employers, and employees is "unique, providing for the full participation of non-governmental occupational organizations in all ILO deliberative bodies and activities, as well as in the drafting of ILO conventions and recommendations and in their implementation."[11]

From the beginning, the ILO's primary focus has been freedom of association, the right of collective bargaining, discrimination in the work place, and the expansion of welfare programs.[12] It is involved in the formulation of international labor standards; the dissemination of cross-national statistics and information on working conditions; technical assistance; and promotional and educational activities.[13] Standards are provided by conventions drawn up by annual sessions of the International Labour Conference and by recommendations that are not legally binding but offer important policy guidelines. Once it ratifies a convention, a state party is required to enact and implement the convention's provisions. As of 2006, 185 conventions had been adopted. However, ILO standard setting was originally applied to pluralist democracies whose labor was politically organized.[14] By contrast, the lack of independence of the worker and employer representatives in communist states like China has presented obstacles to ILO effectiveness.[15]

As the primary principle of the ILO and a major supervisory responsibility of its Governing Body, the right to freedom of association is seen to include a number of principles: the right of all workers and employers to establish organizations that are freely administered; the right of organizations not to be suspended or dissolved; protection against discrimination; the right to collective bargaining; the right to strike; and the right to exercise basic civil rights.[16] The ILO's provisions for freedom of association, as contained in Convention No. 87, consist of a number of articles, of which Article 2 states: "Workers and employers, without distinction whatsoever, shall have the right to establish and, subject only to the rules of the organization concerned, to join organizations of *their own choosing without previous authorisation.*"[17] Worker and employer organizations are seen by the ILO to require specific protection because

> if trade unions have acquired considerable influence in some developed countries, in most of the developing world they remain subject to manipulation and exploitation by governments and by employers. Their leaders are often the subject of arrest and imprisonment, torture and exile. Employers' organizations can also be subject to brutal repression.[18]

ILO monitoring is based on dialogue and persuasion, underpinned by the principles of transparency, continuous improvement, reciprocity, and modeling, the last of which has become more important with the introduction of the Declaration on Fundamental Principles and Rights at Work in 1999. The organization has avoided the dualism afflicting UN human rights bodies between civil/political and economic/social/cultural rights, viewing freedom of association as both a civil right and an economic right. Its procedure for the adoption of conventions has been reportedly more systematic, and its supervisory procedures have been judged to be more effective.[19]

The ILO's main monitoring procedure, like that of other international human rights organs, is based upon reports by states on their compliance with norms they have accepted in the conventions. These reports are made by national governments, but employer and worker organizations are entitled to make written observations that are examined together with the government's reports.[20] A state is not obliged to implement a convention it has not ratified. However, the ILO Constitution (Article 19, Paragraph 5) requests states members to submit unratified conventions to their national "competent authorities" (normally the legislature) for enactment of legislation or other action, and to report on means taken, or contemplated, to give effect to the convention. Nonratified conventions at the very least provide standards for the state and its citizens to aspire to. Conventions and recommendations thus form a kind of "international common law."[21]

The ILO Governing Body Committee on Freedom of Association (CFA), established in 1951, monitors states' implementation of that principle.[22] On the basis of the claim of the ILO Constitution and the appended Declaration of Philadelphia (1944), it has successfully established that all ILO members are subject to its jurisdiction even without the ratification of the relevant conventions, the Freedom of Association and Protection of the Right to Organize Convention (No. 87, 1948), and the Right to Organize and Collective Bargaining Convention (No. 98, 1949). The CFA is a nine-member tripartite committee with nine alternates and an independent chair that reaches its decisions by consensus. It meets three times a year before each session of the ILO Governing Body. It is made up of elected members of the Governing Body, which in turn is authorized to reject or amend Committee findings.[23] Complaints by individuals are not admissible, but they may be submitted to the CFA by workers' or employers' organizations, such as the International Council of Free Trade Unions (ICFTU), or by governments. Complaints are then communicated to the government concerned, which is invited to comment.[24]

Other monitoring mechanisms include constitutional complaints procedures, commissions of inquiry, and "direct contacts." The first two procedures have rarely been used.[25] "Direct contacts" are short, personal visits by ILO officials or an independent person named by the Director-General to ILO member states to resolve problems in the implementation of a ratified convention or other ILO member responsibilities.[26] Because they require the prior consent of the state concerned, they are often seen as the solution of last resort.

China and the ILO before June 1989

In contrast to the delicate coordination required for China's entry into the World Bank and the IMF, and its swift integration into UNEP, China's entry into the ILO was smoothed by the ILO's own initiatives in 1971, but did not become effective for another decade.[27] "China" had been a founding member of the ILO in 1919 and had been elected to the ILO Governing Body in 1934.[28] Before 1949, the ROC had ratified all applicable conventions passed by the annual Conference.[29] After the establishment of the People's Republic in 1949, the ILO, like the UN, chose to validate the credentials of Taiwan.[30] Socialist states in particular regularly challenged those credentials. Once the UN had restored the rights of the People's Republic to the China seat in October 1971, the Director-General placed the question of its ILO entry before the 184th session of the Governing Body, in its role as titular head of the ILO between conferences. Some states, in particular the United States, urged that Resolution 2758 be referred to the Conference at its 1972 session, whereas the Workers' Group, together with socialist and developing states, upheld the competence of the Governing Body. The Governing Body then adopted, by thirty-six votes to three with eight abstentions, a decision as proposed by the Worker's Group, to recognize the government of the People's Republic of China as the official representative government of China.

The Governing Body decision was taken without knowing whether China had the desire or ability to assume the obligations of membership. In fact, not only did China not understand its obligations, it was more than ten years before it began to fully participate in the work of the organization and to contribute financially. This was partly because the destruction of the trade union movement in China during the Cultural Revolution made it difficult to apply the ILO rules of tripartism to China. It was also because, as in the United Nations proper, China declared that it needed time to increase its understanding of the ILO.[31] To some extent, the reason was also ideological: at that point in its history, China saw the relationship between workers and employers as necessarily an oppositional rather than a cooperative one.[32] It regarded ILO standards as too Western to be relevant to a developing socialist country. As Feng Chen has observed, "it was assumed that in a socialist society, where labor was no longer pitted against capital and workers were presumably represented by the 'workers' state, unions' original purpose of representing and defending labor interests was essentially redundant."[33] China thus became a nonactive member (*buhuodong chengyuanguo*).[34]

This situation changed when the ILO's Director-General, Francis Blanchard, sought to bring China into the fold as a fully functioning member.[35] Apart from the value of involving a large and powerful state, he believed that it was preferable to deal with China as an ILO member, subject to the ILO Constitution, rather than to allow it to remain outside the organization.[36] He thus subscribed to a "process-based" compliance approach. Between 1980 and 1982, Blanchard visited China three times to discuss the issue with the government, and in June 1983 China sent its first post-1949 delegation to the sixty-ninth session of the International Labour Conference.[37] At this session, the Conference made a "substantial gesture" by canceling the accrued debt representing China's statutory contribution due since 16 November 1971 (US$37,220,652) and the arrears owed by Taiwan (US$1,624,059).[38]

This decision, based on a Governing Body proposal, was reached in response to China's request to the Director-General that it be relieved of obligations decided unilaterally at a time when it was not taking part in the work of the organization.[39] It was clearly made as a concession to China on the understanding that the case would not constitute a precedent that might be used by others to justify the cancellation of other arrears.

Despite China's formal participation in ILO activities after 1983, it was not until 1986–87 that Premier Zhao Ziyang encouraged a more assertive role in the organization.[40] By this stage, China was thoroughly launched on the restructuring of its economy, a painful process that introduced unprecedented tensions into the relations between state, labor, and management. In this period, it also joined other human rights bodies and ratified the Convention against Torture. In the ILO, it aspired to greater organizational power, whether in the ILO Governing Body or in positions in the committees, and sought increased technical assistance.[41] It took particular interest in ILO meetings and conferences relating to the elimination of racism, the promotion of employment and social security, and the protection of the environment, and increased its participation in ILO activities in the Asian region.[42]

Thereafter, China developed a complicated relationship with the ILO. Still nominally a "workers' state," it has been concerned to maintain its reputation as a compliant and cooperative member.[43] On the other hand, its leaders have been sensitive to the impact industrial rights might have on the consciousness of a vast workforce that, as a result of the 1997 decision to rationalize state-owned enterprises (SOEs), has been radically downsized.[44] For its part, the ILO has benefited from an enhanced legitimacy conferred by China's participation, but has had to maintain a delicate balance between the promotion of Chinese work-ers' interests and the continuation of China's particular role in the organization.

Notwithstanding the importance of the Chinese Foreign Ministry's role, the formal responsibility for China's ILO policy was undertaken by two divisions in the Ministry of Labor's Department of Foreign Affairs, the Division of ILO and the Division of Technical Cooperation.[45] As a gesture to ILO tripartism, regarded as the key to the management of conflict between the state, labor, and management, the All-China Federation of Trade Unions (ACFTU) also played a role, its Secretary, Fang Jiade, becoming Chinese worker representative on the ILO Governing Body. However, despite the radical shift in China's labor rela-tions during the 1980s, the governmental and unitary character of the ACFTU, the single body responsible for all union matters in China affiliated with the Chinese Communist Party (CCP), did not change. Its organization was incom-patible with genuine tripartism, and only compounded the contradiction between acting on behalf of the state and representing workers' interests.[46] Key officials were appointed by the Communist Party, while the higher organs dic-tated the appointments, functions, and powers of lower-level ACFTU bodies.[47] Thus, ACFTU directives to all its subordinate unions in 1990 and 1995 required that "unions at all levels should maintain a high degree of unanimity with the Party politically, in ideas and actions."[48] Chinese workers were thereby effectively denied freedom of association, in the sense of both the right to orga-nize and join trade unions of their choice without previous authorization, and the freedom to organize their unions independently of Communist Party con-trol. After 1989, this incompatibility was the source of the debate between the Chinese government, the ILO Governing Body CFA, and the ICFTU.

Like many other Asian states, China was from the beginning more attuned to the benefits of technical cooperation than to ILO standards. At an ILO Asian-Pacific Symposium on Standards-Related Topics in New Delhi, from 14 to 17 March 1989, Guan Jinghe claimed China's extenuating circumstances in rela-tion to labor standards: "Since China is a large country and only officials respon-sible for handling standards-related matters from departments concerned in the Ministry of Labour grasp the significance of labor standards, it is not possible to meet with the requirement of extensive application of ILO Conventions and Recommendations."[49] China's indifference to standards was reflected in its rati-fication of only a small number of the ILO's 185 conventions. Initially, as an asser-tion of sovereignty, the Chinese Foreign Minister, Wu Xueqian, had notified the ILO in 1984 that, although China would continue to recognize all fourteen con-ventions ratified prior to 1 October 1949, it would abrogate all of the twenty-three conventions subsequently ratified by Taiwan in the name of China.[50] By January 2006, it had ratified only twenty-three, all but nine before 1949, with twenty still in force.[51] In terms of important standards, the number was judged by ILO officials to be extremely small. ILO technical cooperation with China was also relatively restricted given the country's size and importance.[52] Like other states, China was required to report to the ILO on its implementation of the conventions it ratified. Yet, because it did not ratify Conventions 87 and 98, it reportedly assumed that freedom of association standards did not apply to it.

In theory, the government did not reject the fundamental principle of the right to freedom of association, the basic norm of the ILO Governing Body CFA, which monitored Chinese workers' human rights after June 1989. As it insisted, this freedom was guaranteed by the Chinese Constitution. In fact, however, it failed even to declare its support for this critical right. Legal provisions for the right of workers to form and join trade unions were offset by the requirement that this activity should be carried out "according to law." They ignored the key requirement that the unions should be "of their own choosing" and established "without previous authorisation." In effect, China did not even acknowledge the substantive content of the norm in theory.

Before 1989, China's official trade union maintained close contacts with the ICFTU, the world trade union organization enjoying consultative status with the ILO. Established in 1949 in London by seventy trade unions in fifty-three countries, and subsequently based in Brussels, the ICFTU also had a regional organization, the ICFTU Asian and Pacific Regional Organization (APRO).[53] Between 1984 and 1989, almost all national trade unions had also visited Beijing. Prior to the events in Tiananmen, the unitary Chinese trade union was reportedly attempting to address the issue of grievances in the workplace, but not worker participation.[54]

China and the ILO, June 1989–2004

Chinese government suppression of China's Democracy Movement in June 1989 initially jeopardized the ILO's relationship with China and set back the latter's integration into the organization.[55] It also prompted the first strong ILO pressures on China. The presence in Tiananmen Square of the Workers Autonomous Federation (WAF), together with the support and donations given to students and hunger strikers even by the official ACFTU, represented the Chinese government's worst nightmare, the possibility of a merger between students and workers following the model of Poland's Solidarity movement. WAF organizers distributed leaflets criticizing the existing labor policies and the official union structure. Their grievances included the lack of workplace democracy, the lack of genuine worker participation, the wide wage discrepancy between workers and plant managers, poor labor protection and working conditions, and the decline in workers' living standards. At the same time, workers insisted that they wished to organize the WAF according to constitutional means and that they did not oppose the rule of the CCP. By the height of the movement in Beijing, one hundred thousand workers from the manufacturing, service, and building industries, as well as worker intellectuals, from Beijing, the northeast, Tianjin, Shanxi, Jiangsu, Hebei, and Hunan had enrolled in the Beijing federation. During the June crackdown, workers who had attempted to halt the army's advance, and the WAF camp on the northwest side of the square, were attacked. Those people subsequently executed for their involvement in the movement, albeit also charged with acts of physical opposition and destruction, were almost all workers.

The killing or injury of large numbers of workers throughout China during and after the early June events, and the deliberate government attack on the WAF tents in Tiananmen Square on 3–4 June were subsequently deemed by the ILO to be in contravention not only of the basic tenets of freedom of association but also of the ILO Constitution.[56] The June crackdown precipitated a period in which the ILO applied universal standards to China and China began slowly to realize the costs as well as the benefits of organizational participation. The organization drew a fine line in its policies between displays of disapproval to indicate that it was "not business as usual," and avoidance of action that would undermine the fundamental interests of Chinese workers. Existing programs of technical assistance continued, but no new ones were introduced until the CFA had examined the problem. After June 1989, following a ruling that there were to be no further dealings with the government, the Director-General had to personally screen any application for technical assistance to China. However, since real workers were not well represented, it was difficult to determine who was who and to know which activities were *not* governmental.[57] ILO training programs continued in the south of China, because the Director-General believed that they were in the interests of Chinese citizens.

Although technically it would have been possible for the ILO to respond to the crackdown with a fact-finding Commission of Inquiry, the Director-General himself reportedly overruled such an approach.[58] Moreover, although the Chinese government might have given its permission for direct contact, it was decided not to request it, since there were no independent trade unions in China that could have acted as interlocutors against the government's claims.[59] As a result, the ICFTU decided to bring its complaint through the CFA procedure, which in the past had been applied to many other states that had not ratified the relevant conventions.

The first case against China, Case No. 1500, was brought by the ILO Governing Body CFA in response to ICFTU complaints on 19 June, 22 June, and 20 July 1989. The Chinese government was required to supply detailed information in response to allegations of human rights abuses on 3–4 June and after, particularly in respect of the treatment of leaders and members of the WAF set up during the course of the Democracy Movement. At the same time, the ICFTU broke off contacts with the ACFTU. Following the ICFTU decision not to support him, at the June 1990 conference, the Chinese ACFTU member on the ILO Governing Body was not reelected.

When the ICFTU registered its complaints against the Chinese government in June and July 1989, Chinese officials reacted with indignation.[60] Only at the time of the complaints did they realize that all ILO member states were bound by the provisions of Conventions 87 and 98, whether or not they had ratified them. To the surprise of members of the CFA, Chinese officials constantly challenged the procedures of the inquiry and reportedly attempted to influence the Secretariat at all levels.[61] For its part, the committee attempted to persuade the Chinese Mission to comply with its requirements. The Chairman of the Governing Body, Douglas Poulter, reasoned with Chinese officials that to reject CFA monitoring could be regarded as a direct attack on the Governing Body, making it difficult for China to remain within the ILO.[62] Particularly unacceptable to ILO officials was China's claim to the right to noninterference.[63]

In response to CFA Case No. 1500, China initially denied that it was bound by ILO norms and procedures.[64] Between October 1990 and March 1992, however, it supplied information requested by the Committee while formally rejecting outside interference, and thereafter complied with the ILO's procedural requirements without protest. The process of interaction with the Committee, which repeatedly insisted on conformity to its guidelines, finally convinced China that noncompliance was more destructive of its reputation and sovereignty than cooperation. On the other hand, it could not comply substantively, since it was not yet willing to accept the full meaning of the standard of freedom of association.

Soon after the completion of Case No. 1500, a second CFA case on China, No. 1652, was prompted by a further ICFTU complaint. This focused on issues arising from China's new Trade Union Law of 3 April 1992, and examined the more general problems of a unitary trade union, as well as seeking to curtail the ongoing repression of the underground free trade union movement. The principal objections of the ICFTU and CFA to the new Trade Union Law were that it demonstrated China's "utter disregard for the principle of freedom of association"; it denied unions the right to formulate their own programs; it required local unions to be under the control of the ACFTU and the Chinese Communist Party (CCP); and it prevented local unions from acquiring legal personality unless approved by the ACFTU. Yet, from the Chinese perspective, the Trade Union Act brought some progress. It allowed the establishment of basic level union committees by a minimum of twenty-five members of an enterprise or organization, expanded trade union powers, and empowered labor unions to assume the role of mediators in labor disputes within enterprises.[65] It also prohibited antiunion discrimination and was still more progressive in requiring union participation in joint enterprises and wholly foreign-owned enterprises.[66]

Although initially resurrecting its noninterference claims, in Case No. 1652 China moved more quickly toward compliance with its reporting obligations. It also supplied information on the workers for whom the CFA had requested follow-up. However, it did not implement Committee recommendations that it amend the Trade Union Act of 1992 to conform with the right to freedom of association and that it release labor activists imprisoned because of their involvement in the 1989 Democracy Movement.

By 1994, China's disinterest in ILO standards had become an obstacle to its organizational ambitions. In addition to losing its representation on the ILO Governing Body in 1990, its continuing opposition to freedom of association precluded its candidature when the Governing Body's chairmanship rotated to the Asian Group in 1994.[67] In a more positive sense, the consistency of CFA procedures, the relatively fixed process of the examination and the Committee's faithfulness to its body of case law, clearly impressed Chinese authorities.[68] Moreover, China's relationship with the ILO was complex. Although the CFA examination subjected China to a grueling challenge that affected its status within the ILO, this did not inhibit the relationship in all areas. As domestic labor unrest increased, ILO standards provided China with some convenient ideas for resolving industrial disputes.[69] Consequently, by 1994, there were indications of greater Chinese cooperation at the international level, not only in Case No. 1652, but with respect to other ILO standards. Appearing before the Committee on the Application of Standards during the International Labour Conference in June 1994, China's representative expressed renewed interest in those standards, which required "more emphasis on the role of labor legislation in protecting the basic rights of workers."[70] This and other statements revealed the shift in China's attitude since Guan Jinghe's disclaimer in 1989 of its ability to comply.[71]

Legislative and Institutional Implementation

China's new declaratory policy on ILO standards foreshadowed norm internalization at the domestic legislative level. The new Labor Law of the People's Republic of China, promulgated on 5 July 1994 and effective from 1 January 1995, contained no guarantee of the right to strike or the right of workers to form and join the trade union of their own choosing and without prior authorization, as ILO Convention 87 stipulated. However, Article 7 of the new law provided that "trade unions shall represent and safeguard the legitimate rights and interests of laborers, and independently conduct their activities in accordance with the law" (*duli zizhu de kaizhan huodong*).Article 8 also provided that workers shall "take part in democratic management or consult with the employing units on an equal footing about protection of the legitimate rights and interests of laborers."The new law also foreshadowed the development of collective bargaining, accepted the principle of tripartism, and endorsed a list of workers' rights, including "the right to be employed on an equal basis and choose one's occupation." Furthermore, it required the state to "formulate labor standards."[72] For the first time, it also contained a list of penalties in the form of fines, compensation to workers, revocation of business licenses, and criminal liability for violations of its provisions.[73] These provisions indicated selective legislative internalization of some ILO standards.

However, while this law reflected the government's recognition that the new market-oriented economy necessitated special protection of workers' rights, it also provided guidelines for the expansion of the scope of labor contracts to all workers and a range of procedures for dismissals, layoffs, and resignations.[74] It also reiterated the Trade Union Law's position that it was the state's right to guide labor relations, rather than its obligation to facilitate worker independence.And, as the CFA noted, it restricted the freedom of workers and employers when bargaining collectively, and "appear[ed] to codify exactly the same type of mediation and arbitration system as the regulations which the Committee had previously criticised," thereby undermining the right to strike.[75] That is, while paying lip service to workers' rights, it "entrench[ed] the Party-dominated labor union system as the basic mechanism for enforcing workers' rights."[76]

In contrast to the lack of laws empowering workers, legislation was introduced that sought to address their day-to-day conditions and safety, particularly in joint ventures with foreigners.This included Regulations Concerning Minimum Wages in Enterprises (24 November 1993); Regulations on Unemployment Insurance for Staff and Workers of State-Owned Enterprises (4 December 1993); Regulations on the Administration of Labor in Foreign-Invested Enterprises (11 August 1994); Notice Regarding Further Improvement of the Work of Poverty Relief and the Reemployment of Workers (1997); Standards for Examining and Verifying the Vocational Safety and Health Management System (20 December 2001); Measures on the Control over National Occupational Health Standards (1 May 2002); and the Law of the People's Republic of China on Work Safety (1 November 2002).[77]

The institutionalization of ILO norms was partly assisted by the establishment of a small ILO branch in Beijing in 1985.[78] Staffed by a Director, Deputy Director (a former Chinese Ministry of Labor official), and three to four program officers and support staff, its primary task was to represent the ILO in Mongolia, Hong Kong, Macao, and China. Most of its activities emphasized tripartism, with the Ministry of Labor and Social Security representing the government, the ACFTU representing workers, and the employers represented by China Enterprise Confederations. In May 2001, the ILO Director-General also signed a Memorandum of Understanding with China.[79] Its four strategic areas of basic international labor standards, employment promotion, labor market, and social dialogue established a framework of technical cooperation and advisory services. In this way, external organizational pressures were physically internalized. Much effort was expended on employment promotion, social security reform, work injuries, maternal care, unemployment, HIV/AIDS, and medical insurance. In these activities the ILO also liaised with the World Bank and the Asian Development Bank.[80] In addition, in November 2001, the ACFTU established a special department dealing with occupational safety, health, and industrial relations. However, as long as the ACFTU continued to dominate China's industrial relations, it was difficult to institutionalize those core ILO norms that, by virtue of its very rules and structure, the unitary Chinese union was breaching.

Compliance and Cooperation

For all China's legislative and institutional reforms, it exhibited little compliance with core international standards at the domestic level of practical implementation, whether political or social. The marked increase in managerial autonomy within the enterprise, a decline in authority of the official union, and an unclear relationship between the labor contract system and the contract responsibility system were at the source of this weak implementation, as was the "blurred line between the local governments and businesses [which] creates an environment where those designated as the protectors of labor are either intimately connected with or even the same as those who are violating workers' rights."[81] The weakness of worker organization and the effective domination of workers by both the state and the market were other contributing causes.[82]

International NGOs and scholars also perceived a widening gap between China's legislative and practical implementation of labor standards, reflected in government efforts to suppress labor activists, chronically poor labor conditions, and a mounting number of labor disputes.[83] The difficulties of seeking remedies through the courts left workers with few protections, forcing them into more public action.[84] By 2002, industrial unrest and demonstrations had exploded throughout Daqing and the provinces of Sichuan, Hunan, Hubei, and Liaoning, although they were also quickly suppressed.[85] The protests, most of them directed against state-owned enterprises (SOEs), were usually responses to actual or feared job losses, wage or benefit arrears, or allegations of management corruption. Labor disputes, which could be anything from a wage conflict to a full strike, represented another potent indicator of dissatisfaction. From 1992 to 1999, the number of registered disputes in a year increased fourteen times to over 120,000. Thus, in 1995, 32,000 labor disputes were officially registered; in 1997, 97,000 were registered; in 1999, 127,000; and in 2001, 154,621.[86] By late 2005, the number of disputes was estimated by an independent source at some 300,000 a year.[87] Since other cases were not heard and not officially registered, the actual number was probably even higher.[88] In addition, despite a new work safety law enacted in 2002, in September 2003 alone accidents took the lives of 11,449 workers, particularly in the coal industry, an increase of 9 percent over September 2002.[89]

This unprecedented degree of industrial unrest, disputation, and loss of human security reflected the radical economic and social changes China's workers were enduring.[90] With the rationalization of industry and the downsizing of state-owned enterprises, between 1982 and 2000 China was estimated to have laid off 25 million workers.[91] By 2005, the estimate had risen to 40 million workers.[92] Massive retrenchments (*xiagang*) of workers had begun in 1998. Of those laid off, 50 percent had found new jobs in 1998, but by 2002, only 15 percent were reemployed.[93] By 2004, an estimated 26 million people had been laid off because of SOE reform alone: in 2002, 11.8 million workers had lost their jobs in SOEs.[94] Particularly hard-hit were the 40–50-year-old bracket of unskilled workers from the Cultural Revolution generation. Competing with them for jobs were 10 million new graduates entering the market each year and rural to urban migrants, estimated at 140 million people in 2005.[95] These migrants were particularly disadvantaged. They suffered the discrimination created by the *hukou* (urban registration) system, which made them ineligible for education, healthcare, and social security benefits. They were paid lower wages than urban employees, and frequently were not paid at all; they faced harsh working environments; and they had limited access to job opportunities and employment services.[96] Women were also laid off at a higher rate than men, typically at a ratio of 3:2.[97] Unemployment and underemployment in China also afflicted over 30 percent of the rural population. By the end of 2004, the number of surplus workers in rural areas was estimated at more than 150 million.[98] For urban lay-offs, unemployment benefits lasted only one to two years,[99] while the rural unemployed had no coverage. As a result, protests, demonstrations, and mass incidents grew to 87,000 in 2005, a rise of 6.6 percent over the previous year.[100]

In the face of such widespread industrial change, from 2002 the Chinese government worked to adjust its labor policies and improve labor conditions. An amendment to the Constitution, adopted in March 2004, stated that "the State should construct an all-round social security system which goes well with the pace of economic development."[101] By the end of 2004, according to Chinese government estimates, the numbers of people (in a population base of 1.3 billion) participating in basic pension insurance, unemployment insurance, medical insurance, and industrial injury insurance in urban areas had reached 164 million, 106 million, 124 million, and 68.4 million respectively. By contrast, in the rural areas, which still constituted the majority of China's population, only 55 million people participated in the social old-age pension system and only 2.2 million farmers actually received old-age pensions.[102] The government also increased the minimum wage and introduced a plan to directly elect senior union representatives in foreign-invested and privately owned factories with less than 200 employees, even though these unions were still under the leadership of the ACFTU.[103] It introduced legislation to alleviate the conditions of migrant workers, particularly their children, and to offer support to unpaid workers.[104] Increasingly, China cooperated with the ILO branch in Beijing, which sought to alleviate the problems arising from massive unemployment and social need. However, as critics observed, the three prongs of China's attempts to remedy the situation—the new non-state sector as refuge, the "reemployment" project, and the program of social insurance—were either fatally flawed or quite inadequate to the task.[105] For this reason, Chinese lawyers became increasingly active in opposing the violation of the lawful rights of citizens, particularly in relation to property rights and economic and social rights. As the 2005 UNDP report on China pointed out:

> [The social security system] cannot guarantee equal social security rights to all groups. [It] is also biased towards the urban population and concentrates on social insurance, with a tiny proportion for social relief expenditures targeted at the poor. The average social security expenditure per capita in urban areas is 10 times that of rural areas. Thus, the social security premiums of urban employees are continuously increasing, while rural migrant workers, employees of township enterprises and farmers—who represent the majority of Chinese labor—are virtually excluded from the system.[106]

Moreover, a clear imbalance remained between the government's attempts to make adjustments to improve workers' welfare and its failure to comply with the ILO's core labor standards. In an interview in 2002, an official in the ILO Beijing branch asserted that collective bargaining had been implemented in China since October 2001 when the Standing Committee of the NPC adopted amendments to the Trade Union Law. The ACFTU had also reportedly been promoting both collective bargaining and tripartism.[107] In a report to the UN Committee on Economic, Social and Cultural Rights in 2003, the Chinese government, while admitting that "China's trade unions do not agree with strikes," even claimed that China's Constitution, the Trade Union Act, and the Labour Law clearly granted workers freedom of association and the right to form and join trade unions of their own volition.[108] However, in 2004, the ICFTU's annual survey of violations of trade union rights found that not only was there no free-dom of association in China, but that all attempts to establish trade unions had been suppressed, collective bargaining remained ineffective, and tripartite con-sultation was absent.[109] Moreover, despite the limited experiments in more open union elections and decision making, in general the ACFTU continued to be constrained by the innate contradiction between representing the inter-ests of the state and those of workers. It was only able to resolve this impasse with respect to workers' rights by responding to their minimum personal and enterprise-specific needs.[110]

Even Chinese scholars increasingly recognized this situation was inadequate to workers' needs. In their view, economic globalization and the marketization of labor in China meant that, in order to ensure against unfair labor practices, there was a need to strengthen the right to organize, in the sense of the right to negotiate and the right to strike.[111] As a scholar pointed out, "we shouldn't imagine that we can bring China into conformity with capital, management and distribution norms without conforming to labor law, which is likewise part of economic law."[112] Egregious social problems also spawned the New Left (*xin zuopai*), who drew on the writings of Michel Foucault and Edward Said, and whose demand for social justice aligned them with a neo-Marxist critique of capitalism and globalization. The New Left was critical of the neoliberal reform agenda and sought Chinese solutions to social problems.[113] Globalization was interpreted by such thinkers as involving "Americanization and incorporation into multinational corporations," and its purpose as taking orders from the "IMF, World Bank, WTO, UN and other organs controlled by the U.S. government and Federal Reserve Bank."[114] In 2003, one of its number, Wang Hui, published a critique, *China's New Order*, in which he accused China's leaders of coloniz-ing their own citizens in the interests of international capital.[115]

For such reasons, in Geneva the ILO Governing Body CFA continued to focus on China's implementation of the right to freedom of association, both in law and practice, as the only permanent solution to its industrial problems. And, as before, China continued to exhibit a mixed pattern of procedural com-pliance and substantive non-compliance and non-cooperation. Although, for instance, it eventually voted for the 1997 ILO Declaration on Fundamental Prin-ciples and Rights at Work, based on the right to freedom of association and con-taining a follow-up mechanism, it negotiated to keep the obligations involved in the Declaration as weak as possible.[116]

The Declaration

> reaffirm[ed] the commitment of the organization's member states "to respect, to pro-mote and to realize in good faith" the right of workers and employers to freedom of

association and the effective right to collective bargaining, and to work toward the elimination of all forms of forced or compulsory labor, the effective abolition of child labor and the elimination of discrimination in respect of employment and occupation.[117]

These fundamental principles and rights incorporated conventions on forced labor (C. 29 and C. 105), freedom of association (C. 87 and C. 98), discrimination (C. 100 and C. 111), and child labor (C. 138 and C. 182). However, despite its grudging support for the Declaration, as of 2006, China was one of four states that had ratified only three of these (in China's case, C. 100, C. 138, and C. 182).[118] This placed it in the category just ahead of the seven least cooperative states, which had ratified only one or two of the fundamental conventions, namely Armenia, Laos, Myanmar, Oman, Solomon Islands, the United States, and Vanuatu.[119]

The principle of freedom of association also continued to be a sticking point in subsequent CFA cases on China. By 2005, the CFA had heard numerous cases on China (Cases Nos. 1500, 1652, 1819, 1930, 1942 [Hong Kong], 2031, and 2189). In June 1998, in Case No. 1930, the Committee had published a further complaint made by the ICFTU on 4 June 1997 against the Chinese government for violations of the principle.[120] As in previous cases, the ICFTU criticized aspects of China's new labor legislation and called for parts of both the Trade Union Law and the new Labor Law to be amended. However, its attention was focused primarily on the lack of enforcement of the positive aspects of the new laws, particularly new provisions for collective bargaining, and on the continued ill-treatment, and in some cases, torture, of large numbers of independent labor activists who had remained in jail or labor camp since 1989, despite repeated demands by the CFA for their sentences to be reexamined and quashed.

Freedom of association was also the subject of a further ICFTU complaint against China presented on 4 June 1999. Following an earlier Case No. 1819 on behalf of three Chinese seamen who were arrested in China because of a dispute with the owners of a foreign-owned vessel,[121] CFA Case No. 2031 alleged physical assaults and detention of labor activists in China, and their imprisonment for attempts to establish independent trade union organizations or to carry out activities for the defense of workers' interests. Among its main concluding recommendations, the Committee requested the Chinese government, as it had already done in Case No. 1652, to amend sections 4, 5, 8, 9, 11, and 13 of the Trade Union Law in line with freedom of association principles. On this occasion, however, as an indication of its urgent concerns, it also requested China to examine the possibility of an ILO direct contacts mission in order "to examine the pending issues with all the parties concerned."[122] Never before, even after the government's 1989 suppression of the Democracy Movement demonstrations, had the ILO made such a serious request of China.

China's continuing resistance to freedom of association principles was reflected in its statement when ratifying the International Covenant on Economic, Social and Cultural Rights in March 2001 that the application of Article 8.1 (a) of the Covenant "shall be consistent with the relevant provisions of the Constitution of the People's Republic of China, the Trade Union Law of the People's Republic of China and the Labor Law of the People's Republic of China."[123] Yet, as has been noted, in contravention of the right to freedom of association proclaimed in Article 8.1 of the Covenant, China's Trade Union Law gave effective control over the establishment and operations of all legal subsidiary labor organizations to the ACFTU. It was significant that, of all the provisions in the ICESCR to which it might object, China chose only the right to freedom of association on which to declare a reservation. At a more general societal level, the government's antipathy to the principle was expressed in its decision to ban the Falun Gong spiritual movement after its members had staged a large antigovernment demonstration in central Beijing in 1999. It was likely that this ban stemmed not only from traditional fears of peasant rebellions inspired by religious fanaticism, but also from more modern fears that if freedom of association were allowed to any other social group, China's workers might also attempt to invoke it.

The result was that, although in August 2001 the Standing Committee of the National People's Congress announced draft amendments to the Trade Union Law, these did not appear to respond to the Governing Body CFA's recommendations, although they gave greater protection to attempts to organize unions, particularly in the private sector, including foreign investment enterprises (FIEs). Nor did the government consult with the ILO on the proposed changes.[124] Rather, while conceding widespread abuse of workers' rights, it only presented a new policy to empower the existing official trade union "to make representation with enterprises and institutions that seriously infringe on their staff members' and workers' labor rights and interests and to demand that they take measures to make necessary corrections."[125] In addition, despite the Chinese authorities' claim that the revised Criminal Law of 1997 introduced the concept of equality before the law, certain categories of administrative punishment were still targeted against the lower socioeconomic groups—such as vagabonds, itinerants, and the unemployed. Increasingly, according to *China Labour Bulletin*, such punishment was also being applied to "workers who have been left out of, or impoverished by, the reform process."[126]

On 27 March 2002, a further case, No. 2189, was brought against China not only by the ICFTU but by also the International Metalworkers' Federation

(IMF). It related to specific acts of repression by Chinese security forces and police in response to the rising levels of worker discontent. It made allegations with respect to repressive measures, including threats, intimidation, intervention, beatings, detentions, arrests, and other mistreatment of workers occurring in the industrial northeast (Liaoning and Heilongjiang Provinces), in the northwest (Shanxi), and in the southwest (Sichuan) of China. Having considered China's response, the CFA concluded "with regret" that "very little information has been provided in respect of . . . the question of ensuring respect for the basic principles of freedom of association." It reiterated that

> the only durable solution to the apparently increasing social conflict experienced in the country is through full respect for the right of workers to establish organizations of their own choosing by ensuring, in particular, the effective possibility of forming, in a climate of full security, organizations independent of both of those which exist already and of any political party.

Although aware that the Chinese government was not prepared to countenance such a visit, it once again requested the government to allow a direct contacts mission to promote the "full implementation of freedom of association."[127]

Despite this impasse, China's relations with the ILO were improving at a more general level. Partly as a result of the ACFTU's strong campaign for international recognition, in 1996 relations between the ILO and the ACFTU had been restored and technical cooperation between China and the organization had surged.[128] In 1998, the ILO and China developed a program on industrial relations, involving assistance on labor legislation and capacity building, particularly on tripartism, training, and pilot studies.[129] As the two sides concluded their MOU in 2001, China began turning its attention to critical elections for the ILO Governing Body at the June 2002 Conference, for which it had nominated a worker delegate. Its cause had regional support, particularly from Japanese and Singaporean trade unionists. To further bolster its case, China ratified two more conventions, one on labor administration and the other on safety and health in construction, only a few months before the Conference.[130] It also published its first White Paper on labor and social security, the opening sentence of which stated that "the right to work and enjoy social security is a fundamental right of citizens."[131] This claimed that China had established a "new type of labor relations" and that, despite the evidence to the contrary, "after years of trial and effort, a labor and social security system corresponding to the socialist market economy is now basically in place." The White Paper, however, made no mention of workers' rights, of ILO labor standards, of freedom of association, collective bargaining, worker participation, or tripartism. Only once did it refer to the ACFTU and only once to "trade unions," and then only in the context of their organization of annual "heart-warming activities" to help badly off families.

Thus, by June 2002, a dilemma was once again posed for the ILO and its delegates. The delicate balance between the organization's mandate to support and protect China's workers and its need to encourage China's role within the organization was once more imperiled. At stake was the ILO's desire to maintain institutional harmony and universal representation, as against the provision of its Constitution and the Declaration of Philadelphia that, whether or not they had ratified the relevant ILO conventions, all members of the organization, including China, were obliged to respect and implement the core principle of freedom of association. And yet, at the 1999 ILO Conference, the Committee of Experts had acknowledged the Chinese government's preference for "a gradual approach" toward conforming with the principles of freedom of association and ratifying the Convention.[132] At the 2000 Conference, worker delegates from other states had also expressed particular concern about China's lack of commitment to worker interests. Some had complained that China did not promote progressive economic and social policies but, rather, narrowly focused on political issues, such as its efforts in Conference to defend Burma against threatened ILO sanctions.[133] Nevertheless, on 10 June 2002, in accordance with Article 52 of the Standing Orders of the Conference, by a small majority, a divided Workers' Group elected Xu Xicheng (China) as Vice-Chairperson of the Workers' Group of the Governing Body of the International Labour Office for the period 2002–5.[134] The decision, made in the face of China's resistance to the principle of freedom of association, provoked strong protest from leading international unions, including the IUF and the HKCTU.[135]

Meanwhile, Case No. 2189 continued in the CFA. In March 2003, the Committee presented its interim report to the Governing Body, and, on 21 August, the government transmitted additional information.[136] In May, ignoring the ILO's pleas on their behalf,[137] Chinese courts sentenced Yao Fuxin and Xiao Yunliang, leaders of the labor protest in Liaoyang City, which was one of the outstanding matters in question in Case No. 2189, to seven and three years in prison respectively on the charge of "subverting state power."[138] On 5 March 2004, the ICFTU transmitted additional information in a letter to the ILO regarding detained Chinese textile workers. In the same month, the CFA noted with regret that the government had not responded to the Committee's previous recommendations or to the ICFTU allegations and urged it to institute the independent investigations requested and provide all detailed information. Once again, "convinced that the development of free and independent trade unions and employers' organizations is indispensable . . . to enable a government to confront its social and economic problems and resolve them in the best interests of the workers and the nation," it "strongly urged" the government to respond positively to a suggestion for a direct contacts mission. It also called the

Governing Body's special attention to the case, "because of the extreme seriousness and urgency of the matters dealt therein."[139] Its concerns were echoed in May 2005 by the UN Committee on Economic, Social and Cultural Rights, which, in its concluding observations on China's first report to it, "regret[ted] the State party's prohibition of the right to organize and join independent trade unions."[140] It was clear that, while China was complying procedurally with the CFA, it was not doing so substantively. Despite its deep fears about worker unrest, it preferred to alleviate workers' economic and social conditions while maintaining their political subordination, rather than to follow ILO recommendations to grant them greater independence vis-à-vis the state.

The UN Committee against Torture

The principal instrumentalities set up by the UN system for monitoring states' compliance with the prohibition on torture were two treaty bodies, the Committee against Torture and the Human Rights Committee, as well as the Special Rapporteur on Torture appointed by the Commission on Human Rights.[141] The Committee against Torture (CAT), established under Article 17 of the 1984 Convention, began to function on 1 January 1988 and first met in April 1988. Like the Conference on Disarmament, it convenes in the spacious white buildings of the Palais des Nations, overlooking the calm blue waters of Lake Geneva and, in the distance, the floating peak of Mont Blanc. It is a small committee consisting of ten experts, "of high moral standing and recognized competence in the field of human rights, who shall serve in their personal capacity."[142] They are elected by secret ballot from a list of persons nominated by states parties, on an equitable geographical basis, for an initial term of four years.[143] Ideally, they are lawyers and medical specialists but, more recently, their independence has been brought into question by an increase in the nomination and election of recently retired diplomats or serving government officials.[144]

Although the Convention against Torture established four monitoring procedures, the only mandatory one is that states parties are obliged to report to the Committee on the measures they have adopted to implement the Convention. Nonmandatory procedures are provided for by Article 20, under which the Committee can investigate reports of torture on its own initiative through confidential inquiries or fact-finding missions on the state's territory; Article 21, covering interstate complaints; and Article 22, allowing individual complaints. A state party is bound by Article 20 unless at the time of ratification or accession it expressly declares its unwillingness to accept the competence of the Committee, whereas Articles 21 and 22 require an explicit declaration of acceptance of the Committee's competence.[145]

The Committee receives reports from states parties on the measures they have taken to give effect to their undertakings under the Convention and invites them to cooperate in the examination of reliable information on their practice of torture and to make a confidential Committee inquiry if it is warranted. In cases where the state party recognizes the Committee's competence, it also receives and considers communications from a state party that claims that another state party is not fulfilling its obligations under the Convention, or communications from, or on behalf of, individuals subject to its jurisdiction who claim to be victims of a violation of the Convention by a state party.[146] China, however, has not accepted the Committee's competence in either case.[147] Why, therefore, it chose to ratify the Convention so early, at a time when it also had one of the lowest participation rates among human rights treaty instruments, remains an intriguing question. By 1996, just over 50 percent of states (98 of 193) had become parties to the Convention.[148] By January 2006, however, 141 states had become parties to the Convention.[149]

Article 1, Paragraph 1 of the Convention defines torture as follows:

> For the purposes of this Convention, the term "torture" means any act by which severe pain or suffering, whether physical or mental, is intentionally inflicted on a person for such purposes as obtaining from him or a third person information or a confession, punishing him for an act he or a third person has committed or is suspected of having committed, or intimidating or coercing him or a third person, or for any reason based on discrimination of any kind, when such pain or suffering is inflicted by or at the instigation of or with the consent or acquiescence of a public official or other person acting in an official capacity. It does not include pain or suffering arising only from, inherent in or incidental to lawful sanctions.[150]

Article 19 of the Convention obliges each state party to submit to the Committee both an initial report and subsequent periodic reports. The former, which is to be filed within a year of the entry into force of the Convention for the state concerned, should describe in the first part the constitutional and legal framework within which the Convention will be implemented, and detail in the second the means whereby individual articles in the Convention have been implemented, providing specific details of cases and situations where the guarantees have been enforced.[151] The Committee invites representatives of the state party to attend the meetings at which reports are considered, so that they may respond to the questions put in the morning session by the Committee and clarify aspects of the report. The Committee may then make general comments on the report and may indicate whether some of the obligations of the state concerned have not been implemented.

In examining whether a state concerned has violated its obligations under the Convention, and thereby establishing state responsibility, CAT has a quasi-judicial function.[152] It also relies on NGOs for much of its evidence. This international organizational–international civil society linkage is vital in bringing greater transparency and accountability to China's practice since, as Peter Kooijmans, a former UN Special Rapporteur on Torture, has observed, "it is . . . in cases where there is a very authoritarian government not tolerating differences of opinion and where political opposition is next to impossible that torture is the most frequent and may take on a systematic character and where public authorities may be the instigators or prove compliant in this regard."[153]

China and the Committee against Torture

China's relationship with the UN Committee against Torture represented a different form of international organizational participation. Rather than becoming a member of the Committee, China became subject to its jurisdiction as a result of ratifying the Convention, the international instrument that brought the Committee into being.[154] Its voluntary submission to the jurisdiction of the Committee was the culmination of its two-phase process of entry into the international human rights regime.[155]

In the early years of its UN membership, China had limited its human rights involvement to issues of collective human rights that it had supported since 1949, such as the right to self-determination and opposition to apartheid.[156] For this reason, it had refused to participate in the work of the UN Commission on Human Rights but had joined another Economic and Social Council (ECOSOC) functional committee, the Commission on the Status of Women. It was also wary about the Universal Declaration and the two International Covenants, emphasizing as they did the rights of the individual as well as of the collective.[157] Since it did not become party to any of the conventions relating to human rights, it was not subject to the monitoring of these bodies.

China's more proactive involvement in the international human rights regime began when it sent observer delegates to the UN Human Rights Commission's sessions in 1979, 1980, and 1981.[158] By 1981, it had been elected by ECOSOC as a member of the Commission and in 1982 sent an official delegation. It had then joined the Sub-Commission on Prevention of Discrimination and Protection of Minorities, the panel of human rights experts, in 1984. From 1980 to 1989 it successively signed, or signed and ratified, seven human rights conventions and one protocol.[159] It also participated in the working group to draft and formulate the Convention against Torture and Other Cruel, Inhuman or Degrading Treatment or Punishment.[160]

China's ratification of the Convention on 4 October 1988 made it subject to the obligation in Article 2 to "take effective legislative, administrative, judicial or other measures to prevent acts of torture in any territory under its jurisdiction."[161] Yet its ambivalence toward the international human rights regime led it to sidestep the non-mandatory provisions of the Convention. Upon ratification of the Convention on 4 October 1988, China entered the reservation that: (1) "The Chinese Government does not recognize the competence of the Committee against Torture as provided for in article 20 of the Convention,"[162] and that (2) "The Chinese Government does not consider itself bound by paragraph 1 of article 30 of the Convention."[163] The latter paragraph provided for the arbitration of any dispute between states parties concerning the interpretation or application of the Convention.[164] China also failed to make a declaration of acceptance on the competence of the Committee with respect to Articles 21 and 22.[165] This evasion of the complaints mechanism meant that it was bound only by the mandatory procedure for monitoring the implementation of the Convention by states parties, that is, it accepted only the obligation to report to the Committee on the measures it had taken to implement the Convention. For that reason, UN officials have surmised that it became a party to the Convention mainly because of its obligations as a large power.[166] Subsequent developments revealed its basic failure to understand and accept the norms, principles, rules, and obligations flowing from its accession.

Although China's constitutions have not contained provisions explicitly prohibiting torture, Article 32 of the 1979 Criminal Procedure Law provided that "it is strictly prohibited to use torture to coerce statements (*yanjin xingxun bigong*) and to gather evidence by threat, enticement, deceit or other unlawful methods."[167] Yet, all indications suggest that torture remains a systemic problem and is "routine in many Chinese detention centers, prisons and labor camps."[168] The sources of the problem include a long legacy of torture in China's traditional legal system; its prevalence during the Cultural Revolution; a lack of popular awareness of human rights; insufficient supervision of the exercise of judicial power; inadequate education and training of judicial personnel; local and departmental protectionism; corruption; and the use of torture to extract a confession.[169] They all, however, relate to the absence in China of an effective rule of law. Contemporary forms of torture include violent beating; suspending and beating; being handcuffed behind the back; branding; burning with cigarette butts; electric shocks; shining intense light into the eyes at short range; using trained dogs to tear and bite; mock execution by shooting to extort a confession; sexual abuse; force feeding or forcing victim to drink urine; and inquisition through humiliation.[170]

In recent years, the practice of torture has even been expanding because of its use outside the criminal justice system in areas such as family planning and tax collection.[171] It has also assumed new forms, such as psychiatric detention.[172] Part of the problem is that China's conception of "torture" remains narrow. Under the Chinese Criminal Law, torture means to "coerce a statement" (Art. 136), or to subject imprisoned people to corporal punishment and abuse for this purpose (Art. 189).The purposive and temporal specificity of these articles means that they do not apply generally to the periods of detention, arrest, and subsequent imprisonment. At the hearing of the second periodic report before CAT, Ambassador Wu Jianmin admitted that "China's domestic legislation did not incorporate the definition of torture appearing in Article 1 of the Convention." His defense was merely that China's "domestic legislative provisions designated *various forms* of torture as criminal offences."[173]

Another problem is the lack of accurate and consistent statistics. The most useful, if chronologically restricted, source is China's report to CAT in May 1999, which referred to upwards of 400 cases of torture filed for investigation in both 1996 and 1997. This report also recorded that, between January and July 1998, Chinese courts tried 154 cases of torture; that penalties were imposed in 136 out of 150 cases; and that the victims received compensation from the state. It added that in 1997 there were 1.44 million prison inmates guarded by 280,000 law enforcement personnel; and that fifty-five of the latter were prosecuted for verbal or physical abuse of inmates, and fourteen sentenced to prison terms.[174] The figure of roughly four hundred cases filed every year is consistent with the May 1996 admission of China's Ambassador to the United Nations, Wu Jianmin, that between 1993 and 1995 the Supreme People's Procuratorate had investigated 1,194 allegations of torture, and that "hundreds of complaints concerning torture were filed every year."[175] The same can be said of a scholarly estimate of more than 4,000 cases concerning the extortion of confessions by torture between 1979 and 1989, and a further 2,536 cases involving 5,091 persons between 1990 and 1996.[176] Less illuminating is the reference in China's 2004 human rights White Paper to fifty-two prosecutions in 2003 relating to the same offence.[177] The restricted grounds for prosecution suggest that the actual cases of torture, as defined by the Convention, have been far more numerous than even the figure of four hundred cases a year.

China's Reports to the Committee against Torture, 1989–2004

In the ten years from its first report to the Committee in 1989 to its most recent in May 1999, China was engaged in a steep learning curve, which led to the introduction of new provisions on torture in its domestic legislation, and started it on the path toward eventual signature of the International Covenant on Civil and Political Rights (ICCPR).[178] As in its relations with the ILO Governing Body Committee on Freedom of Association (CFA), its most searing experience was its initial contact with the monitoring body. Thereafter, it was subjected to sustained Committee pressures that drew attention to the underlying causes of torture and pointed it in the direction of principles and requirements such as the importance of the rule of law; the non-justifiability of torture; a rejection of the defense of superior orders; the rejection of impunity and amnesties; continuous review of the rules and practices of those involved in law enforcement and supervision; the creation of the offense of torture in domestic law; the investigation of complaints and remedies; and the exclusion of evidence based on torture.[179] The Committee's recommendations, which reflected its habitual principled focus, precluded China's self-justification and focused its attention on the building blocks of a just society.

China's complacent assumptions regarding its status and immunity to criticism were rudely shattered by the Committee's shocked response to its initial 1989 report. This was a document of only eleven pages that, contrary to the guidelines, confined itself to an outline of China's formal constitutional, legal, and regulatory provisions against torture and failed to address serious allegations of actual abuses.[180] It also ignored the requirement to detail the means whereby individual articles in the Convention had been implemented in practice. The reaction of China's representatives to the blunt and somewhat unusual request of the Committee Chairman for a supplementary report was almost truculent. They questioned the Committee's procedures and its competence to pass judgment on the condition of 1.2 billion Chinese citizens,[181] challenged the admissibility of NGO allegations, and stonewalled requests for further information.[182] Although they did not openly accuse the Committee of exceeding its powers, they made complaints to this effect behind closed doors,[183] and subsequently raised similar concerns during the UN General Assembly debates in November 1990. Later, in a more conciliatory mode, the Chinese Ambassador called for understanding from the Committee, asking it to assess China's problems in the context of a country in which medieval concepts and cultural behavior had to be changed.

China's culture shock was compounded by the weighty criticisms of its reports from NGOs such as the International League for Human Rights, Asia Watch, and Amnesty International.[184] Although China vigorously rebutted their criticisms, its subsequent publication of a number of White Papers on human rights containing references to the issue of torture was indicative of its sensitivity.[185]

China's supplementary report, issued in October 1992, adhered religiously to the Committee's guidelines. A large and senior delegation also attended the Committee hearings in April 1993.[186] This was described as the first time that Chinese authorities had recognized that the Committee had the right to question them and that they had the duty to respond.[187] Because of its procedural compliance, the report, a substantial document of thirty-nine pages divided into two parts, was accepted by the Committee.[188]

At the same time, the Committee drew attention to the grave shortcomings of Chinese policy on the ground. It expressed concern about NGO reports of the use of administrative detention and cases of torture, particularly in Tibet, called for the punishment of those responsible, requested further legislation providing extensive guarantees for arrested or detained persons, with particular reference to "limitations on the use of instruments, equipment and weapons by the security forces," and requested the Chinese government to consider making declarations with regard to Articles 21 and 22 of the Convention and withdrawing the reservation to Article 20.[189]

Unlike its supplementary report, China's second periodic report, produced in December 1995, did not address the thorny issue of practical implementation. Rather, it was a programmatic document, full of its future plans for dealing with the issue. Nevertheless, the formal concluding observations of the Committee stated that "the second periodic report of China follows the Committee's guidelines and meets them satisfactorily."[190] They approved its references to recent amendments to the Criminal Procedure Law; its reports of police officials being prosecuted for acts of torture; and the information it provided of new criminal and administrative compensation for victims of abuse. At the same time, the Committee deplored NGO evidence that "torture may be practiced on a widespread basis in China." It made nine recommendations that reflected its emphasis on the rule of law, the separation of powers, and the requirements of due process.

On 5 October 1998, between the second and third periodic reports, China signaled a changing attitude to human rights by signing the ICCPR, which contained specific obligations prohibiting torture. In its third periodic report, due in 1997 but not submitted until 4 May 1999, the first nineteen pages were devoted to developments in China and the final thirty-three to the implementation of the Convention in the Hong Kong Administrative Region. The China section was divided into two parts, the first describing progress made in the implementation of each article of the Convention, the second addressing the additional information that had been requested by the Committee. In form, it therefore complied with reporting requirements. Yet, in substance, it was still not compliant. As on previous occasions, with the exception of the supplementary report of 1992, it focused primarily on the details of legislative provisions rather than on the actual incidence of torture in China, which was the subject of only a few brief, and prima facie misleading, sentences.

During subsequent questioning, Chinese officials conceded that eighty-four Falun Gong adherents had been convicted, but denied charges that they had been tortured. Similarly, they denied allegations of the torture of ethnic minority prisoners in Xinjiang. They cited regulations on the prohibition of extortion of confessions through torture, on the death penalty, on criminal suspects' right to lawyers, on the right to remain silent and on organ donation. One less critical area in which they admitted systemic weakness was the high incidence of domestic violence, where "the government had strengthened the relevant legislation and was working with non-governmental organizations (NGOs) and other associations to combat the problem." Another was the detention system, where there had been "some individual cases where public security organs had exceeded the legal time limit" for detainees' imprisonment.[191]

In its conclusions and recommendations, the Committee welcomed, inter alia, Chinese legislative amendments and action taken with regard to timely access to defense counsel, the presumption of innocence, amendments to the Criminal Law and Procedure on fair trials, and more severe punishment for acts of torture. However, it expressed continued concern about serious incidents of torture, especially involving Tibetan and other national minorities; the absence of detailed information and statistics regarding torture; the failure to implement reforms uniformly and equally; the limitation of prosecution of suspected torturers to serious cases; the continuation of the system of administrative sanctions; the absence of a uniform and effective investigative machinery; and reports of coercive and violent measures by some local officials in implementing China's population policy. As on previous occasions, the Committee recommended that China incorporate a definition of torture into its domestic law and that, in respect of both the mainland and the Hong Kong SAR, it consider declaring in favor of Articles 21 and 22 of the Convention, and withdrawing its reservation under Article 20. It also called on China to waive the requirement for a person in custody to obtain permission to have access to a lawyer; to abolish all forms of administrative detention; to ensure prompt and effective investigation of all allegations of torture; and to include in its next report detailed statistics of the incidence of torture, disaggregated by region and gender.[192] It was clear that many of the Committee's concerns, raised from the beginning, had still not been addressed. By August 2006, China's fourth periodic report, scheduled for 2 November 2001, was almost five years overdue.

Two other developments were notable in China's relations with the Committee at this point. First, during the May 2000 discussions, a Chinese official confirmed that his government was currently considering whether to withdraw its reservations to the Convention and make declarations under Articles 21 and 22.[193] Secondly, the concluding statement by China, though expressing dissatisfaction with "groundless" allegations by NGOs, nevertheless acknowledged that "the Committee had made many pertinent comments and useful recommendations, which would be transmitted to the Chinese government for serious consideration." Surprisingly, China's representative also invited the Committee to visit China so that it could make "an independent and objective judgment on the accusations made."[194]

Such an invitation appeared at odds with China's rejection of repeated attempts by the UN Special Rapporteur on Torture, Nigel Rodley, and his successor, the distinguished scholar and UN human rights expert Theo van Boven, to carry out a fact-finding mission to China. The on-again off-again nature of the intended visit was related to the government's refusal to accept the UN human rights experts' "terms of reference" for fact-finding missions. These were based on the ICRC's methods of work and included access to all prisons and places of detention, the confidentiality of interviews with detainees and an assurance from the government that no persons or officials with whom the Special Rapporteur came into contact would subsequently be harassed, punished, or subjected to judicial proceedings.[195]

Legislative and Institutional Implementation

Between its second periodic report of 1995 and its third in 1999, China undertook sweeping domestic legislative change related to the development of a rule of law, much of which conformed with its obligations under the Convention against Torture. The new Prison Law of December 1994 was promulgated in part to improve treatment of detainees. It included administrative procedures to complain against prison conditions. In February 1995, judges, prosecutors, and the police became more accountable with the passage in the NPC of the Law on Judges, the Law on Procurators, and the People's Police Law.[196] Accountability was also enhanced with the adoption on 12 March 1994 of the State Compensation Law. This stipulated that if the legal rights and interests of citizens were infringed by state organs, the victims had the right to obtain compensation. It made more specific the guarantees in the 1982 Constitution, whereby citizens could file complaints against any state official for "violation of the law or dereliction of duty."[197] The first Lawyers' Law, which took effect in January 1996, allowed lawyers greater independence, and for the first time recognized that they represented their clients rather than the state.[198]

In March 1996, the NPC approved major amendments to the Criminal Procedure Law (CPL) of 1 July 1979, which regulated investigation and trial in criminal cases. The revised CPL was hailed as a breakthrough that represented progress in the protection of the individual and rights of due process.[199] It imposed stricter controls on police powers during detention and allowed longer preparation time for defense lawyers. It stipulated that no criminal suspect was to be held for more than twelve hours continuously, and that, from the day public prosecution was initiated, the criminal suspect had the right to retain a lawyer to offer him legal advice.[200] It freed judges from presenting evidence, allowing them to concentrate on hearing the case and overseeing court procedures. Moreover, under Article 34, as in Article 32 of the 1979 CPL, "the use of torture to coerce statements and the gathering of evidence by threats, enticement, deceit or other unlawful methods [was] strictly prohibited."

The Administrative Punishment Law, which came into force on 1 October 1996, also helped regulate the system of administrative punishment known as reeducation through labor (RETL) that existed parallel to the criminal justice system. The new Criminal Law of 17 March 1997, an amendment of the 1979 Criminal Law, stipulated, under Article 247, that "judicial workers who extort a confession from criminal suspects or defendants by torture, or who use force to extract testimony from witnesses, are to be sentenced to three years or fewer in prison or put under criminal detention. Those causing injuries to others, physical disability, or death, are to be convicted and severely punished according to Articles 234 and 232."[201]

However, many of these apparently enlightened pieces of legislation also had their negative side. For instance, the revised Criminal Law only stipulated that "judicial workers" should not carry out torture, thereby, by implication, excluding the police. Moreover, the difficulty for complainants lay in enforcing those rights. The revisions to the Criminal Law also replaced the concept of "counterrevolutionary" offenses with provisions barring "treasonous acts designed to threaten national security." This suggested that, at the same time as liberalizing the law, China was also using it to enhance state security.

Even the revised CPL had its dark side. Two key issues not addressed in the new legislation, the use of illegally obtained evidence and the presumption of innocence, had consequences for the prohibition of torture. Under the Convention against Torture, China was obliged to prevent, forbid, and criminalize acts of torture. As indicated earlier, China's definition of torture did not cover the official use of torture to punish, intimidate, or coerce a person for any reason.[202] The revised CPL did not encompass this broad definition, nor did it exclude the use of evidence that had been coerced by torture. Not only, therefore, did it fail to prevent torture, it failed to forbid all acts of torture as defined under the UN Convention.[203] It also failed to increase protection against torture in other respects such as prompt and ongoing access to lawyers, judges, or relatives. As the Lawyers' Committee for Human Rights concluded, the revised CPL "represent[ed] a clear failure to bring China into compliance with the Torture Convention."[204]

Subsequently, some advances were made. In 1997, the Supreme People's Court published a separate pamphlet containing the thirteen banned practices of judges, as stipulated in the Judges' Law, which reportedly included extortion of confessions by torture.[205] By 2001, China's *Legal Daily* had begun to give greater scrutiny to torture, publishing comments and criticism by Chinese legal scholars.[206] In a bid to end the use of torture and threats by police to extract confessions, in August 2003 China's Ministry of Public Security also issued a new regulation to bring police activities under stricter controls. The new regulations, which came into force on 1 January 2004, declared confessions extracted through torture unacceptable. They also required that police officers should respect the dignity of suspects when conducting investigations. Interrogation of suspects would be limited to 12 hours at a time, but 24-hour interrogations would be allowed if special permission was granted.[207] In the same year, the government announced that evidence produced through coerced confessions would be excluded in some administrative cases, while some provincial governments also issued regulations stipulating that judges and police using torture to extract confessions would be dismissed. In some cases, such individuals were prosecuted and sentenced.[208] Finally, in December 2005 the government announced plans to make court proceedings on death penalty appeals open to the public from 1 January 2006.[209]

Compliance and Cooperation

Despite such reforms, NGOs continued to report that torture constituted a systemic problem in China. This, as Amnesty International pointed out, was partly because of the state's failure to introduced necessary institutional reforms to ensure enforcement of the new legislation.[210] Moreover, the inadequacy of that new legislation was underlined by the report of the third visit of the UN Working Group on Arbitrary Detention to China in 2004, which stated bluntly that "none of the recommendations that the Working Group formulated in its earlier report have been followed." Thus, it recommended that all laws governing criminal detention "should be reconsidered" and that, in cases of administrative detention, there should be an effective right to challenge the lawfulness of the detention before a court and due process requirements should be provided by law.[211] The most authoritative and detailed evidence of torture in China was provided in the 2004 report of the UN Special Rapporteur on Torture, Theo van Boven. In it, he described in harrowing detail 170 cases of torture.[212] Of these, thirty-one people had reportedly been beaten or tortured to death, or died soon after being tortured. Others had suffered paralysis, disability, and miscarriage. His revelation that the majority of torture victims were either ordinary workers or members of the Falun Gong established an important linkage between the rights to freedom of association and freedom from torture. Both of these groups were being punished for activities involving the exercise of the right to freedom of association. The forms of torture detailed in the report included electric shocks on all parts of the anatomy; hanging by the wrists for days, and in one case, a month; severe beating and burning; suspension upside down; sexual abuse; sleep deprivation; strapping on the "tiger bench"; water torture; force-feeding; piercing of genitals with needles; and blocking of orifices. In addition, outside the UN system, a former Canadian parliamentarian and Crown Prosecutor, David Kilgour, co-wrote a report alleging widespread and forced organ harvesting from Falun Gong practitioners in China.[213]

Chinese scholars also acknowledged the extent of the torture problem. Among them, Chen Yunsheng published a book detailing the extent of the practice and proposing a range of solutions.[214] The Chairman of the Criminal Law Committee of the All-China Lawyers Association, Tian Wenchang, also recommended China's consideration of the anti-torture measures adopted in foreign countries and lacking in China.[215] These included the right to silence; the supervision system that records the entire interrogation process; the requirement that lawyers should be present when investigative organizations interrogate the suspect; the requirement that all evidence obtained by torture should be excluded; and the responsibility of the prosecution for the burden of proof. He concluded that "since the phenomenon of extortion of confessions by torture still exists in China, it may be necessary to accelerate the legislative efforts in the field by China's lawmakers."

Other developments in China's international policy confirmed the impression that, while China was conforming to some extent to the letter of its obligations under the Convention, it remained resistant to cooperation with its fundamental object and purpose. On 3 March 1992, at its forty-eighth session, the Commission on Human Rights had decided, in its Resolution 1992/43, to strengthen the Convention by establishing an open-ended working group to draft an Optional Protocol to it. The aim was to elaborate a mechanism for the inspection of all places of detention of states parties, and, on periodic and ad hoc bases, to examine the treatment of detainees and ensure states were taking adequate measures for the prevention of torture and cruel, inhuman, or degrading treatment. China was heavily involved in the drafting of the Optional Protocol. Here, the fundamental issue was whether, in ratifying the protocol, states were agreeing in advance to prison visits or whether ratifying states could grant or withhold consent to a request for a visit. As in the case of the ILO's Fundamental Principles and Rights at Work, China worked hard to water down the draft Optional Protocol, arguing that the making of visits to prisons and prisoners should be subject to prior consent and national laws.[216]

China's position, and that of Cuba, Mexico, Uruguay, Syria, and Nigeria, threatened the viability of the Optional Protocol, since if states had the option to refuse a visit by the proposed subcommittee, its purpose would be undermined. During negotiations, some unexpected alliances were also formed. Thus, China stood with the United States in favor of allowing reservations to the Optional Protocol, while China and Australia favored a high number of ratifications before the Optional Protocol could enter into force.[217]

China's lack of transparency in these matters, and its insistence on the overriding importance of sovereignty, suggested that torture remained a serious, persistent problem in the country. On 7 November 2002, the text of the draft Optional Protocol to the Convention against Torture was put before the UN General Assembly. In its final form, the Protocol's objective was to establish a system of regular visits to be undertaken by independent international and national bodies to places where people were deprived of their liberty in order to prevent torture and other inhuman and degrading treatment. The Protocol would have no procedure for reservations and would establish a Sub-Committee on Prevention to carry out, in cooperation with states parties, the functions stipulated by the protocol.[218] It was duly approved in the UN General Assembly by a recorded vote of 104 in favor to 8 against, with 37 abstentions. Voting against were China, Cuba, Israel, Japan, Nigeria, Syria, the United States, and Viet Nam. As with its obduracy on the principle of freedom of association, China remained unwilling to allow any renegotiation of its sovereignty on this non-derogable human right, control over which it regarded as integral to leadership survival. Consequently, it did not ratify the Protocol. In addition, it was inaccessible to international bodies seeking to independently monitor the conditions in Chinese prisons; it made no palpable progress in negotiations for an agreement for ICRC access to prisons;[219] and, as a member of the CAT observed, it was among those countries that chose not to contribute to the UN Voluntary Fund for the Victims of Torture.[220]

Despite China's apparent lack of support for the Committee against Torture and for the norms of the Convention, in 1998 Yu Mengjia (China) was elected a member and, in 2004, a Vice-Chairperson, of the Committee.[221] Contrary to the Convention's requirements, Yu was a career diplomat who had been a first secretary in the Chinese mission in Geneva and a Chinese Ambassador and Deputy Permanent Representative to the United Nations.[222] His lack of human rights expertise and his background in officialdom cast doubt upon his suitability as one of the "experts of high moral standing and recognized competence in the field of human rights, who shall serve in their personal capacity." This success for China was soon to become a trend. In 1999, a Chinese woman, Feng Cui, was elected to the Committee on the Elimination of Discrimination against Women (CEDAW), and, in 2001, Tang Chengyuan was elected a member of the Committee on the Elimination of Racial Discrimination (CERD). With a Chinese national on three of the five major human rights treaty bodies to which China was a state party, this was an unusually high record of membership, even though the appointments were only for a fixed term. With the addition of the new Chinese worker representative on the ILO Governing Body in June 2002, it appeared that China had succeeded, for the time being at least, in its goal to achieve representation, status, and influence in the major international committees monitoring the implementation of human rights. Whether it intended to use this new-found authority to enhance or restrict the effectiveness of these bodies remained an open question.

The question also remained open when, nearly a decade after the initial approach, Beijing finally allowed the fact-finding mission of the Special Rapporteur on Torture, now Manfred Nowak, to occur. This visit was marked by both positive and negative signs of China's cooperation on the issue of the eradication of torture. At the commencement of his twelve-day visit from 20 November to 2 December 2005, Nowak acknowledged the significance of Beijing's invitation as symbolizing China's "growing awareness that torture is quite widely practiced in the common criminal proceedings [in China] by the police and that something needs to be done."[223] At the same time, as he ended his visit, he was constrained to point out that some government authorities, such as the Ministries of State Security and Public Security, had "attempted at various times through the visit to obstruct or restrict his attempts at fact-finding."[224]

The mission's aim was, as Nowak pointed out, to commence fact-finding and to start a process of cooperation aimed at eradicating torture in the PRC. To that end, the Special Rapporteur emphasized both the progress China had made, and the systemic obstacles it faced, in the effort to eliminate torture.[225] He welcomed positive developments at the legislative level, and practical measures to combat torture. He also acknowledged that China was among the first states to ratify the Convention. However, while observing that the practice of torture was on the decline in China, he reiterated his belief that it was still widespread. Many of the reasons he gave were familiar: the Chinese definition of torture was inadequate; the essential procedural safeguards to make its prohibition effective, such as the presumption of innocence, timely notice of reasons for arrest, and timely access to counsel, were lacking; there was no independent monitoring mechanism; the complaints mechanism was ineffective; and the judiciary was not independent and suffered from a low status. Ideological constraints included the focus of China's criminal justice system on culpability, and the practice of "the forceful re-education of human beings with deviant behavior through labor and coercion."

Among his preliminary recommendations, Nowak suggested reform of China's criminal procedure law to conform with ICCPR fair trial provisions; the transfer of several functions of the procurators, such as the supervision of

the police, to the courts; the raising of the status and independence of judges
and the courts; the establishment of an individual complaints mechanism; the
abolition of re-education through labor; the limitation of the scope of the death
penalty; the establishment of a national human rights institution; and China's
ratification of the ICCPR and the Optional Protocol to the Convention against
Torture. China's subsequent rejection of his preliminary findings seemed to go
even further than its earlier rejection of Committee monitoring and did not
bode well for its future cooperation with UN human rights bodies.[226]

Conclusion

The two international organizations in this study are key institutions of the
human rights regime that are critical to human security and the rule of law in
China. Their norms, for different political and historical reasons, represent
peculiar difficulties for China. They are also closely connected, in that the
majority of known victims of torture are ordinary workers and members of the
Falun Gong seeking to exercise freedom of association. China's participation
in both these organizations therefore provides a fundamental test not only of
its compliance and cooperation, but also of the applicability of process-based
compliance theory.

From the time China replaced Taiwan as official representative of China in
the ILO in 1971, it moved from a situation in which it claimed special privileges to one in which it accepted, after considerable resistance, the organization's right to monitor its workers' rights. China's interaction with the ILO
Governing Body Committee on Freedom of Association between 1990 and 2004
was a tough, unrelenting process, with ILO officials persisting in applying universal ILO standards against strong, and at times vituperative, Chinese opposition. The repeated CFA cases on China highlighted the country's pervasive and
continuing abuse of workers' rights. However, China also showed increasing procedural compliance, and, at the level of domestic legislation, demonstrated
acceptance of some ILO norms and rules. This gradual change was in line with
the ILO's experience that the internalization of standards was an evolutionary
process.[227]

However, with a few signal exceptions, China failed to comply with the ILO's
core norms, principles, and rules at the level of practical implementation, that
is, at a deep level of compliance. Because it did not in fact accept freedom of
association in its intrinsic sense of allowing workers the freedom to form and
join the trade union of their own choosing without previous authorization, there
was little substantive change in its attitude to this specific and core standard either
at the international or the domestic level. It also continued to arrest, sentence,
imprison, and torture the same workers for whom the ICFTU and the CFA

had pleaded clemency. By the time cases No. 2031 and 2189 were heard (June 1999 to present), China had changed its declaratory policy on standards and had introduced a new Labor Law that incorporated some labor standards, such as tripartism, worker participation, and the right to collective bargaining. However, both CFA cases were brought down in response to continuing complaints about physical abuse and detention of labor activists in China and both requested China's permission, not vouchsafed, to allow an ILO direct contacts mission to investigate the situation.

Therefore, notwithstanding its manifest strengths, the ILO Governing Body CFA faced a tough challenge. This was primarily because the standards integral to the mandate of the ILO Committee were in practice anathema to China's leaders. The new leadership ushered into power in March 2003 has shown itself increasingly concerned about the problems of worker and peasant unrest and has begun work on a social security net.[228] To underline its new approach, it has not only amended the Constitution to recognize the importance of human rights but has also incorporated the provision that "the state establishes and improves a social security system compatible with the level of economic development." It has published a White Paper on China's urban and rural employment situation and has publicized plans to extend to China's poor peasants the subsistence allowance paid to the urban poor, as well as introducing new policies for migrant workers.[229]

However, the Chinese government still fundamentally disagrees with the ILO's own remedies, highlighted and strongly articulated in CFA Case No. 2189, to address the mounting problem of industrial unrest in China by allowing the establishment of independent trade unions. Although improvements have been made in Chinese legislation on related standards, the battle over the basic principles of the right to freedom of association, which, on the one hand, is a matter of life and death for China's workers, and, on the other, a right conceived by China's leaders as a threat to the existing political system, continues to be waged in the ILO Governing Body CFA to this day.

China's relations with the Committee against Torture have been no less fraught. China took the first step in recognizing the importance of the issue, the competence of the Committee, and its own responsibilities as a Permanent Member of the UN Security Council when it voluntarily signed and ratified the Convention against Torture. Beyond that point, it gradually complied at the procedural level with its reporting obligations. As the CAT has acknowledged, in accepting the prohibition against torture and in entrenching that acceptance, to some degree, in domestic legislation, China has made some progress. On the other hand, UN bodies and international NGOs have challenged the adequacy of Chinese legislative implementation. With Chinese authorities themselves, they have also acknowledged the gap between China's procedural compliance at the international level and practical compliance within China.

Thus, while China has complied to a degree with its reporting obligations, that compliance has yet to be translated adequately into the more significant levels of domestic law and, more obviously, of domestic practice, whether political or social. While the prohibition against torture has been addressed by Chinese legislation in different ways, core issues of definition, implementation, monitoring, and enforcement remain unresolved. The limitations on the Committee's effectiveness are suggested by the gap between China's procedural compliance, which the Committee approved, and its failure to implement its obligations in practice. Such was the problem that necessitated the adoption of the Optional Protocol, an instrument China voted against. Some of the other key obstacles to the CAT's effectiveness have clearly been China's denial of the Committee's competence under Article 20 to undertake confidential inquiries or fact-finding missions on its territory; its unwillingness to accede to Article 21, allowing complaints by other states parties, and to Article 22, allowing complaints by individuals; and its refusal to even sign, let alone ratify, the Optional Protocol. Unwillingness to be bound by these voluntary instruments and provisions is a measure of China's failure to cooperate with the object and purpose of the treaty. It provides another example of China's very limited cooperation with the international human rights regime.

It is clear that China has been less responsive to both these international organizations than it has to those in other regimes, including international environmental bodies. Although in theory supporting their norms, in practice it has perceived them as posing unacceptable challenges to its sovereignty. While it has complied with both bodies procedurally, and has accepted some lesser norms, it has resisted the internalization of their core values. Unlike the other case studies examined here, participation in these organizations has not had the effect of encouraging China to redefine its interests in terms that correspond with organizational rules and treaty norms. This is because, in the case of the right to freedom of association and the right to freedom from torture, no organizational pressures or incentives to comply have been powerful enough to overcome the disadvantages that China perceives will accrue from compliance. Unlike its experience in other regimes, China's robust interaction over time with international organizations has affected, but not sufficiently liberalized, China's policies on labor rights and on torture. Rather, China has debated the need to establish a charter of fundamental industrial rights and has sought to block any strengthening of CAT powers. In neither case to date has its activities had a fatal impact on these bodies or their norms. However, in successfully nominating a Chinese national onto the CAT for three years, as well as onto two other leading human rights treaty bodies, and in returning a worker representative to the ILO Governing Body, China has positioned itself to take a preeminent role in the deliberations of these human rights bodies, without having committed itself either to substantive compliance or to cooperation.

What does this say about process-based compliance theories? It is clear that the process of participation in international organizations has important and wide-ranging effects on a state, and that, where the international socialization and integration of an authoritarian state have been achieved, the process of its participation in international institutions will have been the most significant causal influence. No other force has the simultaneous capacity to legitimize a state's sovereignty, to encompass a state with rules, material and normative incentives, pressures of reintegrative shaming, and appeals to reputation and status, as well as to provide the security of reciprocal guarantees between states. At the same time, in critical instances affecting sovereignty or state security, the state's self-interest will prevail over organizational norms. In other words, contrary to the precepts of the Chayes' managerial theory, a significant aspect of self-interest remains exogenous to the participation process. Although normative and reputational factors have been vital to China in the ILO, and even though the ILO's pressures on, and influence within, China have been substantial since 1989, China has resisted its impact in specific areas because of domestic governance concerns. As a result of such least-likely test cases, it is clear that, unless there is substantial convergence between international pressures and domestic interests, participation in international human rights bodies will gradually persuade China to internalize some of their norms and principles, but not those seen as challenging the constitutive norms of the Chinese state. Until compelling pressures to liberalize come from *within* China as well as from without, international organizations will remain the most significant sources of pressure in the international socialization and integration of least-likely states, but, by the same token, as Harold Koh's transnational legal theory suggests, they will also have their limits.

Conclusion

The task of legal analysis is to find a middle ground, conjoining law
to politics without collapsing the one into the other and attaining a
realism that neither expects law to guarantee a peaceful world nor
concludes that law is irrelevant to international peace.

Richard Falk, The Status of Law in International Society *(1970)*

This has been a story of "rogue" states, quasi-revolutionary states, international
exclusion and inclusion, compliance and cooperation, non-compliance and
non-cooperation, North-South harmony, and North-South disagreement. It has
been related within the context of an international order of equally conflicting
tendencies, at once moving toward globalization and localization, toward the
liberalization of international trade and its regionalization and bilateralization,
to increasing dependence on international law and an increasing tendency to
flout it, to the growing interdependence of transnational border issues and a
greater likelihood for states to tread an isolationist path. In this environment of
flux and change, it has nevertheless been possible to test the effeciveness of compliance theories in explaining why nonliberal states also comply with international rules. In this book, the central player has been China, and the stage,
international organizations in the international regimes of security, political
economy, the environment, and human rights—the Conference on Disarmament (CD), the World Bank (IBRD/WB), the International Monetary Fund
(IMF), the United Nations Environment Programme (UNEP), the International Labour Organization (ILO), and the UN Committee against Torture
(CAT). These case studies have explored two main questions. First, has the multilateral system in general, and international organizations and their associated
treaties in particular, been instrumental in persuading a least-likely state, in this
case China, to comply and even cooperate with their norms, principles, and
rules, and if so, how and why? Second, has China at the same time been instrumental in shaping and altering those norms, principles, and rules and, if so, what
are the implications of such changes for China and the international system?

China's Compliance and Cooperation

The evidence presented has been negative as well as positive. To test the negative effects of nonparticipation in international organizations, we have used history to show how China's view of international organizations and international law evolved from imperial to Republican times as China became more involved in international organizations and more inclined to invoke international law. We have also shown how, with the advent of a communist government in 1949, that situation regressed. We have documented China's increasing isolation from, and frustration with, the international system, as the barriers against its participation became more and more all-encompassing. In the tumultuous years of the 1960s, its revolt against international institutions fed into, and was in turn affected by, the revolutionary struggle within its domestic society.

This period contrasted dramatically with the subsequent era of China's international organizational participation. Thus, we have monitored the gradual integration of this erstwhile "rogue," "renegade" or "revolutionary," and now "quasi-revolutionary," state into the international community after 1971, when it finally replaced Taiwan as official representative of "China" in the United Nations. We have also analyzed the changing record of the PRC's compliance with the norms, principles, and rules of the constituent instruments and associated treaties of key international organizations in the areas of international and human security. In an attempt to ascertain "whether" China has complied with its voluntarily assumed obligations, we have distinguished between five levels of compliance. The first three are in the international arena: (1) accession to a treaty or agreement; (2) procedural compliance with reporting and other obligations; and (3) substantive compliance with the norms, principles, and rules of the multilateral body. The last two levels are in the domestic arena: (4) formal compliance, or the implementation of international norms in domestic legislative provisions, in judicial incorporation, and/or in institutional development; and (5) practical compliance at the level of domestic implementation. Practical compliance in turn has been subdivided into (a) political implementation, indicating government policy that responds to an international norm; and (b) social implementation, indicating widespread general obedience to a norm.[1] These levels form a spectrum rather than a continuum. For instance, a state may comply at levels 1, 3, or 5, and not necessarily at levels 2 and 4. The levels are also of different significance, depending on whether one is measuring international or domestic compliance. For the latter purpose, level 5 (b) is clearly the most significant of the indices and the most suggestive of a society's deep domestic compliance and internalization of international norms.

On the other hand, to measure the depth of a state's international compliance, three further indicators test its internalization of international norms, standards, and rules. Of these, the first is the notion that participation in international organizations leads states to redefine their interests in terms that correspond with treaty norms.[2] To obtain a comparative perspective on China, we have first documented its policy on the eve of its entry into each international organization, and then traced its subsequent conceptual and policy changes. A second index of deep international compliance is a state's preparedness to renegotiate its sovereignty and move to a more restrictive interpretation of the principle. A third is the extent to which the state has gradually accepted the "costs" of participation in the regime. Needless to say, these indicators often overlap, and each may apply more usefully in different regimes.

Nevertheless, even at these different levels, the notion of compliance has not proved adequate to explain the nature of China's international integration. To complete the jigsaw puzzle, it has been necessary to look beyond compliance to the question of cooperation. Here, indicators include the readiness of a state to ratify treaties without introducing excessive reservations, to assume nonmandatory obligations, to promote the object and purpose of an organization and its associated treaties, and to encourage other states to do likewise. By contrast, non-cooperation is reflected in self-interested attempts to block, stymie, or otherwise impede attempts to promote the object and purpose of the organization and its treaties. This lack of cooperation, however, must be carefully distinguished from legitimate, democratic attempts to represent the will and interests of a collectivity of developing states in order to shape international law in a way that will eventually benefit international harmony, global interests, and cooperation as a whole. Debate and disagreement and the changing nature of state practice are, and always have been, part of the process intrinsic to international diplomacy and the development of international law. Both sides of this story, non-cooperation and spoiling activities as well as constructive debate and legitimate disagreement, have been told and weighed equally in the balance.

What has been China's record of compliance and cooperation in each regime? We have emphasized that, for all states, compliance generally varies across and even within regimes.[3] Compliance is also a relative matter, in that there is no such thing as perfect compliance. However, within these constraints, there are some states that, because of their culture, history, political philosophy and public policy, are deemed least-likely to comply. Likewise, as Anne-Marie Slaughter has hypothesized, there are others, liberal democracies, that, for the very same reasons, are deemed "most likely" to comply.[4] For a state that has long been identified as belonging to the "least-likely" category, China has made enormous progress. In comparison with its attitude to international law and international organizations in the 1950s, 1960s, and even early 1980s, its acceptance of, and integration into, the international system have been nothing short of extraordinary.

Taking each international organization in turn, in its relations with the Conference on Disarmament and the international security regime as a whole, starting from a very low baseline, China has shown the greatest preparedness to change. It has moved from a policy in 1980 supporting continued nuclear testing and the right of states to acquire nuclear capability to one eventually embracing the principles of nuclear nonproliferation and disarmament and supporting the integrity of international security organizations and their associated treaties. For the most part, it has attained the first four levels of compliance, although a question mark has hovered over its response at the fifth level, domestic practical implementation, as a result of its alleged export of nuclear material and equipment. Nevertheless, in the sphere of domestic legislation and institution building, its record has been reasonable. It has also shown deep international compliance, in the sense of altering its perception of its self-interest to accord with the norms, principles, and rules of the regime, preparing to renegotiate its sovereignty and accepting the costs as well as the advantages of participation. At the same time, it has made clear that its compliance and cooperation remain contingent on the reciprocal behavior of other states, particularly the United States, whose strategic decisions are capable of undermining China's own security. For this reason, China, while ratifying the other major nonproliferation and disarmament treaties, has signed, but not yet ratified, the Comprehensive Test Ban Treaty.

China's lack of cooperation with this regime, on the other hand, has been expressed in other, more subtle ways. It has interpreted the norms and rules of the regime narrowly, failed to commit itself to voluntary and extended controls that accord with the spirit of its obligations, and failed to participate in some voluntary agreements. In matters directly implicating sovereignty, verification measures, and transparency, it has also been less than cooperative and has adopted a policy of "asymmetrical transparency." Nevertheless, it has accepted intrusive controls and verification missions from the International Atomic Energy Agency (IAEA) and the Organization for the Prohibition of Chemical Weapons (OPCW). More recently, it has been one of the world's most outspoken defenders of the existing norms, institutions, and rules of the international security system at a time when that system has been subjected to sustained assault. It has thereby promoted the object and purpose of the treaties. Moreover, although it had long refused to require full-scope safeguards (FSS) as a condition for supply of nuclear exports, which it would be obliged to do if it joined the Nuclear Suppliers Group (NSG), it signaled a new readiness to consider the need for such safeguards when it joined that body in June 2004.[5]

China has also changed in diverse ways as the result of its membership of the World Bank and the IMF. Although initially it did not support the norms of either organization, and found it difficult to adapt to Bank and Fund rules and requirements, it has since become increasingly compliant at both the international and national levels. In the case of the Bank, China has an exemplary record of project management and loan repayment. In the case of the Fund, it has benefited from opening up communication through the Article IV Consultations in broad areas of macroeconomic management and through the development of a Government Financial Management Information System. It has internalized its integration into the two international organizations by implementing their norms and rules in domestic legislation and through domestic institution building. Where, however, their strictures appeared to undermine China's interests, it has adopted a policy of "creative" independence. This freedom, which has been made possible by China's economic importance, has benefited the country in some ways but not in others.

However, while China has complied with its mandatory obligations overall, its cooperation with the international political economy regime has also been open to question. While it has begun to participate in the General Data Dissemination System (GDDS), it has only recently announced its interest in participating in the Fund's Financial Sector Assessment Program. Paradoxically, its very emphasis on legality makes it slow to succumb to such non-mandatory undertakings. It has adhered almost exclusively to the letter of the law, rather than developing its institutional relationships in a cooperative manner according to the spirit of membership and the object and purpose of the Articles of Agreement. To that extent, although it has increasingly accepted the costs of membership, it has not yet accepted the sovereignty constraints entailed in full integration into the Bank and Fund. Critical to the difference between partial and full integration has been the problem of transparency. Thus, although acknowledging China's distinct progress, IMF Directors continue to express frustration over its opacity and its reluctance to accept voluntary constraints on its activities.

As one would anticipate, China has behaved more like a developing state in the international environmental regime. It has been active in negotiating the content of treaties to accord more clearly with its current needs of rapid industrialization. Its compliance, like that of many other states, has been uneven and has varied both between issue areas and within them. In relation to the atmospheric environment, there has been a clear difference between its compliance in the areas of ozone protection, where its obligations are specific, and that of climate change, where they are general and limited. In the former, China has complied internationally with its reporting obligations and in setting voluntary targets. It has also complied domestically in meeting legal and institutional targets and in the practical implementation of many of its reduction targets, even if it has deliberately limited its obligations by failing to ratify the full range of Amendments to the Montreal Protocol. On the other hand, in the climate change regime, China does not have an obligation under the Framework Convention (UNFCCC) and Kyoto Protocol to meet reduction targets and, in ensuing negotiations, has sought to avoid any introduction of such targets. It has been slow to comply with its reporting obligations but has nevertheless worked to bring the Protocol into effect. This at least suggests the beginnings of cooperation with the object and purpose of the Protocol. Moreover, it has ratified the Protocol, acceding before other nonparticipants such as Russia, the United States, and Australia. Despite its lack of obligations at the international level, it has, in the spirit of the norms and rules of the regime, sought to reduce its emission of greenhouse gases relative to GDP. While its record at the international level has been mixed, at the domestic level it has sought to cooperate with the regime.

However, in this area, issues of sovereignty and self-interest have remained paramount for China. For this reason, it has opposed any strengthening of UNEP. It has ratified conventions, but has only ratified their associated protocols once it has ensured that they conform to its interests. Having achieved a satisfactory compromise, it has then been prepared to redefine lesser interests in conformity with the treaty, particularly in the face of evidence that compliance would lead to profit or to technology transfer, or power and influence. Only to that extent has it accepted costs in the regime as well as benefits.

Finally, it is clear, and not surprising, that China has been less responsive to international human rights organizations than to the key institutions of other regimes. Here, as in the environmental regime, it has also worn its "developing state" hat. Although in theory supporting the norms of both the ILO Governing Body Committee on Freedom of Association (CFA), and the UN Committee against Torture (CAT), in practice China has viewed them as unacceptable challenges to its sovereignty. While it has complied with both bodies procedurally, and has adopted some lesser norms, it has resisted the legislative, political, and social implementation of their core values, which go to the heart of its sovereignty. In fact, the more it has shown compliance with the procedural requirements of these bodies and the more it has implemented lesser treaty obligations in its domestic legislation and institutions, the less it has been prepared to comply with their most vital standards. While its compliance in the former respects has been noted by the monitoring agencies, both have decried China's lack of improvement in areas that have been continuing sources of concern to them. China has steadfastly resisted implementing the right to freedom of association, so integral to ILO standards, either in legislation or in practice, whereas it has been prepared to incorporate concepts of tripartism, worker participation, and

TABLE 1

China's Overall Compliance Levels by Organization/Treaties, 1980 and 2005

| Compliance Levels | International Security | | | | Political Economy | | | | Environment (treaties) | | | | Human Rights | | | |
| | CD | | IAEA | | World Bank | | IMF | | UNEP/Ozone | | Climate Change | | CAT | | ILO | |
	1980	2005	1980	2005	1980	2005	1980	2005	1980	2005	1980	2005	1980	2005	1980	2005
Entry/Accession to Treaty	√-	√	x	√	√-	√	√-	√	√-	√	x	√	x	√	√-	√
Procedural compliance with international obligations	x	√	x	√	x	√	x	√	x	√	x	√	x	√	x	√
Substantive compliance with rules/international obligations	x	√	x	√	x	√	x	√	x	√	x	√-	x	√	x	√
Domestic formal/legal implementation	x	√	x	√	x	√	x	√	x	√-	x	√-	x	√-	x	x
Domestic political/social implementation	x	√-	x	√-	x	√-	x	√-	x	√-	x	√-	x	x	x	x

Key:
√ = reasonable
√- = marginal
x = none

collective bargaining into its legislation. Likewise, with respect to CAT, the prohibition against torture has been addressed by Chinese legislation in different ways, but core issues of definition, implementation, monitoring, and enforcement remain unresolved. The human rights system has thus revealed the outer limits of the effective impact of international organizations in cases where international pressures are perceived as threatening critical domestic interests, including the nature of domestic governance.

Nevertheless, to the general question, can and does a least-likely state comply with international norms, the answer must be in the affirmative (see Table 1). In most of these regimes, China has complied with international norms and procedures at the three different international levels: accession to treaties, procedural compliance, and substantive compliance. It has also internalized their norms, if not socially, then at least to the level of implementing them legislatively and politically and incorporating them in domestic institutions. China's initial impulse toward organizational participation was the product of complex motives that did not include the acceptance of the norms of each regime. Accession to treaties was primarily motivated by exogenous self-interest, as rational choice theory would anticipate. However, compliance with international norms, rules, and procedures occurred not immediately as the result of coercion, to which China responded adversely, but in graduated stages, in response to the complementary pressures of authoritative institutional procedures, iterated persuasion and discourse, organizational pressures and incentives, changes in the international environment, and domestic pressures. In an effort to harmonize its domestic law with its membership and treaty obligations, through the intervention of its executive and legislature, China internalized treaty and organizational norms and rules in its domestic law and institutions. The extent of its socialization is today exemplified in journalistic perceptions that, contrary to the view of Adlai Stevenson cited at the beginning of Chapter 1, China is now located among the "civilized" nations:

> Today's world . . . is increasingly divided between the "World of Order"—anchored by America, the EU, Russia, India, China and Japan and joined by scores of smaller nations—and the "World of Disorder." The World of Disorder is dominated by rogue regimes like Iraq's and North Korea's and the various global terrorist networks that feed off the troubled string of states stretching from the Middle East to Indonesia.[6]

To the question, can a least-likely state comply *deeply*, on the other hand, the answer is more complex. There are two aspects to "depth" of compliance. One is the depth of compliance required by a treaty, that is, the extent to which it requires the state to depart from what it would have done in its absence. It seems that, as a result of participating in international organizations and ratifying their associated treaties, China, a former "least-likely" rogue state, has managed, contrary to rational choice theory, to progress toward "deep" international treaty-based compliance and a consequent shift in its international behavior in certain areas. It has ratified treaties and joined international organizations that have required it to make radical changes in its behavior far beyond what it would have done in their absence. Indicators of this behavioral shift have been its redefinition of its interests, its renegotiation of its sovereignty, and its acceptance of substantial costs.

Depth Required by Treaty

China's redefinition of its interests has been evident in organizations such as UNEP, the CD, and the ILO. As a result of its participation in UNEP, and the material and technical assistance obtained under its auspices, China responded to its obligation under the Montreal Protocol to cut CFC and halon emissions. Change was also evident in its participation in the CD, which it joined in 1980. Initially, it supported the right of developing countries to acquire nuclear weapons. However, the essential breakthrough arose from the realization that its existing position on proliferation was not good for global security, and that global security was in its interests. It was this conceptual advance that led to China's accession to the NPT in 1992. Its redefinition of interests has also been clearly reflected in new legislation and institution building in areas corresponding to almost all of the international organizational norms and treaties to which China is a party, whether in international security, international political economy, the environment, or even, to a lesser degree, human rights. Even in the case of the ILO, in the face of domestic and organizational pressures, China's informal compliance with selected ILO labor standards has improved, as has its declaratory policy on ILO standards, such as collective bargaining, tripartism, and worker participation, if not freedom of association.

The PRC's preparedness to renegotiate its sovereignty has been most apparent in the CD. On entering the organization, it ceased atmospheric nuclear testing. It also accepted intrusive controls and verification missions from the IAEA and OPCW as a result of the obligations it assumed under the NPT and CWC. However, even China's participation in international human rights organizations, whose norms present the most serious challenge to its sovereignty, has reflected some flexibility. Most remarkable is the fact that China chose to join the major human rights bodies and to ratify treaties, like the Convention against Torture, whose norms did not appear to coincide with the values of its leadership. In addition, following the suppression of the Democracy Movement, the Chinese government decided to actively engage in the international human rights debate and to embark on vigorous human rights diplomacy. It also traded numerous concessions on sovereignty as a quid pro quo for human rights concessions by the international community. The most important of these were its signature and ratification of the ICESCR and signature of the ICCPR and its continued reporting on the condition of human rights in Hong Kong after takeover.

China's acceptance of costs has also been most clearly revealed in the international security regime. It opposed a comprehensive test ban treaty well into the 1990s but signed the CTBT in 1996, giving up its earlier requirements of "no first use" and the continuation of "peaceful nuclear explosions," thereby agreeing to a global moratorium on testing, whether in the atmosphere, space, or underground, and to more transparency. It ceased nuclear testing in late July 1996, and accepted strict limits on sales of missiles. In addition, it has given a negative assurance that it will not be the first to use or threaten the use of nuclear weapons; it approved extension of the NPT in 1995; and concluded a joint statement with the United States in 1994 to abide by MTCR. At the first Conference on Facilitating the Entry into Force of the Comprehensive Nuclear Test Ban Treaty in Vienna from 6 to 8 October 1999 to urge countries to sign and ratify the CTBT, China promised to speed up its ratification, conditional on a full review of the treaty and the state of the international security environment.[7] Its subsequent failure to follow through is a reflection of its loss of trust in that environment. Even in the UN Committee against Torture and in the ILO Committee on Freedom of Association, China experienced a totally new phenomenon—a tough and unrelenting process of monitoring from 1990 to the present, which exposed it to the reputational costs of embarrassment and shaming. Despite this experience, China did not seek to withdraw from its participation in either of these bodies, and partially conformed to strict reporting requirements.

Depth of Internalization

The second aspect of "deep" compliance is the extent to which treaty norms are internalized in a state's domestic policy. The evidence is that least-likely states do internalize norms, at least legislatively and politically. This internalization is one of the direct and significant outcomes of states' participation in international organizations and treaties, in that they are thereby obliged to harmonize their domestic rules and institutions with their international legal obligations. However, this top-down process does not guarantee comprehensive practical social implementation of treaty norms, in the sense of the widespread general obedience of the civilian population. In the human rights regime, China's extensive labor legislation has not guaranteed the practical implementation of all labor rights, despite the political rhetoric to the contrary, while, in arms control, there are continued charges of non-compliance in relation to arms sales and technology transfer. The same distance between legislative and practical implementation is evident in the case of the atmospheric environment. In this

TABLE 2

China's Overall Attitudes by Regimes, 1949 – 2005

	International Security	Political Economy
Major Phase	CD, IAEA	WB, IMF
1949–71	support for norms until 1960s, then disengagement/opposition	disengagement/opposition to norms
1970s	disengagement/opposition to norms	disengagement/opposition to norms
1980s	engagement→compliance/support	engagement→compliance/support
1990s–present	compliance/support; marginal cooperation	compliance/support; marginal cooperation

regime, not only is there a problem with social internalization, but, within the political realm, leadership policies are often contradictory and ambiguous. Finally, as Thomas Franck would argue, China's commitment to all these international regimes has been dependent on its continued perception of their legitimacy.[8] Initially, for instance, threats of change to the arms control regime, such as the Indian and Pakistani tests and U.S. plans for missile defense, only strengthened China's commitment to nuclear disarmament and nonproliferation. But U.S. challenges to the authority and legitimacy of the ABM Treaty elicited warnings from China that the abrogation of the treaty would imperil international compliance with the norms of the regime.

To date, however, China may be judged to have complied reasonably with the constituent instruments of international organizations and with the norms, principles, and rules of their associated treaties. Indeed, when measured against the base level of its compliance and cooperation in 1980, its progress has been remarkable (see Tables 2 and 3). Nevertheless, its concern to preserve its sovereignty has remained paramount. Although, as we have observed, the bounds of that sovereignty have been renegotiated when national self-interest or normative concerns have required, its lack of international cooperation and, in particular, of transparency, continues to present problems. Its interpretation of the norms, principles, and rules of each international organization has remained legalistic and narrow and has only marginally reflected a sympathy with their object and purpose (see Table 3).

What light does this analysis shed on the general nature of each international organization and regime and on the incentives and enforcement mechanisms of their constituent instruments and treaties? Our findings confirm that the types of "compliance-pull" vary between the different regimes and their key orga-

TABLE 2
(continued)

Environment	Human Rights	
UNEP *(atmospheric)*	CAT	ILO
disengagement/opposition to norms	disengagement/opposition to norms	disengagement/opposition to norms
engagement	disengagement/opposition to norms	disengagement/opposition to norms
engagement→compliance/support	engagement but opposition to implementation	engagement but opposition to norms
compliance/support; marginal cooperation	engagement but non-implementation of norms; little cooperation	engagement but opposition to principal norms; marginal cooperation

nizations. In the UN proper, China's participation has been chiefly motivated by its legitimizing effect and the benefits it confers. In the CD, China has been more influenced by role modeling, status considerations, institutional pressures to conform, and the principle of reciprocity. The quality of treaty rules has been a less important determinant of compliance than the desire to be regarded as a responsible member of the international community shouldering the burdens of a major state. However, as we have observed, the treaty rules themselves have been highly significant in the sense that China, like every other state, has the obligation to harmonize its domestic rules and institutions with its membership and treaty obligations. A reconceptualization of the value to China of the norms of the regime, in conjunction with the changes in the international strategic environment, has also occurred as a result of just "being there," participating in the long drawn-out negotiations in the CD. Reciprocity, on the other hand, has been a two-edged sword that accounts not only for the stability of the international security regime, but also for its precariousness. That is, it explains both China's compliance and non-compliance. For instance, it accounts for China's current ambivalence, in response to changing U.S. policy, toward ratifying the CTBT. As Robert Keohane has pointed out, reciprocity involves "exchanges of roughly equivalent values in which the actions of each party are contingent upon the prior actions of the others in such a way that good is returned for good, and bad for bad."[9]

In the World Bank and the IMF, norms, principles, and rules are important for China. However, both organizations, and particularly the World Bank, involve substantial material benefits for it. The status implications of having an Executive Director with a single country constituency have also encouraged China's compliance, as has an increased quota in the IMF, a prize for which China was

TABLE 3
China's Deep International Compliance and Cooperation Levels by Organization/Treaties, 1980 and 2005

| | International Security | | | | Political Economy | | | | Environment (treaties) | | | | Human Rights | | | |
| | CD | | IAEA | | World Bank | | IMF | | UNEP/Ozone | | Climate Change | | CAT | | ILO | |
Indices	1980	2005	1980	2005	1980	2005	1980	2005	1980	2005	1980	2005	1980	2005	1980	2005
Deep Compliance																
1. Redefinition of interests	×	√	×	√	×	√	×	√	×	√	×	√	×	√	×	√
2. Preparedness to renegotiate sovereignty	×	√	×	√	×	√	×	√	×	√	×	√	×	√	×	√
3. Accepts costs of participation	×	√	×	√	×	√	×	√	×	√	×	√-	×	×	×	×
Cooperation																
Promotes object and purpose of international organizations and treaties	×	√-	×	√	×	√	×	√	×	√	×	√-	×	×	×	×

Key:
√ = reasonable
√- = marginal
× = none

prepared to shoulder greater costs. China takes pride in its reputation for reliable performance and predictability in both bodies. It has also cleverly sidestepped obligations that would infringe on its sovereignty, by avoiding SALs in the World Bank and not borrowing from the IMF. By contrast, in line with the theory of Thomas Franck, the quality of rules and the incentives contained in international treaties have been more significant for China's compliance with the environmental regime. This is because, where no automatic, short-term national advantages and international reciprocity naturally accrue to a state within a regime, the organization and its treaties need to provide them. Following its more favorable consideration of both the Montreal and Kyoto Protocols, China's decision to ratify them suggests that the material incentives provided in the London Amendment to the Montreal Protocol and the enhanced funding provided for the GEF to climate change in 2002 were significant reasons for its new cooperation with the regime. The Kyoto Protocol also introduced reciprocal benefits through the Clean Development Mechanism, which permitted developed states to get emission reduction credits for projects undertaken to reduce carbon emissions in developing countries, and joint implementation, which allowed developed country parties to get credit for projects done in other developed country parties. In the Montreal Protocol, the negative provision that states could only sell ozone-depleting substances (ODS) to other states parties also encouraged its ratification by states such as China.

It is to be noted that in many of these international organizations, contrary to the rational choice theory of George Downs and others that emphasizes coercion, a flexible interpretation of the rules has often proved more effective than a literal one.[10] Thus, for instance, although the formal enforcement mechanisms in the Articles of Agreement of the Bank and Fund and in the atmospheric environmental treaties appear strict, in practice, as interviews attest, monitoring bodies err on the side of leniency in their enforcement of the rules. Negotiators in these regimes report that, while in theory they could deprive states of their access to benefits if they do not comply with the rules, in practice they routinely find that the most effective procedure is to adopt a "softly, softly" approach, such as naming and shaming defaulting states.

In the human rights regime, by contrast, the critical disjunction between the norms of the ILO and the UN Committee against Torture and China's most vital political identity/national interests, has created a situation in which national pride, prestige, and face have been at a premium. Apart from the lack of reciprocity and mutual advantage for states within the human rights regime, the two primary norms of these particular bodies, the principle of freedom of association and the prohibition against torture, are anathema to Chinese leaders, whatever they might legislate or declare in public. Because of its formal identity as a workers' state, China has been primarily concerned in the ILO with matters of status and reputation. In addition to benefiting from technical assistance, it has sought to obtain executive status to offset its "naming and shaming" by the ILO Governing Body CFA. To this end, it has been prepared to show more cooperation. Hence its ratification of two more ILO Conventions, C. 150 and C. 167, just prior to the vote that saw the return of China's worker representative to the ILO Governing Body. It has also been prepared to renegotiate its sovereignty and to accord national recognition to some of the less exacting ILO standards. To deter evasion of its core norms, a recent stratagem of the ILO has been to focus on the fundamental ILO principles, which incorporate a number of the most basic conventions, including Conventions 87 and 98. By recording a chart of ratifications of these fundamental Conventions on its website, in order of the group of states with the least ratifications to those with the most, the organization has exerted a subtle "naming and shaming" pressure on backsliding states, including China.

China's Interaction with the World Trade Organization (WTO) and the World Health Organization (WHO): A Comparison

Perspective will be added to the above findings by contrasting two mini case studies of China's remarkably positive, if as yet brief, involvement with the WTO and its more problematic relationship with the WHO in recent years. Since China's entry into the WTO was so hard won, and since, like the World Bank, it promised China clear material advantages as well as challenges, one would anticipate that, despite domestic obstacles, this issue area would constitute a "most-likely" case of Chinese compliance. The China-WTO record may therefore be invoked as a control against which to test the validity of our general conclusions. By contrast, the China-WHO record offers a test of a least-likely case of compliance, and shows how self-interest can encourage both non-compliance and compliance.

The WTO

Perhaps the most challenging example of China's international organizational participation was its entry into the WTO on 11 December 2001, following fifteen years of difficult negotiations. Status, trading opportunities, the pressures of globalization, and the desire to deepen restructuring within China were all motives behind China's wish to join. It saw the WTO as an "important carrier of globalization," which would allow China to "become a respectable member in the open international economic system," enabling it to enjoy equal trading treatment and to take part in formulating trade regulations. The WTO would also have the crucial function of opening up China's services industry; it would link China with the global economy; "bring about rational allocation of resources"; allow more Chinese enterprises to operate outside the country; and facilitate foreign investment in China.[11] Moreover, since China was not at that point a member of any regional trading bloc, the WTO would help it to remain competitive.[12]

At the same time, China's accession required it to enforce the WTO Understanding, which stipulates that national judicial systems act in compliance with international treaty obligations and norms,[13] thereby, by implication, overriding Chinese domestic judicial decisions and practice. Within the WTO, China also became vulnerable to the WTO dispute system and to pressure for increased legal transparency, and greater political openness and accountability.[14] Other challenges to its sovereignty have been posed by the conditions attached to its entry. In contrast to other WTO members, who undergo a periodic Trade Policy Review every two, four, or six years, China agreed to submit to a decade-long special Transitional Review Mechanism, consisting of an annual review by sixteen subsidiary house bodies, followed by a separate review by the General Council each December.[15]

In terms of its domestic impact, WTO membership also increased competition and further eroded China's central control over commercial policy. It necessitated significant reductions in tariffs, removal of nontariff barriers and quotas, further protection of intellectual property rights, and the elimination of many barriers to trade in agricultural products.[16] In January 2002, China cut tariffs on some 5,300 imported items, lowering them on average from 15 to 12 percent. It also removed non-tariff barriers on 238 product items.[17] In addition, it shouldered short-term legislative expenses. Thus, in March 2000, Premier Zhu announced that the central government was reviewing and would revise existing laws, regulations, and policies that obviously contradicted WTO rules in a bid to guarantee conformity with the latter.[18] A two-year-long review of its laws related to foreign trade ended in April 2004 with amendments to its Foreign Trade Law.[19] Scholars were also dispatched to leading U.S. universities to become experts on WTO law. In general, President Jiang Zemin undertook that "once inside the WTO, China will strictly comply with the universally acknowledged market rules, implement open, transparent and equality-based policies of trade and investment and endeavor to promote a multi-directional and multi-level opening-up in a wide range of areas."[20]

In the short term, however, the social costs associated with such developments have been more obvious than any long-term benefits.[21] Because of the competition to which it has exposed China's urban and rural industries, WTO membership has had critical ramifications for human security in China. As previous chapters have documented, prior to its accession, domestic stability had already become a cause for concern, partly because of China's failure in the 1990s to create a universal social welfare system funded through investments in capital markets to protect the unemployed and other groups rendered vulnerable by accession.[22] As a result, unemployment increased, regional inequalities widened, and social disturbances deepened, particularly in the heavily industrialized northeast and the agriculturally dependent interior.[23] China's accession to the WTO simply exacerbated these problems. Apart from domestically sourced problems of nonperforming loans in the banking system, corruption, and the restructuring and bankruptcy of state-owned enterprises, the globalization of capital within the WTO elevated the rights of shareholders over China's social and political goals at substantial cost to its sovereignty.[24] For these reasons, China's new leaders, ushered into power in March 2003, redirected national attention to the welfare of workers and peasants and finally began work on the establishment of a social security net.[25]

China's accession presented challenges not only for China, but for the whole WTO system. Obstacles to implementing WTO rules included their in-applicability to a non-market economy; the inadequacy of existing surveillance machinery; the cultural mismatch between China and other WTO members, leading to differences of interpretation; the inadequacy of Chinese domestic financial and legal institutions; interference from, and non-compliance of, China's sub-national authorities; and the danger that Western WTO members would engage in excessive dispute resolution with China.[26] If WTO members placed too much pressure on China, if its economic restructuring was pushed too fast and social stability was imperiled, domestic unrest would increase: if, on the other hand, in the interests of domestic stability, China did not fully implement the reforms it had promised within the accepted timetable, it could become embroiled in constant dispute with other WTO members,[27] and glob-alization would be the loser.

What has been China's record of compliance since 2001; how, if at all, has it deviated from its characteristic early pattern of international organizational participation in the 1970s and 1980s; and are any major differences yet discernible in its record of compliance and cooperation? Already, numerous official and scholarly evaluations of China's record in the WTO have been concluded.[28] Prior to 11 December 2004, when most of China's key commitments were sched-uled to be phased in fully, most observers concluded that, despite many tech-nical and practical difficulties, China had made considerable progress in its compliance with WTO rules, and, at least at the central level, was determined to meet its commitments.[29] Achievements included the steps, initiated before accession, to dismantle the protectionist system,[30] the promulgation of laws and regulations that, for the most part, complied with its WTO obligations, efforts to strengthen the regulatory system, and increased transparency.[31] Problems that had also been flagged, however, included the technical and practical obstacles to fair, uniform, and impartial implementation; continuing and significant problems of transparency; areas, such as agriculture, where China was in compliance but had instituted new regulations or standards that restricted market opening; the slow progress of domestic institution and market building; the incomplete development of a system of enforcement, particularly in relation to intellectual property rights (IPR); opposition from local industries that did not initially consent to WTO provisions; and utilization of remedies that were permissible under the WTO such as antidumping and health and safety standards.[32]

In 2005, a year after its key commitments had been phased in, the U.S. Trade Representative Report to Congress made a careful, but equally mixed, evaluation:

> China has not yet fully embraced the key WTO principles of market access, non-discrimination and national treatment, nor has China fully institutionalized market mechanisms and made its trade regime predictable and transparent. While China has made some important progress, it continued to use an array of industrial policy tools in 2005 to promote or protect favored sectors and industries and these tools at times collide with China's WTO obligations.[33]

With the end of country-by-country textile quotas on 1 January 2005, moreover, China's textile exports to the United States and the European Union swelled. An impending trade conflict with the latter was only avoided at the eleventh hour by China's agreement to place voluntary limits on its textile and apparel exports to about 10 percent a year until 2008.[34] Its compliance/cooperation record has therefore been, to say the least, uneven.

At the same time, as Nicholas Lardy has pointed out, some provisions that were actually built into China's WTO commitments have made compliance very difficult. These include China's unique and extensive undertaking, far surpassing those made by other countries, which, for instance, creates problems for low-income Chinese farmers; its extensive commitments in the services sector, which were made without sufficient consultation with the relevant domestic regulators; and the limits to market access for Chinese goods in foreign markets that were accepted by China in its accession package. Some of these "constrain the government's ability to smooth what will inevitably be a socially painful restructuring."[35] These views are strongly endorsed by Chinese critics of China's terms of admission. Yet, despite the international and domestic challenges it faced, in December 2003, China passed its annual review by the world trade body.[36]

At first sight, such problems appear to mirror our findings of China's compliance record in the main case studies. While it adheres to the letter of the law, and has a good record of legislative implementation, China has difficulty with practical implementation, with rule of law issues, with enforcement, and with transparency. As in the case of other international organizations, China is, on the whole, compliant but not wholly cooperative within the WTO. What is unusual in the WTO case, however, is the breadth of China's commitments, in comparison with other developing countries, particularly its agreement to internalize WTO norms and procedures to an unprecedented degree. Most remarkable is its acceptance of more intense foreign and international scrutiny than other WTO members over the next ten years, its agreement to more than 685 trade regime commitments, and its acknowledgement of the need for transparency.[37] This is in striking contrast to its lack of cooperation on issues of transparency and verification in the other international organizations reviewed here.

Another major stumbling block in the past has been China's continual struggle to block Taiwan's membership or participation, in any capacity, in international organizations. Here again, China has made a special exception, allowing Taiwan to join as a "Separate Customs Territory of Taiwan, Penghu, Kinmen and Matsu" and to become a member of the WTO following its own accession. While this may have been for the instrumental reasons of facilitating political and economic reintegration in the long term, in the short term it represented a potential sovereignty cost. The only other cases where China has made such a concession to Taiwan is to approve its participation in the Asian Development Bank and the Asia-Pacific Economic Cooperation (APEC) forum (and then as a region of China under the designation of Taipei, China [in ADB] or Chinese Taipei [in APEC]), both key institutions of the international political economy regime. In other words, in the WTO China has not only reassessed its interests as conforming with WTO norms, but it has accepted unusually high costs and has substantially renegotiated its sovereignty. In these senses its participation appears qualitatively different from that in other international organizations.

In its early relations with the WTO, China has also varied its normal pattern of behavior. In the 1970s and 1980s, it initially adopted a modest, reserved role of learner in international organizations, eschewing leadership. To some extent that learning pattern has been continued in its early relations with the WTO. Yet, shortly after entering the WTO, China joined seven other co-complainants in a case against the United States after Washington had sought to shore up the ailing U.S. steel industry by imposing emergency tariffs of up to 30 percent on imported steel. When the WTO Appellate Body for trade disputes found for the complainants, China indicated that it would cooperate in enforcing the judgment.[38] The subsequent attempt by a spokesman to downplay its involvement as a kind of "on-the-job training . . . to get China familiar with the procedure and techniques," could not conceal China's commitment to the WTO and its rules.[39]

China also took an unusually assertive leadership position at the Doha round at Cancun. By July 2003, it was expressing anxiety about the slow progress, particularly on agricultural issues, of the new round of talks initiated in November 2001.[40] At Cancun, the emergence for the first time of the "G-20 Plus" as a powerful negotiating bloc was largely due to the leadership of Brazil, India, and China, with Brazil taking the initiative.[41] Likewise, China's leadership inspired the formation of an informal alliance among the ninety least-developed states in Africa, the Caribbean, and the Pacific Rim. Whereas its co-appellants in the U.S. steel case consisted of developed and middle income states (EU, Japan, South Korea, Switzerland, Norway, New Zealand, and Brazil), at Cancun, as in its maiden speech upon entry to the WTO, China indicated its intention to primarily emphasize its role as a "developing state." As a result, WTO Director-General Supachai Panitchpakdi even began to promote China as a possible intermediary between the developed and developing world, encouraging further progress in negotiations.[42] By contrast, at the Sixth Ministerial Conference of the WTO in Hong Kong in December 2005, China appeared to be hoist on its own petard, unwilling to offend developed states, particularly the EU, and so wary of championing the interests of developing states. Even its potential as an intermediary between the two sides was not fully explored.[43] Finally, the collapse of the Doha Round talks in Geneva in July 2006, as the result of disagreement between the United States and Europe over farm subsidies and import quotas, confirmed that the fate of the developing states still remained hostage to the interests of the developed world, whatever the new-found negotiating skills of the "G-20 Plus."

Nevertheless, what emerges from the brief period of China's WTO participation is the tentative conclusion that, where its economic interest is at stake, and the ideology of the free market is involved, China is capable of a qualitatively different relationship with the world, one in which regime norms may be internalized, the limits of sovereignty become more elastic, high costs are acceptable, and the intrusion of verification and on-site monitoring is permissible. Such tolerance is partly a function of the chronology of China's entry into international organizations in a period privileging the ethos of the free market. It is also the result of China's own cost-benefit analysis. Where it hopes to gain more, China is prepared to give more.

WHO

China's interaction with the WHO provides a very different test case of compliance. Like the international human rights organizations, it tests the outer limits of the effectiveness of international organizational process. This is because, as in the former cases, China's receptiveness to international pressures, norms, and rules has been diminished when political leaders perceive that those norms and rules constitute a threat to the structure of domestic governance and social stability, as well as the international status, of the Chinese state, and that no incentives exist that outweigh those costs.

Like the WTO, the WHO and its norms and rules have significant implications for human security in China.[44] However, they also have obvious repercussions for global human security. In contrast to China's entry into the WTO, which entailed the restructuring of Chinese policies and institutions well in advance of entry, and involved participation costs, its membership of WHO, commencing in 1972, only revealed the costs many years later. Moreover, those costs arose not from participation in the organization, but, rather, from China's long-term neglect of its responsibilities as a member. This was a case where the impact of international organizational pressures on China developed very slowly, from negligible to overwhelming. As the result of two major and unanticipated crises, the global spread of AIDS and the sudden development on Chinese territory of the acute respiratory disease SARS, China eventually recognized that its response to globalization would not be judged solely by its implementation of WTO rules. The advent of AIDS and SARS highlighted the critical lack of transparency in domestic political culture, which plagued China's relations with most international organizations. It placed a spotlight on China's domestic governance, revealing a syndrome of secrecy and denial as well as a tendency to seek scapegoats for the maladministration issuing from that secrecy. Finally, it highlighted the economic costs and loss of international face that could result from non-compliance.[45]

WHO membership conferred on China multiple benefits of access to health information, health technologies, and technical assistance. China was in turn bound by Articles 61–65 of the WHO Constitution, which obliged it to report annually on the progress achieved in improving the health of its people and in implementing recommendations made to it by the Organization, particularly with respect to conventions, agreements, and regulation. Members were also required to "communicate promptly to the organization important laws, regulations, official reports and statistics pertaining to health which have been published in the State concerned"; to provide statistical and epidemiological reports in a manner to be determined by the Health Assembly; and to "transmit upon the request of the Board such additional information pertaining to health as may be practicable."[46]

China's failure to respond to WHO warnings about AIDS is well documented. From the beginning, it denied the prevalence of the disease in China, ignored the tragic reinjection of infected plasma into the thousands of peasants who had sold their blood as a survival stratagem, and lost years in a battle that it was finally forced to join.[47] This denial lasted from 1989, when the first case of AIDS occurred in the country, until 1998, when China finally accepted WHO findings about the incidence of the disease in the country. Even by October 2002, the UN Secretary-General still felt obliged to warn that it faced a looming epidemic.[48] Only in December 2003, on World AIDS day, did the government take its first real steps toward a full-scale public awareness campaign.[49] The result has been that, by 2010, China will suffer from 6.4 million, and possibly 10 million, cases if the infection rate increases significantly.[50]

Despite its painful awareness that a swifter response could have saved tens of thousands of lives, China did not learn the more general lesson of the need for transparency and accountability in its relations with the WHO. Although the outbreak of SARS occurred as early as November 2002, it was not until 11 February 2003 that China reported five cases to the WHO, insisting at the same time that the disease was "under control." On 7 April, WHO Director-General Gro Harlem Brundtland criticized the Chinese government for not asking earlier for international assistance and, on the same day, the leader of a WHO team that had interviewed health authorities in Guangdong, dismissed Chinese claims that the disease was under control.[51]

SARS presented a peculiar challenge to all states. Although in terms of global epidemics its infection rate was not very high, the fact that it spread so insidiously, that it had no known antidote and that it targeted the medical staff mobilized to treat it, created global anxiety.[52] Moreover, unlike AIDS, it was class-neutral and swiftly crossed all boundaries. Having hitherto refused WHO authorities permission to travel to Guangdong, and forbidden the Chinese media to cover the story, in the face of worldwide panic the Chinese authorities finally apologized on 4 April for not having alerted people to the disease and announced China's participation in a global investigation.[53] By then, 1,220 people had been infected in China alone. On 15 April, admitting 1,418 cases and 64 deaths, Chinese authorities ended their secrecy and called the situation "grave."[54] Despite this, the WHO had still not been told to what extent it would be allowed to help contain the disease.[55] A cover-up was suggested by the revelations of a courageous Chinese medical practitioner that the official statistics supplied for the incidence of the disease in Beijing were incorrect.[56] By 12 May, 240 Chinese had died from SARS and more than 4,900 had been infected, the bulk of the world's total of over 7,000.[57]

Apart from its political culture of non-transparency, China's decision to cover up the mounting crisis was most heavily influenced by its anxieties about its national reputation and the effects of a national epidemic on economic growth and tourism, fears of undermining the peaceful transfer of political power planned for the National People's Congress in March 2003, and, as in the case of AIDS, concerns about its impact on social stability. The human rights of its people were very low on its list of priorities. The case suggested that "China's participation in international organizations d[id] not, on its own, bring about responsible, let alone humane, behavior."[58]

The situation also had important political dimensions. When SARS subsequently reached Taiwan and Taiwan's own crisis deepened, China was obliged to give permission to WHO to play a direct role in its health outcomes, thereby implicitly renegotiating its sovereignty.[59] It also allowed five Taiwanese experts invited by the organization to attend a WHO meeting in Malaysia on SARS.[60] Because of its delay in granting permission, however, and because of its opposition to Taiwan's annual attempts to rejoin WHO, Taiwanese President Chen Shui-bian insisted that China's actions had in fact "widened the gap between the two."[61]

Paradoxically, the very results China's leaders most feared from disclosure ensued from their secrecy. Even though China was declared free of the disease by June 2003, there was always the possibility that it could resurface.[62] Perhaps the most critical result of Beijing's lack of transparency was its impact on international public opinion, producing a widespread realization that the modernization and globalization of China's economy had not been accompanied by a change in attitude. China's mistake had been to adopt perestroika (economic reform) without effective glasnost (openness). In the end, the sudden cessation of reported infections and signs of economic revival restored the faith of the international community. When the infection briefly returned in 2004, moreover, China was quick to report it. In the same year, and again in 2005 and 2006, it also reported outbreaks of the bird flu that had a catastrophic potential to infect humanity at large.[63] Thus, by 2006, China had implicitly acknowledged the truth of Director-General Brundtland's assertion that "the first and most imperative lesson learned from SARS is the need for all disease outbreaks to be reported quickly and openly. . . . In a globalised world, efforts to hide epidemics due to the fear of social and economic consequences will be truly costly."[64] However, the lesson had only been learnt at considerable cost, not so much as the result of international organizational pressures, but by dint of revealing the dire domestic and international consequences of non-compliance. The case defined the outer limits of international organizational effectiveness in cases where a state's perception of its strategic domestic interests ran counter to international organizational norms.

This prompts the penultimate question of why a least-likely, former "rogue," "revolutionary" and now "quasi-revolutionary" state, complies with international norms, principles, and rules. Judging from both the WTO and WHO cases, one could conclude that utilitarian rationalism, the notion that states only follow international law when it is in their interest to do so, is the sole reason for China's compliance. In other words, only where its material interest is at stake is China prepared to cooperate as well as to comply with international rules. Yet, as the cases studies have revealed, China's compliance has, in fact, been determined by a complex mix of normative and instrumental factors and motivations.

To understand this, we must revisit and then expand on the question of why China chose to join the UN proper. The PRC's unremitting efforts from 1949 to replace Taiwan as China's official representative in the UN were initially the primary reason for its interest in international organizations. Legitimation of CCP rule was sought not just through the establishment of diplomatic relations with other countries but, in line with Inis Claude's hypothesis, through the processes of "collective legitimization" conferred by the UN.[65] Both processes entailed the PRC's replacement of Taiwan as the legitimate representative of "China." However, so important was UN endorsement to the PRC that it was prepared to refuse or defer diplomatic relations with those countries that would not also support its entry into the UN. This legitimation was sought not only through the verbal functioning of the UN, as identified by Claude and others, but also through the status derived from executive UN positions. China's second and related core goal was community. Having existed for so long in defensive and angry isolation, it sought a formal role in the international community that had long rejected it. China was just one of those revolutionary actors identified by Richard Falk in 1970 as depending upon mutual contact and communication, not only with developing, but also with developed, states.[66] Finally, it was dependent on a minimally reliable system of international order. Such a system in turn required a rule-impregnated international society, based on the principles of sovereignty and the sovereign equality of states. These three goals were finally realized after 1971, when the PRC succeeded in replacing Taiwan as official representative of China in the United Nations and related international organizations.

However, the core goals of legitimation, community, and a rule-based system are not temporary expedients but stepping stones toward the continuing success of international interaction. For the PRC, the need to continuously legitimize its rule was pressing, given that the government in Taiwan also regarded international organizations as a mutual battleground for the determination of ultimate sovereignty over "China." To realize these core goals on a continuing basis, states must also exhibit a degree of reciprocity by complying adequately with the rules of the game. The need for reciprocity is not necessarily something states are aware of when they enter international society. Only over time, after prolonged interaction, persuasion, and pressure applied by international organizations, did China become aware of, and responsive to, its reciprocal obligations. This was particularly evident in its interaction with the ILO and CAT. Even in such "least-likely" cases, provided that external developments and pressures converged with domestic interests, this complex organizational process brought about the gradual liberalization of official Chinese views. Conversely, as China's SARS crisis and its intransigence over the right to freedom of association and the prohibition against torture suggest, the bottom line defining the limits of its compliance and cooperation was any development that might destabilize China's authoritarian political system, undermine its developmental goals, or threaten its autonomy.

We must also reflect on why China sought to enter the other international organizations under scrutiny here. As we have shown, prior to participation or accession, China made it clear, whether in explicit policy statements, in the reservations it entered in ratifying a treaty, or in the conventions it chose not to ratify, that it disagreed with the principal norms of each organization and its associated treaties. It also became a member of each organization in different periods and under different circumstances. It joined the Conference on Disarmament and replaced Taiwan in the IMF and World Bank in 1980, when it was seeking to expand its membership of international organizations and promote its economic interests. On the other hand, spurred on by participation in the Conference on the Environment in Stockholm that had established UNEP, in a kind of defensive policy-by-default it joined UNEP in 1973, the year of its formation. Although it replaced Taiwan as representative of China in the ILO soon after the latter was ousted from the UN, it did not begin active participation in the ILO until 1983, and then as part of a policy of membership expansion. Finally, it became subject to the supervision of the UN Committee against Torture as a result of voluntarily ratifying the Convention against Torture on 4 October 1988, a decision based primarily on considerations of status and protection of its interests. In only one of these international organizations, the World Bank, did membership promise clear material advantage for China. Even in that case, its leaders recognized some of the costs it would have to bear, and required considerable persuasion from the elite levels of the host organization, as they did in the case of the ILO, to acquiesce in full participation. And yet, some of China's most notable normative, conceptual, and policy advances were made in those very organizations, such as the Conference on Disarmament and the United Nations Environment Programme, that did not initially promise it advantage. Within the CD, China moved from a defensive posture to an increasingly confident and positive role, in which it oscillated between supporting the interests of developing states and joining and supporting the august counsels of the P-5. In UNEP, it ratified major environmental treaties and implemented their rules. While it advanced the interests of developing states, it did so in a broadly community-based and democratic fashion. In addition, as the Tables show, in all of these organizations, apart from human rights bodies, it complied reasonably across the different levels, with the exception of the troubled category of social implementation. How did this happen?

Test of Compliance Theories

Clearly, none of the compliance theories that we have considered provides on its own a necessary and sufficient explanation for the complexity of China's response. Rule-legitimacy theory gives insufficient scope to organizational process, and focuses too closely on the details of rules. Managerial theory pays too little attention to exogenous self-interest, fails to give plausible reasons for China's non-compliance with treaty norms, and virtually ignores the issue of domestic implementation. Likewise, neoliberal institutionalism does not explain the process of China's domestic internalization of norms, and does not consider the potential of interests to undermine, as well as bolster, institutional pressures. Rational choice theory's claim that states are unwilling to pay the costs of deep compliance is disproved by the Chinese experience. By any measure, China has made more than a "modest" departure from what it would have done in the absence of international rules and international organizations. The China case also undermines the argument of Downs and others that "the deeper the agreement is, the greater the punishments required to support it."[67] At most, China has responded to persuasion, shadowed by the possibility of enforcement. The moment the threat has been implemented, however, issues of sovereignty and national pride have come into play and transcended the constraining effects of fear.[68]

Unlike other theories, transnational legal process theory illuminates the essential aspect of domestic internalization, as well as explaining the interaction between the international and the national. Koh is correct when he states that in nonliberal countries, strong executives may internalize international rules. Yet, the Chinese case does not validate his further hypothesis that once these rules are accepted as domestic law in such countries, they begin to trickle down into the system and force domestic change.

Finally, liberal identity theory only explains the behavior of liberal states. As a prescription for future peace and for increased compliance by all states, therefore, it is unlikely to be successful. The specific explanations it gives for state compliance also fail the test of the least-likely case study, since it has been shown that nonliberal states also comply with international norms, but for different reasons. In other words, contrary to the claims of the liberal identity theorists, absence of an entrenched rule of law does not prevent a state from complying, at least at the level of legislative implementation, with the international rule of law.

Putting aside their various inadequacies, however, it is clear, as we have argued throughout, that the process-based theories—managerialism, transnational legal process, constructivism, and the related IR theory of persuasion—when considered together with Inis Claude's legitimization theory, are the most helpful in explaining China's increasingly compliant international behavior. First, as Claude would anticipate, from 1971, the legitimizing power and effects of UN membership entrenched China's involvement in, and identification with, international organizations. From 1949, its struggle to join the United Nations was aimed to win international support for its sovereignty, to benefit from the empowering effects of sovereign equality and to legitimize both its rule and its policies. Second, having decided to join other international organizations for reasons of status, national interests, and the desire to protect its sovereignty, other motivations and influences came into play. Here, Checkel's persuasion theory, that states are more likely to be persuaded when they are either uncertain or novice, helps explain why states like China, despite their "least-likely" status, were to some extent already predisposed to comply with international rules.[69] Beyond that initial tendency, China's compliance evolved gradually, very much as the managerialists, international legal process theorists, and constructivists have argued, as the result of a long drawn-out iterative process of bargaining, "jawboning," and mutual explanation within international institutions, rather than through coercive pressures. This process, which also gradually introduced China to the need for reciprocity, persuaded it to "explore, redefine and sometimes discover" its own, and mutual, interests.[70] Likewise, specific international organizations and their treaties helped increase China's transparency, and, by cutting its transaction costs, building its capacity, and enhancing dispute settlement, further entrenched its organizational dependence.

At the domestic level, transnational legal process theory rightly stresses domestic norm internalization and usefully distinguishes three different forms: legislative, political, and social. Some of its compliance-facilitating agents, namely, governmental norm sponsors, and, to a limited extent, bureaucratic compliance procedures and law-declaring forums, are also helpful in explaining China's attempts to implement norms. The theory, like the pyramid theory of John Braithwaite, also correctly conceives management and the threat of enforcement as complementary, rather than alternative, strategies. It introduces the concept of "presumptive" compliance, which underlines the special effort required for states not to comply. By the same token, Koh's related theory of why liberal states comply helps explain why nonliberal states do not comply.[71] In contrast to liberal states, the lack of strong pressures from domestic NGOs in China and the inaccessibility of China's authoritarian government to public opinion, block the trickle-down of such norms and rules into social practice.

At the same time, liberal and rationalist theories should not be entirely discounted. They also offer complementary, if only partial, explanations. Rule-legitimacy theory explains why China sought external legitimation through its membership of international rule-making institutions and why it complied with legitimate ILO rules and procedures, despite believing that, as a result of its failure to ratify relevant standards, their application to itself was not warranted. The theory also accurately predicts China's respect for the procedural fairness of international forums. Conversely, the commitment "to keep the game going," explains China's unwillingness to opt out of organizations or regimes that have frustrated its interests. Within rationalism, neoliberal institutionalism introduces the necessary extralegal factors, the considerations of interest and reputation so important in China's case, yet places the institutional process at the core of compliance explanations. Rational choice theory, on the other hand, correctly emphasizes the exogenous nature of some aspects of self-interest, a loose cannon that in China's case has both reinforced compliance and produced noncompliance. In particular, it helps explain why China is prepared to make more concessions on sovereignty in relation to the international political economy regime than in relation to the other regimes, and why it decided to comply with the Montreal Protocol, and even finally decided to ratify the Kyoto Protocol.

By contrast, liberal identity theory, like Koh's liberal state theory, offers a useful negative model. By highlighting the compliance processes within liberal states, it exposes the deficits in a nonliberal state, and helps explain why the top-down processes of legislative and political implementation of international norms in China are still insufficient to bring about the social implementation of norms necessary for deep compliance and cooperation. In other words, it illuminates the distinction made by Koh between political and social internalization. It is precisely the disjunction between strong executive policy and legislation imposed from above and the lack of domestic receptivity from below, or a failure of the trickle-down effect, that accounts for China's inability to implement new policies and new laws in practice. Local interests, corruption, interministerial rivalries, a lack of trust between the leaders and the led, and, in particular, the tenuous hold of China's "rule by law," all account for this lack of domestic acceptance and social internalization of new norms, however strong the political directives from above might be. In other words, while authoritarian states may adapt quite well to the international rule of law, the effective implementation, enforcement, and internalization of that law will ultimately be stymied by the lack of a genuine rule of law at the domestic level.

It is also the case, as we have observed, that different compliance theories are more applicable in one regime than another. The different characteristics of the regimes and their associated international organizations and treaties, in particular their different underlying norms and principles, compliance mechanisms, costs and benefits, incentives and disincentives for compliance, make this inevitable. For instance, specific treaty-induced compliance theories, as the work of Thomas Franck, among others, would suggest, are more applicable to the environmental regime, while regime-specific principles, like reciprocity and transparency, together with political considerations such as status and reputation, are more important in explaining China's response to international organizations like the CD, World Bank, and IMF.

Finally, as regards the comparative value of international law and international relations theories of compliance, the former alert international relations theorists to pay more attention to the role of rule legitimacy and institutional process in eliciting state compliance, while the latter highlight the failure of legal theorists to take account of key political variables. However, with the exception of transnational legal process theory and constructivism, both international law and international relations theories fail to adequately incorporate consideration of the domestic implementation of international norms, without which they cannot effectively determine whether "compliance" has in fact occurred. Moreover, the case studies reveal the ultimate poverty of such theories as sufficient explanation for international order. They are conceived too narrowly, and, most important, fail to explore the realms of cooperation and non-cooperation, without which a full appreciation of the complex requirements for international integration is impossible. While state compliance with international norms, principles, and rules is an essential building block of harmonious interstate relations, a state's cooperation with them, in the sense of implementing and promoting their object and purpose in a variety of ways, remains the most reliable predictor of long-term global security. The study of compliance, therefore, remains incomplete unless it is also accompanied by consideration of the broader, more political concept of cooperation. It is these gaps in the literature that this study has sought to fill.

China's Impact and Influence

The second part of the problematic addressed at the outset is the critical question of China's impact on international organizations and their associated treaties. The question of China's compliance with existing international norms throws light on the past and affects the here and now. Its influence on the development of those norms and rules, on the other hand, will be critical to future international order, whether in relation to arms control and disarmament or in relation to matters of human security, including developmental, environmental, and human rights issues. Because of China's size, power, and influence, its impact on international organizations, alone or in concert, is far greater than the principle of sovereign equality would suggest, particularly in institutions like the World Bank and IMF, where the state's power is not based on the principle of "one state, one vote" but is broadly reflective of its economic power.

To take the regimes in turn, in the international security regime, China's impact on the CD has been significant. Initially, other CD members felt that its entry had brought enhanced legitimacy and universal authority to their organization and transformed it into a confidence-building forum within which they could attempt to influence China's nuclear policies and, in particular, express their disapproval of its nuclear testing within a multilateral setting. China's membership also gave the G-21 an often sympathetic, if not representative, voice within the P-5. In particular, its opposition to the abrogation of the ABM Treaty expressed G-21 concerns. Less positively, its policy of "asymmetrical transparency" also influenced the NAM states. Apart from its critical role in the negotiation of treaties, China's specific contribution to debate included its insistence on the need for the United States and the Soviet Union/Russia to make progress in disarmament and nuclear nonproliferation before other NWS were obliged to follow suit. Its "no first use" policy and position on the "complete prohibition and destruction of nuclear weapons" were other specifically Chinese inputs. China's participation in the CD debates also helped mitigate its own shocked response to the Indian and Pakistani tests and thereby helped obviate excessive international tensions. In recent years, its strong declaratory support for the norms and rules of the regime has arguably strengthened it. On the other hand, disagreement between the United States and China is currently impeding the progress and effectiveness of the CD, thereby highlighting the current reciprocity deficit.

In the international political economy regime, both the World Bank and the IMF have been extraordinarily respectful of China's sensitivities about sovereignty, about its status, and about the authoritarian nature of its political system, since these issues have generally formed the basis of the recurring strains in the relationship, just as they have in relations with other international organizations. China's economic clout has had an effect on the Bank's lending policies, while its relative imperviousness to IMF conditionality has allowed it considerable independence as a member. For these reasons, it is difficult to agree that "the rules of the two institutions have not been bent for China any more than they normally are for large new entrants."[72] This relative freedom enjoyed by China has had both negative and positive consequences for it. In terms of human security, its insistence on using Bank funds for growth rather than development is now revealing its shortcomings, whereas its relative financial independence protected it during the 1997 Asian financial crisis. Nevertheless, assessments in 1999 that the integration of China into the world trade, investment, and financial arenas had occurred without significant disruption to the international political economy regime, still appear largely correct.[73] Rather than undermining the basic norms, rules, and principles of these key economic international organizations, China has assisted in their development and evolution, playing, for instance, an important role in influencing the Bank to introduce the idea of country ownership of projects. At the same time, Bank and Fund norms and rules have protected the organizations from excessive demands by China and have lent weight to the importance of modeling, or the positive example set by other complying states.

In the atmospheric environment, China's record of pushing the interests of developing states on the issue of global warming has contrasted with its more compliant approach to the Vienna Convention and the Montreal Protocol. The difference in China's response has both domestic and international origins. For China, compliance with the climate change instruments involves relatively larger domestic economic costs, as it does for all states. Thus, its lack of cooperation has reflected the general reluctance on the part of the entire international community, as well as its perception that compliance could compromise its critical national interests. It has also reflected China's need to champion the interests of developing states when its interests have coincided with theirs. Until the Kyoto Protocol entered into force in February 2005, moreover, there were no detailed, effective mechanisms that could have encouraged states' compliance and cooperation.

Nevertheless, China's influence on this part of the regime, through its support for the position of developing states and its negotiating power, has been substantial. From the time of negotiations on the Vienna Convention and the Montreal Protocol, its insistence that developed states assume initial responsibility for the state of the atmospheric environment and that they assist developing states to attain a capacity to follow suit in due course, has influenced the norms, principles, and rules of this regime. On the other hand, in the last few years, China has redefined its interests to accord more closely with the norms of the atmospheric environment. Its ratification of the Kyoto Protocol in 2002 may have even influenced Canada's and Russia's ultimate decisions to follow suit. Such encouragement of others falls into the category of promoting the object and purpose of the Protocol. However, the ongoing tension between China's need to rapidly industrialize and its gradual recognition of the devastating effects of environmental degradation will continue to determine its ambivalent attitude to atmospheric environmental protection, and its readiness to act and negotiate in the interests of the G-77.

In the international human rights regime, by contrast, China has been more consistently negative. It has contested the need to establish a charter of funda-

mental industrial rights, in particular resisting acceptance of the right to freedom of association, and has sought to block any strengthening of CAT powers. To date, its activities have not had a fatal impact on these bodies or their
norms.[74] However, as we have observed, in successfully nominating a former
Chinese Foreign Ministry official onto the Committee's panel of human rights
experts, as well as a Chinese national onto two other international human rights
treaty bodies, and in returning a worker representative to the ILO Governing
Body, China has positioned itself to take a leading role in the future deliberations of these bodies, without having committed itself to either compliance or
cooperation.

The outlook for China's impact on international organizations and their
associated treaties is therefore mixed. In the CD, the IBRD, and IMF, China's
influence has been largely positive and broadly supportive of their goals and purposes. Despite its role as a club of one, its shared interests with both developed
and developing states in these organizations are symptomatic of its integrated role
within them. Where its efforts have given support to the needs of developing
states, they have not generally been to the detriment of other members, except
perhaps India. By contrast, in matters affecting the environment and human rights,
particularly the atmospheric environment and labor and health rights, China's
identification with, and championship of, the interests of the developing world
have created challenges for existing international standards as well as for national
standards adopted within the developed world. This, among other reasons, is
because non-state actors like multinationals exploit differences in national standards globally to transfer investment and employment to those states with lower
standards, thereby supporting the race to the bottom. Even developed state
actors have exploited China's position by, for instance, using its refusal to assume
initial responsibility for global warming as an excuse not to sign or ratify the
Kyoto Protocol themselves. The dangers of such lowest-common-denominator
politics are clear, particularly at a time when China's power, both regional and
international, is rapidly increasing. Since China is one of the weak links in the
chain of labor, health, and environmental standards, its further international integration and socialization are critical to the maintenance of international standards of human security and sustainable development. The fact that it has already
changed so much in a period of relatively stable multilateralism is a cogent argument for maintaining the stability of those standards now and in the future. While
it is still in a learning mode, it is also critical to ensure that it has strong and stable role models in other states. The most harmful lesson it could learn would be
that states, particularly powerful ones, are free to make their own rules as they
go along, and that reciprocity no longer counts.[75]

In conclusion, what does this book say about how best to treat renegade, rogue, and even quasi-revolutionary states? And what does it say about the power of international organizations? In an era of heightened international tension and asymmetrical power, when the risks of unilateral action are enhanced, it reminds us of the critical importance of international organizations in maintaining international order and enhancing international prosperity and global security. The international multilateral system, despite its much publicized flaws, has been successful in numerous publicized and unpublicized ways. It has assisted in the integration and socialization of nonliberal states in the international community; it has enlarged and enhanced their capacities; and it has encouraged their increased compliance with international law. It has also demonstrated the importance and benefits of reciprocal compliance and cooperation. Under this benign influence, as this study has shown, least-likely states will and do comply with the norms, principles, and rules of international organizations and international treaties, and internalize many of their values in legal and political practice. The basic need for international legitimation, international community, and a stable system of international rules is shared by all states. If least-likely states are given a stake in the international system, they will join it. Eventually, like China, they will even begin to promote that system, which in turn will benefit from their participation.

Such a conclusion, however, in no way precludes the continuing role and importance of international politics. Multilateral institutions and international rules are a prerequisite of international order, not an ultimate guarantor of it. Rather, as in a domestic setting, international institutions and rules provide the springboard from which that order can be negotiated in a rule-governed, relatively egalitarian, and predictable manner. As Inis Claude has observed, "collective legitimization may stimulate legal changes that will make international law more worthy of respect and more likely to be respected, but it may also encourage behavior based upon calculation of what the political situation will permit rather than consideration of what the principles of order require."[76] The close intertwining of international politics and international law in the world of international organizations has ensured that, whether we are dealing with nonliberal states or liberal states, it will be ever thus. That China and other least-likely states will also seek to influence and shape the international system is in the nature of international politics, particularly where it involves a large power. The essential requirement for the health and security of the international system, however, is that all states should be present at the negotiating table. However great their differences, these are more likely to be resolved by an ongoing multilateral conversation in an international institutional setting.

List of Abbreviations

ABM	anti-ballistic missile
ACFTU	All-China Federation of Trade Unions
ADB	Asian Development Bank
AMCs	asset management companies
APLs	anti-personnel landmines
APRO	Asian and Pacific Regional Organization
ARF	ASEAN Regional Forum
ARPLA	Asian and Pacific Regional Centre for Labour Administration
BCP	Basle Core Principles
BIS	Bank for International Settlements
BWC	Biological Weapons Convention
CAS	Country Assistance Strategy
CAT	United Nations Committee against Torture
CAT	Convention against Torture and Other Cruel, Inhuman or Degrading Treatment or Punishment
CCP	Chinese Communist Party
CD	Conference on Disarmament
CDF	Comprehensive Development Framework
CDM	Clean Development Mechanism
CEDAW	Committee on the Elimination of Discrimination against Women
CER	Certified Emissions Reduction
CERD	Committee on the Elimination of Racial Discrimination
CFA	Committee on Freedom of Association

CFCs	chlorofluorocarbons
CIAE	China Institute of Atomic Energy
CITES	Convention on International Trade in Endangered Species of Wild Fauna and Flora
CMS	Convention on the Conservation of Migratory Species of Wild Animals
CO_2	carbon dioxide
COP	Conference of the Parties
COSTIND	Commission on Science, Technology and Industry for National Defense
CPA	counterpart agency
CPL	Criminal Procedure Law
CSD	United Nations Commission on Sustainable Development
CTBT	Comprehensive Test Ban Treaty
CWC	Chemical Weapons Convention
EC	European Commission
ECOSOC	Economic and Social Council
EEC	European Economic Community
ENDC	Eighteen Nation Committee on Disarmament
ESAF	Enhanced Structural Adjustment Facility
EU	European Union
FAO	Food and Agricultural Organization
FDI	foreign direct investment
FIEs	foreign investment enterprises
FMCT	Fissile Material Cut-off Treaty
FSAP	Financial Sector Assessment Program
FSS	full-scope safeguards
G-7	Group of Seven (the seven major industrialized democracies, consisting of Canada, France, Germany, Italy, Japan, the United Kingdom, and the United States, refers to the meeting of the respective Finance Ministers and Governors of the Central Banks)
G-8	Group of Eight (the above states plus Russia)
G-21	Group of Twenty-One (the non-aligned nations in the Conference on Disarmament)
G-77	Group of Seventy-Seven (a loose coalition of developing nations, now comprising 132 member states)
GAD	General Armaments Department
GATT	General Agreement on Tariffs and Trade
GDDS	General Data Dissemination System

GDP	gross domestic product
GEF	Global Environment Facility
GHG	greenhouse gases
GONGO	government-organized NGO
HBFCs	hydrobromofluorocarbons
HCFCs	hydrofluorocarbons
HKCTU	Hong Kong Confederation of Trade Unions
IAEA	International Atomic Energy Agency
IBRD	International Bank for Reconstruction and Development (World Bank)
ICAO	International Civil Aviation Organization
ICBM	intercontinental ballistic missile
ICCPR	International Covenant on Civil and Political Rights
ICESCR	International Covenant on Economic, Social, and Cultural Rights
ICFTU	International Council of Free Trade Unions
ICSID	International Centre for Settlement of Investment Disputes
IDA	International Development Association
IEG	Intergovernmental Working Group on International Environment Governance
IEO	Independent Evaluation Office
IFC	International Finance Corporation
IGO	intergovernmental organization
IL	international law
ILO	International Labour Organization
IMF	International Metalworkers' Federation
IMF	International Monetary Fund
IMO	International Maritime Organization
IMS	International Monitoring System
INGO	international nongovernmental organization
IPCC	Intergovernmental Panel on Climate Change
IPR	intellectual property rights
IR	international relations
ITU	International Telecommunication Union
IUF	International Union of Food, Agricultural, Hotel, Restaurant, Catering, Tobacco and Allied Workers' Associations
KIEOs	keystone international economic organizations
LCHR	Lawyers' Committee for Human Rights
LSG	Leading Small Group
MFA	Ministry of Foreign Affairs of the People's Republic of China

MIGA	Multilateral Investment Guarantee Agency
MLF	Multilateral Fund
MOF	Ministry of Finance of the People's Republic of China
MOFTEC	Ministry of Foreign Trade and Economic Cooperation of the People's Republic of China
MOP	Meeting of the Parties
MOU	Memorandum of Understanding
MTCR	Missile Technology Control Regime
NAM	Non-Aligned Movement
NEPA	National Environmental Protection Agency
NGO	nongovernmental organization
NMD	national missile defense
NNWS	nonnuclear weapon states
NPC	National People's Congress
NPT	Nuclear Nonproliferation Treaty
NSG	Nuclear Suppliers Group
NTM	national technical means
NWFZ	nuclear weapon free zone
NWS	nuclear weapon states
OECD	Organisation for Economic Co-operation and Development
OED	Operations Evaluation Department
ODP	ozone-depleting potential
ODS	ozone-depleting substance
OPCW	Organization for the Prohibition of Chemical Weapons
OSI	on-site inspection
P-4	Permanent Four (four of the five Permanent Members of the UN Security Council)
P-5	Permanent Five (the five Permanent Members of the UN Security Council)
PAROS	prevention of an arms race in outer space
PLA	People's Liberation Army
PMO	Project Management Office
PNE	peaceful nuclear explosion
PRC	People's Republic of China
PSI	Proliferation Security Initiative
PTBT	Partial Test Ban Treaty
QAG	Quality Assessment Group
RETL	reeducation through labor
RMB	renminbi (unit of Chinese currency)
ROC	Republic of China

ROK	Republic of Korea
ROSCs	Reports on the Observance of Standards and Codes
RSAL	Rural Sector Adjustment Loan
SALs	structural adjustment loans
SALT	Strategic Arms Limitation Talks
SARS	severe acute respiratory syndrome
SCBs	state commercial banks
SDDS	Special Data Dissemination Standards
SDR	Special Drawing Right ("Basket" currency used by IMF for internal accounting purposes)
SEPA	State Environmental Protection Administration
SDI	Strategic Defense Initiative
SCO	Shanghai Cooperation Organization
SMA	State Meteorological Administration
SOE	state-owned enterprise
START	Strategic Arms Reduction Talks
TMD	theater missile defense
UNCED	United Nations Conference on Environment and Development
UNCTAD	United Nations Conference on Trade and Development
UNDP	United Nations Development Programme
UNEP	United Nations Environment Programme
UNESCO	United Nations Educational, Scientific and Cultural Organization
UNFCCC	United Nations Framework Convention on Climate Change
UNGA	United Nations General Assembly
UNIDO	United Nations Industrial Development Organization
UNROCA	United Nations Register on Conventional Arms
UNSSOD	United National Special Session on Disarmament
UNSSOD1	United Nations First Special Session on Disarmament
WAF	Workers Autonomous Federation
WFC	World Food Council
WHO	World Health Organization
WIPO	World Intellectual Property Organization
WMD	weapons of mass destruction
WMO	World Meteorological Organization
WSSD	World Summit on Sustainable Development

Notes

INTRODUCTION

1. For relationship between state security and human security, see Sadako Ogata and Johan Cels, "Human Security: Protecting and Empowering the People," *Global Governance* 9 (2003), 274–75. See also Commission on Human Security, *Human Security Now: Protecting and Empowering People* (New York: Commission on Human Security, 2003). The commission has defined human security as "protecting the vital core of all human lives in ways that enhance human freedoms and human fulfillment."

2. Ann Kent, *China, the United Nations and Human Rights: The Limits of Compliance* (Philadelphia: University of Pennsylvania Press, 1999), 2.

3. For the significance of a least-likely state to the testing of compliance, see Harry Eckstein, "Case Study and Theory in Political Science," in Fred I. Greenstein and Nelson W. Polsby, eds., *Strategies of Inquiry*, Handbook of Political Science, vol. 7 (Reading, MA: Addison-Wesley, 1975), 118–19.

4. As late as 1998, Harold Koh included China among a small group of rogue states. See Harold Hongju Koh, "The 1998 Frankel Lecture: Bringing International Law Home," *Houston Law Review* 35 (Fall 1998), 675–76.

5. This figure does not include Hong Kong which, in the same period, was a member of eleven conventional IGOs and 1,279 conventional INGOs. See Union of International Associations, ed., *Yearbook of International Organizations: Guide to Global Civil Society Networks, 2004–2005* (Munich: K. G. Saur, 2004), vol. 5, 45. For definition of conventional IGOs and INGOs, see Appendix 7 in ibid., 397–98.

6. Kent, *China, the United Nations and Human Rights.*

7. As Richard Bilder has argued, the path of future research is also to go beyond compliance theories to empirical studies that "explore the relation between international norms and state behavior" and test the meaning and essence of compliance and cooperation as well as the applicability of the theories to the real world. See Richard B. Bilder, "Beyond Compliance: Helping Nations Cooperate," in Dinah Shelton, ed., *Commitment and Compliance: The Role of Non-Binding Norms in the International Legal System* (Oxford: Oxford University Press, 2000), 73.

8. See Elizabeth Economy and Michel Oksenberg, eds., *China Joins the World: Progress and Prospects* (New York: Council on Foreign Relations Press, 1999); Alastair Iain Johnston and Robert S. Ross, eds., *Engaging China: The Management of an Emerging Power* (London: Routledge, 1999); David M. Lampton, ed., *The Making of Chinese Foreign and Security Policy in the Era of Reform* (Stanford, CA: Stanford University Press, 2001); David Zweig, *Internationalizing China: Domestic Interests and Global Linkages* (Ithaca, NY: Cornell University Press, 2001); David S. G. Goodman and Gerald Segal, eds., *China Rising: Nationalism and Interdependence* (London: Routledge, 1997); Susan L. Shirk, *How China Opened Its Door: The Political Success of the PRC's Foreign Trade and Investment Reforms* (Washington, DC: Brookings Institution, 1994); and Thomas W. Robinson and David Shambaugh, eds., *Chinese Foreign Policy: Theory and Practice* (Oxford: Clarendon Press, 1994). While the authors in the last-mentioned volume discuss China's cooperation with the international system in some detail, they do not address cooperation theory.

9. See, for instance, Harold K. Jacobson and Michel Oksenberg, *China's Participation in the IMF, the World Bank and GATT: Toward a Global Economic Order* (Ann Arbor: University of Michigan Press, 1990); Alastair Iain Johnston, "The Social Effects of International Institutions on Domestic (Foreign Policy) Actors," in Daniel W. Drezner, ed., *Locating the Proper Authorities: The Interaction of Domestic and International Institutions* (Ann Arbor: University of Michigan Press, 2003), 145–96; Michel Oksenberg and Elizabeth Economy, "China: Implementation under Economic Growth and Market Reform," in Edith Brown Weiss and Harold K. Jacobson, eds., *Engaging Countries: Strengthening Compliance with International Environmental Accords* (Cambridge, MA: MIT Press, 1998), 353–94; and Jeannette Greenfield, *China's Practice of the Law of the Sea* (Oxford: Clarendon Press, 1992).

10. Hilary Charlesworth, "International Law: A Discipline of Crisis," *Modern Law Review* 65 (May 2002), no. 3, 388–92. Notable exceptions to this general rule are the writings of Richard Falk and Abram and Antonia Chayes.

11. Charlesworth, "International Law," 391.

12. Louis Henkin, *How Nations Behave: Law and Foreign Policy* (London: Pall Mall Press, 1968), 42. See also J. L. Brierly, *The Law of Nations: An Introduction to the International Law of Peace* (Oxford: Clarendon Press, 1963), 6th ed., 72.

13. These include most of the theories cited in the following pages. Scholars who have recently challenged the Henkin thesis include Benedict Kingsbury, "The Concept of Compliance as a Function of Competing Concepts of International Law," *Michigan Journal of International Law* 19 (Winter 1998), 345–72; and Oona A. Hathaway, "Do Human Rights Treaties Make a Difference?" *Yale Law Journal* 111 (June 2002), no. 8, 1935–2042.

14. See, for instance, Robert O. Keohane, "International Relations and International Law: Two Optics," *Harvard International Law Journal* 38 (Spring 1997), no. 2, 487–502.

15. Harold Hongju Koh, "Why Do Nations Obey International Law?" *Yale Law Journal* 106 (1997), no. 8, 2611, 2613.

16. Kal Raustiala, "Compliance and Effectiveness in International Regulatory Cooperation," *Case Western Reserve Journal of International Law* 32 (Summer 2000), 400–409; and Hathaway, "Do Human Rights?" 1942–61.

17. See Henkin, *How Nations Behave*, 45–83; Oran R. Young, *Governance in World Affairs* (Ithaca, NY: Cornell University Press, 1999), 106–7; and Oran R. Young, *Compliance and Public Authority: A Theory with International Applications* (Baltimore: Johns Hopkins University Press, 1979), 18–28.

18. Abram Chayes and Antonia Handler Chayes, *The New Sovereignty: Compliance with International Regulatory Agreements* (Cambridge: Cambridge University Press, 1995), 28.

19. Chayes and Chayes, cited in George W. Downs, David M. Rocke, and Peter N. Bar-

soom, "Is the Good News about Compliance Good News about Cooperation?" *International Organization* (henceforth *IO*) 50 (1996), no. 3, 379–406, at 2.

20. Chayes and Chayes, *The New Sovereignty*, 10; and Abram Chayes and Antonia Handler Chayes, "On Compliance," *IO* 47 (Spring 1993), no. 2, 188. Cf. Downs et al., who mistakenly cite the third cause identified by the Chayes as "uncontrollable social or economic changes." See Downs, Rocke, and Barsoom, "Is the Good News?" 381.

21. Thus, Henkin observes, Hitler accepted the Munich Pact while, conversely, "a nation particularly concerned to observe law may be more hesitant about accepting new law in the first instance." See Henkin, *How Nations Behave*, 34; and Hathaway, "Do Human Rights?"

22. See Harold Koh, book review: "The New Sovereignty," *American Journal of International Law* (henceforth *AJIL*) 91 (April 1997), no. 2, 390–91.

23. Philip Alston and James Crawford, eds., *The Future of UN Human Rights Treaty Monitoring* (Cambridge: Cambridge University Press, 2000); and Thomas Risse, Stephen C. Ropp, and Kathryn Sikkink, eds., *The Power of Human Rights: International Norms and Domestic Change* (Cambridge: Cambridge University Press, 1999), 93–94.

24. Koh, "Why Do Nations Obey?" 2651.

25. Ibid., 2655.

26. Young, *Governance in World Affairs*, 98.

27. Koh, "Why Do Nations Obey?" 2650.

28. Ibid.

29. Koh, "The New Sovereignty," 391.

30. The emphasis here is on a graduated response from speaking very softly to wielding a big stick, in order to achieve the desired outcome by the least coercive, most cooperative means. See Ian Ayres and John Braithwaite, *Responsive Regulation: Transcending the Deregulation Debate* (New York: Oxford University Press, 1992), 39.

31. Koh, "Bringing International Law Home," 645–53, 662–80, 675–76.

32. Andrew Hurrell, "International Society and the Study of Regimes," 59, cited in Koh, "Why Do Nations?" 2634.

33. These entail internal liberalization by leaders in response to domestic/transnational pressures. See Risse, Ropp, and Sikkink, eds., *The Power of Human Rights*, 20–33.

34. Jeffrey T. Checkel, "Why Comply? Social Learning and European Identity Change," *IO* 55 (Summer 2001), no. 3, 553.

35. As Checkel points out, "My focus on persuasion dovetails with a revitalization of the 'international legal process' tradition within international law." Ibid., 564, f.39. See also Jutta Brunée and Stephen J. Toppe, "Persuasion and Enforcement: Explaining Compliance with International Law," *Finnish Yearbook of International Law* (2002).

36. Alastair Iain Johnston, "Treating International Institutions as Social Environments," *International Studies Quarterly* 45 (December 2001), iss. 4, 488.

37. Checkel, "Why Comply?" 562–63.

38. J. D. Armstrong, *Revolution and World Order: The Revolutionary State in International Society* (Oxford: Clarendon Press, 1993); Charles E. Ziegler, *Foreign Policy and East Asia: Learning and Adaptation in the Gorbachev Era* (Cambridge: Cambridge University Press, 1993); and Stephen Chan and Andrew J. Williams, eds., *Renegade States: The Evolution of Revolutionary Foreign Policy* (Manchester: Manchester University Press, 1994).

39. Richard Falk, *The Status of Law in International Society* (Princeton, NJ: Princeton University Press, 1970); and Inis L. Claude, "Collective Legitimization as a Political Function of the United Nations," *IO* 20 (1966), no. 3, 367–79.

40. Claude, "Collective Ligitimization," 372.

41. Ibid., 376. On the other hand, international lawyers argue that membership of the

UN "entails a presumption of statehood which it would be very difficult to dislodge." See Martin Dixon, *Textbook on International Law* (London: Blackstone Press, 2000), 4th ed., 106.

42. Claude, "Collective Legitimization," 373–75.

43. Ibid., 379.

44. Thomas M. Franck, *The Power of Legitimacy among Nations* (New York: Oxford University Press, 1990); Thomas M. Franck, *Fairness in International Law and Institutions* (Oxford: Clarendon Press, 1997); Anne-Marie Slaughter, "International Law in a World of Liberal States," *European Journal of International Law* 6 (1995), no. 4, 503–38; Anne-Marie Burley, "Law among Liberal States: Liberal Internationalism and the Act of State Doctrine," *Columbia Law Review* 92 (December 1992), no. 8, 1907–96; and Anne-Marie Slaughter Burley, "International Law and International Relations Theory: A Dual Agenda," *AJIL* 87 (1993), no. 2, 205–39.

45. Franck, *The Power of Legitimacy*, 45.

46. See, for instance John Braithwaite and Peter Drahos, *Global Business Regulation* (Cambridge: Cambridge University Press, 2000); Edith Brown Weiss, ed., *Environmental Change and International Law: New Challenges and Dimensions* (Tokyo: United Nations University Press, 1992); and Martti Koskenniemi, "Breach of Treaty or Non-Compliance? Reflections on the Enforcement of the Montreal Protocol," *Yearbook of International Environmental Law* 3 (1992), 123–70.

47. Franck, *The Power of Legitimacy*, 206, 46, 49, 43.

48. Ibid., 64–65, 202, 196, 181.

49. Koh, "Why Do Nations Obey?" 2645.

50. Keohane, "International Relations and International Law," 493.

51. See Slaughter, "International Law in a World of Liberal States"; and Burley, "Law among Liberal States."

52. See Andrew Moravcsik, "Taking Preferences Seriously: A Liberal Theory of International Politics," *IO* 51 (1997), no. 4, 513–53.

53. Slaughter, "International Law in a World of Liberal States," 504.

54. Ibid., 511.

55. José E. Alvarez, "Do Liberal States Behave Better? A Critique of Slaughter's Liberal Theory," *European Journal of International Law* 12 (2001), no. 2, 183–246.

56. Such works include Harold Hongju Koh, "Transnational Legal Process," *Nebraska Law Review* 75 (1996), no. 1, 181–207; Koh, "Why Do Nations Obey?"; Koh, "Bringing International Law Home"; Robert O. Keohane, *International Institutions and State Power: Essays in International Relations Theory* (Boulder, CO: Westview Press, 1989); Alston and Crawford, eds., *The Future of UN Human Rights Treaty Monitoring*; and Young, *Governance in World Affairs*.

57. As José Alvarez has observed in his masterly critique, if not a meta theory, liberal identity theory can be understood, and appreciated, as a partial, particularistic theory. In this sense it could have usefulness. See Alvarez, "Do Liberal States?" 241.

58. Keohane, "International Relations and International Law," 487–502.

59. Downs, Rocke, and Barsoom, "Is the Good News?" 379–406. See also George W. Downs, "Enforcement and the Evolution of Compliance," *Michigan Journal of International Law* 19 (1998), 319–44.

60. Henkin, *How Nations Behave*, 34.

61. Downs, Rocke, and Barsoom, "Is the Good News?" 383.

62. Ibid., 386.

63. See Shirley V. Scott, "Beyond 'Compliance': Reconceiving the International Law–Foreign Policy Dynamic," *Australian Yearbook of International Law* 19 (1998), 35–48.

64. Christine Parker, *The Open Corporation: Effective Self-regulation and Democracy* (Cambridge: Cambridge University Press, 2002).

65. Neil Gunningham and Darren Sinclair, *Leaders and Laggards: Next-Generation Environmental Regulation* (Sheffield: Greenleaf, 2002), 10.

66. As Oran Young defines it, "the term compliance refers to all behavior by subjects or actors that conforms to the requirements of behavioral prescriptions or compliance systems. . . . A compliance mechanism is any institution or set of institutions (formal or informal) established by a public authority . . . for the purpose of encouraging compliance with one or more behavioral prescriptions of a compliance system." See Young, *Compliance and Public Authority*, 4–5. Ronald Mitchell puts it more simply: "I define compliance as an actor's behavior that conforms to a treaty's explicit rules." See Ronald B. Mitchell, "Compliance Theory: An Overview," in James Cameron, Jacob Werksman, and Peter Roderick, eds., *Improving Compliance with International Environmental Law* (London: Earthscan, 1996) 5.

67. Joseph M. Grieco, *Cooperation among Nations: Europe, America and Non–Tariff Barriers to Trade* (Ithaca, NY: Cornell University Press, 1990), 69–70.

68. *The Oxford Compact Dictionary and Thesaurus* (Oxford: Oxford University Press, 1997), 160. This definition self-evidently excludes instances where there is a legal requirement to cooperate, for instance, as stipulated in a treaty provision.

69. Braithwaite and Drahos, *Global Business Regulation*, 22.

70. I thank Don Greig for his valuable comments on this point and on other parts of the section and chapter.

71. Arthur A. Stein, *Why Nations Cooperate: Circumstance and Choice in International Relations* (Ithaca, NY: Cornell University Press, 1990), 174.

72. See ibid.; Jennifer Sterling-Folker, *Theories of International Cooperation and the Primacy of Anarchy: Explaining U.S. International Policy-Making after Bretton Woods* (Albany, NY: SUNY Press, 2002); Lisa L. Martin, *Coercive Cooperation: Explaining Multilateral Economic Sanctions* (Princeton, NJ: Princeton University Press, 1992); and Stephen Zamora, "The Cultural Context of International Legal Cooperation," *Journal of Legal Education* 51 (September 2001), no. 3, 462–68.

73. Henkin, *How Nations Behave*, 17–20.

74. According to Union of International Associations, ed., *Yearbook of International Organizations 1999/2000* (Munich: K. G. Saur, 2000), vol. 2, "an organization is intergovernmental if it is established by signature of an agreement engendering obligations between governments, whether or not that agreement is eventually published." By contrast, according to ECOSOC Res. 288 (X), an international nongovernmental organization (INGO) is one not established by intergovernmental agreement. It must also be genuinely international in character. See ibid., 1477.

75. See José E. Alvarez, *International Organizations as Lawmakers* (Oxford: Oxford University Press, 2005); José Alvarez, "International Organizations: Then and Now," *American Journal of International Law* 100 (April 2006), no. 2, 324–42; C. F. Amerasinghe, *Principles of the Institutional Law of International Organizations* (Cambridge: Cambridge University Press, 1996); Philippe Sands, *Lawless World: America and the Breaking of Global Rules* (Melbourne: Allen Lane / Penguin, 2005); Jan Klabbers, *An Introduction to International Institutional Law* (Cambridge: Cambridge University Press, 2002); Christopher C. Joyner, ed., *The United Nations and International Law* (Cambridge: American Society for International Law and Cambridge University Press, 1997); and Shirley V. Scott, *International Law in World Politics: An Introduction* (Boulder, CO: Lynne Rienner, 2004).

76. Klabbers, *An Introduction*, 7–13.

77. See Susan Ariel Aaronson, *Trade and the American Dream: A Social History of Postwar Trade Policy* (Lexington: University Press of Kentucky, 1996), 3. See also Milton Churche, "The Havana Charter for an International Trade Organization of 1948 and the World Trade Orga-

nization in Comparative Perspective," Economic History Seminar, 7 September 2001, Australian National University, Canberra.

78. Klabbers, *An Introduction*, 344.

79. Samuel S. Kim, "China's International Organizational Behaviour," in Robinson and Shambaugh, eds., *Chinese Foreign Policy*, 405.

80. Dinah Shelton, "The Impact of Economic Globalization on Compliance," in Alexandre Kiss, Dinah Shelton, and Kanami Ishibashi, eds., *Economic Globalization and Compliance with International Environmental Agreements* (The Hague: Kluwer Law International, 2003), 39.

81. Dixon, *Textbook on International Law*, 106.

82. See Christian Reus-Smit, "Obligation and the Political Authority of International Law," Canberra: Department of International Relations Working Paper, Australian National University 2002/2, 33. Others see it as helping to "solve coordination problems, persuade other states to change their preferences or help enforce bargains." See Jon C. Pevehouse, "Democratization, Credible Commitments, and Joining International Organizations," in Drezner, ed., *Locating the Proper Authorities*, 27.

83. Falk, *The Status of Law*, 67 (emphasis added).

84. Andrew Hurrell, "International Society and the Study of Regimes: A Reflective Approach," in Volker Rittberger, ed., *Regime Theory in International Relations* (Oxford: Clarendon Press, 1993), 59.

85. Chayes and Chayes, *The New Sovereignty*, 271–85.

86. Ibid., 4–5, 25 (emphasis added).

87. Friedrich Kratchowil and Edward D. Mansfield, eds., *International Organization: A Reader* (New York: HarperCollins, 1994), xiii.

88. Stephen Krasner, "Structural Causes and Regime Consequences: Regimes as Intervening Variables," *IO* 36 (Spring 1982), no. 2, 187.

89. Braithwaite and Drahos, *Global Business Regulation*, 18–19.

90. See discussion in Michael Byers, *Custom, Power and the Power of Rules: International Relations and Customary International Law* (Cambridge: Cambridge University Press, 1999), 19–13.

91. See Don Greig, "'International Community': 'Interdependence' and All That . . . Rhetorical Correctness?" in Gerard Kreijen et al., eds., *State, Sovereignty and International Governance* (Oxford: Oxford University Press, 2002), 583.

92. Here I draw, with significant variations, on the insights of David Kennedy at his seminars, "Special Topics in International Law," 30 June–2 July 2000, Faculty of Law, Australian National University, Canberra. See also David Kennedy, "The Move to Institutions," *Cardozo Law Review* 8 (1987), 841–989; and Alvarez, "International Organizations."

93. Churche, "The Havana Charter."

94. Kennedy, "Special Topics."

95. Braithwaite and Drahos, *Global Business Regulation*, 114–20.

96. See table 20.1, ibid., 476–77.

97. Kennedy, "Special Topics."

98. Cf. International law uses "hard" and "soft" to indicate whether or not an international legal instrument or decision is legally binding.

99. Robert E. Goodin, "International Ethics and the Environmental Crisis," *Ethics and International Affairs* 4 (1990), 92.

100. Stein, *Why States Cooperate*, 208.

101. Martin Dixon and Robert McCorquodale, *Cases and Materials on International Law* (London: Blackstone, 2000), 3rd ed., 486.

102. Ibid.

103. See Daniel Bodansky, "The Legitimacy of International Governance: A Coming Challenge for International Environmental Law?" *AJIL* 93 (July 1999), no. 3, 604.

104. Dixon and McCorquodale, *Cases and Materials*, 183–84.

105. Ibid., 525.

106. Hathaway, "Do Human Rights?"

107. Falk, *The Status of Law*, 332.

108. José Alvarez, at "Workshop on Liberalism in International Law," Centre for International and Public Law, Faculty of Law, Australian National University, July 2000.

109. See also Kent, *China, the United Nations and Human Rights*, 7, 236.

110. Koh, "Why Do Nations Obey," 2656. Koh distinguishes between legal, political, and social internalization, but in the present book legislative implementation is conceived as the fourth level of implementation and is differentiated from practical implementation.

111. Chayes and Chayes, *The New Sovereignty*, 4–5, 25. As Keohane has observed, "Institutions matter, even if they cannot enforce rules from above, *because they change actors' conceptions of their interests.*" See Robert O. Keohane, "International Relations, Old and New," in Robert E. Goodin and Hans-Dieter Klingeman, eds., *A New Handbook of Political Science* (Oxford: Oxford University Press, 1996), 470 (emphasis in original).

112. For differing standards in the international human rights regime, for instance, see Kent, *China, the United Nations and Human Rights*, 255 f.32.

113. Chayes and Chayes, *The New Sovereignty*, 17–22.

114. See John Jackson, *World Trade and the Law of GATT* (Indianapolis: Bobbs-Merrill, 1969), 163.

115. Chayes and Chayes, *The New Sovereignty*, 17–18.

116. See, for instance, Sidney Blumenthal, *The Clinton Wars: An Insider's Account of the White House Years* (London: Viking 2003), 629–99.

117. See Jimmy Carter, "Just War—or a Just War?" *New York Times*, 9 March 2003. For some of the most impassioned critiques, see Senate floor speeches of U.S. Senator Robert Byrd, at http://byrd.senate.gov/byrd_speeches/byrd_speeches; and comment by Kurt Campbell, former U.S. Deputy Assistant Secretary of Defense, in reference to the UN Security Council: "I think many in the hardline camp have very little use for some of these institutions [UN Security Council] and believe that if anything they undermine American purpose rather than enhance it." Find at http://abc.net.au/4corners/content/2003/transcripts/s801456.htm (accessed 12 March 2003). For U.S. difficulty in adhering to the international rule of law, see John T. Murphy, *The United States and the Rule of Law in International Affairs* (Cambridge: Cambridge University Press, 2004), in particular, 349–59.

118. See also José E. Alvarez, "Why Nations Behave," *Michigan Journal of International Law* 19 (Winter 1998), 303–17; and Ann Kent, "The Unpredictability of Liberal States: Australia and International Human Rights," *International Journal of Human Rights* 6 (Autumn 2002), no. 3, 55–56.

119. See explanation in Ann Kent, "Influences on National Participation in International Institutions: Liberal v Non-Liberal States," in Hilary Charlesworth, Madelaine Chiam, Devika Hovell, and George Williams, eds., *The Fluid State: International Law and National Legal Systems* (Sydney: Federation Press, 2005), 251–76.

120. See "China's Remarks to the UN," *New York Times*, 5 February 2003; and "Authority of UN Security Council Should Not Be Hurt," *People's Daily*, 28 February 2003, at http://english.peopledaily.com.cn (accessed 4 March 2003).

121. Chayes and Chayes, "On Compliance," 197.

122. Risse, Ropp, Sikkink, eds., *The Power of Human Rights,* 5–6.

123. See Sir Anthony Mason, "The Internationalisation of Domestic Law," *Law and Pol-*

icy Papers No. 4, (Canberra: Centre for International and Public Law, Australian National University, 1996).

124. Young, *Governance in World Affairs*, 91–92.

125. Dixon and McCorquodale, *Cases and Materials*, 109.

126. See Hathaway, "Do Human Rights?"; and critique in Ryan Goodman and Derek Jinks, "Measuring the Effects of Human Rights Treaties," *European Journal of International Law* 14 (February 2003), no. 1, 171–83.

127. Marc A. Levy, Oran R. Young, and Michael Zurn, "The Study of International Regimes," *European Journal of International Relations* 1 (September 1995), no. 3, 294, citing Donald Campbell and Julian Stanley, *Experimental and Quasi-Experimental Designs for Research* (Chicago: Rand McNally, 1966). On the micro-macro approach, see Braithwaite and Drahos, *Global Business Regulation*, 13–14.

128. Examples include Raymond Frech Mikesell, *The Bretton Woods Debates: A Memoir* (Princeton, NJ: Economics Department, Princeton University, 1994); and Devesh Kapur, John P. Lewis, and Richard Webb, *The World Bank: Its First Half Century* (Washington, DC: Brookings Institution, 1997), 2 vols.

CHAPTER I

1. Truong Buu Lam, "Intervention versus Tribute in Sino-Vietnamese Relations, 1788–1790," in John King Fairbank, ed., *The Chinese World Order: Traditional China's Foreign Relations* (Cambridge, MA: Harvard University Press, 1968), 179.

2. Tseng Yu-hao, *Modern Chinese Legal and Political Philosophy* (Shanghai: Commercial Press, 1930), 163.

3. See Jerome Alan Cohen and Hungdah Chiu, eds., *People's China and International Law: A Documentary Survey* (Princeton, NJ: Princeton University Press, 1974), 5. "Traces" of international law may be found in ancient China, but such law did not fall under the normal definition of "law between sovereign and equal states based on the common consent of those states." See Li Zhaojie, "How International Law Was Introduced into China," in Ma Chengyuan et al., *Guoji falü wenti yanjiu* ("Research on Issues of International Law") (Beijing: Zhongguo zhengfa daxue chubanshe, 1998), 54–76; and Keyuan Zou, "Chinese Approaches to International Law," in Weixing Hu, Gerald Chan, and Daojiong Zha, eds., *China's International Relations in the 21st Century: Dynamics of Paradigm Shifts* (Lanham, MD: University Press of America, 2000), 171–72.

4. Cohen and Hungdah Chiu, eds., *People's China*, 6.

5. The Tsungli Yamen was China's first foreign affairs office. For this early exposure, and China's reaction to it, see Li Zhaojie, "How International Law," 77–135. See also Keyuan Zou, "Chinese Approaches," 171–72.

6. Tseng Yu-hao, *Modern Chinese Legal*, 163; Keyuan Zou, "Chinese Approaches," 172.

7. See Cohen and Hungdah Chiu, eds., *People's China*, 1286–87.

8. For the League's response to Japanese action and China's diplomacy, see Chih Meng, *China Speaks: On the Conflict between China and Japan* (London: Macmillan, 1932), 156–95. See also Report of a Study Group, China Institute of International Affairs, *China and the United Nations* (New York: Manhattan, 1959), 6–8.

9. See Xie Qimei and Wang Xingfang, eds., *Zhongguo yu Lianheguo: Jinian Lianheguo chengli wushi zhounian* ("China and the United Nations: Commemorating the Fiftieth Anniversary of the Founding of the United Nations") (Beijing: Shijie zhishi chubanshe, 1995), 12. For details of China's participation in the preparatory conferences, see ibid., 8–18.

10. For the Republic of China's role, see China Institute, *China and the United Nations*.

11. See Penny Wensley, "Australia and the United Nations: Challenges in the New Millennium," *Law and Policy Paper* 14 (Sydney: Federation Press, 2000), 3.

12. See his son's account of Roosevelt's view of China in Elliot Roosevelt, *As He Saw It* (New York: Duell, Sloan and Pearce, 1946), 129–30, 143, 249.

13. UN Doc A/1123. See especially Hungdah Chiu and R. R. Edwards, "Communist China's Attitude toward the United Nations: A Legal Analysis," *American Journal of International Law* (hereafter *AJIL*) 62 (January 1968), no. 1, 20–50; "China and the United Nations: Three Approaches," articles in *International Organization* (hereafter *IO*) 20 (Autumn 1966), no. 4, 1966; Byron S. J. Weng, *Peking's UN Policy: Continuity and Change* (New York: Praeger, 1972); Guo Qun, *Lianheguo* ("The United Nations") (Beijing: Shijie zhishi she, 1956); and United Nations, *Yearbook of the United Nations* (New York: Department of Public Information, United Nations), 1950–71 editions.

14. See collected documents in Cohen and Hungdah Chiu, eds., *People's China*, 267–313.

15. Ibid., 1290.

16. Xie Qimei and Wang Xingfang, eds., *Zhongguo yu Lianheguo*, 30.

17. See also letter, dated March 8, 1950, addressed to the President of the Security Council from the Secretary-General, and Text of Memorandum on the Legal Aspects of the Problem of Representation in the United Nations, in Andrew W. Cordier and Wilder Foote, eds., *Public Papers of the Secretaries-General of the United Nations: Trygve Lie, 1946–1953* (New York: Columbia University Press, 1969), 265.

18. For early history, see ibid., 17–20.

19. Ibid., 259.

20. In the Security Council vote on China's representation, U.S. Ambassador Ernest A. Gross indicated he would vote against the Soviet proposal but declared that the United States would accept the decision of the majority in the Security Council, since the United States considered the question procedural rather than substantive. See Security Council Official Records (5th year), 460th meeting, 12 January 1950, 6.

21. Thus, on 12 July, the Secretary-General stated: "The dispute over the representation of China would not have assumed such dangerous proportions had it not been for the overriding crisis in world affairs." Text in Cordier and Foote, *Public Papers*, 329.

22. See S/1511 and S/1588, in *Yearbook of the United Nations, 1950*, 222–30; Cordier and Foote, *Public Papers*, 329.

23. See David Brook, *The UN and the China Dilemma* (New York: Vantage, 1956), 66–69.

24. For Chinese division of the pre-1971 era into three periods, see Wu Baoding, ed., *Guojifa yu guoji shiwu lun* ("On International Law and International Affairs") (Hefei: Anhui daxue chubanshe, 1999), 130–31.

25. Wu Xiuquan, *Eight Years in the Ministry of Foreign Affairs, January 1950–October 1958: Memoirs of a Diplomat* (Beijing: New World Press, 1985), 46–53.

26. Hungdah Chiu and Edwards, "Communist China's Attitude," 38–40.

27. For the Chinese argument, see Xie Qimei and Wang Xingfang, eds., *Zhongguo yu Lianheguo*, 30–35. For the impact of Korean War in the United States, see Stanley D. Bachrack, *The Committee of One Million: "China Lobby" Politics, 1953–1971* (New York: Columbia University Press, 1976), 43–102.

28. See Wang Taiping, ed., *Xin Zhongguo waijiao 50 nian* ("Fifty Years of Chinese Foreign Policy") (Beijing: Beijing chubanshe, 1999), vol. 1, 71.

29. Byron S. Weng, "Communist China's Changing Attitudes toward the United Nations," *IO* 20 (Autumn 1966), no. 4, 685.

30. Wang Jiajun, *Shenma shi Lianheguo?* ("What Is the United Nations?") (Beijing, 1957), 40–42, transl. in Cohen and Hungdah Chiu, eds., *People's China*, 1335.

31. Dong Biwu, "The Tenth Anniversary of the United Nations," *People's China* 14 (16 July 1955), 6–8, in Cohen and Hungdah Chiu, eds., *People's China*, 1292.

32. Wang Jisi, "International Relations Theory and the Study of Chinese Foreign Policy: A Chinese Perspective," in Thomas W. Robinson and David Shambaugh, eds., *Chinese Foreign Policy: Theory and Practice* (Oxford: Clarendon Press, 1994), 493.

33. Steven I. Levine, "Perception and Ideology in Chinese Foreign Policy," in ibid., 37–38.

34. Hungdah Chiu, "Communist China's Attitude toward International Law," *AJIL* 60 (1966), 248.

35. Huan Xiang, cited in Kong Qingjiang, "Enforcement of WTO Agreements in China," unpublished conference paper, 2002. See also Hungdah Chiu, "Communist China's Attitude," 266. Particularly offensive to China was the general tendency among Western writers to define international law as a body of legally binding rules governing relations among "civilized states." See ibid., 250.

36. Zhu Liru, "Refute the Absurd Theory Concerning International Law by Ch'en T'i-ch'iang," *People's Daily*, 18 September 1957, cited in Hungdah Chiu, "Communist China's Attitude," 248–49.

37. Cohen and Hungdah Chiu, eds., *People's China*, 12–13.

38. See analysis of texts in Hungdah Chiu, "Communist China's Attitude," 258–59.

39. Zhou Gengsheng, *Xiandai YingMei guojifa de sixiang dongxiang* ("Trends in Modern English and American International Legal Thought") (Beijing: Shijie zhishi chubanshe, 1963), 67, 84–85.

40. Wang Yaotian, *Guoji maoyi tiaoyue he xieding* ("International Trade Treaties and Agreements") (Beijing, 1958), 9–10, 12–14, in Cohen and Hungdah Chiu, eds., *People's China*, 1118–20. In the final quote, Wang was citing Russian scholar F. I. Kozhevnikov.

41. Keyuan Zou, "Chinese Approaches to International Law," 180.

42. Ibid.

43. Yang Xin and Chen Jian, "Expose and Criticize the Imperialists' Fallacy Concerning the Question of State Sovereignty," *Zhengfa yanjiu* (1964), no. 4, 6–11, transl. in Cohen and Hungdah Chiu, eds., *People's China*, 110.

44. Ibid., 111–12.

45. Ibid., 112.

46. This latter, more restrictive notion of sovereignty was articulated in 1999 by the UN Secretary General: "State sovereignty, in its most basic sense, is being redefined by the forces of globalization and international cooperation. The State is now widely understood to be the servant of its people, and not vice versa. At the same time, individual sovereignty—and by this I mean the human rights and fundamental freedoms of each and every individual as enshrined in our Charter—has been enhanced by a renewed consciousness of the right of every individual to control his or her destiny." See "Secretary-General Presents His Annual Report to General Assembly," UN Press Release SG/SM/7136 GA/9596, 20 September 1999.

47. See Jiang Weiyu, *Xiandai guojifa yuanli jiexi* ("Analysis of Principles of Modern International Law") (Beijing: Zhongguo renmin gongan daxue chubanshe, 2002), 74.

48. Ibid.

49. See statement by U.S. Secretary of State, William Rogers, in August 1971, cited in Blythe Foote Finke, *China Joins the United Nations* (New York: SamHar, 1973), 6. See also China Institute, *China and the United Nations*, 17.

50. Thus, in 1959, the report of the Study Group acknowledged: "*There is a widespread impression* that, since 1950, the Chinese delegation has lost all its influence and weight in the United Nations and has been reduced to a nonentity or 'fiction.' This statement is too

sweeping and an inaccurate description of the state of affairs. While it is undeniable that *the Chinese delegation today does not enjoy the prestige it once did, it has not quite lost all its moral influence and force.* For example, in the Security Council, China still has its veto power which even the Soviet Union cannot ignore." See China Institute, *China and the United Nations*, 17 (emphasis added).

51. Nagendra S. Singh, *Termination of Membership of International Organizations* (New York: Praeger, 1958), 155.

52. Philippe Ardant, "Chinese Diplomatic Practice during the Cultural Revolution," in Jerome Alan Cohen, ed., *China's Practice of International Law: Some Case Studies* (Cambridge, MA: Harvard University Press, 1972), 91.

53. Guo Qun, *Lianheguo*, 37.

54. Of these, the 1954 Geneva Conference has been called "the first important international conference that New China had attended with the big states." See Wang Taiping, ed., *Xin Zhongguo*, vol. 2, 1275–76.

55. These included: the International Organization for the Cooperation of Railways; the Organization for Postal and Telecommunications Cooperation among Socialist Countries; the Fisheries Research Commission for the Western Pacific; the Warsaw Treaty Organization; and the Council for Mutual Economic Aid. See Cohen and Hungdah Chiu, eds., *People's China*, 1400–1401.

56. For instance, see commentary in ibid.

57. Weng, *Peking's UN Policy*, 322.

58. For a Chinese refutation of these arguments, see Zhou Gengsheng, "China's Legitimate Rights in the United Nations Must Be Restored," *Renmin ribao*, 5 December 1961, 5, transl. in Cohen and Hungdah Chiu, eds., *People's China*, 275–83.

59. Guo Qun, *Lianheguo*, 36.

60. Kong Meng, "A Criticism of the Theories of Bourgeois International Law Concerning the Subjects of International Law and Recognition of States," *Guoji wenti yanjiu* (1960), no. 2, 44–53, in Cohen and Hungdah Chiu, eds., *People's China*, 98.

61. Ibid., 94.

62. For Chinese version of these events, see Zhou Gengsheng, "China's Legitimate Rights," in Cohen and Hungdah Chiu, eds., *People's China*, 277–80.

63. Sixteenth Session General Assembly Debate on Agenda Items 90 and 91 December 1, 1961, Question of the Representation of China in the United Nations Restoration of the Lawful Rights of the People's Republic of China in the United Nations, in Richard A. Falk and Saul H. Mendlovitz, *The Strategy of World Order: The United Nations* (New York: World Law Fund, 1966), vol. 3, 144.

64. See Weng, *Peking's UN Policy*, 179–80.

65. *Peking Review* 8 (29 January 1965), no. 5, 5–6, cited in Weng, "Communist China's Changing Attitudes," 698–99. Foreign Minister Chen Yi also proclaimed: "During the U.S. war of aggression against Korea, the United Nations adopted a resolution naming China as an aggressor. How can China be expected to take part in an international organization which calls her an aggressor? . . . The question now is how to reform the UN in accordance with the purposes and principles of its Charter and to free it from the control of the United States and other big powers. If the task of reforming the United Nations cannot be accomplished, conditions will no doubt gradually ripen for the establishment of a revolutionary United Nations." See *Peking Review* 8 (8 October 1965), no. 41, 7–14.

66. Lin Biao, "Long Live the Victory of People's War," *Peking Review* 8 (3 September 1965), no. 36, 9–30.

67. For best description, see Ardant, "Chinese Diplomatic Practice," 86–128.

68. See Barbara Barnouin and Yu Changgen, *Chinese Foreign Policy during the Cultural Revolution* (London: Kegan Paul International, 1998), 98–112.

69. Report of a National Policy Panel established by the United Nations Association of the United States of America, "China, the United Nations and United States Policy: An Analysis of the Issues and Principal Alternatives with Recommendations for U.S. Policy," *IO* 20 (Autumn 1966), no. 4, 705.

70. Lincoln P. Bloomfield, "China, the United States, and the United Nations," *IO* 20 (Autumn 1966), no. 4, 657.

71. See Melvin Gurtov, "The Foreign Ministry and Foreign Affairs in the Chinese Cultural Revolution," in Thomas W. Robinson, ed., *The Cultural Revolution in China* (Berkeley: University of California Press, 1971), 313–66; Barnouin and Yu Changgen, *Chinese Foreign Policy*, 1–34; and Ardant, "Chinese Diplomatic Practice," 86–128.

72. Before 13 January 1950, when the Security Council first voted on the question of Chinese representation, twenty-one governments, including five members of the Council, had extended recognition to the PRC and by the end of June 1950, five more governments had recognized it. See Weng, *Peking's UN Policy*, 77. However, by 1961, China had still only established relations with thirty-nine, mainly developing, states. See Cohen and Hungdah Chiu, eds., *People's China*, 1296, citing secret PLA document.

73. Barnouin and Yu Changgen, *Chinese Foreign Policy*, 98.

74. Samuel S. K. Kim, *China, the United Nations and World Order* (Princeton, NJ: Princeton University Press, 1979), 103.

75. See also Michel Oksenberg and Elizabeth Economy, "China: Implementation under Economic Growth and Market Reform," in Edith Brown Weiss and Harold K. Jacobson, eds., *Engaging Countries: Strengthening Compliance with International Environmental Accords* (Cambridge, MA: MIT Press, 1998), 355–56.

76. The automatic nature of this vote was experienced by the author herself, when the Australian Department of External (now Foreign) Affairs held its annual departmental discussion on whether to vote to support PRC representation in the UN. Officers were encouraged to provide reasons for or against, but even if no argument was made against, the head of the East Asia Branch always concluded that the U.S. draft resolution opposing PRC representation should be supported.

77. See Kim, *China, the United Nations*, 102–3.

78. A/L.632 and Add.1, 2. See United Nations, *Yearbook of the United Nations, 1971*, 131, 136.

79. Resolution 2758 (XXVI), A/L.630, adopted by the General Assembly. See text in ibid., 135–37. For details of the debate, see Xie Qimei and Wang Xingfang, eds., *Zhongguo yu Lianheguo*, 44–49; Peter A. Poole, *China Enters the United Nations: A New Era Begins for the World Organization* (New York: Franklin Watts, 1974); Finke, *China Joins*; and Kim, *China, the United Nations*, 99–105.

80. Poole, *China Enters the United Nations*, 6–7.

81. Cited in Finke, *China Joins*, 11.

82. See United Nations, *Yearbook of the United Nations, 1971*, 133.

83. Ibid.

84. See "Chinese Vice-Premier on China's 50 year Diplomacy," Xinhua News Agency, 24 September 1999, Reuters China News Agency, 24 September 1999.

85. See Samuel S. Kim, "China's International Organizational Behaviour," in Robinson and Shambaugh, eds., *Chinese Foreign Policy*, 431, 425.

86. Wu Baoding, *Guojifa*, 131.

87. See Tian Jin et al., *Zhongguo zai Lianheguo: Gongtong dizao geng meihao de shijie* ("China in the United Nations: Together Building a Better World") (Beijing: Shijie zhishi chubanshe, 1999), 36.

88. Xie Qimei and Wang Xingfang, eds., *Zhongguo yu Lianheguo*, 42–43.

89. Cited in Finke, *China Joins*, 12.

90. "Huang Hua Urges UN and All Related Organizations to Cease Immediately All Contacts with Chiang Kai-shek Clique," NCNA, United Nations, 13 January 1972, cited in Kim, *China, the United Nations*, 346. See details in ibid.

91. Discussion with Gwenda Matthews, Canberra, 12 March 2004. Mathews was a legal specialist at the UN Office for Law of the Sea and Ocean Affairs in 1971. For the former Taiwanese staff this even involved nominating a "home" in China, a country some had never even visited, for leave purposes.

92. Thus, they voted in favor of a resolution warning that the United States would be violating its obligations under the UN Charter if congressional action permitted chrome imports from Rhodesia, accused India of interfering in Pakistan's domestic affairs, and defended China's right to test nuclear weapons in the atmosphere.

93. Cited in Finke, *China Joins*, 17.

94. Ibid.

95. Cohen and Hungdah Chiu, eds., *People's China*, 1365.

96. Discussion with Gwenda Matthews.

97. Ardant, "Chinese Diplomatic Practice," 91.

98. Kim, *China, the United Nations*, 122.

99. Ibid., 114.

100. This constituted US$12 million for the regular budget for 1970–71 and US$18 million in bonds to cover UN police action in Belgian Congo. Ibid., 146.

101. See Don Shannon, "Peking Offers to Raise UN Contributions—With a Catch," *Los Angeles Times*, 10 October 1972, 1, in Cohen and Hungdah Chiu, eds., *People's China*, 1364.

102. This would return China's contribution to the original figure allotted to China in 1946 on the basis of its population and production, a figure reduced when it had been unable to pay.

103. In October 1972, Xing Songyi, the Chinese delegate, told the UN General Assembly's Administrative and Budgetary Committee that Peking was prepared to increase its contribution from 4 percent to 7 percent of the world organization's annual budget, and at the same time demanded that Chinese be made a "working language" of the UN by 1974. According to a U.S. estimate, this would add $5 million to the annual budget. See Shannon, "Peking Offers to Raise UN Contribution," 1363.

104. Kim, *China, the United Nations*, 148–49.

105. United Nations, *Yearbook of the United Nations, 1971*, 133–35.

106. Kim, *China, the United Nations*, 348.

107. Oksenberg and Economy, "China: Implementation," 356.

108. For history of its entry into these organizations, and subsequent participation, see Kim, *China, the United Nations*, 348–402.

109. Gerald Chan, *China and International Organisations: Participation in Non-Governmental Organisations since 1971* (Hong Kong: Oxford University Press, 1989), 17–18.

110. Ibid., 17.

111. See details of entry into INGOs in ibid.

112. In the IMF, for instance, countries' voting rights were based on their quotas, whose

size was roughly determined by their share of world trade. In the ILO, on the other hand, voting was based on a tripartite system of representation, in which governmental representatives shared power with employers and workers. To obtain power in such organizations required extensive negotiation.

113. Meng Yan, "China Opposes US Measure," *China Daily*, 14 July 2003.

114. Kim, "China's International Organizational Behaviour," 422.

115. See Benjamin Schwartz, *Communism and China: Ideology in Flux* (New York: Atheneum, 1970), 71, cited in Levine, "Perception and Ideology," 32.

116. See Harold K. Jacobson and Michel Oksenberg, *China's Participation in the IMF, the World Bank and GATT: Toward a Global Economic Order* (Ann Arbor: University of Michigan Press, 1990), 18–20.

117. For India's special treatment, see Edward S. Mason and Robert E. Asher, *The World Bank since Bretton Woods: The Origins, Policies, Operations, and Impact of the International Bank for Reconstruction and Development and the Other Members of the World Bank Group* (Washington, DC: Brookings Institution, 1973), 675–76. Later, however, disenchantment set in and India lost its special status in the organization. See Jochen Kraske with William H. Becker, William Diamond, and Louis Galambos, *Bankers with a Mission: The Presidents of the World Bank, 1946–1991* (New York: IBRD/Oxford University Press, 1996), 144–45.

118. For China's behavior generally, see Kim, *China, the United Nations*, 159–61, 402–3.

119. Kim, "China's International Organizational Behaviour," 431, 425.

120. For Chinese thinking, see Wang Jisi, "International Relations Theory," 498; and Alastair Iain Johnston, *Cultural Realism: Strategic Culture and Grand Strategy in Chinese History* (Princeton, NJ: Princeton University Press, 1995).

121. See also Avery Goldstein, "The Diplomatic Face of China's Grand Strategy: A Rising Power's Emerging Choice," *China Quarterly* 168 (December 2001), 835–64; and Evan S. Medeiros and M. Taylor Fravel, "China's New Diplomacy," *Foreign Affairs* 82 (November–December 2003), iss. 6, 22–35.

122. Mely Caballero-Anthony, "Looking North: Southeast Asia and China Put Sovereignty Aside to Pursue Regionalism," *South China Morning Post*, 10 January 2003.

123. Its founding members were China, Russia, Tajikistan, Kyrgyzstan, Kazakhstan, and Uzbekistan. See Zhang Jian, "The Shanghai Cooperation Organisation and Its Future," Australia and Security Cooperation in the Asia-Pacific Region, *AUS-CSCAP Newsletter* No. 14 (November 2002), 12–15.

124. An Wei and Li Dongyan, eds., *Shizi lukou'r shang de shijie: Zhongguo zhuming xuezhe tantao 21 shiji de guoji jiaodian* ("World at the Crossroads: China's Leading Scholars Explore Critical International Issues of the Twenty-first Century") (Beijing: Zhongguo renmin daxue chubanshe, 2000), 261.

125. Although some scholars believe the improvement in U.S.-China relations began in mid-2001 with the new, tough line adopted by the Bush administration, it was only after September 11 that the United States and China concurred in seeing the need to reduce mutual tensions.

126. Supachai Panitchpakdi, cited in "China Briefing: WTO Seeks Mediation from China," *Far Eastern Economic Review*, 20 November 2003, at http://global.factiva.com/en/arch/display.asp.

127. David E. Sanger, "Bush Lauds China Leader as 'Partner' in Diplomacy," *New York Times*, 10 December 2003. Bush said: "At a time when the WTO faces an impasse, we need China to use its influence to be a bridge between developed and developing countries."

128. See *China Quarterly* (2002) for a detailed study of Chinese think tanks in the foreign policy research institutes, the economic research institutes, and the public security

research institutes. See in particular, David Shambaugh, "China's International Relations Think Tanks: Evolving Structure and Process," *China Quarterly* 171 (September 2002), 575–96. See also Medeiros and Fravel, "China New Diplomacy," 22–35; and articles by Sharon Liang, Liu Xiaobo, Human Rights in China, Bobson Wong, Erping Zhang, and Stacey Mosher in "The Rise of Civil Society," *China Rights Forum* (2003), no. 3, 11–44, 81–84.

129. Articles by Sharon Liang et al. in "The Rise of Civil Society."

130. See Medeiros and Fravel, "China's New Diplomacy."

131. See Harold Hongju Koh, "The 1998 Frankel Lecture: Bringing International Law Home," *Houston Law Review* 35 (Fall 1998), 675; J. D. Armstrong, *Revolution and World Order: The Revolutionary State in International Society* (Oxford: Clarendon Press, 1993), 297; and Stephen Chan and Andrew J. Williams, eds., *Renegade States: The Evolution of Revolutionary Foreign Policy* (Manchester: Manchester University Press, 1994). Harold Koh includes China in the category of "rogue" states, David Armstrong speaks of "revolutionary" states, and Stephen Chan and Andrew Williams refer to "renegade" states.

132. The critical difference between China and the post-revolutionary states of Eastern Europe is that the former is still an authoritarian political system. For this reason, within the UN system China is not categorized as a post-revolutionary state.

133. Thus, Kenichi Ohmae claims that China is well on the way to becoming "China Inc.," "an entirely new geopolitical model—the country as corporation," which, by promoting economic growth, will "provide China's people with the necessary education in the ways of capitalism [and will] give the Chinese people an appetite for self-determination and participation." See Kenichi Ohmae, "The China Shop," *Australian Financial Review Boss* 3 (2004), no. 4, 54–57. This ignores the more likely scenario that economic modernization will continue, as it has since its initiation in 1978, to be compartmentalized from the political system.

134. For instance, Bobson Wong, "A Matter of Trust: The Internet and Social Change in China," *China Rights Forum* (2003), no. 3, 41–43.

135. Tom Zeller, Jr., "China, Still Winning against the Web," *New York Times*, 15 January 2006.

136. For these tests of the degree of *liberalization*, see Charles E. Ziegler, *Foreign Policy and East Asia: Learning and Adaptation in the Gorbachev Era* (Cambridge: Cambridge University Press, 1993), 166–69.

137. Others have identified its continued tendency to maintain flexibility and avoid enduring commitments and entangling alliances within international society; to free-ride and seek influence without shouldering responsibility; to make compliance with China's objectives a test of another state's "friendship"; to mobilize support among developing nations; to take advantage of the ambiguities in the norms of international regimes; to capture the moral high ground, thereby placing the international interlocutor on the defensive; to maintain secrecy and opacity; and to enter into international agreements before China has the institutions to implement them, as a way of obtaining the support of the international organization in building its institutional capacity. See Elizabeth Economy and Michel Oksenberg, eds., *China Joins the World: Progress and Prospects* (New York: Council on Foreign Relations Press, 1999), 25.

138. For examples of this highly systematized analytical approach in contemporary literature, see the views of leading scholars in An Wei and Li Dongyan, eds., *Shizi lukou'r shang.*

139. I thank Gerry Simpson for this point and for his general insights. This point has also been made by Su Changhe, "China in the World and the World in China: The Domestic Impact of International Institutions on China's Politics, 1978–2000," Research Agenda for the Center for China and International Organizations, School of International Relations and Public Affairs, Fudan University, 2004, 18.

140. Armstrong, *Revolution and World Order*, 297.

141. See also Ann Kent, "China's International Socialization: The Role of International Organizations," *Global Governance* 8 (July–September 2002), no. 3, 343–64; and Kent, "China's Participation in International Organisations," in Yongjin Zhang and Greg Austin, eds., *Power and Responsibility in Chinese Foreign Policy* (Canberra: Asia Pacific Press, 2001), 132–66.

142. Yoichi Funabashi, Michel Oksenberg, and Heinrich Weiss, *An Emerging China in a World of Interdependence* (New York: Trilateral Commission, 1994), 55.

143. Rao Geping, "Guanyu guoji zuzhi yu guoji zuzhifa de jige wenti" ("Some Questions on International Organizations and the Law of International Organizations"), in Ma Chengyuan et al., *Guoji falü wenti yanjiu* ("Research on Issues of International Law") (Beijing: Zhongguo zhengfa daxue chubanshe, 1998), 214; and Rao Geping, *Quanqiuhua jincheng zhong de guoji zuzhi* ("International Organizations in the Process of Globalization") (Beijing: Beijing daxue chubanshe, 2005).

144. See Wu Baoding, ed., *Guojifa*, 132.

145. Ye Zongkui and Wang Xingfang, eds., *Guoji zuzhi gailun* ("An Introduction to International Organizations") (Beijing: Zhongguo renmin daxue chubanshe, 2001), 23.

146. See Wu Baoding, *Guojifa*, 132. For Deng Xiaoping's policies toward international organizations, see Ye Zongkui and Wang Xingfang, eds., *Guoji zuzhi*, 24.

147. Ibid., 23.

148. Lu Ning, *The Dynamics of Foreign Policy Decision-Making in China* (Boulder, CO: Westview, 1997), 20–21.

149. Lu Ning, "The Central Leadership, Supraministry Coordinating Bodies, State Council Ministries and Party Departments," in David M. Lampton, ed., *The Making of Chinese Foreign and Security Policy in the Era of Reform, 1978–2000* (Stanford, CA: Stanford University Press, 2001), 50–51.

150. Ibid.

151. For instance, in relation to voting in the Security Council on the situation in Sudan, China's ambassador to the United Nations, Wang Guangya, stated: "I can't say anything about what the voting position that my government will give to me but at least I can see there are some difficulties in the current draft. . . . All I can say is that the draft as it stands now poses difficulties for China." See video, "Media Stakeout: Comments to the Press by the Permanent Representative of China," 16 September 2004, at www.un.org/webcast/sc.html. While such dependence on government instructions is normal in the context of the Security Council, in China's case it was also apparent in less-political bodies and was observed by the author at the August 1993 session of the UN Human Rights Subcommission, Geneva, and confirmed more generally in discussion with diplomats.

152. Rao Geping, "Guanyu guoji zuzhi," 214.

153. Ibid., 214–15. On the other hand, this research void is rapidly being filled. See Su Changhe, "China in the World"; Li Tiecheng, ed., *Shiji zhi jiao de Lianheguo* ("The United Nations between Centuries") (Beijing, Renmin chubanshe, 2002); Su Changhe, "Zhongguo yu guoji zhidu" ("China and the International System"), *Shijie jingji zhengzhi* ("World Economics and Politics") (October 2002), no. 10, 5–10; and Su Changhe, "Faxian Zhongguo xin waijiao" ("Discovering China's New Foreign Policy"), *Shijie jingji zhengzhi* (2005), no. 4, 11–15. For research by international lawyers, see particularly Rao Geping, ed., *Quanqiuhua*; and Rao Geping, ed., *Guoji zuzhi fa* ("The Law of International Organizations") (Beijing: Beijing daxue chubanshe, 1996).

154. Rao Geping, "Guanyu guoji zuzhi," 215.

155. Wang Jisi, "International Relations Theory," 498; and Johnston, *Cultural Realism*.

156. See Anonymous, "Measuring Globalization: Who's Up, Who's Down?" *Foreign Policy* (January–February 2003), iss. 134, 60–73.

157. Ibid.

158. See Wang Yanjun, "Xuexi Jiang Zemin guanyu xianghu yicun de lunshu" ("Study Jiang Zemin's Remarks on Interdependence"), in *Waijiao xueyuan xuebao* ("Journal of the Foreign Affairs Institute") (1999), no. 2, 36–40.

159. See, for instance, Qin Yaqing, "Guoji zhidu yu guoji hezuo—fanxiang xinziyou zhidu zhuyi" ("International Regimes and International Cooperation—Neorealism Revisited"), *Waijiao xueyuan bao* ("Journal of the Foreign Affairs Institute") (1998), no. 1, 45–46.

160. For best overview of China's view of globalization, see Yong Deng and Thomas G. Moore, "China Views Globalization: Toward a New Great-Power Politics?" *Washington Quarterly* 27 (Summer 2004), no. 3, 117–36. See also Russell Leigh Moses, "Chinese Views on Globalization," ChinaOnLine Commentary, www.chinaonline/commentary (accessed 26 June 2000); and Nick Knight, "Imagining Globalization: The World and Nation in Chinese Communist Party Ideology," *Journal of Contemporary Asia* 33 (2003), no. 3, 327.

161. See views of Li Tiecheng, Li Shaojun, and many other scholars in An Wei and Li Dongyan, eds., *Shizi lukou'r shang*, 188, 193, and, more generally, 178–209. See also Xie Qimei, "Foreword," in Xie Qimei and Wang Xingfang, eds., *Zhongguo yu Lianheguo*, 1; and Su Changhe, "China in the World."

162. The critical impact of the bombing of Kosovo in changing China's world view is explored in Zhang Yunling, "Whither the World Order?" in Zhang Yunling and Guo Weihong, eds., *China, US, Japan and Russia in a Changing World* (Beijing: Social Sciences Documentation Publishing House, 2000), 3–30. See also Gao Feng, "China and Sovereign Equality in the 21st Century," in Sienho Yee and Wang Tieya, eds., *International Law in the Post-Cold War World: Essays in Memory of Li Haopei* (London: Routledge Studies in International Law, 2001), 235–38.

163. See, for instance, Li Shaojun cited in An Wei and Li Dongyan, eds., *Shizi lukou'r shang*, 191.

164. See Li Tiecheng cited in An Wei and Li Dongyan, eds., *Shizi lukou'r shang*, 181–88.

165. See Pang Zhongying cited in An Wei and Li Dongyan, eds., *Shizi lukou'r shang*, 193.

166. See Yong Deng, "Hegemon on the Offensive: Chinese Perspectives on U.S. Global Strategy," *Political Science Quarterly* 116 (Fall 2001), 35–51.

167. Ibid.; and David Shambaugh, "China Engages Asia: Reshaping the Regional Order," *International Security* 29 (Winter 2004), no. 3, 64–99. See also Frank Frost, *Directions in China's Foreign Relations—Implications for East Asia and Australia* (Canberra: Parliament of Australia, 2005); Wang Jisi, "China's Search for Stability with America," *Foreign Affairs* 84 (September–October 2005), no. 5, 39–76; and Chen Zhimin, "Nationalism, Internationalism and Chinese Foreign Policy," *Journal of Contemporary China* 14 (February 2005), 35–53.

168. See "Position Paper of the People's Republic of China on the United Nations Reforms," China View, 7 June 2005, 2, at www.globalpolicy.org/msummit/millenni/2005/chinaposition.htm (accessed 8 February 2006).

169. Kong Qingjiang, "Enforcement of WTO Agreements," unpublished paper, 4.2.4.

170. Ibid.

171. See, for instance, Ye Zongkui and Wang Xingfang, eds., *Guoji zuzhi gailun*, 23.

172. For details, see Kong Qingjiang, "Enforcement of WTO Agreements in China," in Deborah Cass, Brett Williams, and George Barker, eds., *China and the World Trading System* (Cambridge: Cambridge University Press, 2003), 149–50.

173. Kong Qingjiang points out that "in the Chinese context, one has difficulty defin-

ing whether the State belongs to the Monist or Dualist system. On the one hand, there exists no statutory provisions that characterize treaties as part of the domestic legal system; on the other, from time to time, international treaties are directly applicable in practice." See Kong Qingjiang, "Enforcement of WTO Agreements," unpublished paper, 6.4.

174. Cited in ibid. This provision is not entrenched in China's Constitution which, in Art. 67.14, simply states that the Standing Committee of the National People's Congress has the power "to decide on the ratification and abrogation of treaties and important agreements concluded with foreign states." See the Constitution of the People's Republic of China, in *People's Republic of China Yearbook, 1997* (Chinese version) (Beijing: Editorial Department of the PRC Yearbook, 1997), vol. l.

175. UN Committee against Torture, 4th Sess., Summary Record of the 51st Meeting, Geneva, 27 April 1990, UN Doc. CAT/C/SR.51 (4 May 1990), 2.

176. Debate on this matter is now proceeding apace in China, with international lawyers urging the government to make amendments to the Constitution that will facilitate the harmonization of international and municipal law.

177. Keyuan Zou, "Chinese Approaches," 180.

178. See Huang Lie, "The Relation between International Human Rights Treaties and China's Domestic Law," in *EU-China Dialogue, Lisbon, 8–9 May 2000* (Lisbon: Faculdade de Direito da Universidade Nova de Lisboa, February 2002), 151–54.

179. Kong Qiangjiang, "Enforcement of WTO Agreements," 6.3.

180. Ibid.

181. Ibid.; and Ann Kent, *China, the United Nations and Human Rights: The Limits of Compliance* (Philadelphia: University of Pennsylvania Press, 1999).

182. Kong Qingjing, "Enforcement of WTO Agreements," 4.2.3.

183. This conflict is noted by both international organizations and scholars in many issue areas. It is exacerbated by the "bureaucratic tendency" observed by Kong Qingjiang that "once a law is passed, the problem which the law is supposed to address is assumed to have been addressed."

CHAPTER 2

1. Arturo Colorado Castellari, *The Cultural Legacy of the Palais des Nations: The Murals by José Maria Sert* (United Nations: New York, 1985), 9. The importance of the setting was remarked on by many delegates. Thus, U.S. representative Rostow commented: "Being in this beautiful room is always a moving and a chastening experience. The memories of many battles lost and won hover in the air, reminding us that good intentions are not enough." See CD/PV.152 (9 February 1982), 7.

2. See "China's Contributions to Nuclear Disarmament," Chinese government site available at www.china.org.cn/e-caijun/e-caijun.htm; and Monterey Center for Nonproliferation Studies (henceforth MCNS), "China and International Agreements, Organizations and Regimes," available at www.nti.org/db/china.

3. See Statement by UN Secretary-General Perez de Cuellar in CD/PV.194 (15 February 1983), 8.

4. See, for instance, Derek Boothby, "The United Nations and Disarmament," *International Relations Studies and the United Nations Occasional Papers,* 2002, no. 1.

5. Interview with Rebecca Johnson of Acronym, Geneva, 3 September 1998.

6. CD/PV.336 (4 February 1986), 10.

7. Interview with Rebecca Johnson, Geneva, 3 September 1998.

8. For complex history of its origins, see Rudiger Wolfrum and Christian Philipp, eds., *United Nations: Law, Policies and Practice* (Dordrecht: Martinus Nijhoff, 1995), vol. 1, 407–9.

9. For details of organization of the CD, see Conference on Disarmament, "Rules of Procedure of the Conference on Disarmament," CD/8/Rev.7 (27 June 1996).

10. For institutionally based articles, see in particular Alastair Iain Johnston and Paul Evans, "China's Engagement with Multilateral Security Institutions," in Alastair Iain Johnston and Robert S. Ross, eds., *Engaging China: The Management of an Emerging Power* (London: Routledge, 1999), 235–72; Michael D. Swaine and Alastair Iain Johnston, "China and Arms Control Institutions," in Elizabeth Economy and Michael Oksenberg, eds., *China Joins the World: Prospects and Progress* (New York: Council of Foreign Relations, 1999), 90–135; and Alastair Iain Johnston, "The Social Effects of International Institutions on Domestic (Foreign Policy) Actors," in Daniel W. Drezner, ed., *Locating the Proper Authorities: The Interaction of Domestic and International Institutions* (Ann Arbor: University of Michigan Press, 2003), 145–96. A great deal of both primary and secondary material is also available at the MCNS website, at www.nti.org/db/china.

11. Swaine and Johnston, "China and Arms Control Institutions," 105.

12. See Johnston and Evans, "China's Engagement," 248.

13. See Johnston, "The Social Effects," 185.

14. This is also the view of Risse and Sikkink, in Thomas Risse, Stephen C. Ropp, and Kathryn Sikkink, eds., *The Power of Human Rights: International Norms and Domestic Change* (Cambridge: Cambridge University Press, 1999), 37–38.

15. See Piet de Klerk, "Strengthening the Nonproliferation Regime: How Much Progress Have We Made?" *Nonproliferation Review* 6 (Winter 1999), no. 2, 52–58.

16. Hans Blix, "The Role of the IAEA and the Existing NPT Regime," in Sadruddin Aga A. Khan, ed., *Nuclear War, Nuclear Proliferation, and Their Consequences* (Oxford: Clarendon Press, 1986), 62.

17. Text in Jerome Alan Cohen and Hungdah Chiu, eds., *People's China and International Law: A Documentary Study* (Princeton, NJ: Princeton University Press, 1974), 123. See also the approval of the UN arms control and disarmament activities expressed by Guo Qun in 1956, in Guo Qun, *Lianheguo* ("The United Nations") (Beijing: Shijie zhishi she, 1956), 59–60.

18. See Zhu Mingquan, "The Evolution of China's Nuclear Nonproliferation Policy," *Nonproliferation Review* 4 (Winter 1997), no. 2, 1–33; and Yuan Jingdong, "The Evolution of Chinese Nonproliferation Policy, 1989–1999: Progress, Problems and Prospects," paper delivered at International Studies Association, available at www.cc.columbia.edu/sec/dlc/ciao/yujo1. For a Chinese statement, see "Statement of the Chinese Government, 31 July 1963," *Peking Review* 6 (2 August 1963), no. 31, 7–8, in Cohen and Hungdah Chiu, eds., *People's China*, 1622–27.

19. Wu Yun, "China's Policy towards Arms Control and Disarmament," *Pacific Review* 9 (1996), no. 4, 578–79.

20. Ibid; and Tian Jin et al., *Zhongguo zai Lianheguo: Gongtong dizao geng meihao de shijie* ("China in the United Nations: Together Building a Better World") (Beijing: Shijie zhishi chubanshe, 1999), 106–15.

21. For above, see Zhu Mingquan, "The Evolution of China's Nuclear Nonproliferation Policy," 1–5.

22. Jean-Pierre Cabestan, "La position chinoise sur le désarmament depuis Mao Zedong" ("The Chinese Position on Disarmament since Mao Zedong") *Défense Nationale* 40 (March 1984), 96–97; Tian Jin et al., *Zhongguo zai Lianheguo*, 115.

23. Johnston, "The Social Effects."

24. Johnston and Evans, "China's Engagement," 240.

25. CD/PV.54 (4 February 1980), 25.

26. Interview with Foreign Ministry official, Geneva, September 1998.

27. Li Changhe, "Statement at the Plenary Meeting of the Conference on Disarmament," 2 September 1999, Geneva, available at MCNS website (23 September 2002), 2; see Note 2, above.

28. Conflict flared as early as February 1980, in China's first speech before the CD. See Zhang Wenjin in CD/PV.53 (5 February 1980), 19–27.

29. The Soviet delegate stated that, although his country had always assumed that China's participation was "desirable," "we already had serious doubts about the Chinese representatives' readiness to collaborate in working out concrete disarmament measures [and] are forced to note that the statement of the Chinese delegation gives no grounds for optimism." See CD/PV.54 (5 February 1980), 25.

30. See CD/PV.81 (24 April 1980), 24; and CD/PV.179 (17 August 1982), 28.

31. CD/PV.188 (17 September 1982), 10–14, 17.

32. For statement of these issues, see Tian Jin in CD/PV.176 (5 August 1982), 18–21.

33. CD/PV.281 (14 August 1984), 14.

34. See, for instance, CD/PV.334 (29 August 1985), 11.

35. See CD/PV.176 (5 August 1982), 19; and CD/PV.160 (4 March 1982), 22.

36. By March 1985, China was claiming that "multilateral negotiations and bilateral negotiations are mutually complementary." See CD/PV.302 (26 March 1985), 16.

37. CD/PV.292 (19 February 1985), 23.

38. See CD/PV.118 (26 March 1981), 25.

39. CD/PV.176 (5 August 1982), 19 (emphasis added).

40. See working paper on chemical weapons (CD/102), a working paper on technical issues of chemical warfare agents (CD/CW/CTC/3), and a working document on chemical weapons (CD/443).

41. UN Doc. A/39/35.

42. See MCNS, "Biological Weapons Convention," at www.nti.org/db/china/bwcorg .htm.

43. Ibid. Its instrument of accession was accompanied by a statement that criticized the Convention for failing to explicitly prohibit the use of biological weapons and for lacking the concrete measures for supervision and verification and "forceful measures of sanctions in the procedure of complaint against instances of violation of the Convention." For text, see http://domino.un.org/Treaty/Status.nsf.

44. See National Report of the PRC on the Implementation of the Treaty on the Non-proliferation of Nuclear Weapons, NPT/CONF.1995/18 (17 April 1995).

45. CD/PV.282 (16 August 1984), 36.

46. CD/PV.292 (19 February 1985), 30, 32. Qian's announcement was warmly received by all delegates apart from the representative of the Soviet Union, who, insisting that "this is not a birthday party," expressed skepticism as to whether China would be prepared to cease testing its own nuclear weapons "on a basis of reciprocity." "This is by no means meant to please anybody," Qian responded. "We are prompted only by the interest of our common cause, that is, disarmament." See CD/PV.293 (21 February 1985), 23.

47. CD/PV.317 (2 July 1985), 20.

48. CD/PV.339 (13 February 1986), 30.

49. Ibid., 31.

50. This comprised the strictures that: (1) the ultimate goal of nuclear disarmament should be the complete prohibition and thorough destruction of nuclear weapons; (2) the United

States and the Soviet Union should take the lead in nuclear disarmament; (3) all nuclear weapon states should undertake not to be the first to use nuclear weapons; (4) reduction of medium-range nuclear missiles deployed by the United States and Soviet Union should be simultaneous and balanced; (5) there should be a parallel drastic reduction of conventional arms; (6) outer space should be used exclusively for peaceful purposes and an international agreement on the complete prohibition of space weapons should be concluded as soon as possible; (7) an international convention on the complete prohibition and thorough destruction of chemical weapons should be concluded at an early date; (8) disarmament agreements should provide for "the necessary and effective measures of verification"; and (9) disarmament should not be monopolized by a few big powers but all countries should enjoy "equal rights to participate in the discussions and settlement of problems related to disarmament." For this and Zhao's statement on nuclear tests in atmosphere, see CD/PV.350 (25 March 1986), 6–7.

51. Xie Qimei and Wang Xingfang, eds., *Zhongguo yu Lianheguo: Jinian Lianheguo chengli wushi zhounian* ("China and the United Nations: Commemorating the Fiftieth Anniversary of the Founding of the United Nations") (Beijing: Shijie zhishi chubanshe, 1995), 187–88.

52. For details, see CD/WP.286 (24 July 1987); and CD/WP. 341 (12 April 1988), cited in CD/PV.457 (14 April 1988), 39–40.

53. CD/PV.530 (29 August 1989), 14.

54. Robert A. Manning, Ronald Montaperto, and Brad Roberts, *China, Nuclear Weapons and Arms Control: A Preliminary Assessment* (New York: Council on Foreign Relations, 2000), 65. See also CD/PV.538, 6.

55. *National Report of the People's Republic of China.*

56. A/39/59 and CD/PV.292 (19 February 1985), 32.

57. CD/PV.466 (19 July 1988), 11–13.

58. CD/PV.525 (10 August 1989), 21–24.

59. CD/PV.538 (27 February 1990), 6.

60. See MCNS, "Nuclear Non-Proliferation Treaty: China," www.nti.org/db/china/nptorg.htm.

61. Interview with disarmament expert, Geneva, 18 September 1998.

62. Savita Pande, "China's Nuclear Doctrine," *Strategic Analysis* 23 (March 2000), no. 12, 13.

63. Interview with disarmament expert, Geneva, 18 September 1998.

64. Thus, it claimed: "China maintains that the prevention of proliferation of nuclear weapons is not an end in itself. . . . Only when substantial progress is made in the field of nuclear disarmament can the proliferation of nuclear weapons be checked most effectively." For full text, see http://domino.un.org/TreatyStatus.nsf.

65. Pande, "China's Nuclear Doctrine," 13.

66. See *National Report of the People's Republic of China*; and Information Office of the State Council of the People's Republic of China, *China: Arms Control and Disarmament* (Beijing, November 1995).

67. See Rebecca Johnson, *Acronym Report* (Geneva, 27 April–8 May 1998), no. 11, 1.

68. See Patricia Hewitson, "Nonproliferation and Reduction of Nuclear Weapons: Risks of Weakening the Multilateral Nuclear Nonproliferation Norm," *Berkeley Journal of International Law* 21 (2003), no. 3, 405–94.

69. See MCNS, "International Atomic Energy Agency," available at www.nti.org/db/china/iaeaorg.htm (accessed 29 September 2002). This also states that the three-module centrifuge plant will be under IAEA safeguards. See also John F. Murphy, "Force and Arms," in Christopher C. Joyner, ed., *The United Nations and International Law* (Cambridge: Cambridge University Press, 1997), 125.

70. Interview with disarmament expert, Geneva, 18 September 1998.

71. Ibid.; and MCNS, "Chemical Weapons Convention," (20 September 2002).

72. For text, see http://domino.un.org/Treaty/Status.nsf.

73. "China Earnest in Implementing the Chemical Weapons Convention," *People's Daily*, 17 January 2001; and Information Office of the State Council of the People's Republic of China, *China's Endeavors for Arms Control, Disarmament and Non-Proliferation* (Beijing: Information Office of the State Council, 2005), chapt. 3.

74. Information Office, *China's Endeavors for Arms Control*.

75. Sha Zukang, "China's Perspective on Non-Proliferation," in Joseph Cirincione, ed., *Repairing the Regime: Preventing the Spread of Weapons of Mass Destruction* (New York: Routledge, 2000), 130.

76. Zou Yunhua, *China and the CTBT Negotiations* (Stanford: Center for International Security and Cooperation, Stanford University, December 1998), 4, available at http://cisac.stanford.edu/publications/china_and_the_ctbt_negotiations.

77. Interview with Rebecca Johnson of Acronym, Geneva, 3 September 1998.

78. Zou Yunhua, *China and the CTBT*, 4.

79. See, for instance, criticisms by Norway, Japan, and Argentina in CD/PV.706 (1 June 1995). For Chinese justifications, see CD/PV.645 (4 February 1993), 12; CD/PV.717 (August 1995), 4; CD/PV.724 (8 February 1996), 29.

80. Comment from Western disarmament specialist, Geneva, 18 September 1998.

81. In her carefully documented analysis of the negotiations, Zou Yunhua has highlighted China's particular concerns and the adjustments it made during negotiations from 1994 to 1996. See Zou Yunhua, *China and the CTBT*, 5–21.

82. Interview with disarmament expert, Geneva, 18 September 1998.

83. Interview with arms control negotiator, Geneva, 4 September 1998. This occurred because of Indian blocking tactics in the CD in response to the insistence of China, and, to a lesser extent, Russia and the UK, that the three threshold states, particularly India, had to be necessary parties for the CTBT to enter into force. See Thomas Graham, Jr., *Disarmament Sketches: Three Decades of Arms Control and International Law* (Seattle: University of Washington Press, 2002), 253–54; and Joseph Cirincione, "History of the CTBT Negotiations," Arms Control Press Conference, 20 September 1996, at www.clw.org/pub/clw/coalition/jcctbt.htm.

84. Interview with disarmament expert, Geneva, 8 September 1998.

85. Zou Yunhua, *China and the CTBT*, 21–24.

86. Interview with disarmament expert, Geneva, 18 September 1998.

87. Bates Gill, "Two Steps Forward, One Step Back: The Dynamics of Chinese Nonproliferation and Arms Control Policy-Making in an Era of Reform," in David M. Lampton, ed., *The Making of Chinese Foreign Policy and Security Policy in the Era of Reform* (Stanford, CA: Stanford University Press, 2001), 263–64.

88. Zou Yunhua, *China and the CTBT*, 8.

89. Interview with disarmament expert, Geneva, 18 September 1998.

90. Interview with arms control negotiator, Geneva, 4 September 1998.

91. Interview with disarmament expert, Geneva, 18 September 1998.

92. Xinhua News Agency, 7 October 1999, Reuters China News, 7 October 1999.

93. Kyodo News, 25 April 2000; and Information Office of the State Council of the People's Republic of China, *China's National Defense in 2000* (Beijing, October 2000), part 4, available at www.china.org.cn/e–white.

94. For text of statement, see http://domino.un.org/Treaty/Status.nsf. For other statements, see MCNS website.

95. Interview with Chinese Foreign Ministry official, Department of Arms Control and Disarmament, Chinese Foreign Ministry, Beijing, 14 May 2002.

96. Hewitson, "Nonproliferation and Reduction of Nuclear Weapons," 465 (emphasis added).

97. Zou Yunhua, *China and the CTBT*, 6–7.

98. See also Johnston, "The Social Effects," 185; and Gill, "Two Steps Forward," 267–87.

99. Information Office of the State Council of the PRC, *China's National Defense* (Beijing, July 1998), chapt. 5.

100. Interview with disarmament negotiator, Geneva, 4 September 1998.

101. Interview with Rebecca Johnson, Geneva, 3 September 1998.

102. Discussion with BBC journalist, Beijing, May 2002.

103. Interview with Foreign Ministry official, Geneva, September 1998.

104. Manning, Montaperto, and Roberts, *China, Nuclear Weapons*, 32–33, 41.

105. Sha Zukang, "China's Perspective," 127.

106. CD/1508 (15 May 1998).

107. See statements in CD/PV.799 (25 June 1998), 5, 15; CD/PV.798 (18 June 1998), 3, 5; CD/PV.796 (4 June 1998), 2–6: and CD/PV.795 (2 June 1998).

108. Author's notes from Final Plenary Session, CD, Geneva, September 1998.

109. CD/PV.680 (2 June 1994), 30.

110. CD/PV.770 (26 June 1997), 66.

111. Ibid., 11. Nevertheless, it acceded to the amended landmines protocol (Protocol II) to the Convention on Conventional Weapons (CCW).

112. CD/PV.676 (24 February 1994), 18–19.

113. Interview with Rebecca Johnson, Geneva, 3 September 1998.

114. It signed and ratified Protocols I and III to the Treaty of Rarotonga for South Pacific Nuclear Free Zone, signed and ratified Protocol I and II to the Pelindaba Treaty (Africa), and signed Protocol II to the Treaty of Tlatelolco (Latin America).

115. Information Office, *China's National Defense in 2000*, part 6.

116. CD/PV.910 (15 August 2002), 5.

117. Interview of Foreign Ministry official, Geneva, September 1998.

118. For details, see MCNS, "Fissile Material Cut-Off Treaty."

119. See Li Song, "Views on the Prospects of Multilateral Arms Control and the Conference on Disarmament," EANP Conference Abstracts, 23 September 1998, available at http://cns.miis.edu/cns/projects/eanp/beijing/agenda (accessed 17 September 1999).

120. These observations are based on interviews in Geneva in August–September 1998.

121. See, for instance, Information Office, *China's National Defense in 2000*, chapt. ll.

122. Manning, Montaperto, and Roberts, *China, Nuclear Weapons*, 2, 16–21. By contrast, new research suggests that even 400 devices may be an overestimate. Thus, according to Robert Norris and Hans Kristensen, "We estimate that China has an arsenal of some 200 nuclear warheads, down from an estimated 435 in 1993. This change is due to new information about the arsenal. . . . U.S. intelligence and defense agencies predict that over the next decade, China may increase the number of warheads targeted primarily against the United States from 20 to about 75–100." See Robert S. Norris and Hans M. Kristensen, "Global Nuclear Stockpiles, 1945–2006," *Bulletin of the Atomic Scientists* 62 (July/August 2006), no. 4, 64–66.

123. Interview with arms control negotiator, Geneva, 4 September 1998.

124. Interview with Chinese Foreign Ministry official, Geneva, September 1998.

125. For critique of U.S. activity, see, in particular, James E. Goodby, "Doing America's Work at the UN," *International Herald Tribune*, 30 October 2002.

126. For details of research, see report in Julian Borger, "US 'Has Secret Bio-weapons Programme,'" *Guardian Weekly*, 167 (31 October–6 November 2002), no. 19, 1.

127. You Ji, "The PLA, the CCP and the Formulation of Chinese Defence and Foreign Policy," in Yongjin Zhang and Greg Austin, eds., *Power and Responsibility in Chinese Foreign Policy* (Canberra: Asia Pacific Press, 2001), 116.

128. Manning, Montaperto, and Roberts, *China, Nuclear Weapons*, 51.

129. See, for instance, Sha Zukang, "China's Perspective," 127–32.

130. See Sha Zukang cited in *People's Daily*, 21 February 2001, and 14 March 2001.

131. Tang Jiaxuan, opening statement at conference, "A Disarmament Agenda for the 21st Century," Chinese Foreign Ministry, Beijing, 2–4 April 2002, 3, at http://disarmament .un.org/ddapublications/po6contents.htm (accessed 11 October 2002).

132. CD/PV.892 (7 February 2002), 3 (emphasis added).

133. This was the impression gained from the author's discussions with Chinese disarmament experts in Beijing in May 2002.

134. For Russian response, see Hewitson, "Non-Proliferation and Reduction," 126–27.

135. This account is based on an interview at the Department of Arms Control and Disarmament, Chinese Foreign Ministry, Beijing, 14 May 2002.

136. See statement by Hu Xiaodi at the Plenary of the Conference on Disarmament, Geneva, 15 February 2002, CD/PV.892, 5–6. On missile defense, see also Hu's statements to the CD on 14 September 2000 and 24 February 2000; and Li Changhe's statement on 11 March 1999.

137. CD/1679 (28 June 2002).

138. See press releases, UN News Centre, 15 August 2002, 22 August 2002.

139. Interview at Department of Arms Control and Disarmament, Chinese Foreign Ministry, Beijing, 14 May 2002.

140. Rebecca Johnson, "CD Closes 2002 Still Deadlocked," *Disarmament Diplomacy* (October–November 2002), no. 67, at www.acronym.org.uk, 10–11.

141. CD/PV.910 (15 August 2002), 3. For specific details of this policy, see *Position Paper of the People's Republic of China on the United Nations Reforms*, 7 June 2005, www.globalpolicy .org/msummit/millenni/2005/chinaposition.htm (8 February 2006), 7–10.

142. In his final year as Secretary-General of the Conference on Disarmament, Vladimir Petrovsky stated: "We at the CD feel very strongly that what is lacking today is not so much an efficiency of machinery, as it may look on the surface, . . . but the political will and in particular, minimal degree of harmony among Member States, in particular those who are often referred to as major players." See United Nations Press Release DG/01/13 (15 May 2001). For NGO assessments, see Rebecca Johnson, "Conference Remains Deadlocked after First Part of 2002 Session," *Disarmament Diplomacy* (May–June 2002), no. 64; and Johnson, "CD Closes 2002," 9–10.

143. Shirley V. Scott, *International Law in World Politics: An Introduction* (Boulder, CO: Lynne Rienner, 2004), 47.

144. Johnson, "CD Closes 2002," 2.

145. See "Revitalising Conference on Disarmament Requires Renewed Political Will, Determination, Says Secretary-General," UN Press Release SG/SM/8584, DCF/420, 21 January 2003; and "Conference on Disarmament Adopts Annual Report, Concludes 2003 Session," UN Press Release, 9 September 2003, at www.unog.ch/news.

146. Information Office of the State Council of the People's Republic of China, *China's National Defense in 2004* (Beijing: December 2004), chapt. 10.

147. See Tanya Ogilvie-White, "China's Response to Nuclear Break-out and Non-Compliance: Pursuing 'Harmony without Uniformity,'" paper presented to the Annual Conference of the Australian and New Zealand Society of International Law (ANZSIL), ANU, Canberra, 18–20 June 2004.

148. "China to Join NSG to Boost Nonproliferation Efforts," Kyodo News, 28 January 2004.

149. See Ministry of Foreign Affairs of the People's Republic of China, "Second Round of China–MTCR Dialogue Held in Beijing," 3 June 2004, at www.fmprc.gov.cn; and Anil K. Joseph, "China Ready to Control Missile Proliferation," rediff.com at http://ushome.rediff .com (accessed 3 June 2004).

150. Rebecca Johnson, "The Miserable Failure of the NPT to Contain the Nuclear Spectre," Acronym Report on NPT Review Conference Day 3, 4 May 2005.

151. These it listed as the pursuit of unilateralism, the advocacy of a preemptive strategy, the listing of other countries as targets of nuclear strike, terrorism, the proliferation of WMD, the abrogation of the ABM Treaty, the dilution of the prospect of entry into force of the CTBT, and the paralysis of the CD, undermining the possibility of negotiating an FMCT and PAROS. See "Statement by Zhang Yan, Head of the Chinese Delegation in the General Debate at the 2005 NPT Review Conference," New York, 4 May 2005, 1, at www.un.org/ events/npt2005/statements03may.html (accessed 9 January 2006).

152. For details, see NTI, Country Overviews, "China: Nuclear Overview" (November 2005), at www.nti.org/e_research/profiles/China (accessed 6 January 2006).

153. Zhen Huang, "China's Strategic Nuclear Posture by 2010: Minimum or Limited Deterrence? Likely Impact of U.S. Missile Defense," paper prepared for the 8th ISODARCO-Beijing Seminar on Arms Control, Beijing, China (14–18 October 2002), copy on file with author; and Li Bin, "The Impact of U.S. NMD on Chinese Nuclear Modernization," (April 2001), www.pugwash.org/reports/rc/rc8e.htm.

154. Thus, the 2004 report to Congress on PRC military power stated that China was building up its short-range and long-range ballistic missile production. It reported: "[In China], a ballistic missile modernization program is under way to upgrade all classes of missiles, both qualitatively and quantitatively. Beijing intends this program to improve its nuclear deterrence by increasing the number of warheads that can target the United States and augmenting the nuclear force's operational capabilities for contingencies in East Asia." See U.S. Secretary of Defense, *Annual Report on the Military Power of the People's Republic of China* (Washington, DC, 2004), 37. The 2005 *Annual Report* (Washington, DC, 2005) even claims that China's improvements to its strategic missile force "could provide a credible, survivable nuclear deterrent and counterstrike capability." For details of missiles, see U.S. Secretary of Defense, *Annual Report on the Military Power of the People's Republic of China* (Washington, DC, 2005), 28–30. For overall assessment, see Desmond Ball, "The Probabilities of 'On the Beach': Assessing 'Armageddon Scenarios' in the 21st Century," paper prepared for the conference, "Science and Ethics: Can *Homo Sapiens* Survive?" Manning Clark House, Canberra, 17–18 May 2005. For similar estimate of 400 nuclear weapons, see NTI, "China: Nuclear Overview" (November 2005) (6 January 2006). By contrast, see much lower 2006 estimate in Norris and Kristensen, "Global Nuclear Stockpiles," 64–66. For U.S. build-up, see Ralph Vartabedian, "U.S. Nuclear Scientists Back in Race," *Los Angeles Times* reported in *Sydney Morning Herald*, 1–2 July 2006, 17.

155. Complaining about China's expansion of its missile forces, and its projection of its power, U.S. defense secretary Donald Rumsfeld declaimed: "Since no nation threatens China,

one must wonder: Why this growing investment? Why these continuing large and expanding purchases? Why these continuing robust deployments?" See Reuters, "Rumsfeld Says China Needlessly Projects Power," *New York Times*, 4 June 2005. This reaction is to misunderstand the nature of the arms control regime and the effect of U.S. unilateralism in undermining mutual trust and reciprocal compliance between states.

156. See details in Kirsten Speidel, "Major Chinese Arms Control Organizations," in Economy and Oksenberg, eds., *China Joins the World*, appendix B, 339–41; Gill, "Two Steps Forward," 285–87; and Swaine and Johnston, "China and Arms Control Institutions," 104–5.

157. See MCNS website www.china.org.cn/e-caijun/e-caijun.htm, "PRC Laws and Regulations" under "List of Statements and Documents: Chinese Government"; Information Office, *China's Endeavors*, annex 2; and Yuan Jingdong, "Strengthening China's Export Control System" (Monterey: Monterey Institute of International Studies, 2002), available at http://cns.miis.edu/research/china/chiexp/prcxc.htm (accessed 6 November 2002), 2–6. According to Fu Cong of the Department of Arms Control and Disarmament in the Ministry of Foreign Affairs, "the Regulations stipulate that the State does not support, encourage or engage in the proliferation of nuclear weapons and does not assist other countries in the development of such weapons. Nuclear exports shall be limited to peaceful purposes only and shall be subject to IAEA safeguards." Fu Cong, "An Introduction (to) China's Export Control System," at the Tokyo Workshop on Nonproliferation Export Control Regimes," 11–12 December 1997.

158. For comparison between provisions in regulations and MTCR, see Phillip C. Saunders, *Preliminary Analysis of Chinese Missile Technology Export Control List*, (Monterey, CA: Center for Nonproliferation Studies, Monterey Institute of International Studies, 6 September 2002).

159. Information Office, *China's National Defense* (2004), chapt. 10.

160. Ibid., chapt. 5.

161. These were all published by the Information Office of the State Council of the People's Republic of China: *China: Arms Control* (Beijing, November 1995); *China's National Defense* (Beijing, July 1998); *China's National Defense in 2000* (Beijing, October 2000); *China's Space Activities* (Beijing, November 2000); *China's National Defense in 2002* (Beijing, December 2002); *China's Non-Proliferation Policy and Measures* (Beijing, December 2003); *China's National Defense 2004*; and *China's Endeavors*. All available at www.china.org.cn/e–white. See also PRC State Council, *China's National Report on the Implementation of the Treaty on the Nonproliferation of Nuclear Weapons* (Beijing, December 2003). For analysis of the "circumscribed" transparency of these White Papers, see Gill, "Two Steps Forward," 277–80.

162. Yuan Jingdong, "Strengthening China's Export Control System," 1.

163. Jonathan D. Pollack, "The Cox Report's 'Dirty Little Secret,'" *Arms Control Today* (April–May 1999), available at www.armscontrol.org/act/1999.

164. For detailed studies of these claims and their supporting evidence, or lack of it, see Shirley A. Kan, "China's Proliferation of Weapons of Mass Destruction and Missiles: Current Policy Issues," *CRS Issue Brief*, 25 July 2002 (#1B2056), available at www.fas.org/spp/starwars/crs; Shirley A. Kan, *China and Proliferation of Weapons of Mass Destruction and Missiles: Policy Issues*, CRS Report for Congress (#RL31555) (Washington, DC: Congressional Research Service, 6 September 2002); Yuan Jingdong, "Strengthening China's Export Control System," 1–9; Robert G Sutter, *Chinese Nuclear Weapons and Arms Control Policies: Implications and Options for the United States*, Report for Congress, 94–422 S (Washington, DC: Congressional Research Service Report, 25 March 1994), at www.fas.org/spp/starwars/crs/94–422s .htm; Gary Klintworth, "China and Arms Control: A Learning Process," in Yongjin Zhang and Austin, eds., *Power and Responsibility*, 219–49; Manning, Montaperto, and Roberts, *China, Nuclear Weapons*; MCNS, "U.S.-China Convergence and Friction on Arms Control/Nonproliferation Issues"; MCNS, "Arms Control and Nonproliferation Sanctions against China," at www.cns.miis

.edu/cns/projects/eanp/fact/posconc.htm; and Reuters, "China Links with Saudi, Pakistan a U.S. Concern," 15 February 2004, at www.nytimes.com/reuters.

165. MCNS, "Arms Control and Nonproliferation Sanctions against China"; and Yuan Jingdong, "Strengthening China's Export Control System," 4–6.

166. See, respectively, *The Hindu*, 3 July 2000 and *New York Times*, 2 September 2001; Judith Miller, "Bush Puts Penalties on Nuclear Suppliers," *New York Times*, 2 April 2004; and David E. Sanger, "U.S. to Punish 9 Companies Said to Help Iran on Arms," *New York Times*, 28 December 2005.

167. See, for instance, U.S. claims that Chinese state-owned corporations have engaged in "transfer activities" with Pakistan, Iran, North Korea, and Libya that "are clearly contrary to China's commitments to the U.S." See "China's Non-Proliferation Policies: Statement by US Assistant Secretary of State Paula DeSutter," 24 July 2003, at www.acronym.org.uk/docs.

168. Distinction made in Yuan Jingdong, "Assessing Chinese Nonproliferation Policy: Progress, Problems and Issues for the United States," prepared statement for the U.S.-China Security Review Commission Hearing on China's Proliferation Policies, 12 October 2001, at http://cns.miis.edu, 9. For summary of specific U.S. criticisms of China's nonproliferation policies, see Shirley A. Kan, *China and Proliferation of Weapons of Mass Destruction and Missiles: Policy Issues*, CRS Report for Congress (#RL31555), updated 17 July 2006; and Joseph Cirincione with Jon B. Wolfsthal and Miriam Rajkumar, *Deadly Arsenals: Tracking Weapons of Mass Destruction* (Washington, DC: Carnegie Endowment for International Peace, 2005), 141–62.

169. For detailed analysis, see Kan, *China and Proliferation* (2002), 3–16.

170. Cirincione et al., *Deadly Arsenals*, 149; and Joby Warrick and Peter Slevin, "Beijing Linked to Nuclear Hawkers," *Sydney Morning Herald*, 16 February 2004.

171. "China Links with Saudi, Pakistan a U.S. Concern," Reuters, 15 February 2004, at www. nytimes.com; and Sanger, "U.S. to Punish 9 Companies."

172. Manning, Montaperto, and Roberts, *China, Nuclear Weapons*, 34.

173. For instance, as an arms control specialist remarked in an interview in Geneva in September 1998, in relation to the NPT, the UK and Germany have also sent sensitive material to Iraq.

174. See Swaine and Johnston, "China and Arms Control Institutions," 120 (emphasis added). Johnston and Swaine conclude that participation in these forums may have encouraged a rethinking of China's interests, even though international security institutions "simply do not demand much from most of their participants." See also Johnston and Evans, "China and Multilateral Security Institutions," 265.

175. Kan, *China and Proliferation* (2002), 1–2, 21.

176. Klintworth, "China and Arms Control," 241–43.

177. Yuan Jingdong, "Assessing Chinese Nonproliferation Policy," 2–5.

178. Yuan Jingdong, "Missile Export Controls Significant Step for Beijing," *South China Morning Post*, 29 August 2002, 12. For China's explanations of its failure to join these bodies, see Sha Zukang, "China's Perspective," 128–30.

179. "China to Join NSG to Boost Nonproliferation Efforts," Kyodo News, 28 January 2004.

180. Manning, Montaperto and Roberts, *China, Nuclear Weapons*, 6.

181. Yuan Jingdong, "Assessing Chinese Nonproliferation Policy," 5, 10.

182. Tom Allard and Hamish McDonald, "Nuclear Arms Race Fuels New Standoff," *Sydney Morning Herald*, 6–7 September 2003, 1.

183. CD/PV.892 (7 February 2002), 21 and 27.

184. These exceptions include its voluntary acceptance of IAEA supervision of its civilian nuclear reactors.

185. Full-scope safeguards require IAEA inspections of all other declared nuclear facilities in addition to the facility importing supplies to prevent diversions to weapons programs.

186. Thus, China's Government White Paper, *China's National Defense* (2004) states that: "The proliferation of WMD and their means of delivery is detrimental to world peace and security, so is it to China's own security. Non-proliferation is in the common interests of all countries, including China."

187. Mohamed ElBaradie, "Act Now on Nukes or Risk Self-Destruction," *Sydney Morning Herald*, 16 February 2004 (emphasis added).

188. Susan V. Lawrence, "China Rejects Offer to Join Missile Accord—Move Threatens to Erode US-European Efforts to Control North Korea," *Asian Wall Street Journal*, 8 November 2002, available at Factiva.

189. Jayantha Dhanapala, "The State of the Regime," in Cirincione, ed., *Repairing the Regime*, 21.

190. China is not the only source of this perception. See Dan Plesch, "Iraq First, Iran and China Next," *Guardian*, 13 September 2002.

191. Interview with Rebecca Johnson, Geneva, 3 September 2002.

192. Zhu Mingquan, "The Evolution of China's Nuclear Nonproliferation Policy," 10.

193. Johnston and Evans, "China and Multilateral Security Institutions," 239–40.

194. See also ibid., emphasizing the role of "path dependency."

195. See "word-deed" gap in Yuan Jingdong, "Missile Export Controls," 12.

196. As Jayantha Dhanapala has pointed out, "If countries are perceived to derive certain benefits from ignoring . . . fundamental global norms, the risk could grow that others will either follow suit or seek various forms of compensation for continued participation in the regime." See Dhanapala, "The State of the Regime," 17.

CHAPTER 3

1. See, in particular, Devesh Kapur, John P. Lewis, and Richard Webb, *The World Bank: Its First Half Century* (Washington, DC: Brookings Institution, 1997), vols. 1–2; K. Sarwar Lateef, "The First Half Century: An Overview," in K. Sarwar Lateef, ed., *The Evolving Role of the World Bank: Helping Meet the Challenge of Development* (Washington, DC: World Bank, 1995), 1–35; and Harold K. Jacobson and Michel Oksenberg, *China's Participation in the IMF, the World Bank and GATT: Toward a Global Economic Order* (Ann Arbor: University of Michigan Press, 1990), 1–3.

2. Raymond F. Mikesell, "The Bretton Woods Debates: A Memoir," *Essays in International Finance* No. 192 (Princeton, NJ: Department of Economics, Princeton University, 1994), 58.

3. See Stephen Zamora, "Economic Relations and Development," in Christopher C. Joyner, ed., *The United Nations and International Law* (Cambridge: American Society of International Law and University of Cambridge, 1997), 236–75.

4. Nicholas R. Lardy, "China and the International Financial System," in Elizabeth Economy and Michel Oksenberg, eds., *China Joins the World: Progress and Prospects* (New York: Council on Foreign Relations Press, 1999), 207–8. Lardy argues that the market is "the principal source of the norms of behavior."

5. Mikesell, *The Bretton Woods Debates*, 22–23, 36.

6. "China's Principled Stand on Relations of International Economy and Trade," *Peking Review* 15 (28 April 1972), no. 17, 11–14, in Jerome Alan Cohen and Hungdah Chiu, eds., *People's China and International Law: A Documentary Study* (Princeton, NJ: Princeton University Press, 1974), 1373, 1376–77.

7. Jacobson and Oksenberg, *China's Participation*, 61.

8. Xie Qimei and Wang Xingfang, eds., *Zhongguo yu Lianheguo: Jinian Lianheguo chengli wushi zhounian* ("China and the United Nations: Commemorating the Fiftieth Anniversary of the Founding of the United Nations") (Beijing: Shijie zhishi chubanshe, 1995), 266.

9. Jacobson and Oksenberg, *China's Participation*, 64–65, 70.

10. Kapur, Lewis, and Webb, *The World Bank*, vol. 2, 605, 1190.

11. Jochen Kraske, William H. Becker, William Diamond, and Louis Galambos, *Bankers with a Mission: The Presidents of the World Bank* (New York: IBRD / Oxford University Press, 1996), 178–79. During McNamara's visit to China in April 1980, Deng Xiaoping told him: "We are very poor. We have lost touch with the world. We need the World Bank to catch up. We could do it without you, but with you we can do it better and quicker." See citation of World Bank records in Pieter Bottelier, "China on the World Stage: Reexamining Expectations," speech at the National Press Club, 28 October 1999, at www.chinaonline .com/ commentary_analysis/wtocom/currentnews/secure/c91119, 2 (accessed 6 September 2004).

12. The following account is based on this classic work. See Jacobson and Oksenberg, *China's Participation*, 70–77.

13. Interview of Shahid Hussain, cited in Kraske et al., *Bankers with a Mission*, 179.

14. Ibid., 178.

15. Jacobson and Oksenberg, *China's Participation*, 78–79. The result was that, following a general increase in the World Bank's authorized capital in 1988, China's voting power in the Bank ranked 3.19 percent of the total.

16. Kapur, Lewis, and Webb, *The World Bank*, vol. 1, 1190.

17. The following account is based on ibid., 550–51, 1190.

18. Lateef, "The First Half Century," 15–31.

19. World Bank Group, "What Does the World Bank Do?" at www.worldbank.org/ html/extdr/about/role (accessed 16 November 1999).

20. See IBRD, *IDA Eligibility, Terms and Graduation Policies* (Board Report, 7 August 2003), available at www-wds.worldbank.org/servlet/WDS-Ibank_Servlet?.

21. See IBRD, Articles of Agreement, Art. III, at www.worldbank.org/html/extdr/ backgrd/ibrd/art3.htm.

22. Zamora, "Economic Relations and Development," 240, 277.

23. These are: Art. 1: Purposes; Art. II: Membership in and Capital of the Bank; Art. III: General Provisions Relating to Loans and Guarantees; Art. IV: Operations; Art. V: Organization and Management; Art. VI: Withdrawal and Suspension of Membership: Suspension of Operations; Art. VII: Status, Immunities and Privileges; Art. VIII: Amendments; Art. IX: Interpretation; Art. X: Approval Deemed Given; Art. XI: Final Provisions. See IBRD, Articles of Agreement.

24. See *Guidelines: Procurement under IBRD Loans and IDA Credits* (Washington, DC: World Bank, 2004), available at www.worldbank.org/html/opr/procure/guideli.html (accessed 6 September 2004).

25. See IBRD, Articles of Agreement.

26. Zamora, "Economic Relations and Development," 277.

27. Interview, World Bank, Washington, DC, 7 November 2000.

28. IBRD, "The World Bank's Role," at www.worldbank.org/html/extdr/backgrd/role, 4 (accessed 11 June 1999).

29. World Bank Group, "Operations Evaluation Department: Overview," at www.world bank.org/oed/oed_overview.html (accessed 6 September 2004).

30. See Lucia Palpal-latoc, "Amnesty Calls for Rights Tie for Loans," *Hong Kong Standard*, 24 September 1997, Reuters China News, 24 September 1997.

31. See Larry Elliot, "Protesters Win a Battle, But Not the War," *Guardian Weekly*, 3–9 October 2002, 11; and Joseph E. Stiglitz, *Globalization and Its Discontents* (London: Penguin, 2002), xv.

32. Stiglitz, *Globalization*, 89–132; Bertram S. Brown, "IMF Governance, the Asian Financial Crisis, and the New International Financial Architecture," in Sienho Yee and Wang Tieya, eds., *International Law in the Post–Cold War World: Essays in Memory of Li Haopei* (London: Routledge Studies in International Law, 2001), 139–40; and Martin Feldstein, "A Self-Help Guide for Emerging Markets," *Foreign Affairs* 77 (March–April 1998), iss. 2, 93–110.

33. See, for instance, Stanley Fischer, "In Defense of the IMF: Specialized Tools for Specialized Tasks," *Foreign Affairs* 98 (July–August 1998), no. 4, 103–6; Kenneth Rogoff, "The IMF Strikes Back," *Foreign Policy* 134 (January–February 2003), 38–49; and Joseph Kahn, "World Bank, in Report, Defends Its Use of Aid," *New York Times*, 12 March 2002.

34. World Bank Group, *The World Bank: Knowledge and Resources for Development* (Washington, DC: World Bank, September 1999), 5.

35. Stiglitz, *Globalization*, 49.

36. See Larry Elliot, "World Bank Paints Picture of Catastrophic Global Future," *Guardian Weekly*, 29 August–4 September 2002, 11.

37. See David Zweig, *Internationalizing China: Domestic Interests and Global Linkages* (Ithaca, NY: Cornell University Press, 2002), 226–38; and Tian Jin et al., *Zhongguo zai Lianheguo: Gongtong dizao geng meihao de shijie* ("China in the United Nations: Together Building a Better World") (Beijing: Shijie zhishi chubanshe, 1998), 154–70.

38. As the Bank's official historians have noted, "the Bank—like other external sources of assistance—was appalled by India's poverty, dazzled by its size and by the prestige of being active there, and impressed by the articulateness of its political leaders and top-level civil servants and by the high priority they accorded to economic development. . . . A decade later the mood had changed to one of disenchantment—with planning, with India, with infrastructure." See Edward S. Mason and Robert E. Asher, *The World Bank since Bretton Woods*, (Washington, DC: Brookings Institution, 1973), 682–83.

39. Bottelier, "China on the World Stage," 1.

40. International Monetary Fund, *People's Republic of China: 2005 Article IV Consultation—Staff Report; Staff Supplement and Public Information Notice on the Executive Board Discussion*, IMF Country Report No. 05/411 (November 2005), annex 5.

41. Lateef, "The First Half Century," 28–29.

42. Jacobson and Oksenberg, *China's Participation*, 21 (emphasis in original).

43. For summary, see Ann Kent, *Between Freedom and Subsistence: China and Human Rights* (Hong Kong: Oxford University Press, 1993), 160–66.

44. See distribution in Jacobson and Oksenberg, *China's Participation*, 119. See also Bottelier, "China on the World Stage," 1.

45. Alan Gelb, Gary Jefferson, and Inderjit Singh, "Can Communist Economies Transform Incrementally? China's Experience," *Policy Research Working Paper* (Washington, DC: World Bank, September 1993), 18–21 (emphasis in original).

46. Interview, World Bank, Washington, DC, November 2000.

47. J. Richard Baumgarner, cited in Kapur, Lewis, and Webb, *The World Bank*, 538.

48. Xie Qimei and Wang Xingfang, eds., *Zhongguo yu Lianheguo*, 268. See also "Premier Tells World Bank of Hopes for Continuing Cooperation," Xinhua News Agency, 21 September 1997, Reuters China News, 22 September 1997.

49. Lateef, "The First Half Century," 28–29. For its part, China believes the lessons that

can be drawn by other Bank members from its model of development include the gradual approach to change; the decision to commence reform in the rural areas; and the establishment of special economic zones (SEZs). Interview, IMF, Washington, DC, 13 November 2000.

50. Bottelier, "China on the World Stage," 2.

51. Vinod Thomas and Peter Stephens, *The East Asian Economic Miracle* (Washington, DC: World Bank), 18.

52. Gelb, Jefferson, and Singh, "Can Communist Economies Transform Incrementally?" 18–21.

53. For details, see Jacobson and Oksenberg, *China's Participation*, 111–12.

54. As an interviewee put it in relation to the Bank's environmental assistance, "China gets more money because it has better ideas, better capacity and better management skills." Interview, World Bank, Washington, DC, 7 November 2000.

55. Kapur, Lewis, and Webb, *The World Bank*, 1105, 1154–55.

56. World Bank Group, "The World Bank and China," 2 (16 November 1999).

57. See World Bank Group, "World Bank in China: Economic Achievements and Current Challenges," at www.worldbank.org.cn/English/Overview/overview_brief.htm, 3 (accessed 1 September 2004).

58. Zweig, *Internationalizing China*, 236–37.

59. Bottelier, "China on the World Stage," 4.

60. World Bank Group, "The World Bank and China," 2 (12 October 2001).

61. Bottelier, "China on the World Stage," 4.

62. For these assessments and a fascinating insight into the interaction in this period, see Pieter Bottelier, "China and the World Bank: How a Partnership Was Built," draft paper (3 January 2006), on file with author.

63. See Stiglitz, *Globalization*, 91.

64. See Yushu Feng, "China and the Multilateral Investment Guarantee Agency," *World Bank Policy Research Working Paper* No. 1763, 13.

65. "World Bank to Support China," *South China Morning Post*, 27 April 1997, Reuters China News, 29 April 1997.

66. IBRD, "Foreign Investment, Remittances Outpace Debt as Sources of Finance for Developing Countries—World Bank," Press Statement, 2 April 2003, at www.worldbank.org .cn/English/content/460a6377587.shtml, 1.

67. James Kynge, "World Bank Rethinks Loans," *Financial Times*, 7 December 1999.

68. Bottelier, "China on the World Stage," 1 and 4.

69. Ibid., 4; and Interview, World Bank, Washington, DC, 27 October 2000.

70. Interview, World Bank, Washington, DC, 26 October 2000. This view, however, is contested by another former Bank official.

71. Andrew Batson, "World Bank to Cut Lending to China to 1984 Levels," Dow Jones Newswires, 29 March 2001. Even with that reduction, according to Yukon Huang, director of the World Bank's China Program, China will still be among the Bank's largest borrowers and will probably continue to be the largest borrower for investment projects.

72. "World Bank to Lend $3 Billion to China," *Asia Pulse*, 30 March 2001.

73. *Memorandum of the President of the International Bank for Reconstruction and Development and the International Finance Corporation to the Executive Directors on a Country Assistance Strategy of the World Bank Group for the People's Republic of China*, Report No. 25141 (22 January 2003), 28–29.

74. "World Bank to Support China."

75. World Bank Group, "IFC in China," at www.worldbank.org.cn/English/ifc/ overview_ifc.htm, 68 (accessed 1 September 2003).

76. Kynge, "World Bank Rethinks."

77. IBRD, *Memorandum of the President*, 22.

78. See detailed documentation of these challenges in World Bank, *China 2020: Development Challenges in the New Century* (Washington, DC: World Bank, 18 September 1997); World Bank, *East Asia: Recovery and Beyond* (Washington, DC: World Bank, 2000), 125–32; and World Bank Group, "The World Bank in China," at www.worldbank.org.cn/English/ IBRD/IBRDOverview.shtml (accessed 7 September 2004).

79. Carl J. Dahlman and Jean-Eric Aubert, *China and the Knowledge Economy: Seizing the 21st Century* (Washington, DC: World Bank, October 2001), 16. According to the report, between 1995 and 2000 Chinese cities created 5.5–6.5 million jobs a year. But 8–9 million a year would be needed, as many employees in state-owned enterprises and small rural companies were laid off. Moreover, "other projections estimate the amount of new jobs to be created at a much higher level—in the range of 200 to 300 million in the next ten years, *due to the potential for lay-offs of half of the population currently working in agriculture, SOEs and town and village enterprises* (TVEs)." Ibid. (emphasis added).

80. "World Bank Says China's Economic Challenge Mounting," *China Securities Bulletin*, 18 June 1997, Reuters China News, 18 June 1999.

81. World Bank Group, "The World Bank and China," *Country Brief*, at www.worldbank .org/html/extdr/offrep/eap/china.htm (accessed 8 November 2001).

82. See United Nations Development Programme, *China Human Development Report 2005*, 1–2, 13, available at www.undp.org (accessed 15 January 2006). See also Shang-Jun Wei, "Is Globalization Good for the Poor in China?" *Finance and Development* 39 (September 2002), no. 3, available at www.imf.org/external/pubs (accessed 26 August 2003).

83. IBRD, *Memorandum of the President*, 16–17.

84. World Bank Group, "World Bank in China," (4 September 2004).

85. Yukon Huang, "'Unique' China Defies World's Predictions—*China Daily* Interviews Mr Yukon Huang, World Bank's China Program Director," 21 June 2004, at www.worldbank.org.cn, 6.

86. Interviews, World Bank, 26–27 October 2000; and World Bank, *The World Bank Group in China: Facts and Figures* (Beijing: World Bank Office, July 2000), 5-1.

87. World Bank, *The World Bank Group in China*, 5-2.

88. World Bank, *The World Bank and the Global Environment* (Washington, DC: Environment Department, World Bank, May 2000), 27. The ozone depletion potential (ODP) is a relative measure that compares the expected impact on stratospheric ozone per unit mass emitted to the atmosphere to the impact of the same unit mass of chlorofluorocarbon-11, integrated over time. For details of World Bank's early ODS Phaseout Projects in China, see also O. Yoshida, *The International Legal Regime for the Protection of the Stratospheric Ozone Layer* (The Hague: Kluwer Law International, 2001), 272.

89. The CER credits count toward a state's Kyoto commitments by investing in clean technologies that reduce carbon emissions in developing countries. See World Bank Group, "Launch of Study Signals a Proactive Approach to Clean Development Mechanism in China," at http://web.worldbank.org/WBSITE/EXTERNAL/NEWS (accessed 7 September 2004).

90. Interview, World Bank, Washington, DC, 7 November 2000.

91. Thus, for the 2001 IBRD report, SEPA submitted five pages of comment to the Bank's draft, to be followed by a joint Bank-China meeting.

92. IBRD, *Memorandum of the President*, at CAS annexes C–F.

93. IBRD, "World Bank Supports Civic Engagement Activities of Chinese NGOs," at www.worldbank.org.cn/English/ (accessed 17 August 2004).

94. World Bank, "World Bank Joined by DFID and CIDA to Finance a SARS and Infectious Diseases Response Program for China," 7 July 2003, available at www.worldbank.org .cn/English/Content/sars.htm.

95. "World Bank Chief Economist Praises China's Macroeconomic Policies," Xinhua News, 24 July 1999, Reuters China News, 24 July 1999, 2 parts. See also Stiglitz, *Globalization*; and Yukon Huang, "'Unique' China."

96. "World Bank Chief Economist Praises."

97. See, for instance, Ann Kent, "China's Growth Treadmill: Globalization, Human Rights and International Relations," *Review of International Affairs* 3 (Summer 2004), no. 4, 524–43.

98. "Chinese Dissident Slams World Bank over Corruption," Reuters China News, 24 September 1997.

99. Interview, World Bank, Washington, DC, 26 October 2000.

100. Calculated in millions of 1944 US$.

101. IBRD, "Votes and Subscriptions," at www.worldbank.org/about/organization/ voting/kibrd.htm (accessed 18 December 2001).

102. Interview, World Bank, Washington, DC, 27 October 2000.

103. Bottelier, "China on the World Stage," 4.

104. "Statement by Mr Dai Xianglong, Governor of the People's Bank of China at the 1998 Annual Meeting of the International Monetary Fund and the World Bank," 6 October 1998, Press Release No. 14, 4.

105. "Statement by the Hon. Xiang Huaicheng, Governor of the Bank for the People's Republic of China, at the Joint Annual Discussion," 28 September, 1999, Board of Governors 1999 Annual Meetings, Washington, DC, Press Release No. 15 (28–30 September 1999), 3.

106. Bottelier, "China on the World Stage," 4–5. Bottelier comments that "the provision of effective advice today requires a much higher level of technical expertise and experience than 10 or 15 years ago. Staying ahead of the learning curve in China has become quite a challenge for the Bank," 4–5.

107. IBRD, *Memorandum of the President*, at 43–44.

108. "Cracks Appearing in the China Syndrome: Commentary," *Times*, 19 September 1997, Reuters China News, 19 September 1997. This finding was replicated in the author's own experience in interviews with Bank officials, while IMF officials were more relaxed. David Zweig has also commented on the Bank's secrecy in its dealings with China, and its wish to avoid antagonizing its leaders. See Zweig, *Internationalizing China*, 234.

109. "Letters to the Editor: China Is Not on the World Bank's Dole," *Wall Street Journal Europe*, 5 August 2001.

110. Bottelier, "China and the World Bank," 10.

111. United Nations, *World Economic and Social Survey 2000: Trends and Policies in the World Economy* (New York: Department of Economic and Social Affairs, United Nations, 2000), 214.

112. For above account, see Zweig, *Internationalizing China*, 220, 234, 258.

113. Lardy, "China and the International Financial System," 211.

114. Margaret Pearson, "China's Integration into the International Trade and Investment Regime," in Economy and Oksenberg, eds., *China Joins the World*, 188–89.

115. World Bank Group, "The World Bank in China," 1.

116. Jacobson and Oksenberg, *China's Participation*, 119–21.

117. World Bank, undated report, cited in Zweig, *Internationalizing China*, 236–37.

118. According to a former Bank official, China had the reputation as the only major Bank borrower that distrusted SALs.

119. Lardy, "China and the International Financial System," 212.

120. "Statement by John M. Niehuss, Senior Deputy Assistant Secretary for International

Economic Policy, Department of the Treasury before the Sub-Committee on International Development, Finance, Trade and Monetary Policy, Committee on Banking, Finance and Urban Affairs, House of Representatives, 8 May 1990," in "World Bank Lending to the People's Republic of China," *Hearing before the Sub-Committee on International Development, Finance, Trade and Monetary Policy of the Committee on Banking, Finance and Urban Affairs, House of Representatives, 101st Congress* (Washington, DC: U.S. Government Printing Office, 1990), 42.

121. Jacobson and Oksenberg, *China's Participation*, 117–18.

122. Tian Jin et al., *Zhongguo zai Lianheguo*, 168.

123. Kapur, Lewis, and Webb, *The World Bank*, 532–33.

124. "Statement by John M. Niehuss," 43–44.

125. Lardy, "China and the International Financial System," 209.

126. Tian Jin et al., *Zhongguo zai Lianheguo*, 168.

127. World Bank Group, "The World Bank Lending to China," at www.worldbank.org .cn/English/Project/Overview.shtml (accessed 12 October 2001).

128. Interviews, World Bank, Washington, DC, 7 November 2000.

129. World Bank Group, "The World Bank in China."

130. Bottelier, "China on the World Stage," 1.

131. Interview, World Bank, Washington, DC, November 2000.

132. Yukon Huang, "'Unique' China."

133. Bottelier, "China on the World Stage," 5.

134. Speaking at the Joint Annual Discussion of the World Bank and IMF on 28 September 1999, the Governor of the Bank for the PRC, Xiang Huaicheng, called on all member countries and major shareholders to "respect and protect the Bank's Articles of Agreement with a view to creating a better environment for the Bank to fulfill its development mandate."

135. For revised policy, see "Information Disclosure," www1.worldbank.org/operations/ disclosure/index.html, 1 (accessed 7 September 2004).

136. See IBRD, *Memorandum of the President*, 16.

137. Ibid., 15–16, 19–20.

138. See Executive Summary in Asian Development Bank, *Country Assistance Program Evaluation in the People's Republic of China* (Manila: Asian Development Bank, December 1998), 2–6.

139. Joseph Goldberg memorandum, cited in Kapur, Lewis, and Webb, *The World Bank*, 444.

140. Interview, World Bank, Washington, DC, 7 November 2000. Bank contributions have to be matched by a local counterpart contribution of from 30 to 70 percent. Since many counties are technically bankrupt, farmers also have to make a contribution. The rate may be: province, 50 percent; county, 30 percent; and farmers, 20 percent.

141. Interview, World Bank, Washington, DC, 8 November 2000.

142. For most detailed account of the incident, in which he was initially involved, see Pieter Bottelier, "Was World Bank Support for the Qinghai Anti-Poverty Project in China Ill Considered?" *Harvard Asia Quarterly* 5 (Winter 2000/2001), no. 1, 47–55.

143. Paul Eckert, "World Bank Says China Scheme Funding 'Uncertain,'" Reuters News Service, 17 June 1999.

144. Cited in Government of Tibet in Exile, "The World Bank Backed China's Western Poverty Reduction Project and Its Impacts," at www.tibet.com/NewsRoom/worldbank17 .html.

145. Interview, World Bank, Washington, DC, 27 October 2000.

146. World Bank, "China to Implement Qinghai Component of the China Western

Poverty Reduction Project with Its Own Resources," News Release 2001/004/EAP. See also Inspection Panel Report (emphasis added).

147. "Statement by the Hon. Dai Xianglong, Governor of the Fund for the People's Republic of China at the Joint Annual Discussion," 2000 Annual Meeting, Prague, Press Release No. 18, 26–28 September 2000, 2.

148. Interviews, World Bank, October 2000. This comment was made by a Bank official. It recalls a similar observation made about India in the 1950s and 1960s by the Bank's historians. See Mason and Asher, *The World Bank*, 682–83.

149. Thus, the ADB's Country Strategy and Program Update (2003–7) has programmed a total loan assistance of US$4.6 billion for the period 2004–7, amounting to an annual average lending of about $1.5 billion. See IMF, *People's Republic of China: 2005 Article IV Consultation*, 64.

150. Jacques Pollak, "The World Bank and the IMF: A Changing Relationship," in Kapur, Lewis, and Webb, *The World Bank*, vol. 2, 473. For the following account, see 474–79.

151. For example, Brown, "IMF Governance," 131–47. For Stiglitz's critique, see Stiglitz, *Globalization*, 40–48, 122–26, 137–38, 180–81.

152. See Stephen Zamora, "Articles of Agreement of the International Monetary Fund," in Stephen Zamora and Ronald A. Brand, eds., *Basic Documents of International Economic Law* (Chicago: Commerce Clearing House, 1990), 316.

153. International Monetary Fund, *Annual Report 2000* (Washington, DC: International Monetary Fund, 2000), 16–40.

154. See Jacobson and Oksenberg, *China's Participation*, 122.

155. As a Chinese respondent said of IMF loans, "China is keen to paddle its own canoe."

156. Interviews, IMF, 8–9 November 2000.

157. "Camdessus Says China Needs No IMF Help in Coming Years," *China Securities Bulletin*, 6 January 1998, Reuters China News, 6 January 1998.

158. See www.imf.org.

159. The above is based on interview, IMF, Washington, DC, 13 November 2000.

160. Interview, IMF, Washington, DC, 9 November 2000. For similar perceptions in 1998, see Tian Jin et al., *Zhongguo zai Lianheguo*, 168.

161. ESAF is a lending program at highly subsidized rates for very poor states.

162. Interview, IMF, Washington, DC, 13 November 2000.

163. Interview, IMF, Washington, DC, 9 November 2000.

164. "Statement by Dai Xianglong," 6–8 October 1998, 1–2.

165. "Statement by the Hon. Xiang Huaicheng," 4.

166. "China Supports Mahathir's Call to Reform Financial System," *Bernama Daily Malaysian News*, 24 November 1999, Reuters China News, 24 November 1999.

167. "China 'Willing' to Consider East Asia Monetary Fund," 25 November 1999, Xinhua News Agency, 25 November 1999.

168. "Chinese Premier Urges Greater Regional Cooperation at Recent ASEAN Summit," Xinhua News Agency, 28 November 1999, Reuters China News, 30 November 1999, 2.

169. "Statement by the Hon. Dai Xianglong," 2000.

170. The decision provided that China should pay 25 percent of the quota increase, SDR420.5 million (about US$545 million) in SDRs or usable currency specified by the IMF, with the remainder paid in China's own currency, bringing its total IMF quota to SDR212.4 billion (about US$275 billion). See International Monetary Fund, "IMF Board of Governors Approves Quota Increases for China," News Brief No. 01/17, 8 February 2001.

171. See statistics in *IMF Survey* 30 (19 February 2001), no. 4, 55, at www.imf.org/imfsurvey.

172. See related "Laws and Regulations" at the Chinese Ministry of Foreign Trade and Economic Cooperation website, www.moftec.gov.cn (accessed 8 March 1999).

173. Lardy, "China and the International Financial System," 214.

174. International Monetary Fund, "IMF Concludes 2001 Article IV Consultation with the People's Republic of China," Public Information Notice (PIN) No. 01/91, 24 August 2001.

175. In particular, it was applauded for its formation of the Council of Financial Regulators to reduce vulnerabilities from cross-market systemic shocks; its merger of stock and futures exchanges and clearing houses to increase the transparency of securities markets; and its adaptation of financial legislation to keep up with modern financial practices and institutions. See IMF, "Opening of the IMF's Hong Kong SAR Resident Representative Office," 11 January 2001 at www.imf.org/external/np/speeches/2001.

176. Interview, IMF, Washington, DC, 13 November 2000.

177. See Jacobson and Oksenberg, *China's Participation*, 123.

178. "IMF Fails to Win Release," *Daily Telegraph*, 20 September 1997, Reuters China News, 20 September 1997.

179. According to Art. IX.8, "All Governors, Executive Directors, Alternates, members of committees, representatives appointed under Article XII, Section 3 (j), advisors of any of the foregoing persons, officers, and employees of the Fund (1) shall be immune from legal process with respect to acts performed by them in their official capacity except when the Fund waives this immunity."

180. Lardy, "China and the International Financial System," 210.

181. IMF, "People's Republic of China Accepts Article VIII Obligations," Press Release No. 96/58, 4 December 1996.

182. IMF, "Camdessus Welcomes China's Acceptance of Article VIII," News Brief No. 96/15, 27 November 1996.

183. Interview, IMF, Washington, DC, 13 November 2000.

184. Wang Huiling, "Beijing Has Learnt from Financial Crisis," *Straits Times*, 9 May 1998, Reuters China News, 9 May 1998.

185. Stiglitz, *Globalization*, 125–26.

186. As the *Guardian* commented at the time: "The cheer-leaders of the free market seem not to have noticed that the most stable Asian economy is that which has most consistently spurned free-market nostrums." See "Forget Tigers, Keep an Eye on China," *Guardian*, 17 December 1997.

187. Wang Huiling, "Beijing Has Learnt," citing China's Vice-Minister and Trade Representative, Long Yongtu.

188. Interview, IMF, Washington, DC, 13 November 2000.

189. See Nicholas Lardy cited in Wang Huiling, "Beijing Has Learnt." See also "Chinese Scholars on Asian Financial Crisis," Xinhua News Agency, 31 July 1998, Reuters China News, 31 July 1998; Benjamin Kang Lim, "China Vows Crackdown on Financial Institutions," Reuters News Service, 14 August 1997; and Joseph Stiglitz, cited in "World Bank Praises China, Keeps RMB Stable," China Business Information Network, 22 July 1998, Reuters China News, 22 July 1998.

190. Lardy, "China and the International Financial System," 213, 222.

191. Pearson, "China's Integration," 172.

192. See, for instance, International Monetary Fund, *Experimental IMF Report on Observance of Standards and Codes: People's Republic of China–Hong Kong Special Administrative Region*, August 1999, at www.imf.org/external/np/rose/hkg/index.htm, 3–4 (accessed 22 August 2000).

193. See Jin Liqun, "China: One Year into the WTO Process," Washington, DC, 22 October 2002, available at www.imf.org (accessed 25 August 2003).

194. See, for example, International Monetary Fund, *IMF Concludes 2001 Article IV Consultation with the People's Republic of China*, Public Information Notice (PIN) No. 01/91, 24 August 2001, at www.imf.org/external/np/sec/pn/2001/pn0191.htm.

195. International Monetary Fund, *IMF Concludes 2001*, 4. FSAP are reports of members' observance of standards.

196. IMF, *IMF Concludes 2002 Article IV Consultation with the People's Republic of China*, Public Information Notice (PIN) No. 02/97, 3 September 2002, 1 and 4, at www.imf.org/external/np/sec/pn/2002/pn0297.html.

197. IMF, *IMF Concludes 2003 Article IV Consultation with the People's Republic of China*, Public Information Notice (PIN) No. 03/136, 18 November 2003, 4–6.

198. See Jin Liqun, "China"; and IMF, "China Formally Begins Participation in the IMF's General Data Dissemination System," News Brief No. 02/36, 19 April 2002. For GDDS report by China, see IMF, "GDDS as Provided by the People's Republic of China as a Participant in the GDDS," available at http://dsbb.imf.org/Applications/web/gdds/gddscountrycategorylist.

199. Interview, IMF, Washington, DC, 8 November 2000.

200. On its return from the country being consulted, the IMF staff produces a written report that is discussed by the Executive Board, summarized by the Managing Director, and sent back to the country under study. If the country's Executive Director agrees, this summary text is publicly released, together with background material, as a Public Information Notice (PIN). In Beijing, it is then distributed to the government, to different agencies, and sometimes to the State Council.

201. Interview, IMF, Washington, DC, 13 November 2000.

202. "Statement by Xiang Huaicheng," 1999, 4.

203. International Monetary Fund, *People's Republic of China: 2005 Article IV Consultation*; and International Monetary Fund, *People's Republic of China: 2004 Article IV Consultation—Staff Report; Staff Supplement and Public Information Notice on the Executive Board Discussion*, IMF Country Report No. 04/351 (November 2004).

204. Jin Liqun, "China."

205. Jacobson and Oksenberg, *China's Participation*, 128.

206. Thus, the assessments by Margaret Pearson and Nicholas Lardy in 1999 that the integration of China into the world trade, investment, and financial arenas has occurred without significant disruption to the international political economy regime, still appear largely correct. As Pearson states, "the dominant trend has been for [China's] reformers to adjust their rules to fit those of the regime," rather than vice versa. See Pearson, "China's Integration," 184, 188–89. See also Lardy, "China and the International Financial System," 207.

207. See Stiglitz, *Globalization*, 125–26.

CHAPTER 4

1. See "Global Village of Beijing and the Development of Chinese Environmental NGOs," at www.gvbchina.org/English/WSSD (accessed 27 August 2002).

2. Marvin S. Soroos, "Global Institutions and the Environment: An Evolutionary Perspective," in Norman J. Vig and Regina S. Axelrod, eds., *The Global Environment: Institutions, Law and Policy* (Washington, DC: Congressional Quarterly, 1999), 31, 39.

3. Shafqat Kakakhel, "The Role of International Organizations in the Development of Environmental Law: A Case of UNEP," remarks by the Deputy Executive Director, United Nations Environment Programme, at the International Conference on International Law in

the New Millennium: Problems and Challenges Ahead (New Delhi, 4–7 October 2001), at www.unep.org/Documents.

4. See Elizabeth Economy, "The Impact of International Regimes on Chinese Foreign Policy-Making: Broadening Perspectives and Policies . . . But Only to a Point," in David M. Lampton, ed., *The Making of Chinese Foreign and Security Policy in the Era of Reform, 1978–2000* (Stanford, CA: Stanford University Press, 2001), 230–53; Michel Oksenberg and Elizabeth Economy, "China: Implementation under Economic Growth and Market Reform," in Edith Brown Weiss and Harold K. Jacobson, eds., *Engaging Countries: Strengthening Compliance with International Environmental Accords* (Cambridge, MA: MIT Press, 1998), 353–94; Miranda A. Schreurs and Elizabeth Economy, eds., *The Internationalization of Environmental Protection* (Cambridge: Cambridge University Press, 1997); Ben Boer, Ross Ramsay, and Donald R. Rothwell, *International Environmental Law in the Asia Pacific* (London: Kluwer Law International, 1998); Jimin Zhao and Leonard Ortolano, "The Chinese Government's Role in Implementing Multilateral Environmental Agreements: The Case of the Montreal Protocol," *China Quarterly* 175 (2003), 708–25; and Tao Zhenghua and Rudiger Wolfrum, eds., *Implementing International Environmental Law in Germany and China* (The Hague: Kluwer Law International, 2001).

5. See, for instance, Economy, "The Impact of International Regimes," 235.

6. They embody transparency, the greater specificity of rules, rewards for self-reporting and on-site monitoring, analysis of data, action by international organizations to provide mechanisms for burden-sharing for financing, and "sanctions" for violations, including publicity for non-compliance and the dissemination of self-reported and independently gathered information. See Ronald Mitchell, "Compliance Theory: An Overview," in James Cameron, Jacob Werksman, and Peter Roderick, eds., *Improving Compliance with International Environmental Law* (London: Earthscan, 1996), 3–28. See also Harold K. Jacobson and Edith Brown Weiss, "Assessing the Record and Designing Strategies to Engage Countries," in Weiss and Jacobson, eds., *Engaging Countries*, 515.

7. For an excellent comparison of these instruments, see Elizabeth R. DeSombre, *The Global Environment and World Politics* (London: Continuum, 2002), 95–118.

8. Hans W. Maull, "Japan's Global Environmental Policies," in Andrew Hurrell and Benedict Kingsbury, eds., *The International Politics of the Environment: Actors, Interests and Institutions* (Oxford: Clarendon Press, 1992), 360.

9. Wilfred Beckerman, "Global Warming and International Action: An Economic Perspective," in ibid. 274.

10. See Philippe Sands, ed., *Greening International Law* (New York: New Press, 1994), 70–71. See also Soroos, "Global Institutions," 27–51.

11. See UNGA Res. 2997 (XXVII), 15 December 1972, in United Nations Environment Programme, *Handbook of Environmental Law* (UNEP, 1996), 2–7; and Soroos, "Global Institutions," 37.

12. This was made up of thirteen seats for Asian states; sixteen for African states; six for Eastern European states; ten for Latin American states; and thirteen for West European and other states.

13. Insights from David Kennedy at his seminars, "Special Topics in International Law," 30 June, 1–2 July 2000, Faculty of Law, Australian National University, Canberra.

14. See Martin Dixon and Robert McCorquodale, *Cases and Materials on International Law* (London: Blackstone, 2000), 3rd ed., 485–86; and Edith Brown Weiss, "Our Rights and Obligations to Future Generations for the Environment," in Weiss and Jacobson, eds., *Engaging Countries*, 490. For weaknesses of the compliance mechanisms, see Lawrence E. Susskind,

Environmental Diplomacy: Negotiating More Effective Global Agreements (New York: Oxford University Press, 1994), 11–42.

15. Dixon and McCorquodale, *Cases and Materials*, 485.

16. Subsequently, a large office in Geneva, the UNEP Regional Office for Europe was set up, while numerous UNEP programs and Treaty Secretariats are also located in Geneva.

17. Paul C. Szasz, "Restructuring the International Organizational Framework," in Edith Brown Weiss, ed., *Environmental Change and International Law: New Challenges and Dimensions* (Tokyo: UNUP, 1992), 351–52.

18. See UNEP, *Handbook*, 42–51.

19. For details, see Szasz, "Restructuring," 342–43.

20. See Soroos, "Global Institutions," 39.

21. See Allen L. Springer, *The International Law of Pollution: Protecting the Global Environment in a World of Sovereign States* (Westport, CT: Quorum Books, 1983), 31–33, in Dixon and McCorquodale, *Cases and Materials*, 487–88.

22. The "Rio conventions" refer to the treaties on biodiversity, global climate change, and desertification signed at Rio de Janeiro in 1992.

23. See *Earth Negotiations Bulletin* (henceforth *ENB*) 16 (8 February 1999), no. 6, 1, 11, available at www.iisd.ca.

24. *ENB* 16 (18 July 2001), no. 17, 1–2.

25. See, for instance, Judith Shapiro, *Mao's War against Nature: Politics and the Environment in Revolutionary China* (Cambridge: Cambridge University Press, 2001).

26. "Chinese Delegation Makes Statement on 'Declaration on Human Environment,'" *Peking Review* 15 (23 June 1972), no. 25, 8–9, in Jerome Alan Cohen and Hungdah Chiu, eds., *People's China and International Law: A Documentary Survey* (Princeton, NJ: Princeton University Press, 1974), 1377–80. The following analysis is based on this article.

27. "China's Ten Cardinal Principles on Amending 'Declaration on Human Environment,'" *Peking Review* 15 (23 June 1972), no. 25, 9–11, in Cohen and Hungdah Chiu, eds., *People's China*, 1381–83.

28. *Summary Report of Australian Delegation to the United Nations Conference on the Human Environment*, (Stockholm, 5–16 June 1972), 5.

29. Wang Xi, "China," in Terri Mottershead, ed., *Environmental Law and Enforcement in the Asia–Pacific Rim* (Hong Kong: Sweet & Maxwell, 2002), 103.

30. Samuel S. Kim, *China, the United Nations and World Order* (Princeton, NJ: Princeton University Press, 1979), 489.

31. *Shijie zhishi nianjian, 2000/2001* ("The Yearbook of World Knowledge, 2000/2001") (Beijing: Shijie zhishi chubanshe, 2001), 1129.

32. Together with UNDP and UNIDO, the other implementing agencies of the Multilateral Fund set up to finance the Montreal Protocol, from the 1990s it offered complementary, and sometimes competing, services.

33. *Shijie zhishi nianjian, 2000/2001*, 1129.

34. Wang Xi, "China," 103.

35. Information Office of the State Council, *Environmental Protection in China* (Beijing, June 1996), at www.china.org.cn/e–white/environment/index.htm, chapt. 7.

36. Zhonghua renmin gongheguo waijiaobu waijiaoshi bianjishi, ed., *Zhongguo waijiao gailan 1991* ("Survey of China's Foreign Relations") (Beijing), 407. The various editions of the *Zhongguo waijiao gailan* are hereafter cited as *ZGWJGL*.

37. The Convention on Biological Diversity (signed, 11 June 1992, rat. 5 October 1993); the Basel Convention (Transboundary Movement of Hazardous Wastes and Their Disposal)

(rat. 17 December 1991); and the Convention on International Trade in Endangered Species of Wild Fauna and Flora (CITES) (acc. 8 January 1981). China is not a party to the Convention on the Conservation of Migratory Species of Wild Animals (CMS).

38. Wang Xi, "China," 103.

39. *ZGWJGL 1992*, 478.

40. *ZGWJGL 1993*, 491–92.

41. Information Office of the State Council, *Environmental Protection*, chapt. 7.

42. The following account is based on Song Guotao et al., *Zhongguo guoji huanjing wenti baogao* ("A Report on Problems in China's International Environment") (Beijing: Chinese Academy of Social Sciences, 2002), 430–31.

43. See *China's Agenda 21: White Paper on China's Population, Environment and Development in the 21st Century* (25 March 1994) at www.cei.gov.cn/cnenvir/paipishu/chnwp2.html.

44. Fu Jing, "Climate Changes to Hammer China Hard," *China Daily*, 13 September 2002.

45. Chen Ming, "Judges' Symposium Delegate Says China Protecting Environment through Law," Xinhua News Agency, BBC Monitoring Asia Pacific, 19 August 2002.

46. See "Global Village of Beijing."

47. For affiliated groups, see www.chinagate.com.cn/english/514.htm (accessed 3 June 2002).

48. List available at www.unep.org.

49. "Mainland NGOs to Attend Johannesburg Development Summit," China News Digest, 21 August 2002, at www.cnd.org/Global. In addition, various websites provided extensive information on environmental matters. See, for instance, www.enviroinfo.org.cn; and www.china.org.cn/sepa.

50. Elizabeth Economy, "China's Environmental Movement," Testimony before the Congressional Executive Commission on China Roundtable on Environmental NGOs in China: Encouraging Action and Addressing Public Grievances, Washington, DC, 7 February 2005, 1.

51. See www.enviroinfo.org.cn; and www.china.org.cn/sepa.

52. See debates in the twentieth and twenty-first sessions of the Governing Council and the sixth and seventh Special Session of the UNEP Governing Council, summarized in *ENB* 16 (February 1999–February 2002), nos. 6–24.

53. Ozone depletion is caused by the interaction of certain industrial chemicals with ozone molecules in the stratosphere, thereby creating a chain reaction that destroys large numbers of molecules. See DeSombre, *The Global Environment*, 96.

54. Ibid. 98, 103. See also Mostafa K. Tolba, "Facing a Distant Threat," Statement to the Opening Session of the Conference of Plenipotentiaries on the Protection of the Ozone Layer, Vienna, 18 March 1985, 2–3.

55. For detailed analysis of the compliance mechanism, see Philippe Sands, *Principles of International Environmental Law: Frameworks, Standards and Implementation* (Manchester: Manchester University Press, 1995), vol. 1, 167–68.

56. For excellent analysis of the characteristics of the Protocol, and a comparison with other environmental instruments, see Weiss and Jacobson, "Assessing the Record," in Weiss and Jacobson, eds., *Engaging Countries*, 524–52.

57. Interview with official Australian negotiator, Canberra, June 2002.

58. For details of contracting parties to both, see Maria Clara Maffei et al., eds., *Participation in World Treaties on the Protection of the Environment: A Collection of Data* (London: Kluwer Law International, 1996).

59. This account is based on Liu Wei, "Zhongguo baohu chouyang ceng shinian xing" ("China's Ten Years Protecting the Ozone Layer"), *Zhongguo huanjing bao* ("China's Environment News"), 13 September 2001, 1.

60. Ibid.

61. These were Light Industry, which manufactured refrigerators; Chemical Industry, which manufactured ODS; Public Security, which manufactured and used halons; Electronics, which used ODS; Commerce; and Aeronautics. Later they were joined by the State Administration of Tobacco and Cigarettes, the State Science and Technology Commission, and the Ministry of Foreign Affairs. See Oksenberg and Economy, "China: Implementation," 384–85.

62. See Qu Geping, "The Mending of the Sky by Present-Day Nu Wa—A Magnificent Feat of Our Time," 5 October 2000, 2, statement on file with author.

63. UNEP/OzL.Pro.3/11, 21 June 1991, 24.

64. Oksenberg and Economy, "China: Implementation," 384–85.

65. This account is based on Qu Geping, "The Mending of the Sky," 2–3.

66. See UNEP/Ozl.Pro.WG.1V/5, 17 May 1990. See also Peter H. Sand, "The Potential Impact of the Global Environment Facility of the World Bank, UNDP and UNEP," in Rudiger Wolfrum, ed., *Enforcing Environmental Standards: Economic Mechanisms as Viable Means?* (Berlin: Springer, 1996), 490–92. By July 2001, the Multilateral Fund, managed by an Executive Committee assisted by the Fund secretariat, had received contributions from some thirty-two industrialized countries amounting to US$1.3 billion. Projects and activities supported by the fund were implemented by UNEP, the World Bank, UNDP, and UNIDO.

67. UNEP/OzL.Pro.3/11, 24. See also Oksenberg and Economy, "China: Implementation," 385–86.

68. *ZGWJGL 1991*, 459.

69. In its official publication, the Chinese Foreign Ministry states: "The passage of the amendment to the Montreal Protocol removed the obstacles to China's participation in the international activity protecting the ozone layer." See *ZGWJGL* 1992, 475.

70. DeSombre, *The Global Environment*, 112.

71. Anita Margrethe Halvorssen, *Equality among Unequals in International Environmental Law: Differential Treatment for Developing Countries* (Boulder, CO: Westview, 1999), 172.

72. UNEP/OzL.Pro.3/11, 14.

73. Ibid., 25.

74. See UNEP/OzL.Pro.LG.1/3, 14 July 1989, 8–9.

75. Qu Geping, "The Mending of the Sky," 3.

76. For full account of conflict, see Liu Wei, "Zhongguo baohu," 2–3.

77. Qu Geping, "The Mending of the Sky," 3.

78. Letter from UNEP official, 10 May 2002.

79. World Bank, *China: Air, Land and Water—Environmental Priorities for a New Millennium* (Washington, DC: World Bank, August 2001), xvi.

80. This right, entrenched in Arts. 6 and 41, has been increasingly exercised since 1989. See Anna Brettell, "Bounded Accountability: The Environmental Complaints System," *China Rights Forum* (2002), no. 4, 8–15.

81. For detailed analysis, see Wang Xi, "China," 107–9.

82. See *China's Agenda 21*, chapt. 18.

83. Interview with Chinese expert, Washington, DC, 31 October 2000.

84. Interview, World Bank, Washington, DC, 7 November 2000.

85. Interview with Chinese expert, Washington, DC, 31 October 2000. See also Wang Xi, "China," 105. Other scholars have noted that the Ministries of Light Industry, Electronics and Chemical Industry were considered to be more "advanced" in their outlook, whereas the Ministries of Domestic Trade and Commerce had been "less aggressive in working to reduce consumption of ODS." See Oksenberg and Economy, "China: Implementation," 389.

86. *ZGWJGL 2000*, 710.

87. Hamish McDonald, "Chinese Watchdog Calls Halt to Power Projects," *Sydney Morning Herald*, 21 January 2005, 8.

88. World Bank, *China: Air, Land and Water*, 116–17, 136.

89. Ibid., xvi.

90. Lester Ross, "China and Environmental Protection," in Elizabeth Economy and Michel Oksenberg, eds., *China Joins the World: Progress and Prospects* (New York: Council on Foreign Relations, 1999), 313.

91. World Bank, *China: Air, Land and Water*, 117.

92. Qu Geping, "The Mending of the Sky."

93. DeSombre, *The Global Environment*, 115.

94. UNEP, *Country Programme: China, Report to the Executive Committee of the Multilateral Fund for the Implementation of the Montreal Protocol*, UNEP/OzL. Pro. 5/12.

95. In its country report, China indicated that forty enterprises produced CFCs. The domestic production capacity was 47,000 tons. In addition China imported 15,000–20,000 tons of CFCs. See ibid.

96. See O. Yoshida, *The International Legal Regime for the Protection of the Stratospheric Ozone Layer* (The Hague: Kluwer Law International, 2001), 271, citing 1995 World Bank report.

97. Jimin Zhao and Ortolano, "The Chinese Government's Role," 714.

98. See LEAD-China Associates, Cohort 2, "Environment, Technology Transfer and China's Responsibility—Case of CFCs Substitution of Refrigerator Industry" (no date) available at www.ied.org.cn/Case/en/cpaper2.html (accessed 23 July 2002).

99. IBRD, *Clear Water, Blue Skies: China's Environment in the New Century* (Washington, DC: World Bank, 1997), 11.

100. Ibid. Despite this, the World Bank called China's role in the ozone regime "a model of international cooperation."

101. Yoshida, *The International Legal Regime*, 171; and Economy, "Impact of International Regimes," 243.

102. Jimin Zhao and Ortolano, "The Chinese Government's Role," 715.

103. "Baohu chouyang ceng Zhongguo zai xingdong" ("China's Actions to Protect the Ozone Layer"), *Zhongguo huanjing bao* ("China's Environment News"), 13 September 2001.

104. Qu Geping, "The Mending of the Sky," 4.

105. "Baohu chouyang ceng."

106. Figures supplied by Environment Australia, August 2002. Copy on file with author. The assistance covered projects to totally phase out ODS in China's halon and CFC production, solvents, tobacco, and foam manufacturing sectors. China has received assistance from all four of the MLF's international implementing agencies (UNEP, UNIDO, UNDP, World Bank) as well as France, Germany, Canada and Australia, in implementing MLF-financed projects.

107. Liu Wei, "Zhongguo baohu."

108. Ibid.

109. As against this apparent uncertainty, on the previous page the report stated: "Through its participation in implementing the provisions of the Montreal Protocol, China also successfully froze ODS production and consumption in 1999 at the average of the levels achieved between 1995 and 1997." See World Bank, *China: Air, Land, and Water*, 84–85 (emphasis added).

110. Assessment of July 2002 produced by Environment Australia, on file with author.

111. Ibid. Thus, while a 20 percent reduction was required for methyl bromide by 1 January 2005, as at July 2002 it had increased consumption from freeze level by 91 percent and production by 85 percent. On HCFCs, it was required to freeze consumption/production

by 1 January 2016, but as at July 2002, it had increased consumption from freeze level by 220 percent and production by 856 percent.

112. UNEP/OzL.Pro/ImpCom/29/3 (26 November 2002), 5-6; UNEP/OzL.Pro/ImpCom/31/3 (11 November 2003), 5; Report of the Technology and Economic Assessment Panel, May 2004, at www.unep.org; UNEP/OzL.Pro/ImpCom/35/10 (2 February 2006), 48; UNEP/OzL.Pro/ImpCom/36/7 (10 July 2006), 13.

113. See "Summary of Extraordinary Meeting of the Parties to the Montreal Protocol: 24–26 March 2004," *ENB* 19 (29 March 2004), no. 34, 6.

114. *ENB* 19 (29 November 2004), no. 40, 6.

115. World Bank, *China: Air, Land and Water*, 84–94.

116. Interview, World Bank, Washington, DC, 26 October 2000.

117. Liu Wei, "Zhongguo baohu."

118. See *China's Agenda 21*, chapt. 18.

119. Wang Xi, "China," 128. For other assessments, see Jimin Zhao and Ortolano, "The Chinese Government's Role," 718–24.

120. See Susmita Dasgupta, Mainul Huq, and David Wheeler, "Bending the Rules: Discretionary Pollution Control in China," at http://wbln0018.worldbank.org/Research/.

121. Liu Wei, "Zhongguo baohu."

122. See Liu Yi, "Strengthening ODS Licensing System, Make Sure Fulfillment of their Commitment by the Developing Countries," paper delivered at Earth Forum, Washington, DC, 31 October 2000.

123. The following account is based on an interview with a Chinese expert, Washington, DC, 31 October 2000.

124. Jimin Zhao and Ortolano, "The Chinese Government's Role," 714–18.

125. Interview, World Bank, Washington, DC, 26 October 2000.

126. Cited in DeSombre, *The Global Environment*, 103. The increased greenhouse gases in the atmosphere absorb radiation from the sun that would otherwise be released, thereby increasing the global temperature. Associated weather effects lead to an increase in frequency and severity of storms, changing rainfall patterns, the melting of polar ice caps and an expected rise in sea level. Ibid., 97.

127. Ibid., 98.

128. Under Art. 4 of the Framework Convention, all parties undertook a range of responsibilities, including publishing national inventories of anthropogenic substances, establishing national programs containing measures to mitigate climate change, cooperating in preparing for adaptation to the impacts of climate change, and taking climate change into account in relevant social, economic, and environmental decisions. However, only the developed country parties listed in Annex 1 had the obligation to submit information on action taken under the Protocol and to return greenhouse gas emissions to their 1990 level.

129. DeSombre, *The Global Environment*, 101–2.

130. See Helen Dewar, "Senate Advises against Emissions Treaty That Lets Developing Nations Pollute," *Washington Post*, 26 July 1997, A11, cited in ibid., 115.

131. See Susskind, *Environmental Diplomacy*, 31–32.

132. See "Issues in the Negotiating Process: Compliance under the Kyoto Protocol," available at http://maindb.unfccc.int. The compliance mechanism, based on similar mechanisms adopted by the Montreal Protocol, the ILO, and other UN bodies, had been developed by the Joint Working Group. At COP-6 part II, parties had adopted the Bonn Agreements, which stated the consequences for a party of non-compliance with its emission commitments in the Kyoto Protocol. These were: deduction from that party's assigned amount from the second commitment period of emissions equal to 1.3 times the amount of excess emissions;

development of a compliance action plan; and suspension of eligibility to make transfers under emissions trading.

133. The GEF was set up to provide concessional multilateral funding for ozone depletion, climate change, biodiversity, and international waters, administered mainly by the World Bank and operating separately from its "soft-loan" affiliate, the International Development Association (IDA). For details, see Peter S. Thacher, "The Role of the United Nations," in Hurrell and Kingsbury, eds., *The International Politics of the Environment*, 199–200. Between 1991 to 1999, the GEF had already allocated US$884 million to 227 climate change projects and activities. See www.gefweb.org/Projects/focal_areas/focal_areas.html (accessed 14 August 2002).

134. This analysis is based on interviews with experienced atmospheric environment negotiators, Canberra, June 2002.

135. Interview, World Bank, Washington, DC, 26 October 2000.

136. See alarming forecasts of environmental impact on China by Ding Yihui, former Cochair of Intergovernmental Panel on Climate Change (IPCC), in Yao Weijie, "China's Warming Climate Worries Experts," *Science Times*, 30 May 2002, available at www.china.org.cn (accessed 3 June 2002).

137. *China's Agenda 21*, chapt 18.

138. See *ENB* 12 (10 April 1995), no. 21, 5.

139. Thus, at a 1993 conference, China and developing states criticized the developed states' use of the joint implementation mechanism to avoid their obligations under the Convention and to transfer the responsibility to developing states. In 1995, at the First Conference of the Parties (COP-1) to the Convention, China and India negotiated the setting up of a Working Group of the Parties to discuss post-2000 activities that focused on the responsibilities of developed states. At the 1997 COP-3, China argued for equitable rules and, with India, succeeded in delaying the pace at which trading would come into effect and in eliminating an article on voluntary commitments. At COP-4, the G-77 and China maximized their leverage for financial and technical assistance, while avoiding any conditionalities that might draw them into new commitments. In 1998 and 1999, in discussions on the principles, rules, methods, and direction of the Clean Development Mechanism, joint implementation and emissions trading, China and the G-77 opposed the arguments of developed states for their speedy establishment and implementation. See *ZGWJGL 1994*, 597; *ZGWJGL 1996*, 685; *ENB* 12 (13 December 1997), no. 76, 12, 15; *ENB* 12 (16 November 1998), no. 97, 14; *ZGWJ* (original title altered to *Zhongguo waijiao*), 1999, 672; and *ZGWJ*, 2000, 710–11. For details of the Protocol, and China's position during negotiations, see also Liu Zhenmin, "The Kyoto Protocol to the Convention on Climate Change: Commitments, Implementation, and Mechanisms," in Tao Zhenghua and Wolfrum, eds., *Implementing International Environmental Law*, 133–39.

140. "Fada guojia ying lüxing 'gongyue' suo chengdan de yiwu" ("Developed States Should Fulfill the Obligations They Have Undertaken under the 'Protocol'"), *Keji ribao* ("Science and Technology Daily"), 4 November 1999.

141. It noted: "In 2003, there were frequent climatic disasters. Typhoons and sandstorm disasters were less serious than the previous several years; but droughts, storms, floods, heat, unbroken spell of rainy weather, and hail were more serious. The climatic disasters of 2003 were 'slightly more severe than medium level.'" See State Environmental Protection Agency, *Report of the State of the Environment in China 2003* (Beijing, 2004).

142. Former Cochair of Intergovernmental Panel on Climate Change (IPCC), Ding Yihui, for instance, found that it would reduce the water supply in Northwest China by 20 billion cubic meters, ten times the water stored in Miyun Reservoir in Beijing, and lead to

the thickening of sand layers in that region. Grain output and forest area would be reduced, particularly in Northeast China, while disasters such as mud-rock flow and landslides would increase in Southwest China. See interview of Ding Yihui, in Yao Weijie, "China's Warming Climate Worries Experts."

143. See Fu Jing, "Climate Changes to Hammer China."

144. Economy, "Impact of International Regimes," 249–50.

145. See Chinese analysis of progress in *ZGWJ 2001*, 666–67.

146. He acknowledged that China's emission rate was now second highest in the world, behind that of the United States, and referred to the forthcoming challenge of China's entry into the WTO. See "Wo jiang dali zhili eryanghuatan paifang" ("We Will Energetically Control CO_2 Emissions"), *Guangming ribao*, 28 December 2001.

147. "Climate Changes Key to Sustainable Development," Xinhua News Agency, 5 April 2002.

148. *ENB* 12 (27 November 2000), no. 163, 13.

149. See *ENB* 12 (12 November 2001), no. 189, 15–16.

150. These included biodiversity, international waters, replacement of ozone-depleting chemicals, desertification, and persistent organic pollutants. See GEF, "Donor Countries Agree to the Highest Replenishment Ever for the Global Environment Facility (GEF)," Press Release, Washington, DC, 7 August 2002, at www.gefweb.org.

151. Statement by H.E. Mr. Zhu Rongji at the World Summit on Sustainable Development, Johannesburg, South Africa, 3 September 2002, available at www.un.org/events/wssd/statements/chinaE.htm (accessed 6 November 2002). Four days before, on 30 August 2002, the NPC had quietly approved China's ratification of the Kyoto Protocol.

152. For summary of COP-11 achievements, see *ENB* 12 (12 December 2005), no. 291, 18.

153. Ibid., 19.

154. China's representative stated: "We really feel pity that the U.S. has not yet, and is not going to join the Kyoto Protocol, not only because of the size of its total emissions, but also because of its higher per capita emissions." See "China Urges US to Join Kyoto Treaty," Associated Press 30 November 2005, at www.nytimes.com/aponline/international/ (accessed 2 December 2005); and Andrew C. Revkin, "US, Under Fire, Eases Its Stance in Climate Talks," *New York Times*, 10 December 2005.

155. For details of this effort, see Economy, "Impact of International Regimes," 244–45.

156. Song Guotao et al., *Zhongguo guoji*. Scientists estimated that air pollution, in the form of coal burning, industrial waste gas, and vehicle tail gas, cost China RMB 20 billion (US$2.4 billion) a year, almost 10 percent of its total environmental costs.

157. Interview, Canberra, June 2002.

158. "Summary of the UNFCCC Workshop on the Preparation of National Communications from Non–Annex 1 Parties: 26–30 April 2004," *ENB* 12 (3 May 2004) no. 232, 2; and *ENB*, 12 (11 December 2004), no. 254, 2.

159. Thus, the Party newspaper, the *People's Daily*, cited a news bulletin in which Klaus Topfer of UNEP praised China for reducing its CO_2 emissions by 12 to 17 percent since 1996. See Wang Jingzhong, "Lianheguo huanguizhu deng jigou fabiao gongbao canyang Zhongguo nuli jianshao wenshi qiti paifang liang" ("UNEP and Other Organs Publish a Report Praising China for Its Energetic Efforts to Reduce Global Warming Emissions"), *Renmin ribao*, 4 August 2001.

160. See FCCC/AGBM/1997/CRP.5, 30 November 1997, 1.

161. World Bank, *China: Air, Land, and Water*, 84.

162. Ibid.

163. Keith Bradsher, "China's Boom Adds to Global Warming Problem," *New York Times*, 22 October 2003.

164. See World Bank, *China: Air, Land, and Water*, 84.

165. Ibid., 88–89.

166. See Jeffrey Logan, "Chinese Energy and Carbon Trends: Assessing Statistical Uncertainties at the Turn of the Century," unpublished paper (2000), on file with author. Logan suggests that the statistics leave unanswered questions, such as "available information does not clearly explain where energy use has declined."

167. David Zweig and Bi Jianhai, "China's Global Hunt for Energy," *Foreign Affairs* 84 (September–October 2005), iss. 5, 25.

168. Ibid.; and J. E. Sinton and D. G. Friedly, *What Goes Up: Recent Trends in China's Energy Consumption*, Lawrence Berkeley National Laboratory Report No. 1BL-44283, Berkeley, CA, 2000. Paper on file with author.

169. Bradsher, "China's Boom."

170. For the above, see ibid.; and Logan, "Chinese Energy and Carbon Trends."

171. See "China Strengthens Control on Coke Production," *China Chemical Reporter* 16 (2005), no. 18, 481; "China to Gradually Reduce Coke Exports," Xinhua News Agency, 25 June 2005; and "China Says Coal Imports Up 59 Percent as Energy Demand Soars," *Canadian Press*, 24 June 2005.

172. For increase, see Keith Bradsher and David Barboza, "China's Toxic Brew Hits Its Neighbours," *New York Times* in *Sydney Morning Herald*, 17–18 June 2006; and "China Draws Line in Sand to End Pollution for Good," Reuters, 16 August 2006, www.nytimes/reuters/world/international-environment-china.html. See also Zweig and Bi Jianhai, "China's Global Hunt," 25.

173. Teresa Chea, "China's Growing Pollution Reaches U.S.," *San Francisco Chronicle*, 28 July 2006; James Rose, "Self-Congratulatory Australian Officials Failing the Asia Test," *Canberra Times*, 19 January 2006, 15; and "China Draws Line in Sand."

174. See, for instance, Economy, "Impact of International Regimes," 247.

175. George Monbiot, "America's War on Itself," *Guardian Weekly*, 7–13 January 2005, 14.

176. See Song Guotao et al., *Zhongguo guoji*, 430.

CHAPTER 5

1. See also description of the ILO as "the first of the modern international regulatory agencies," in Abram Chayes and Antonia Handler Chayes, *New Sovereignty: Compliance with International Regulatory Agreements* (Cambridge, MA: Harvard University Press, 1996), 230.

2. David Strang and Patricia Mei Yin Strang, "The International Labour Organization and the Welfare State: Institutional Effects on National Welfare Spending, 1960–80," *International Organization* 47 (Spring 1993), no. 2, 240. See also Hector G. Bartolomei de la Cruz, Geraldo von Potobsky, and Lee Swepston, *The International Labor Organization: The International Standards System and Basic Human Rights* (Boulder, CO: Westview, 1996); and Lee Swepston, *The Universal Declaration of Human Rights and ILO Standards* (Geneva: International Labour Organization, 1998).

3. See Art. 20 of the Universal Declaration of Human Rights, and Art. 23, para. 4, which states that "everyone has the right to form and to join trade unions for the protection of his interests." The International Covenant on Civil and Political Rights (ICCPR) provides for the right to freedom of association and the right to form and join trade unions in Art. 22;

the ICESCR is even more explicit. See United Nations Centre for Human Rights, *Human Rights: A Compilation of International Instruments* (New York: UN, 1993), vol. 1, part 1, 5. Under Art. 8, the ICESCR provides for: "(a) The right of everyone to form trade unions and join the trade union of his choice, subject only to the rules of the organization concerned, for the promotion and protection of his economic and social interests. No restrictions may be placed on the exercise of this right other than those prescribed by law and which are necessary in a democratic society in the interests of national security or public order or for the protection of the rights and freedoms of others; (b) The right of trade unions to establish national federations or confederations and the right of the latter to form or join international trade union organizations; (c) The right of trade unions to function freely subject to no limitations other than those prescribed by law and which are necessary in a democratic society in the interests of national security or public order or for the protection of the rights and freedom of others; and (d) The right to strike, provided that it is exercised in conformity with the laws of the particular country." See ibid., 11.

4. See General Comment 24 on Reservations to the International Covenant on Civil and Political Rights, Human Rights Committee, 1994, in D. J. Harris, ed., *Cases and Materials on International Law* (London: Sweet and Maxwell, 1998), 798–99.

5. See Peter Kooijmans, UN Special Rapporteur on Torture, cited in UN Doc. E/CN.4/1986/15, para. 3, 1.

6. UN instruments prohibiting torture include the 1949 Abolition of Corporal Punishment in Trust Territories, the 1955 Standard Minimum Rules for the Treatment of Prisoners, the 1961 Draft Principles on Protection against Arbitrary Arrest and Detention, and the Code of Conduct for Law Enforcement Officials. Art. 7 of the International Covenant of Civil and Political Rights (ICCPR) of 1967 repeated Art. 5 of the Universal Declaration and added: "In particular, no one shall be subjected without his free consent to medical or scientific experimentation." See Andrew Byrnes, "The Committee against Torture," in Philip Alston, ed., *The United Nations and Human Rights: A Critical Appraisal* (Oxford: Clarendon Press, 1992), 520.

7. UN Centre for Human Rights, "The Committee against Torture," *Human Rights Factsheet* No. 17 (Geneva, 1992), 1.

8. Section 5, "Freedom from Torture," consisted of eight paragraphs, describing the act of torture as "one of the most atrocious violations against human dignity," which "destroys the dignity and impairs the capability of victims to continue their lives and their activities." It reaffirmed that freedom from torture was a right that must be protected "under all circumstances" and "urge[d] all states to put an immediate end to the practice of torture," calling on them to cooperate fully with the Special Rapporteur on Torture. See "Vienna Declaration and Programme of Action," in Australian Department of Foreign Affairs and Trade, *Human Rights Manual* (Canberra: Australian Government Publishing Service, 1993), para. 5.55, 195.

9. United Nations Treaty Collection Website: Database *Status of Multilateral Treaties Deposited with the Secretary-General*, at http://untreaty.un.org.

10. While summarizing the earlier period, this comparative analysis concentrates on post-1997 developments. The earlier period is analyzed in greater detail in Ann Kent, *China, the United Nations and Human Rights: The Limits of Compliance* (Philadelphia: University of Pennsylvania Press, 1999), 84–145.

11. Rachel Brett, "The Contribution of NGOs to the Monitoring and Protection of Human Rights in Europe: An Analysis of the Role and Access of NGOs to the Intergovernmental Organizations," in Arie Bloed, Liselotte Leicht, Manfred Nowak, and Allan Rosas, eds., *Monitoring Human Rights in Europe: Comparing International Procedures and Mechanisms* (Dordrecht: Martinus Nijhoff, 1993), 131.

12. United Nations General Assembly, World Conference on Human Rights Preparatory Committee, *Contribution from the International Labour Organization*, Addendum to Status of Preparation of Publications, Studies and Documents for the World Conference, UN Doc. A/CONF. 157/PC/61/Add. 10 (3 March 1993), 4.

13. Strang and Strang, "The International Labour Organization," 240–41.

14. de la Cruz, von Potobsky, and Swepston, *The International Labour Organization*, 166.

15. Ernest B. Haas, *Beyond the Nation State: Functionalism and International Organizations* (Stanford, CA: Stanford University Press, 1964), 447–48.

16. See Lee Swepston, "Human Rights Complaints Procedures of the International Labor Organization," in Hurst Hannum, ed., *Guide to International Human Rights Practice* (Philadelphia: University of Pennsylvania Press, 1984), 86. See also International Labour Office, *International Labour Standards: A Worker's Education Manual* (Geneva: ILO, 1990), 3rd ed., 103; and International Labour Office, *Freedom of Association: Digest of Decisions and Principles of Freedom of Association Committee of the Governing Body of the ILO* (Geneva: ILO, 1985).

17. Convention (No. 87) Concerning Freedom of Association and Protection of the Right to Organize, 9 July 1948, in United Nations Centre for Human Rights, *Human Rights: A Compilation of International Instruments* (Geneva, 1994), ST/HR/Rev. 4, vol. 1, part 1, no. 2, 422 (emphasis added).

18. United Nations General Assembly, *Contribution from the International Labour Organization*, 4.

19. Virginia A. Leary, "Lessons from the Experience of the International Labour Organization," in Alston, ed., *The United Nations and Human Rights*, 581.

20. Theo van Boven, "The International System of Human Rights: An Overview," in UN Centre for Human Rights, *Manual on Human Rights Reporting under Six Major International Human Rights Instruments* (New York: UN, 1971), 8.

21. Nicolas Valticos, "The Sources of International Labour Law: Recent Trends," in Wybo P. Heere, ed., *International Law and Its Sources* (Deventer: Kluwer Law and Taxation Publishers, 1989), 184–85.

22. For description of CFA, see Ernst B. Haas, *Human Rights and International Action: The Case of Freedom of Association* (Stanford, CA: Stanford University Press, 1970), 26–36; and Breen Creighton, "Freedom of Association," in R. Blanpain, *Comparative Labour Law and Industrial Relations in Industrialised Market Economies* (Deventer: Kluwer Law and Taxation Publishers, 1990), vol. 2, 19–45.

23. Letter from then Australian representative to the ILO, Canberra, 21 February 1996.

24. Swepston, "Human Rights Complaints Procedures," 87.

25. In 1950, a Fact Finding and Conciliation Commission on Freedom of Association was set up, but because it only functioned with the consent of the government concerned, it was used sparingly. See International Labour Office, *International Labour Standards*, 106–8.

26. Leary, "Lessons," 609–11.

27. For more detail, see Kent, *China, the United Nations and Human Rights*, 124–25.

28. Ming K. Chan, *Historiography of the Chinese Labour Movement, 1895–1949: A Critical Survey and Bibliography of Selected Chinese Source Materials at the Hoover Institution* (Stanford, CA: Hoover Institution Press, 1981); *Guoji laodong zuzhi gaiyao ji qi yu Zhongguo zhi guanxi* ("The International Labour Organization and Its Relations with China") (Shanghai: ILO China Branch Office, 1934); *Guoji laodong zuzhi yu Zhongguo* ("The International Labour Organization and China") (Shanghai: ILO Branch Office, 1948).

29. Ming K. Chan, *Historiography*, 16.

30. For account, see Victor-Yves Ghebali, *The International Labour Organization: A Case*

Study on the Evolution of UN Specialised Agencies (Dordrecht: Martinus Nijhoff, 1989), 116; and United Nations, *Yearbook of the United Nations, 1971* (New York: Department of Public Information, United Nations, 1972), 122–33.

31. International Labour Conference, 1984, PR9, at 3, cited in Ghebali, *The International Labour Organization*, 125.

32. Interview, ILO Office, Beijing, 17 May 2002.

33. Feng Chen, "Between the State and Labour: The Conflict of Chinese Trade Unions' Double Identity in Market Reform," *China Quarterly* 176 (December 2003), 1009.

34. For Chinese view of early history of relationship, see "Guoji laodong zuzhi" ("International Labour Organization"), in *Shijie zhishi nianjian, 1994/1995* ("World Knowledge Yearbook, 1994/1995") (Beijing: Shijie zhishi nianjian chubanshe, 1995), 814; and yearly surveys in Zhonghua renmin gongheguo waijiaobu waijiaoshi bianjishi ("Editorial Department, China's Diplomatic History, Chinese Foreign Ministry"), *Zhongguo waijiao gailan* ("A Survey of China's Foreign Relations") (Beijing: Shijie zhishi chubanshe), vols. 1987– present.

35. Interviews with a number of ILO officials and government representatives have suggested that the Director-General saw China's integration into the ILO as an important achievement.

36. Telephone interview with Australian representative to the ILO, Canberra, 6 December 1995.

37. "Guoji laodong zuzhi," 814; and interview, ILO Office, Beijing, 17 May 2002.

38. Ghebali, *The International Labour Organization*, 125.

39. Ibid.

40. Interviews with ILO officials; and *ZGWJGL 1988*, 438; and ibid., 1987, 427 and 428.

41. Interview with Australian government representative to the ILO, Canberra, 21 February 1994.

42. *ZGWJGL 1987*, 427. For details of its varied activities in the 1980s and early 1990s, see Xie Qimei and Wang Xingfang, eds., *Zhongguo yu Lianheguo: Jinian Lianheguo chengli wushi zhounian* ("China and the United Nations: Commemorating the Fiftieth Anniversary of the Founding of the United Nations") (Beijing: Shijie zhishi chubanshe, 1995), 368–73.

43. See "Guoji laodong zuzhi," 814; and Han Nianlong, Qian Qichen, Zheng Weizhi, and Zhou Nan, eds., *Diplomacy of Contemporary China* (Hong Kong: New Horizon, 1990), 406.

44. China's concern was reflected in its condemnation of leading labor dissident Han Dongfang for his involvement with the organization. See International Labour Office, *292nd Report of the Committee on Freedom of Association*, G.B. 259/7/14 (Geneva, March 1994), paras. 385–86, 95.

45. For organizational structure of China's Ministry of Labor, which in March 1998 was enlarged as the Ministry of Labor and Social Security, see International Labour Organization, Asian and Pacific Regional Centre for Labour Administration (ARPLA), *Labour Administration: Profile on the People's Republic of China* (Geneva: ILO, December 1989), 1–6, 69–71; and Guan Jinghe, "Country Paper on China," in ILO, *Report on the ILO Asian-Pacific Symposium on Standards-Related Topics* (New Delhi, 14–17 March 1989), ILO Regional Office for Asia and the Pacific, Bangkok (Geneva: ILO, 1989), 56.

46. Feng Chen, "Between the State and Labour," 1007.

47. "The Fable of 'Calling a Deer a Horse': An Analytical Report on the All-China Federation of Trade Unions and the Repression of Independent Trade Unions," *China Labour Bulletin* 27 (November 1995), 3.

48. See ACFTU, "Opinion on the Implementation of the Circular from the CPC Central Committee on the Strengthening and Improvement of the Leadership of the Communist

Party of China (CPC) in the Work of Trade Unions, the Communist Youth League and the All-China Federation of Women," 15 April 1990; and statement by Zhang Dinghua, General Secretary of the ACFTU, April 1995, *Workers' Daily*, 19 April 1995, both cited in "The Fable."

49. Guan Jinghe, "Country Paper on China," 56.

50. *ZGWJGL 1987*, 427.

51. See ILO, *List of Ratifications of International Labour Conventions*, "China," at http://webfusion.ilo.org/public/db/standards/normes/appl/ (accessed 27 January 2006).

52. Interview with ILO official, Geneva, 30 August 1993. As of May 1993, all but one of the ongoing projects had been decided before 1989, and were valued at US$17,570,836. Information provided by ILO, August 1993.

53. Union of International Associations, ed., *Yearbook of International Organizations, 1995/1996* (Munich: K.G. Saur, 1996), vol. 1, 863.

54. Interview with ICFTU official, Geneva, 19 August 1993.

55. Interviews with ILO official, Geneva, 6 August 1993; and with Australian representative to the ILO, Canberra, 21 February 1994. For a partial account of these post-1989 developments, see also Ann Kent, "China, International Organizations and Regimes: The ILO as a Case Study in Organizational Learning," *Pacific Affairs* 70 (Winter 1997–98) no. 4, 31–47. For account below, see George Black and Robin Munro, *Black Hands of Beijing: Lives of Defiance in China's Democracy Movement* (New York: John Wiley & Sons, 1993), 320; and Lu Ping, ed., *A Moment of Truth: Workers' Participation in China's 1989 Democracy Movement and the Emergence of Independent Unions* (Hong Kong: Asia Monitor Resource Center, 1990), 15.

56. Telephone interview with Australian representative to the ILO, Canberra, 6 December 1995.

57. Interview with ILO officials, Geneva, 11 and 30 August 1993.

58. Interview with ILO official, Geneva, 6 August 1993.

59. Interview with ICFTU official, Geneva, 19 August 1993.

60. This account is based on interviews with Australian representative and ILO officials, Canberra and Geneva, August 1993; comments of then Australian representative to the ILO, 21 February 1996; interviews in Geneva in September 1998; and interviews in Beijing in May 2002.

61. China's complaint to the Director-General is also recorded in Xie Qimei and Wang Xingfang, eds., *Zhongguo yu Lianheguo*, 371.

62. Interview with former ILO official, Canberra, 6 December 1995.

63. Interview with ILO official, Geneva, 11 August 1993.

64. For details of the initial cases, see Kent, *China, the United Nations and Human Rights*, 130–36.

65. See Zhonghua renmin gongheguo guohui fa ("Trade Union Act of the People's Republic of China"), Art. 12, in Jin Qi, ed., *Gonghuifa zidian* ("Trade Union Act Dictionary") (Beijing: Zhongguo zhengfa daxue chubanshe, 1992), 806–7; and Art. 20, 808.

66. Art. 33, 809. This stipulated that in questions of immediate concern such as wages, welfare benefits, production safety, labor protection, and labor insurance, the complaints/objections/views of the trade union should be heard (*yingdang tingqu gonghui yijian*).

67. Interview with ILO delegate, Canberra, 26 July 1994.

68. Interview with representative to ILO, Canberra, 21 February 1994.

69. Interviews with ILO and government officials, Geneva, August–September 1993 and 1995.

70. International Labour Conference, *Provisional Record*, 81st session 25 (Geneva 1994), 25/82–25/83.

71. Guan Jinghe, "Country Paper on China," 56.

72. People's Republic of China Labour Law, 5 July 1994, *China Law and Practice* 8 (29 August 1994).

73. See ibid., Arts. 89–105, 34–36.

74. Mary Gallagher, "An Unequal Battle: Why Labor Laws and Regulations Fail to Protect Workers," *China Rights Forum* (Summer 1997), 12–13.

75. International Labour Office, GB.272/5, paras. 343–48, 75–76.

76. Pitman B. Potter, "The Chinese Legal System (?): Continuing Tensions over Norms and Enforcement," in Joseph Y. S. Cheng, ed., *China Review 1998* (Hong Kong: Chinese University Press, 1998), 35–36. See also Pitman Potter, *The Chinese Legal System: Globalization and Legal Culture* (London: Routledge, 2001), 91–108.

77. For laws, see www/qis.net/chinalaw/prclaw9.htm; and www.isonolaw.com/jsp/law/LAW.

78. See ILO, "The ILO in China," at www.ilo.org/public/english/region/asro/beijing/inchina.htm (accessed 3 August 2004).

79. See "Memorandum of Understanding for Cooperation between the International Labour Office and the Ministry of Labour and Social Security of the People's Republic of China," 17 May 2001, Beijing; and Joint Committee on Cooperation, International Labour Office and the Ministry of Labour and Social Security of the People's Republic of China, "Proposals for a Technical Cooperation Programme," Beijing, December 2001.

80. Interview, ILO office, Beijing, 17 May 2002.

81. See Gallagher, "An Unequal Battle," 13.

82. Marc J. Blecher, "Hegemony and Workers' Politics in China," *China Quarterly* 170 (2002), 283–303.

83. See Gallagher, "An Unequal Battle"; and Anita Chan, "Workers' Rights Are Human Rights," *China Rights Forum* (Summer 1997), 4–7. Chan cites cases of forced and bonded labor; control of workers' bodily functions and physical mistreatment; subsistence or sub-subsistence wages; and violence committed by the police and private security guards.

84. "China Politics: Taking to the Streets," Economist Intelligence Unit Country Briefing, 12 December 2005; and Philip Pan, "The Working Stiffed: Despite Upsurge in Litigation, China's Courts Fail to Redress Labor Abuses," *Washington Post*, 2 July 2002. As a worker who tried litigation stated at the end of the process, "The laws are good, but the legal system doesn't work. If we had to do it again, we would just protest." Sourced from Factiva.

85. See Human Rights Watch, *Paying the Price: Worker Unrest in Northeast China* 14 (New York, August 2002), no. 6 (C).

86. For above statistics, see ILO, "The ILO in China," 1–2.

87. Jonathan Fenby, "Why Chinese Workers Are Getting Restless," *The Business*, 2 October 2005.

88. Interview, ILO office, Beijing, 17 May 2002. See also Murray Scot Tanner, "China Rethinks Unrest," *Washington Quarterly* 27 (Summer 2004), no. 3, 137–56; and Albert Keidel, "The Economic Base for Social Unrest in China," Third European-American Dialogue on China, George Washington University, 26–27 May 2005. For peasant protest, see series of articles in *New York Times* (2004), "The Great Divide." For court cases dealing with urban and rural disorder, see the Dui Hua Foundation, *Selections of Cases from the Criminal Law*, vols. 1–20, in particular, vol. 18 (April 2005).

89. Joseph Kahn, "Workplace Deaths Rise in China Despite New Safety Legislation," *New York Times*, 24 October 2003.

90. Dorothy J. Solinger, "Labour Market Reform and the Plight of the Laid-off Proletariat," *China Quarterly* 170 (2002), 307–25; Erik Eckholm, "Workers' Rights Suffering as China Goes Capitalist," *New York Times*, 22 August 2001; and "The Condition of the Working Class

in China," *Dissent Magazine* (Summer 2004), at www.dissentmagazine.org/menutest/articles/su04/china.htm (accessed 23 July 2004).

91. Interview, ILO office, Beijing, 17 May 2002.

92. United Nations Development Programme, *China Human Development Report 2005*, 2, available at www.undp.org (accessed 15 January 2006).

93. Cai Fang, "Employment Pressure Facing China," paper presented at "Update 2003 China: New Engine of World Growth," Asia Pacific School of Economics and Government, Australian National University, Canberra, 25 September 2003.

94. ILO, "The ILO in China," 1.

95. UNDP, *China Human Development Report 2005*, 2.

96. Ibid.

97. ILO, "The ILO in China," 1.

98. UNDP, *China Human Development Report 2005*, 39.

99. Qun Shi, "Reforms and Challenges of the Social Security System," in Ross Garnaut and Ligang Song, eds., *China: New Engine of World Growth* (Canberra: Asia Pacific Press, 2003), 335.

100. "China Leaders Mine Vein of Unrest to Press Rural Reform" Reuters, 13 February 2006, citing China's Ministry of Public Security figures, www.nytimes.com/reuters/international/international-china-parliament-rural.html (accessed 14 February 2006).

101. UNDP, *China Human Development Report 2005*, 61.

102. Information Office of the State Council, *China's Progress in Human Rights in 2004* (Beijing, April 2005), chapt. 4.

103. Ibid. However, the U.S. State Department has played down these, describing them as limited experiments in more open union elections and decision making, which have included the free election, by secret ballot, of the leaders of ACFTU unions in several foreign-owned enterprises in Guangdong and Fujian Provinces. See U.S. Department of State, "China" (2004 report), 33.

104. See Joseph Kahn, "China to Drop Urbanite-Peasant Legal Differences," *New York Times*, 3 November 2005; "Chinese Migrant Workers' Payment to be Guaranteed by Law in 2006—Minister," BBC Monitoring, 27 December 2005; Yan Hao and Fan Xi, "China Calls on Protecting Rights of Nearly 20 Million Migrant Children," Xinhua News Agency, 18 December 2005; and "Hotline Offer Support to Unpaid Workers," Xinhua News Agency, 27 December 2005.

105. Solinger, "Labour Market Reform," 307–25.

106. UNDP, *China Human Development Report 2005*, 62.

107. Interview, ILO office, Beijing, 17 May 2002.

108. See People's Republic of China, *Implementation of the International Covenant on Economic, Social and Cultural Rights: Initial Reports Submitted by States Parties under Articles 16 and 17 of the Covenant*, E/1990/5/Add. 59 (4 March 2004), 28–33. This, of course, omitted the critical ILO stipulation "without previous authorization."

109. ICFTU, *China, People's Republic: Annual Survey of Violations of Trade Union Rights* (2004) (Country Reports: Annual Survey of Trade Union Rights, 6 January 2004), 3–6, at www.icftu.org.

110. Feng Chen, "Between the State and Labour," 1026.

111. Chang Kai, "Lun bu dang laodong xingwei lifa" ("On Legislation with Regard to Unfair Labor Practices"), *Zhongguo shehui kexue* ("Social Sciences in China") 5 (September 2000), 71–82.

112. Chang Kai interviewed by Ma Wei, "The WTO and Chinese Labor Rights," *Gongren ribao* ("Workers' Daily"), transl. in *China Rights Forum* (2005), no. 3, 40.

113. Joseph Fewsmith, "The Political and Social Implications of China's Accession to the WTO," *China Quarterly* 167 (September 2001), 584.

114. Di Yinqing and Guan Gang, "Meiguo wei shenme jiyu yu Zhongguo chongkai ruguan tanpan" ("Why is the U.S. Anxious to Reopen Negotiations on Entering the WTO?"), *Gaige neican* (20 April 1999), 39–42, cited in ibid., 586–87.

115. See Joseph Kahn, "China's Leaders Manage Class Conflict Carefully," *New York Times*, 25 January 2004.

116. Interview with ILO official, Geneva, 9 September 1998.

117. International Labour Office, "Clearing the Final Hurdle: ILO Conference Adopts the Rights Declaration, Seeks End to Child Labour Abuses," *World of Work* 25 (1998), 13.

118. In 2002, it was reportedly also considering Convention 111 and, within 3–5 years, would consider C. 29 and C. 105. Interview, ILO office, Beijing, 17 May 2002.

119. For details, see http://webfusion.ilo.org/public/db/standards (accessed 17 September 2003).

120. See International Labour Office, *272nd Report of the Committee on Freedom of Association*, Case No. 1930 (China), GB.272/5, 272nd sess. (Geneva, June 1998), paras. 271–367, 64–84.

121. For details, see International Labour Office, *304th Report of the Committee on Freedom of Association* GB.266/5, 266th sess. (Geneva, June 1999), 31–42; and Kent, *China, the United Nations and Human Rights*, 134.

122. International Labour Organization, *Complaint against the Government of China Presented by the International Confederation of Free Trade Unions (ICFTU)* Report No. 321, Case No. 2031, at www.ilolex.ch:1567/cgi–lex.

123. See United Nations High Commissioner for Human Rights, "Status by Treaty," 3, at www.unhchr.ch/tbs/docs.nsf, 2001 (accessed 29 November 2002).

124. Interview, ILO office, Beijing, 17 May 2002.

125. Xinhua News Agency, 27 August 2001.

126. "Between Crime and Error," *China Labour Bulletin* 38 (September–October 1997), 3.

127. Interview, ILO office, Beijing, 17 May 2002; and Committee on Freedom of Association Report, *China (Case No. 2189)*, Report No. 333 (Geneva, March 2004), 387 (g), available at http://webfusion.ilo.org/public/db/standards/normes/.

128. For instance, between 1998 and 2002, the ACFTU had received some 333 delegations from foreign unions, involving 2,647 delegates, and had sent abroad 303 delegations with some 1,625 delegates. See People's Republic of China, *Implementation of the International Covenant*, 32–33.

129. The latter involved a proposal to select 100 enterprises from five principal cities to model an improved form of industrial relations and to establish mediation, conciliation, and arbitration committees at different administrative levels. Interview, ILO office, Beijing, 17 May 2002.

130. These were: C. 150, Labour Administration Convention, 1978 (rat. 07.03.2002); and C. 167, Safety and Health in Construction Convention, 1988 (rat. 07.03.2002). Following the Conference, it also ratified C. 182, Worst Forms of Child Labour Convention, 1999 (rat. 08.08.2002).

131. See Information Office of the State Council, *Labour and Social Security in China* (Beijing: State Council, 29 April 2002), 1, available at www.china.org.cn/e-white/.

132. CEACR General Report 1999, 87th sess., para. 142.

133. This opinion was confirmed in interviews that suggested that China could be an example to other developing countries but that it did not use this power.

134. People's Republic of China, *Implementation of the International Covenant*, 33.

135. See International Union of Food, Agricultural, Hotel, Restaurant, Catering, Tobacco and Allied Workers' Associations (IUF), "Confusion at the ILO? China's Government Elected to Governing Body as Worker Delegate," Geneva, 19 June 2002; and HKCTU, "A Major Defeat for Workers Struggling for Freedom of Association in China," Hong Kong, 12 June 2002, both at www.china.labour-origin.hk.

136. ILO Governing Body Committee on Freedom of Association, "China (Case No. 2189)," *Report No. 330* (Vol. 86, 2003, Series B, no. 1), paras. 385–87, especially 387 (g).

137. On 10 January, the ICFTU requested the personal intervention of the ILO Director-General, Juan Somavia, in the case. See ICFTU, "Letter to Juan Somavia (ILO Director General): China: Request for Personal Intervention," 10 January 2003, at www.icftu.org (accessed 9 August 2004).

138. ILO Governing Body Committee on Freedom of Association, *Report No. 330*, paras. 368–84.

139. ILO Governing Body Committee on Freedom of Association, "China (Case No. 2189)," *Report No. 333* (Vol. 88, 2004, Series B, No. 1), para. 4, and paras. 363–87.

140. Committee on Economic, Social and Cultural Rights, *Concluding Observations of the Committee on Economic, Social and Cultural Rights: People's Republic of China (Including Hong Kong and Macao)*, E/C.12/1/Add.107 (13 May 2005), 4.

141. For details on role of Special Rapporteur and his interaction with China, see Kent, *China, the United Nations and Human Rights*, 106–10.

142. Art. 17.1, Convention against Torture and Other Cruel, Inhuman or Degrading Treatment or Punishment, in UN Centre for Human Rights, *Human Rights*, vol. 1, part 1, 298–99.

143. Arts. 17.2 and 17.5, Convention against Torture, in UN Centre for Human Rights, *Human Rights*, vol. 1, part 1. For details on states parties and members of the Committee, see UN High Commissioner for Human Rights, "Status by Treaty."

144. Andrew Byrnes, "The Committee against Torture," in Philip Alston, ed., *The United Nations and Human Rights* (forthcoming), 2nd ed., 3. This chapter cites both the article by Byrnes in the existing book, Alston, ed., *The United Nations and Human Rights*, and his manuscript in the second and forthcoming edition of the same book. The latter will be henceforth identified as 2nd ed.

145. Byrnes, "The Committee against Torture," 530.

146. See Arts. 19–24, in UN Centre for Human Rights, *Human Rights*, vol. 1, part 1, 300–304.

147. Australian Department of Foreign Affairs and Trade, *Human Rights Manual* (Canberra: Australian Government Publishing Service, 1993), 71.

148. Philip Alston, *Final Report on Enhancing the Long-term Effectiveness of the United Nations Human Rights Treaty System*, UN Doc. E/CN.4/1997/74 (Geneva, 27 March 1996), para. 16, 6.

149. See in *Multilateral Treaties Deposited with the Secretary-General*, at http://untreaty.un.org/ENGLISH/bible.englishinternetbible/bible.asp.

150. UN Centre for Human Rights, *Human Rights*, vol. 1, part 1, 293–94. This definition widened the application of the prohibition against torture from that hitherto utilized, since it included "discrimination" as one of the sources, changed the earlier term, "government official," to "public official" and further broadened its scope by adding in Art. 1.2 that "this article is without prejudice to any international instrument or national legislation which does or may contain provisions of *wider* application." See also Chen Yunsheng, *An End to Torture in Modern China*, transl. of Chen Yunsheng, *Fan kuxing: Dangdai Zhongguo de fazhi he ren-*

quan baohu ("Opposing Torture: China's Contemporary Legal System and the Protection of Human Rights") (Beijing: Shehui kexue wenxian chubanshe, 2000), at www.human rights.dk/publications/all/anendtotorture, 5.

151. For guidelines for initial reports, which have been revised on a number of occasions, see A/46/44 (1991), and for second and subsequent reports, A/46/44 (1991), annex 8; and Committee against Torture, "Rules of Procedure," CAT/C/3/Rev.4 (9 August 2002); Byrnes, "The Committee against Torture," 525. For guidelines, see also UN Centre for Human Rights, "The Committee against Torture," 3–5.

152. It has also been seen to have a judicial role vis-à-vis Art. 22. Letter from UN human rights expert, 14 February 1996.

153. Cited in UN Doc. E/CN.4/1988/15, para. 11, 3 (transl. from French version).

154. See *Report of the Committee against Torture*, UN Doc. A/49/44 (1994), 30, 34; Pang Sen, *Dangdai renquan ABC* ("Contemporary Human Rights ABC") (Chengdu: Sichuan renmin chubanshe, 1992), 210; and Zhonghua renmin gongheguo guowuyuan xinwen bangongshi ("Information Office of the State Council of the People's Republic of China"), *Zhongguo de renquan zhuangkuang* ("Human Rights in China") (Beijing: Zhongyang wenxian chubanshe, October 1991), 66. Although there are sections on China's human rights activities in the United Nations and on China's relations with the ILO in the Chinese Foreign Ministry's publication *Zhongguo waijiao gailan* ("Survey of China's Foreign Relations"), the yearly volumes do not discuss China's relations with the Committee against Torture.

155. For details, see Kent, *China, the United Nations and Human Rights*, 40–48.

156. According to *ZGWJGL 1989*, 459–60, China believed the UN should give priority to issues of racism, colonialism, and foreign aggression and occupation, national self-determination, and development.

157. UN Doc. E/AC.7/SR.748 (13 May 1974), 156–57, cited in Samuel S. K. Kim, *China, the United Nations and World Order* (Princeton, NJ: Princeton University Press, 1979), 486.

158. For this account, see Pang Sen, *Dangdai renquan*, 210.

159. Following is the chronological order of signature [Key: Y: China accepted (ratification, accession, or succession); S: China signed but not yet ratified; R: China made reservations]: Convention on the Elimination of All Forms of Discrimination against Women: Y (1980), R (Para. 1 of Art. 29); International Convention on the Elimination of All Forms of Racial Discrimination: Y (1981), R (Art. 22); Protocol Relating to the Status of Refugees: Y (1982), R (Art. 4); Convention Relating to the Status of Refugees: Y (1982), R (Art. 14.16); Convention on the Prevention and Punishment of the Crime of Genocide: Y (1983), R (Art. 9); International Convention on the Suppression and Punishment of the Crime of Apartheid: Y (1983); International Convention against Apartheid in Sports: S (1987); Convention against Torture and Other Cruel, Inhuman or Degrading Treatment or Punishment: Y (1988), R (Art. 20, Para. 1 of Art. 30). See United Nations, *Multilateral Treaties Deposited with the Secretary-General. Status as at 31 December 1989* (New York: UN, 1990), ST/LEG/ SER.E/8. For discussion of China's position on these treaties, see Xie Qimei and Wang Xing-fang, eds., *Zhongguo yu Lianheguo*, 343–53.

160. Pang Sen, *Dangdai renquan*, 210.

161. See Art. 2.1 in Convention against Torture and Other Cruel, Inhuman or Degrading Treatment or Punishment, in UN Centre for Human Rights, *Human Rights*, vol. 1, part 1, 294.

162. As of April 2002, only 8 of the 129 states parties were not subject to this procedure, while only 49 and 46 states parties respectively had accepted the optional Arts. 21 and 22 procedures. See Byrnes, "The Committee against Torture," 2nd ed., 11.

163. See Convention against Torture, in *Multilateral Treaties Deposited with the Secretary-General.*

164. It read: "Any dispute between two or more States parties concerning the interpretation or application of this Convention which cannot be settled through negotiation shall, at the request of one of them, be submitted to arbitration. If within six months from the date of the request for arbitration the Parties are unable to agree on the organization of the arbitration, any one of those Parties may refer the dispute to the International Court of Justice by request in conformity with the Statute of the court."

165. *Report of the Committee against Torture,* UN Doc. A/49/44 (1994), para. 426, at 67. A state party is bound by Art. 20 unless at the time of ratification or accession it expressly declares its unwillingness to accept the competence of the Committee, whereas Arts. 21 and 22 require an explicit declaration of acceptance of the Committee's competence.

166. Interview with UN official, Geneva, 6 August 1993.

167. *The Criminal Law and the Criminal Procedure Law of the People's Republic of China* (Beijing: Foreign Languages Press, 1984), Chinese text, 180.

168. Human Rights in China, *Words without Substance: The Implementation of the Convention against Torture in the People's Republic of China* (New York: Human Rights in China, April 1996).

169. See ibid., 4–21. Other reasons include: (1) Failings in the legal system, including an incomplete conception of torture; the lack of an independent judicial system; the denial of the right of the accused to early access to legal counsel; the acceptance by trial judges of evidence obtained by torture; and the prevalence of administrative detention, outside the purview of the criminal law; (2) Aspects of judicial practice, wherein cases of torture have been handled in an "overly tolerant manner"; and (3) Chinese Communist Party policies on law enforcement, wherein the Public Security Bureau and State Security organs are given vast powers to maintain social order and to investigate crimes without adequate monitoring.

170. Chen Yunsheng, *An End to Torture in Modern China,* 34–49. The sources for this graphic description are mainly drawn from Chinese media.

171. Amnesty International, *People's Republic of China: Torture—A Growing Scourge in China—Time for Action* (London: AI, 7 April 2001), 1, at http://web2.amnesty.org/library.

172. Robin Munro, *Dangerous Minds: Political Psychiatry Today and Its Origins in the Mao Era* (New York: Human Rights Watch, August 2002).

173. Committee against Torture, *Summary Record of the 251st Meeting: China. 06/05/96,* UN Doc. CAT/C/SR.251 (Geneva, 5 June 1996), para. 5, 3 (emphasis added).

174. See CAT/C/39/Add.2, 11–12.

175. Committee against Torture, *Summary Record of the Public Part of the 252nd Meeting: China,* CAT/C/SR.252/Add.1 (Geneva, 8 May 1996); and Committee against Torture, *Summary Record of the 251st Meeting,* 3.

176. Chen Yunsheng, *An End to Torture,* 122.

177. See Information Office of the State Council of the People's Republic of China, *Progress in China's Human Rights Cause in 2003* (Beijing, March 2004), 15, at www.china.org.cn/e-white/.

178. The first three reports, the initial report (December 1989), a supplementary report required by the Committee (October 1992), and the second periodic report (December 1995), have been described in detail in Kent, *China, the United Nations and Human Rights,* 91–105.

179. Byrnes, "The Committee against Torture," 2nd ed., 34–36.

180. It only acknowledged: "As with other criminal offences, so torture, an act which endangers society, has yet to be eliminated completely in China. Due to a weak sense of legal system, the serious influence of privileges and the rather low professional level among some

State functionaries, the phenomena [sic] of torture still exists in some localities." See Committee against Torture, *Consideration of Reports Submitted by States Parties under Article 19 of the Convention: Initial Reports of States Parties due in 1988*, Addendum, "China," UN Doc. CAT/C/7/Add. 5 (Geneva, 1989), para. 53, 11.

181. Interview with UN official, Geneva, 6 August 1993.

182. Interview with UN human rights expert, Vienna, 25 June 1993.

183. Interview with UN official, Geneva, 6 August 1993. The following observations come from this interview.

184. International League for Human Rights, *Torture in China: Comments on the Official Report of China to the Committee against Torture* (New York: ILHR, April 1990); Asia Watch, *Torture in China* (New York: Asia Watch, July 1990); Amnesty International, *Torture in China*, ASA 17/55/92 (London, December 1992); and Amnesty International, *Torture and Ill-Treatment: Comments on China's Second Periodic Report to the UN Committee against Torture*, ASA 17/51/96 (Geneva: AI, April 1996).

185. Information Office of the State Council, *Human Rights in China* (Beijing, November 1991), 22. This stated that "it is strictly prohibited to extort confessions by torture (*xingxun bigong*)." The second White Paper, *Criminal Reform in China*, stated that "it is strictly forbidden to torture (*yanjin dui zuifan shijia kuxing*), insult, or otherwise maltreat prisoners." It also stated that "criminals have the right to protection against assault on their human dignity or personal safety under all circumstances. In response to any illegal action on the part of a warden or guard, such as obtaining a confession by torture (*xingxun bigong*), administering corporeal punishment or otherwise maltreating a prisoner, the victim has the right to appeal to the people's procuratorate, the people's court, the people's government or any other institution to expose and report such treatment." See Information Office of the State Council, *Criminal Reform in China* (Beijing, August 1992), 7. Subsequently, China published five more human rights White Papers, available at www.China.org.cn/e-white/.

186. See Committee against Torture, *Summary Record of the Fifth Part (Public) of the 146th Meeting*, "Supplementary Report of China (cont.)," UN Doc. CAT/C/SR.146/Add. 4, para. 5, 4.

187. Interview with UN human rights expert, Vienna, 25 June 1993.

188. Committee against Torture, *Initial Reports of States Parties Due in 1989*, Addendum, "China," Supplementary Report, 8 October 1992, UN Doc. CAT/C/7/Add. 14 (1993), part 1 at 3–16, part 2, 17–32; and interviews with UN human rights expert, Vienna, 25 June 1993 and UN official, Geneva, 6 August 1993.

189. UN Doc. A/49/44 (1994), paras. 425–28, 67.

190. Committee against Torture, *Concluding Observations of the Committee against Torture: China*, UN Doc. A/51/44 (Geneva, 9 July 1996), paras. 138–50.

191. CAT/C/SR.419 (9 May 2000), 4 and 7; and A/55/44 (2 January 2001), paras. 107–30.

192. *Summary Record of the Second Part (Public) of the 423rd Meeting: China 9 May 2000*, CAT/SR.423/Add.1.

193. CAT/C/SR.419, 10; and A/55/44, paras. 106–45 (including Hong Kong).

194. CAT/SR.423/Add.1, ix.

195. Human Rights in China, "The Human Rights Situation in China and the Dialogue on Human Rights," Submission to the Foreign Affairs Committee of the House of Commons, 28 July 2000, 7.

196. These came into effect on 1 July 1995. For texts, see *BBC Summary of World Broadcasts*, SWB/FE/2259 and SWB/FE/2261.

197. See Lin Feng, *Administrative Law Procedures and Remedies in China* (Hong Kong: Sweet

and Maxwell, 1996); and Amnesty International, "United Nations Committee against Torture," 3 May 1996, ASA 17/56/96, 9–10.

198. For analysis of the rights implications of this law, see Lawyers' Committee for Human Rights (LCHR), *Lawyers in China: Obstacles to Independence and the Defense of Rights* (New York, March 1998). See excerpts in "Lawyers: No Longer Servants of the State But Not Quite Independent," *China Rights Forum* (Summer 1998), 32–37.

199. Cited in *China Daily*, 27 February 1996, Reuters China News, 1 March 1996.

200. Part 2, Chapt. 2, Arts. 92 and 96, Amended PRC Criminal Procedure Law, 17 March 1996, text in Xinhua News Agency, 23 March 1996, Reuters China News, 19 April 1996.

201. According to Art. 234, whoever intentionally causes a person's serious injury is sentenced to not less than three years and not more than ten years of fixed-term imprisonment; if he "causes a person's death or causes a person's serious deformity by badly injuring him with particularly ruthless means, he is to be sentenced to not less than 10 years of fixed-term imprisonment, life imprisonment, or death." The PRC Criminal Law Amended by the 5th Session, 8th NPC, *FBIS Daily Report*, 14 March 1997. FBIS-CHI-97-056 (17 March 1997).

202. Amnesty International, *No One Is Safe: Political Repression and Abuse of Power in the 1990s* (London, March 1996), 79.

203. Lawyers' Committee for Human Rights (LCHR) (Jonathan Hecht), *Opening to Reform? An Analysis of China's Revised Criminal Procedure Law* (New York, October 1996), 63.

204. Ibid., 69.

205. See *Third Periodic Reports of States Parties Due in 1997: China*, CAT/C/39/Add.2 (5 January 2000), 6.

206. One article argued that the problem was that solving criminal cases wins acclaim and promotion for officials, "no matter what methods are used"; another article by a Beijing University scholar criticized the courts for routinely accepting confessions obtained through torture. Cited in Erik Eckholm, "China Begins to Turn Light on Wide Use of Torture," *New York Times*, 13 February 2001.

207. Jonathan Watts, "China Bans Police Torture of Suspects," *Guardian*, 11 September 2003.

208. United States Department of State, "China" in *Country Reports on Human Rights Practices* (Washington, DC, 25 February 2004), 4, at www.state.gov.

209. "China Reforms Death Penalty Appeals Process," Associated Press, 8 December 2005.

210. Thus, Amnesty International stated that "torture and ill-treatment continued to be reported in a wide variety of state institutions despite the introduction of several new regulations aimed at curbing the practice." See Amnesty International, "China," *Amnesty International Report 2005* (London, 2005), 1. In its human rights report, the U.S. State Department also observed of China that "recommendations from the May 2000 report of the UN Committee against Torture still had not been fully implemented by year's end." United States Department of State, "China" in *Country Reports on Human Rights Practices* (Washington, DC, 25 February 2005), 4, at www.state.gov.

211. See *Report of the Working Group on Arbitrary Detention*: Addendum, "Mission to China," E/CN.4/2005/6/Add.4 (29 December 2004), 19–20.

212. See *Torture and Other Cruel, Inhuman or Degrading Treatment or Punishment: Report of the Special Rapporteur, Theo Van Boven*, E/CN.4/2004/56/Add.1 (23 March 2004).

213. David Matas and David Kilgour, *Report into Allegations of Organ Harvesting of Falun Gong Practitioners in China*, 6 July 2006, at http://OrganHarvestInvestigation.net.

214. Chen Yunsheng, *An End to Torture*.

215. Tian Wenchang, "Laws Aim to End Confessions under Torture," *People's Daily*, 4 April 2003.

216. For these statements, see UN Commission on Human Rights, *Report of the Working Group on the Draft Optional Protocol to the Convention against Torture and Other Cruel, Inhuman or Degrading Treatment or Punishment*, UN Doc. E/CN.4/1997/33 (Geneva, 23 December 1996), paras. 34 and 46.

217. "Working Group on the Draft Optional Protocol to the Convention against Torture," (Geneva, 13–24 October 1997), 6th sess., *Human Rights Monitor* (1997) 39–40, 21–23.

218. UN Press Release, "General Assembly to be Asked to Adopt Protocol on Torture Convention, Setting up Inspection Regime for Implementation of Its Terms," Fifty-seventh General Assembly, Third Committee, 40th Meeting, 7 November 2002.

219. U.S. Department of State, "China," 6.

220. See UN Press Release, "China Opposes and Prohibits Torture, Delegation Affirms," Committee against Torture, 24th session (4 May 2000), at www.unhchr.ch/huricane/huricane/.

221. See "Committee against Torture Opens Thirty-second Session, Hears Address by Acting High Commissioner for Human Rights; Elects Chairperson and Officers," UN Press Release, 3 May 2004.

222. For profiles of Yu and other Chinese experts, see Office of the High Commissioner for Human Rights, "Committee Members by Treaty," at www.unhchr.ch/tbs/doc.nsf.

223. "UN Investigator Says Torture Widespread in China, But Praises Beijing," 22 November 2005, at AsiaNews.it.

224. United Nations Press Release, "Special Rapporteur on Torture Highlights Challenges at End of Visit to China," Beijing, 2 December 2005.

225. Ibid.

226. Foreign Ministry spokesman Qin Gang said that the Special Rapporteur's conclusion that torture was widespread "lacks an objective foundation and does not accord with reality." He observed that "China has already made this position clear to the Rapporteur and requested that he correct his conclusion." See Joseph Kahn, "China Disputes UN Envoy on Widespread Use of Torture," *New York Times*, 7 December 2005.

227. Telephone interview with former Australian representative to the ILO, Canberra, 8 February 1996.

228. "Premier Preoccupied with Rural Areas, Unemployment, Poverty," Xinhua News Agency, 18 March 2003.

229. Art. 14, additional fourth paragraph. According to reports, the Legal Committee of the NPC also discussed the possibility of restoring the right to strike to the Constitution. For White Paper, see Information Office of the State Council, *China's Employment Situation and Policies* (Beijing, April 2004), available at www.China.org.cn/e-white/.

CONCLUSION

1. This subdivision represents an adaptation of Harold Koh's theory dividing practical implementation into three distinct levels of legislative, political, and social implementation. See Harold Hongju Koh, "Why Do Nations Obey International Law?" *Yale Law Journal* 106 (1997), no. 8, 2656. Here, however, legislative implementation is treated as a separate category indicative of formal implementation, to be distinguished from practical implementation in the form of political or social implementation. This adaptation is necessary to highlight the extreme gap that persists in China between formal legislative implementation and the practical implementation and enforcement of those laws.

2. See Abram Chayes and Antonia Handler Chayes, *The New Sovereignty: Compliance with International Regulatory Agreements* (Cambridge, MA: Harvard University Press, 1995). As Keohane has observed, "Institutions matter, even if they cannot enforce rules from above,

because they change actors' conceptions of their interests." See Robert Keohane, "International Relations, Old and New," in Robert Goodin and Hans-Dieter Klingeman, eds., *A New Handbook of Political Science* (Oxford: Oxford University Press, 1998), 470 (emphasis in original).

3. See also Dinah Shelton, "The Impact of Economic Globalization on Compliance," in Alexander Kiss, Dinah Shelton, and Kanami Ishibashi, eds., *Economic Globalization and Compliance with International Environmental Agreements* (The Hague: Kluwer Law International, 2003), 35.

4. Anne-Marie Slaughter, "International Law in a World of Liberal States," *European Journal of International Law* 6 (1995), no. 4, 511.

5. "China to Join NSG to Boost Nonproliferation Efforts," Kyodo News, 28 January 2004.

6. Thomas L. Friedman, "Vote France off the Island," *New York Times*, 9 February 2003.

7. The CTBT cannot take effect until after forty-four countries in the Conference on Disarmament with nuclear reactors or research programs ratify it. As of January 2006, only thirty-three, excluding China and the United States, have done so.

8. Thomas M. Franck, *The Power of Legitimacy among Nations* (New York: Oxford University Press, 1990), 20–21, 111–16.

9. Robert O. Keohane, *Neorealism and Its Critics* (New York: Columbia University Press, 1986), 8.

10. George W. Downs, David M. Rocke, and Peter N. Barsoom, "Is the Good News about Compliance Good News about Cooperation?" *International Organization* 50 (1996), no. 3, 379–406, at 2.

11. Gong Wen and Zhang Xiangchen, "Comment on General Trend of China's Entry into WTO," *People's Daily*, 7 May 1999, 1–2.

12. See Shi Guangsheng, Minister of Foreign Trade and Economic Cooperation, reported in "China's Stance on WTO Accession Unchanged," *People's Daily*, 13 March 2001.

13. Pitman B. Potter, "China and the WTO: Tensions over Dispute Resolution Processes," 10–12 July 1998, Geneva, unpublished paper. See also Pitman B. Potter, *The Chinese Legal System: Globalization and Local Legal Culture* (New York: Routledge, 2001).

14. Pitman B. Potter, "The Legal Implications of China's Accession to the WTO," *China Quarterly* 167 (September 2001), 603–8.

15. Mike Moore, *A World without Walls: Freedom, Development, Free Trade and Global Governance* (Cambridge: Cambridge University Press, 2003), 144.

16. For instance, under the agricultural agreement, brokered in Washington in April 1999, the United States won substantial concessions, cutting the average tariff for agricultural products to 17 percent from 21.2 percent, with the average tariff for U.S. priority products falling to 14.5 percent. Quantitative restrictions, except for major agricultural products such as wheat, rice, corn, cotton, and table sugar, were to be eliminated. See Paul Mooney, "Post-WTO Shocks for China's Farmers," ChinaOnLine, 17 January 2000, at www.chinaonline.com.

17. Moore, *A World without Walls*, 143.

18. "Chinese Premier—China Must Rapidly Prepare for WTO Entry," Xinhua News Agency, Beijing, 5 March 2000, Reuters China News, 5 March 2000.

19. Meng Na and Zhao Lei, "Foreign Trade Amendments Approved, Ending China's Law Amending Process Involving WTO Commitments," Xinhua News Agency, 6 April 2004.

20. See text of Jiang's speech in *People's Daily*, 21 October 2001.

21. Joseph Fewsmith, "The Political and Social Implications of China's Accession to the WTO," *China Quarterly* 167 (September 2001), 589; and Cai Chongguo, "The Social Costs of China's Accession to the WTO," *China Labour Bulletin*, 19 December 2005, at http://iso.clb.org.hk.

22. See Economist Intelligence Unit, "Financial Reforms Delayed," at www.chinaonline

.com; and Premier Zhu Rongji, "Report on the Work of the Government," 5 March 2000, *Beijing Review* 43 (3 April 2000), no. 14, part 7, 25–27.

23. Murray Scot Tanner, "China Rethinks Unrest," *Washington Quarterly* 27 (Summer 2004), no. 3, 137–56. See also "China Risk: Labour Market Risk," and "Risk Overview," *Economist Intelligence Unit* (12 January 2005); Erik Eckholm, "Tide of China's Migrants: Flowing to Boom, or Bust?" *New York Times*, 29 July 2003; and Reuters, "Village Suicides Underscore Plight of China Farmers," 13 August 2003, at www.nytimes.com.

24. John D. Langlois, Jr., "The WTO and China's Financial System," *China Quarterly* 167 (2001), 611.

25. "Chinese Premier Says Agriculture, Farmers' Income 'Major Problem' for Cabinet," Xinhua News Agency, 18 March 2003; and report on improved social security system in Information Office of the State Council, *China's Progress in Human Rights in 2004* (Beijing, April 2005), chapt. 4.

26. See Pieter Bottelier, "The Impact of WTO Membership on China's Domestic Economy," parts 1 and 2, at www.chinaonline.com/commentary (accessed 3 January 2001); and Zhao Wei, "China's WTO Accession: Commitments and Prospects," *Journal of World Trade* 32 (1998), 51–75. For particularly valuable insights, see Deborah Z. Cass, Brett G. Williams, and George Barker, eds., *China and the World Trading System: Entering the New Millennium* (Cambridge: Cambridge University Press, 2003); and Kong Qingjiang, *China and the World Trade Organization: A Legal Perspective* (Singapore: World Scientific, 2002).

27. See Bottelier, "The Impact of WTO Membership."

28. See, in particular, WTO Director-General Supachai Panitchpakdi, "China and the WTO: Challenges and Opportunities for the Future," 2 December 2004, at www.wto.org (accessed 28 January 2005); United States Trade Representative, *2004 Report to Congress on China's WTO Compliance* (Washington, DC, 11 December 2004); United States Trade Representative, *2002 Report to Congress on China's WTO Compliance* (Washington, DC, 11 December 2002); and American Chamber of Commerce, People's Republic of China, *WTO Implementation* 20 August 2002, at www.amcham-china.org.cn/wto/wto_1.htm. For background, see World Trade Organization, *Accession of the People's Republic of China: Decision of 10 November 2001*, WT/L/432, 23 November 2002; World Trade Organization, *Report of the Working Party on the Accession of China*, WT/MIN(01)/3, 10 November 2001; and Pitman Potter, "Asia in the World Trading System," *Asia Pacific Report*, Special Issue, 20–21 October 2000. For China's self-assessment, see Jin Liqun, Vice-Minister of Finance, "China: One Year into the WTO Process," Washington, DC, 22 October 2002, available at www.imf.org.

29. See evaluations in above citations; and Nicholas Lardy, "Survey—China and the World Trade Organization: Problems on the Road to Liberalisation," *Financial Times*, 15 March 2002; Rick Gladstone, "China's Freshman Year in World Trade," *New York Times*, 8 December 2002; U.S. Chamber of Commerce, "U.S. Chamber Report Grades China's Trade Progress—Some Early Progress but More Remains to be Done," Press Release, 12 September 2002; "U.S. Trade Rep Says WTO Concerns Remain," Associated Press, 12 February 2004; and *China Rights Forum* (2002), no. 1, Special Issue: WTO: Profit . . . and Loss?; and *China Rights Forum* (2003), no. 1, Special Issue: China as Partner to the World.

30. Thus, for instance, by the time China had entered the WTO its tariffs had already fallen by three-quarters, to an average of only 15 percent, and it had committed to reducing its average tariff to only 9 percent by 2005. Lardy, "Survey—China and the World Trade Organization," 1.

31. See evaluations cited in Notes 28–29, above. These include extensive revisions to China's Foreign Trade Law, which came into force on 1 July 2004.

32. See Note 28, above.

33. United States Trade Representative, *2005 Report to Congress on China's WTO Compliance* (Washington, DC, 11 December 2005), 3.

34. David Barboza and Paul Meller, "China to Limit Textile Exports to Europe," *New York Times*, 11 June 2005.

35. Lardy, "Survey—China and the World Trade Organization," 1. See also United States Trade Representative, *2005 Report to Congress*, 3.

36. "WTO Pledges Kept, Say Trade Officials," *China Daily*, 20 December 2003.

37. See Sharon K. Hom, "China and the WTO: Year One," *China Rights Forum* (2003), 18; and Geoff Raby, "Entry into the WTO: Commitments and Implementation," in Ross Garnaut and Ligang Song, eds., *China: New Engine of World Growth* (Canberra: Asia Pacific Press, 2003), 131–40. Lin Xinyi, Taiwan's chief delegate to the WTO meeting in Doha, stated: "The event not only illustrates the support and acknowledgment we receive from the WTO members, but also represents the trust and commitment of our 23 million people towards the multilateral trading system embodied by the WTO." See "Taiwan's Membership Application to WTO Approved," Central News Agency, 1 November 2001, in BBC Monitoring Asia Pacific, 12 November 2001.

38. Meng Yan, "WTO Opposes US Measure," *China Daily*, 14 July 2003.

39. Ibid.

40. "Backgrounder—New Round of WTO Talks and China's Stance," Xinhua News Agency, 20 July 2003.

41. Steven Chase, "WTO Talks Bog Down over Subsidies: Cancun Meeting Thrown into Disarray by New Bloc Led by Brazil, India, China," *Globe and Mail*, 13 September 2003.

42. Supachai Panitchpakdi stated: "At a time when the WTO faces an impasse, we need China to use its influence to be a bridge between developed and developing countries." Cited in "China Briefing: WTO Seeks Mediation from China," *Far Eastern Economic Review*, 20 November 2003, at http://global.factiva.com/en/arch/display.asp.

43. "China Keeps a Low Profile," *Indian Express*, 19 December 2005; and "Commerce Minister Bo Xilai has Defended the Mainland's Virtual Absence from . . . ," *South China Morning Post*, 20 December 2005.

44. See also Ann Kent, "China's Growth Treadmill: Globalization, Human Rights and International Relations," in Ronald C. Keith, ed., *China as a Rising World Power and Its Responses to "Globalization"* (London: Routledge, 2005), 533–38.

45. Joseph Kahn, "China Discovers Medical Secrecy Is Expensive," *New York Times*, 13 April 2003.

46. See text of WHO Constitution at www.wpro.who.int/public/policy/cons_chap XlV.asp (accessed 23 April 2003). David Fidler has argued that, because the scope of WHO's International Health Regulations is so narrow, China had no obligation under Art. 62 to report the SARS outbreak to WHO or any other state. See David P. Fidler, "SARS and International Law," *ASIL Insights*, American Society of International Law, April 2003, at www.asil.org/insights/insigh101.htm (accessed 19 May 2003). However, according to Don Greig, a case can be made that the functions of the Organization under Art. 2 of its Constitution to act as the directing and coordinating authority on international health work are so broad that it would be impossible for the Organization to carry out those functions effectively unless there were an implied obligation upon member states to keep it informed of all major national developments relevant to its mandate.

47. See *New York Times* articles: Elisabeth Rosenthal, "AIDS Scourge in Rural China Leaves Villages of Orphans," 25 August 2002; Elisabeth Rosenthal, "China Frees AIDS Activist after Month of Outcry," 21 September 2002; Nicholas D. Kristof, "China's Deadly Cover-up," 29

November 2002; and Elisabeth Rosenthal, "Despite Law, China's HIV Patients Suffer Bias," 14 January 2003.

48. "Annan Warns China of an AIDS Epidemic," *New York Times*, 15 October 2002.

49. Jim Yardley, "China Tells Its Public of Enormity of AIDS Toll," *New York Times*, 3 December 2003. For evidence of secrecy, see Alice Park Kunming, "China's Secret Plague: How One US Scientist is Struggling to Help the Government Face up to an Exploding AIDS Crisis," *Time*, 15 December 2003.

50. Bates Gill, Jennifer Chang, and Sarah Palmer, "China's HIV Crisis," *Foreign Affairs* 80 (March–April 2002), no. 2, 97. See also Hu Jia, "The Tale of Two Crises: SARS vs. AIDS," *China Rights Forum* (2003), no. 3, 56–63.

51. Thomas Crampton, "With SARS on the Rise, China Disputes UN's Travel Warning," *International Herald Tribune*, 5 April 2003.

52. Thanks to Charles Guest for his insights.

53. "China Apologizes as WHO Tracks SARS Path," Associated Press, 4 April 2003, at www.aponline.com.

54. Thomas Crampton, "China Admits SARS Is Spreading," *International Herald Tribune*, 15 April 2003.

55. Denise Grady, "SARS: From China's Secret to a Worldwide Alarm," *International Herald Tribune*, 8 April 2003; and "WHO: China Too Slow in Reporting SARS," VOA News, 7 April 2003.

56. John Pomfret, "Doctor Says Health Ministry Lied about Disease," *Washington Post*, 10 April 2003.

57. See Erping Zhang, "SARS: Unmasking Censorship in China," *China Rights Forum* (2003), no. 3, 44–49; and Hu Jia, "The Tale of Two Crises," 56–63.

58. Ellen Bork, "China's SARS Problem, and Ours," *Daily Standard*, 4 April 2003.

59. Joseph Kahn with Keith Bradsher, "China Allows UN Agency to Help Fight Illness on Taiwan," *New York Times*, 4 May 2003.

60. "China Welcomes Taiwan Presence at WHO SARS Meeting," Xinhua News Agency, 17 June 2003.

61. "Taiwan Leader Says China Talks Unlikely to Resume," Reuters News, 4 July 2003.

62. See Fred Guteri, Sarah Schafer, and Alexandra Seno, "How to Prevent Another Outbreak: Severe Acute Respiratory Syndrome Affected 8,098 People in 2003, 774 Died," *Newsweek International*, 15 December 2003.

63. Alan Sipress, "Fears over Use of Human Flu Drug," *Sydney Morning Herald*, 20 June 2005, 7; and "WHO Warns China to Prepare for Possible New Bird Flu Human Cases in Winter," Xinhua News Agency, 23 December 2005.

64. "WHO Chief Says Need for Openness Key SARS Lesson," Reuters News, 11 July 2003.

65. Inis L. Claude, "Collective Legitimization as a Political Function of the United Nations," *International Organization* 20 (1966), no. 3, 372.

66. Richard Falk, *The Status of Law in International Society* (Princeton, NJ: Princeton University Press, 1970), 67.

67. Downs, Rocke, and Barsoom, "Is the Good News?" 386.

68. This reaction was particularly noticeable in its response to the international sanctions imposed after Tiananmen.

69. Jeffrey T. Checkel, "Why Comply? Social Learning and European Identity Change," *International Organization* 55 (Summer 2001), no. 3, 562–63.

70. Chayes and Chayes, *The New Sovereignty*, 1–33.

71. Harold Hongju Koh, "The 1998 Frankel Lecture: Bringing International Law Home," *Houston Law Review* 35 (Fall 1998), 662–80.

72. Harold K. Jacobson and Michel Oksenberg, *China's Participation in the IMF, the World Bank and GATT: Toward a Global Economic Order* (Ann Arbor: University of Michigan Press, 1990), 127–28.

73. Nicholas R. Lardy, "China and the International Financial System," in Elizabeth Economy and Michel Oksenberg, eds., *China Joins the World: Progress and Prospects* (New York: Council on Foreign Relations, 1999), 207; and Margaret M. Pearson, "China's Integration into the International Trade and Investment Regime," in ibid., 184.

74. On the other hand, its negative influence on more political human rights bodies has been significant. See impact on UN Human Rights Commission in Kent, *China, the United Nations and Human Rights*, 74-83.

75. I am grateful for discussions I have had on such possibilities with Borge Bakken.

76. Claude, "Collective Legitimization as a Political Function of the United Nations," 379.

Index

Studies in Asian Security

A SERIES SPONSORED BY THE EAST-WEST CENTER

Muthiah Alagappa, Chief Editor
Director, East-West Center Washington

Why Taiwan? Geostrategic Rationales for China's Territorial Integrity
By Alan M. Wachman, Forthcoming 2007

Shaping Chinese Foreign Policy
By Evan S. Medeiros, Forthcoming 2007

Beyond Compliance: China, International Organizations, and Global Security
By Ann Kent, 2007

Dangerous Deterrent: Nuclear Weapons Proliferation and Conflict in South Asia
By S. Paul Kapur, 2007

Minimum Deterrence and India's Nuclear Security
By Rajesh M. Basrur, 2006

Rising to the Challenge: China's Grand Strategy and International Security
By Avery Goldstein, 2005

*Unifying China, Integrating with the World: Securing Chinese Sovereignty in
the Reform Era*
By Allen Carlson, 2005

Rethinking Security in East Asia: Identity, Power, and Efficiency
Edited by J. J. Suh, Peter J. Katzenstein,
and Allen Carlson, 2004

The authorized representative in the EU for product safety and compliance is:
Mare Nostrum Group
B.V Doelen 72
4831 GR Breda
The Netherlands

www.ingramcontent.com/pod-product-compliance
Lightning Source LLC
Chambersburg PA
CBHW022347280326
41935CB00007B/108